002191286

DATE DUE

GAYLORD			PRINTED IN U.S.A.

The 2000s in America

The 2000s in America

Volume 2

Gaiman, Neil—Private militias

Editor
Craig Belanger
University of Advancing Technology

SALEM PRESS
A Division of EBSCO Publishing
Ipswich, Massachusetts

GREY HOUSE PUBLISHING

Cover photos (clockwise from top left) : World Trade Center, New York City on September 11, 2001 (Getty Images); Barack Obama (left) and George W. Bush (©Gerald Herbert/AP/Corbis); Apple iPhone (©Adriana Williams/Corbis); Michael Phelps with his gold medal for the 400 meter individual medley at the Athens 2004 Summer Olympic Games (Getty Images).

Title page photo: President Barack Obama and first lady Michelle Obama walk in the Inaugural Parade on January 20, 2009 in Washington, DC. (© Getty Images)

The 2000s in America, 2013, published by Grey House Publishing, Inc., Amenia, NY, under exclusive license from EBSCO Publishing, Inc.

∞ The paper used in these volumes conforms to the American National Standard for Permanence of Paper for Printed Library Materials, Z39.48 1992 (R1997).

Library of Congress Cataloging-in-Publication Data

The 2000s in America / editor, Craig Belanger, University of Advanced Technology.
    volumes cm
  Includes bibliographical references and index.
   ISBN 978-1-4298-3883-2 (set) -- ISBN 978-1-4298-3884-9 (volume 1) -- ISBN 978-1-4298-3885-6 (volume 2) -- ISBN 978-1-4298-3899-3 (volume 3) 1. United States--Civilization--1970---Encyclopedias. 2. United States--Civilization--21st century--Encyclopedias. 3. United States--History--1969---Encyclopedias. 4. Two thousands (Decade)--Encyclopedias. I. Belanger, Craig. II. Title: Two thousands in America.
  E169.12.A178 2013
  973.93--dc23
                                                                                                    2012045422

◼ Contents

■ Complete List of Contents

Volume 1

Volume 2

Volume 3

The 2000s
in America

■ Gaiman, Neil

Identification: Author and graphic novelist
Born: November 10, 1960; Porchester, United Kingdom

Neil Gaiman is the acclaimed author of several books and graphic novels, including the popular Sandman series. Gaiman has built a career around his work in comic books. In doing so, he has helped bring validity to a genre that was once easily dismissed. His books have earned him many coveted awards and he has achieved a cult-like following among fans of genre literature.

When most people think of comic books, they don't think of sophisticated, epic stories about a family of immortal god-like beings and their connection to the human world. Yet, this is the world Neil Gaiman created in his Sandman series (1989–96), itself a reimagining of DC Comics' 1974–76 series of the same name. Although Gaiman's original series was published in the 1980s and 90s, different editions and spin-offs of the series have been published during the 2000s. In 2007, *Entertainment Weekly* named the Sandman series a "new classic," one of the one hundred best reads from 1983 to 2008.

Gaiman has enjoyed many awards for his work over the years both in his native United Kingdom as well as abroad. His novel *American Gods*, published in 2001, won top prizes in science fiction and fantasy writing in, including a Hugo Award (2002), a Nebula Award (2002), and the Horror Writers' Association's Bram Stoker Award for best novel (2001).

With his frequent collaborator, illustrator Dave McKean, Gaiman also created several children's books, including *Coraline* (2002), which was adapted as 2009 animated film and released in February 2009, and *The Wolves in the Walls* (2003), which tells the story of the monsters that live in the rooms of little boys and girls. While *Coraline* won the Horror Writers' Association award for best work for younger readers

Neil Gaiman. (Courtesy Elena Torre)

(2003), some critics maintain that while these books are actually written for children, such frightening content probably makes them better suited for adults. Gaiman continues to produces various works for younger audiences. He released the graphic novel *Batman: Whatever Happened to the Caped Crusader?* in July 2009.

Impact

Many critics have stated that Gaiman's writing makes weighty subjects such as mythology, spirituality, and mortality seem absorbing and fresh. At the same time, he has helped make the world of comic books and graphic novels more accessible to a wider audience. The film adaptation of his novel *Coraline*, directed by Henry Selick, grossed over $100 million.

Further Reading

Goodyear, Dana. "Kid Goth." *New Yorker.* Condé Nast, 25 Jan. 2010. Web. 29 Oct. 2012.

Grossman, Lev. "Geek God." *Time.* Time Inc., 26 July 2007. Web. 29 Oct. 2012.

"Neil Gaiman: By The Book." *New York Times Sunday Book Review* 6 Apr. 2012: BR8. Print.

Tanya Brown

■ Galifianakis, Zach

Identification: American actor and comedian
Born: October 1, 1969; Wilkesboro, North Carolina

Comedian Zach Galifianakis started out in the underground alternative comedy scene, eventually breaking into the Hollywood mainstream with roles in movies such as The Hangover, Dinner for Schmucks, *and* Due Date. *He became known for his off-brand style of comedy and for often mining inappropriate or uncomfortable situations for their humor.*

Zacharius Knight Galifianakis had an early exposure to the arts—his mother oversaw a community arts center—and he began acting attending college at North Carolina State University. After college, Galifianakis moved to New York City to pursue acting, a move that eventually led him into comedy and then to Los Angeles.

Early on, Galifianakis's career consisted of bit parts in minor films and on sitcoms, including the short-lived NBC series *Boston Common.* In 2002, he landed his own comedy show on VH1, *Late World with Zach,* styled after late-night talk shows, but the show was cancelled after only a few weeks on the air. In its aftermath, Galifianakis made the decision to grow his iconic beard and landed a recurring role on the television drama *Tru Calling,* which ran from 2003 to 2005. However, after joining "The Comedians of Comedy" tour in 2004—later made into a film documentary with the same name—Galifianakis became known as one of America's leading "underground" comedians. The stand-up artist was soon delivering his eccentric brand of comedy across several forms of media, from making a music video for rap artist Kanye West's song "Can't Tell Me Nothing" in 2007 to an over-the-top advertising campaign for Absolut Vodka in 2008. Galifianakis also made several appearances on the outlandish comedy-sketch show *Tim and Eric Awesome Show, Great Job!* beginning in 2007.

Zach Galifianakis with The Hangover *costar Heather Graham, 2009.* (©iStockphoto.com/Robert Marquardt)

After starring in the independent film *Visioneers* in 2008, Galifianakis landed a supporting role in the feature film *The Hangover* (2009), from *Old School* director Todd Phillips. For many, Galifianakis's scene-stealing portrayal of the neurotic and socially awkward Alan Garner was a revelation; for Galifianakis, mainstream success quickly followed. Galifianakis also lent his voice to the Disney animated film *G-Force* (2009), landed a starring role in the 2010 comedy *Due Date,* and hosted an episode of *Saturday Night Live* on March 6, 2010. All the while, the comedian maintained his brand of alternative comedy, particularly on the Internet—a comedy sketch series titled "Between Two Ferns with Zach Galifianakis" is a fixture on the Will Ferrell–founded website Funny or Die. In 2011, Galifianakis reprised his role in *The Hangover* in a sequel titled *The Hangover: Part II.*

Impact

Galifianakis—along with contemporaries like David Cross, Michael Ian Black, and Sarah Silverman—is one of the many comedians leading the shift of what has traditionally been called "alt comedy" into the mainstream. Coupled with his expansive Internet presence, Galifianakis's work in big-budget Holly-wood films has brought many new fans to the under-ground comedy world.

Further Reading

Eells, Josh. "The High Times and Surreal Life of Zach Galifianakis." *Rolling Stone* 23 June 2011: 60–68. Print.

Markovitz, Adam. "Zach Galifianakis." *Entertainment Weekly* 20 Apr. 2012: 84–85. Print.

Stein, Joel. "Zach Galifianakis Hates To Be Loved." *Time* 30 May 2011: 46–50. Print.

Bill Rickards

■ Gates, Bill and Melinda

Identification: American business executives and phi-lanthropists

Bill Gates
Born: October 28, 1955; Seattle, Washington

Melinda Gates
Born: August 15, 1964; Dallas, Texas

The merger of the Gates Learning Foundation and the William H. Gates Foundation in 2000 created a powerful new entity. As cochairs of the Bill and Melinda Gates Foundation, the couple took on a host of international problems in search of solutions and encouraged others to support their efforts.

Bill Gates was born October 28, 1955, in Seattle, Washington; Melinda French was born August 15, 1964, in Dallas, Texas. The couple met at Gates's company, Microsoft, and married in 1994. They soon turned their attention to global health and social issues. They contributed almost $16 billion to their philanthropic foundation, the Bill and Melinda Gates Foundation, to combat what they regarded as a global failure—poor people dying of treatable diseases.

Education, global health, and libraries were among the focuses of the foundation. The Global Microbicide Project was formed in 2001 to fight infectious diseases, and in 2002 Bill Gates made appearances with such celebrities as musician-activist Bono to raise awareness of economic, health, and social issues in Africa. Grants supported projects in

Bill and Melinda Gates. (Courtesy Kjetil Ree)

more than thirty countries as the foundation encouraged researchers to find workable solutions to problems.

In 2003, Bill and Melinda Gates visited infants infected with malaria in Africa. The foundation increased its efforts in fighting the often fatal disease, and the Gateses in 2007 called for the eradication of malaria. *Time* magazine named Bill and Melinda Gates, along with Bono, 2005 persons of the year for their work. In 2006 the Gateses and their foundation increased efforts to fight tuberculosis, and Bill Gates significantly reduced his role at Microsoft, the business he cofounded, to focus on philanthropy. He addressed the United Nations General Assembly in 2008, announcing grants to fight hunger and $168 million to combat malaria.

In its efforts toward education, the foundation committed to putting computers in many US public libraries and increasing public access to the Internet. Melinda Gates, in a 2009 speech before the Hispanic nonprofit group the National Council of La Raza, described education inequality as a civil rights issue. The foundation invested in teacher recruitment and training efforts in urban school systems.

Impact

The Bill & Melinda Gates Foundation's careful funding of programs has reaped rewards. A new vaccine against malaria and aggressive mosquito eradication programs have been developed, reducing childhood deaths caused by the parasitic disease. The Gateses' focus on maximum impact through careful funding sets an example for researchers and philanthropists. They encourage research in promising areas with a goal of benefitting many communities.

Further Reading

Fleishman, Joel L. *The Foundation: A Great American Secret; How Private Wealth Is Changing the World.* New York: Public Affairs, 2007. Print.

Kinsley, Michael, ed. *Creative Capitalism: A Conversation with Bill Gates, Warren Buffett, and Other Economic Leaders.* New York: Simon, 2008. Print.

Josephine Campbell

■ Gates, Robert

Identification: American secretary of defense
Born: September 25, 1946; Wichita, Kansas

Gates became the first secretary of defense to serve under presidents of different political parties. Under his leadership, the United States made significant changes to its approach to the wars in Iraq and Afghanistan. Gates proposed new approaches to defense spending that set in motion a reshaping of the goals and capabilities of US armed forces.

Robert Gates was asked by President George W. Bush to become secretary of defense in November 2006, shortly after midterm elections produced Democratic majorities in both houses of Congress. The election sent a strong message to the White House that the public was displeased with events related to the ongoing war in Iraq. The selection was unusual but not unprecedented. Gates had a successful twenty-six-year career in the Central Intelligence Agency (including two years as director), and had served on the National Security Council. Some were surprised when he accepted President Bush's offer. A year earlier, he turned down the opportunity to become the nation's first Director of National Intelligence, indicating that he preferred to remain as President of Texas A&M University, a position he assumed in 2001. In March 2006, Gates agreed to join the Iraq Study Group, organized to provide advice to the president on the conduct of the war. This position gave Gates a working knowledge of conditions in Iraq. An equally important factor in the president's decision to choose Gates was the fact that he was both temperamentally and ideologically different from the outgoing secretary, Donald Rumsfeld. It is likely that

Cadet First Capt. Marc Beaudion greets Defense Secretary Robert M. Gates. (U.S. Army/Photograph by Tommy Gilligan)

in selecting Gates, the Bush administration was seeking a culture change, one that would replace Rumsfeld's terse and aggressive nature.

Service in the Bush Administration

When Gates became secretary of defense on December 18, 2006, the United States had reached a low point in its war in Iraq. Continuing attacks on US military personnel by local insurgents and elements of al-Qaeda in Iraq had overshadowed the successful overthrow of Iraqi dictator Saddam Hussein. American forces continued to conduct operations from strongholds isolated from the Iraqi population, foraying into cities and villages to ferret out enemy combatants, and then returning to secure base camps. Gates moved rapidly to change the course of the conflict. He named General David Petraeus, the Army's foremost expert on counterinsurgency operations, as the new commander in Iraq. Gates also championed a surge, or temporary increase, in combat forces in Iraq. US troops were repositioned to Iraqi population centers to help root out pockets of enemy resistance, and speed up transition of all operations to Iraqi forces. Gates responded promptly and honestly to Congressional leaders skeptical of the new strategy.

Gates became known quickly as a no-nonsense leader, who demanded accountability from high-ranking military officials. When he discovered serious problems at Walter Reed Army Medical Center, the hospital's commanding general was fired. When remedial actions did not proceed quickly enough for him, he removed the Army's surgeon general and the secretary of the army. Gates took similar action against Air Force officials who were hesitant in supporting his plan to shift strategic priorities from conventional conflicts to asymmetric warfare. Following an embarrassing incident in which the Air Force lost track of several nuclear warheads, Gates fired the Air Force chief of staff and the secretary of the Air Force. By 2008, he had begun to unravel the Defense Department's aged procurement system, and challenge the long-held notion that the United States should continue to prepare vigilantly for conventional, land-based warfare. Gates's actions brought praise from Democrats and Republicans in Congress, who appreciated his ability to make substantive changes within the Pentagon bureaucracy.

Service in the Obama Administration

After his election in November 2008, President Barack Obama surprised many in both political parties by asking Gates to remain as secretary of defense in his administration. Gates accepted, and at Obama's request, moved to close down military operations in Iraq and ramp up action in Afghanistan. Gates proved willing to make hard choices to accomplish his goals. Not satisfied with progress in Afghanistan, in 2009 he relieved General David McKiernan, who had been in command for only one year, and selected General Stanley McChrystal as his replacement, a career special forces officer. Gates supported McChrystal's politically unpopular request for an increase in US forces in Afghanistan, aimed at stabilizing the country. Several months later, when McChrystal made public comments that questioned the strategy and competency of President Obama and civilian leaders, Gates took swift action to replace him with General Petraeus.

As defense secretary, Gates lobbied for closer ties between the Defense Department and Department of State, going so far as to advocate increases in the State Department budget to support what he called "soft power" operations in countries like Iraq and Afghanistan. At the same time, he undertook a major strategic overhaul of current and future Pentagon spending, most of which was focused on major weapons systems and conventional warfare. In his

2010 budget proposal, prepared during 2009, Gates recommended eliminating or reducing thirty-three programs, including new aircraft for the Air Force, ships for the Navy, and an integrated fighting system for the Army. He shifted funds to support current operations and purchase less expensive weapons and equipment more useful for the kind of smaller scale, urban warfare being conducted by US forces. Gates was successful in getting Congress to accept many of his recommendations. At the same time, he argued against the Obama administration's plan to make real cuts in defense spending as a means of reducing the national debt.

Impact

Gates's leadership helped reverse the course of the conflicts in Iraq and Afghanistan, materially improving the United States military's ability to conduct successful operations and organize an orderly withdrawal from Iraq and a build-up of forces in Afghanistan. His strong leadership inside the Pentagon restored confidence in the Department of Defense, both within the military and in Congress. His revolutionary budget proposals helped refocus strategic military thinking away from a long-dominant Cold-War mentality to concentrate on preparedness for smaller wars against less capable enemies who nevertheless pose significant threats to peace and prosperity throughout the world. He remained secretary of defense until July 2011, when he retired and was succeeded by former CIA director Leon Panetta. During his retirement ceremony, Gates received the Presidential Medal of Freedom, the country's highest civilian award.

Further Reading

Boot, Max. "Mr. Gates's Farewell." *Commentary* 132.2 (2011): 36–41.

Easterbrook, Greg. "Waste Land." *New Republic* 241.19 (2010): 20–23.

Gates, Robert M. *Understanding the New U.S. Defense Policy Through the Speeches of Robert M. Gates, Secretary of Defense.* Rockville: Manor, 2008.

Herman, Arthur. "The Re-Hollowing of the Military." *Commentary* 130.2 (2010): 11–17.

Rubin, Elizabeth. "The Survivor." *Time* 175.6 (2010): 26–35.

Shimko, Keith L. *Iraq Wars and America's Military Revolution.* Cambridge: Cambridge UP, 2010.

Laurence W. Mazzeno

■ Gawker Media

Definition: A private company that owns a number of gossip and news blogs, including *Gawker*

Gawker Media is a start-up blogging and news company that began an upward and international climb throughout the 2000s.

Gawker Media was founded by Nick Denton, a British journalist who, unlike many, made and kept millions of dollars from the dot-com boom of the 1990s. He sold an events company called First Friday that connected entrepreneurs and venture capitalists just before the bubble burst. At the time *Gawker* was officially launched in December 2002, blogging was still seen as an unprofitable hobby. Indeed, as a start-up, Gawker Media earned an early reputation for long hours and underpaid employees. But Denton's efforts caught the attention of several big advertisers—Audi, Nike, and Absolut Vodka, to name a few—as early as the fall of 2003.

In interviews, Denton was dismissive of blogging as a serious medium while at the same time he pursued expanding Gawker Media, with niche blogs like *Gizmodo* (technology), *Fleshbot* (pornography), and *Lifehacker* (tips for better living). Despite Denton's public protestations, *Gawker* was one of the first blogs to try to turn a profit—by openly pursuing readers—and Denton is considered a pioneer of blogging as a commercial venture. By the end of the 2000s, *Gawker*, lauded as "provocative" and "wildly entertaining," was named the Blog of the Decade by *Adweek* in December 2009. *Gizmodo*, *Deadspin* (a Gawker Media sports blog), and *Lifehacker* were all finalists for the award. As *Mediaite* reported, Denton's "scrappy outsiders" had built an empire on irony, page views, and unadulterated gossip.

Impact

The blog *Gawker*—whose tagline is "Today's gossip is tomorrow's news"—began and has continued to be primarily a commentary on East Coast living. Denton chose twenty-five-year-old Elizabeth Spiers as the site's first editor. New to New York City, Spiers delighted in artfully denigrating the city's elite, even when, as Carla Blumenkranz of *n+1* pointed out, those elite were not known outside of New York media culture. Though Spiers moved on to other publications early in *Gawker*'s history, most notably

Nick Denton, Arianna Huffington, and author John Gapper at a book party. (Courtesy *The Financial Times*/Photograph by Grace Villamil)

the *New York Observer*, she is credited with imbuing *Gawker* with its irreverent and nasty tone, solidifying the blogosphere's gold standard: snark.

Further Reading

Blumenkranz, Carla. "Gawker: 2002–2007: Pageviews to the People." *n+1*. n+1 Foundation, 3 Dec. 2007. Web. 14 Dec. 2012.

Quigley, Robert. "The Gawker Decade: How Gawker Media Defined the 2000s." *Mediaite*. Mediaite, 16 Dec. 2009. Web. 14 Dec. 2012.

Sorkin, Andrew Ross. "Building a Web Media Empire on a Daily Dose of Fresh Links." *New York Times*. New York Times, 17 Nov. 2003. Web. 14 Dec. 2012.

Molly Hagan

■ Geithner, Timothy

Identification: The seventy-fifth US secretary of the Treasury
Born: August 18, 1961; Brooklyn, New York

Timothy Geithner is a prominent American public policymaker and economist. He has held positions with the United States Department of the Treasury under three separate presidential administrations and was a senior official with the International Monetary Fund (IMF) before being tapped in 2009 to be President Barack Obama's choice for secretary of the Treasury.

Timothy Geithner first joined the Department of the Treasury in 1988, where he held a number of positions, ultimately serving under five different secretaries of the Treasury. Geithner's most prominent position with the Treasury in the early 2000s was that of undersecretary of the Treasury for international affairs, a post he held from 1999 until 2001, during the later years of President Bill Clinton's administration. In this role, he would be a central figure in addressing a number of financial crises involving regional markets. In 2001, Geithner's experience in international financial issues served him well, as he became the director of the Policy Development and Review Department at the IMF, a post he retained until 2003.

On November 17, 2003, Geithner was appointed to become the ninth president and chief executive officer of the Federal Reserve Bank of New York. In this capacity, he served as vice chair of the Federal Open Market Committee, an organization that is largely responsible for developing the financial policies of the United States. He held this position for six years. During his tenure as president, Geithner was faced with the beginnings of one of the worst fiscal crises the country had seen since the Great Depression. In March 2008, he oversaw one of the largest bailouts of a financial institution seen at the time, the purchase of Wall Street giant Bear Stearns by JP Morgan Chase, a move that entailed a $29 billion loan from the US Federal Reserve. He was also among the first to voice a concern that the country's financial system needed more government oversight as the US economy stood on the brink of recession.

In 2009, President-elect Barack Obama nominated Timothy Geithner as secretary of the Treasury. President Obama cited Geithner's work during the early stages of the recession as evidence of his capability in addressing the deepening crisis of the time. Geithner's nomination was not without controversy, however. First, it was revealed that Geithner owed more than $34,000 in federal taxes that had not been paid for several years. Geithner repaid the debt, a point he emphasized during his confirmation hearings. He was also grilled for the legality of papers filed for an individual who worked at his residence. Still, Geithner's confirmation hearings would conclude successfully, and Geithner was sworn in as the secretary of the Treasury on January 26, 2009.

In 2009, the recession that was already developing while Geithner was still at the Federal Reserve Bank of New York had taken root. Expectations remained high as to whether the Obama administration would be able to address the issues that had contributed to the ongoing crisis. Geithner's years with IMF, the Federal Reserve, and the US Treasury helped quell some of the concerns that he was not equal to the mammoth tasks at hand. Others, however, cited his presence at these organizations during the beginnings of the crisis as suspect, and many critics questioned whether Geithner could have done more while holding these posts to address those issues in their early stages. As secretary, Geithner oversaw the allocation of billions of dollars from the Troubled Asset Relief Program, efforts to regulate US financial institutions, and negotiations over the debt ceiling.

Impact

Geithner played a key role in shaping the economic landscape of the United States and the world in the first decade of the 2000s. He is considered a central figure in the mitigation of a number of financial crises involving several major corporations. Geithner's policies and actions in his various government roles have come under heavy scrutiny over the years, and the effectiveness of his efforts remains a point of debate and controversy.

Further Reading

Bandyk, Matthew. "Timothy Geithner." *U.S. News & World Report* Mar. 2009: 26. Print.

Timothy Geithner. (U.S. Treasury Department)

Gross, Daniel. "Timothy Geithner." *Newsweek* 5 Jan. 2009: 50–52. Print.

Scheiber, Noam. "The Escape Artist." *New Republic* 10 Feb. 2011: 13–17. Print.

Michael P. Auerbach, MA

■ Genetically modified foods

Definition: Genetically modified (GM) foods are those that have had foreign genes injected into their genetic codes in order to produce, modify, and enhance different specific traits

The rise of the genetic modification of foods caused much controversy in the 2000s as consumers, scientists, and government regulators argued over the possible benefits and risks of consuming these products. GM foods commonly refer to crop plants and animals that have been genetically modified in order to boost certain traits, such as nutritional content and resistance to herbicides. Concerns over the possible health risks of consuming GM foods caused much debate on the federal level. The US Food and Drug Administration (FDA) put several regulations in place to ensure GM foods are government approved before being sold to the public.

Origins and Implementation

Innovations in biotechnology prior to the 2000s provided scientists with the ability to extract specific genes from one source and introduce them into other organisms. This process allowed scientists to enhance, modify, or introduce specific traits that were not possible through traditional breeding. The majority of early modifications were aimed at developing crops' resistant to herbicides, which would allow farmers to safely spray their crops to eliminate weeds and other pests. Other crops were modified to be resistant to certain bacteria and viruses.

GM animals are altered to produce a desirable trait or introduce a new one, such as a larger body, resistance to disease, or a higher nutritional content. Some animals are altered to produce a human or an animal pharmaceutical from their bodily substances, such as milk or blood.

The genetic engineering of plants began during the 1980s when an antibiotic-resistant tobacco plant was manufactured. Before the 2000s, scientists developed GM potatoes, soybeans, canola oil, and several other products that received approval from the FDA. These developments were concerned with herbicide resistance and shorter ripening times. Not until 2000 did scientists used genetic engineering to increase the nutritional value of a food.

The first nutritionally enhanced food was golden rice. Scientists enhanced the beta-carotene content within the product, which boosted the vitamin A level. The goal of these modifications was to produce a food product that could be easily grown in areas of the world such as Africa, where vitamin A deficiency was leading to thousands of deaths.

The rise of GM plants in the United States increased sharply during the 2000s. By 2004, the percentage of modified corn grown in the country reached 45. During the same year, the percentage of GM soybeans in the United States reached 85. States that adapted the quickest to growing GM food were Mississippi and South Dakota. By the end of the decade, the FDA had approved the commercial growing of twenty-five GM crops, and the United States led the world in the production of GM crops, harvesting two-thirds of the world's GM crops.

Regulations

The US Department of Agriculture's Animal and Plant Health Inspection Service agency, the Environmental Protection Agency (EPA), and the FDA strictly regulate GM food in the United States. The agency with the most regulation over GM foods is the FDA. These agencies require that GM food pass regulatory inspections before they can be sold to the public. The FDA states that the same regulations are used for both GM food derived from plants and animals. Oftentimes, more than one agency will have to authorize a GM food before it is released.

In January 2009, the FDA released its final guidance for regulating GM animals under animal drug provisions of the Federal Food, Drug and Cosmetic Act. The guidance put forth was titled "The Regulation of Genetically Engineered Animals Containing Heritable rDNA Constructs." This guidance provides producers of GM animals recommendations to help them follow regulations.

Regulations were also put into effect on some local levels. On March 2, 2004, Mendocino County, California, became the first jurisdiction in the United States to pass a ban on the production and distribution of GM foods. Local farmers and environmentalists who worried about the environmental and health risks of GM products promoted the ban and helped get it passed into law.

Debate

One of the key issues of debate during the last half of the 2000s was the labeling of GM food. Critics argued that GM food should be labeled so consumers would know if they were purchasing altered food. Also, some religious groups disallow the consumption of items found in GM food, such as animal DNA. Throughout the decade, mandatory regulations to label GM food were proposed on the national and state levels were introduced to the US Congress, but they were never put into law. Those who are against labeling argued that it would be expensive and logistically problematic to label GM foods, since no valid differences have been found between GM food and unaltered food. They also state that foods labeled certified organic are already guaranteed unaltered, making a GM label redundant.

Those in favor of GM foods stated that modified foods could help increase the harvest of foods all over the world. They argued that regions around the globe that suffer from difficult growing conditions brought on by weather or soil conditions could benefit greatly from GM foods developed to flourish in harsh conditions. They also stated that modifying food not only makes it more abundant but also more nutritious.

In September 2000, a highly publicized controversy started when it was discovered that a variety of GM corn known as StarLink was being used in products meant for human consumption. This corn was modified to resist the *Bacillus thuringiensis* (Bt) pesticide. Previously, regulatory authorities only permitted the commercial sale of StarLink corn seed as long as it would not be used to produce human food. The FDA restricted it this way because of concerns that some humans could develop allergies to the corn. A Taco Bell brand of taco shells sold at grocery stores was discovered to contain StarLink corn. An immediate recall went into effect at Taco Bell as well as at other manufacturers and distributors that may have been affected. Critics used this incident to argue against the genetic altering of food, and since then, corn produced in the United States has been heavily monitored.

There were also some concerns over the effect of the Bt-corn pollen on monarch butterflies, which sometimes feed in and around corn fields. Critics were angered that the FDA would allow the release of the GM corn without first testing if monarch butterflies were allergic to it. Tests made by the US Department of Agriculture found that only one variety of Bt-corn was toxic to the butterflies.

Impact

The implementation of GM foods in the 2000s had a tremendous effect on the agriculture and livestock industries in the United States. The increase of their use has caused a large amount of controversy as consumers and agencies worried about both the long-term effects on human health and agriculture and ethical issues. The debates also helped bring worldwide attention to the problem of world hunger. The issue of labeling GM foods continued to be a major issue into the following decade. Despite the debates, by the end of the decade, the United States led the world in the production of GM food.

Further Reading

Hart, Kathleen. *Eating in the Dark: America's Experiment with Genetically Engineered Food.* New York: Pantheon, 2002. Print. Written by an environmental journalist, this book looks at the early stages of the debate over GM food.

McWilliams, James E., and Pamela C. Ronald. "The Value of Genetically Engineered Foods." *New York Times* 14 May 2010. Web. 6 Nov, 2012. Looks at research done at the beginning of the 2010s about the cultivation of and the ongoing debates about GM food.

Morin, Monte. "Science Group Opposes Labeling of Genetically Modified Foods." *Los Angeles Times* 26 Oct. 2012. Web. 6 Nov. 2012. Examines the major issue of labeling genetically modified foods in the United States and it how it continued in the 2000s.

Smith, Jeffrey M. *Seeds of Deception: Exposing Industry and Government Lies about the Safety of the Genetically Engineered Foods You're Eating.* Fairfield: Yes, 2003. Print. Explores the possible negative effects of GM foods on health and industry.

Weasel, Lisa H. *Food Fray: Inside the Controversy over Genetically Modified.* New York: AMACOM, 2008. Print. Written by a biologist, this book examines both sides of the GM foods argument, interviewing scientists, farmers, and activists.

Patrick G. Cooper

■ Gibson, Mel

Identification: American actor and director
Born: January 3, 1956; Peekskill, New York

Best known for his work as an actor, Mel Gibson directed the controversial 2004 film The Passion of the Christ. *He also directed the 2006 film* Apocalypto. *Throughout the 2000s, Gibson experienced several controversies and issues in his personal life that cast a shadow over his career achievements.*

Mel Gibson started the 2000s with two very different roles: the lead in the humorous romantic comedy *What Women Want* (2000) and a voice role in the animated film *Chicken Run* (2000). He returned to more familiar roles with *The Patriot* (2000) and *We Were Soldiers* (2002). He then starred in M. Night Shyamalan's alien film *Signs* (2002), with Joaquin Phoenix, Rory Culkin, and Abigail Breslin.

During the next few years, the actor failed to secure any acting roles that brought him box-office success. After the film *The Singing Detective* (2003), he turned to directing. As a director, he stirred controversy with his film *The Passion of the Christ* (2004), which depicted the events leading up to the death of Jesus. Before its release, the film incited controversy after critics deemed it anti-Semitic. Comments made by Gibson's father Hutton regarding the September 11 terrorist attacks and the Holocaust served to stoke the controversy surrounding the film. Because the film failed to attract any backers, Gibson financed it himself. *The Passion of the Christ* became one of the most profitable independent films ever made. Reviews of the film, however, were mixed.

Gibson's next project, *Apocalypto* (2006), proved to be another controversial directorial effort. Gibson employed unknown actors for the film, who spoke in an ancient Mayan language—moviegoers we afforded a translation in subtitles. Prior to the release of *Apocalypto* in July 2006, Gibson was arrested on charges of driving under the influence of alcohol (DUI). His mug shot appeared on the covers of tabloid magazines and other media. During the DUI incident, Gibson allegedly shouted anti-Semitic slurs at the police officers who arrested him. He was also accused of verbally assaulted a police officer after being taken to jail. Gibson apologized for the incident, blaming an alcohol dependency problem. Despite the apology, and the fact

Mel Gibson. (©iStockphoto.com/Kevin Winter)

that he briefly entered an alcoholism treatment program, the arrest episode caused significant damage to Gibson's reputation. *Apocalypto* was finally released, but it failed to capture significant attendance numbers at the box office.

In 2009 Gibson and his wife, Robyn Moore, announced their divorce after a three-year separation. The actor also announced he was expecting a child with singer Oksana Grigorieva, whom he met while filming *Edge of Darkness* (2010).

Impact

Although Gibson enjoyed considerable professional success in the 2000s, in particular with the film *The Passion of the Christ*, his standing in the entertainment industry and his public persona were negatively impacted by his drunk-driving arrest and allegations of anti-Semitism. Further controversies, including allegations of spousal abuse, plagued his career during the late 2000s and early 2010s.

Further Reading

Clarkson, Wensley. *Mel Gibson: Man on a Mission.* London: Blake, 2004. Print.
Perry, Roland. *Lethal Hero: The Mel Gibson Biography.* [USA]: Oliver, 1993. Print.

Angela Harmon

■ Giuliani, Rudolph

Identification: Former mayor of New York City
Born: May 28, 1944; Brooklyn, New York

New York City mayor Rudolph "Rudy" Giuliani restored order to the city and inspired calm across the nation in the aftermath of the terrorist attacks of September 11, 2001, in which the World Trade Towers were destroyed and more than two thousand people were killed in Manhattan alone. Giuliani's actions catapulted him to international prominence; he would go on to establish a lucrative consulting firm and run for the presidency of the United States in 2008.

In 2000 Rudolph Giuliani was nearing the end of his second term as mayor of New York City and experiencing the lowest point in a career that extended over three decades. In 1994 the predominantly Democratic voters of New York City had elected Republican Giuliani as mayor, principally because of his impressive record as US attorney for New York, during which time he prosecuted organized crime figures, Wall Street stock speculators, and corrupt public officials. By 2000, however, the popularity he had achieved during his first term as mayor—through bold initiatives to reduce crime and to restore the beauty and civility of the city—had withered away as Giuliani became embroiled in a number of confrontations with other city officials and his reputation was tainted by various incidents of police misconduct. The publicity surrounding Giuliani's separation and eventual divorce from his second wife eroded his standing with many ordinary citizens. To make matters worse, he was forced to abandon a campaign for the US Senate in 2000 when he was diagnosed with prostate cancer. Nevertheless, he continued to govern the city in the aggressive fashion that provoked many local civic and union leaders and strengthened the opinion that his days in public office were numbered. That perception changed radically on September 11, 2001.

The September 11 Attacks: Responding to Crisis
When the first hijacked plane struck the North Tower of New York's World Trade Center (WTC) complex, Giuliani rushed to the city's emergency command center, which he had established in 1996. While he and other city officials were formulating plans to respond to the crisis, a second plane struck the South Tower and, shortly thereafter, the towers began to collapse. The command center, located in Building 7 of the WTC, had to be evacuated. Following the evacuation, Giuliani immediately began directing rescue and recovery efforts. The media was eager to report

on his calm demeanor and willingness to speak about the city's inherent resiliency.

Although subsequent investigations revealed that Giuliani and his administration made several poor decisions prior to the attack, the mayor's popularity catapulted him into the international spotlight. In contrast to other public officials, including President George W. Bush, Giuliani was seen as the personification of America's strength in the face of adversity. He was praised by virtually every news outlet and was awarded an honorary knighthood by the Queen Elizabeth II of England in 2002. World-famous talk show host Oprah Winfrey dubbed him "America's Mayor." Ironically, while Giuliani's bold steps to restore the city to normalcy won him almost universal praise, subsequent moves to change the term-limits law so that he could run for a third term as mayor were rebuffed, as was an effort to have his term extended ninety days. On December 31, 2001, he left office and began a career in the private sector.

Giuliani Partners
After Giuliani left office, he announced the formation of Giuliani Partners LLC, a private consulting firm specializing in crisis management and security. A number of his partners were former staffers who had worked for Giuliani during his terms as major. Giuliani's high profile drew a number of important clients, including Purdue Pharma, Nextel, and Entergy. In 2004 Giuliani Partners bought Ernst & Young Corporate Finance and began offering financial management services as Giuliani Capital Advisors. In 2005, Giuliani became a partner in the Texas law firm of Bracewell & Patterson. Strong backers of Republican causes, the firm had significant ties to the energy industry and specialized in government relations. Giuliani's appeal was so powerful that the firm changed its name to Bracewell & Giuliani. Within a short time, he amassed significant wealth; in 2006, Giuliani made $16.8 million in income. In addition to his consulting business, he was a sought-after speaker who commanded $100,000 fees for a single engagement.

Not all went smoothly for Giuliani in the private sector. A number of his clients found that work done by Giuliani Partners did little to improve their security. Most notable among these was the government of Mexico City, which saw little effect on the rate of violent crimes after implementing some of the firm's recommendations. Furthermore, consultants were

Rudy Giuliani: 9/11 Speech to the United Nations

October 1, 2001

Thank you, President of the General Assembly, Dr. Han Seung-Soo, and Secretary General Annan. And thank you very much for the opportunity to speak, and also for the consideration you showed the City in putting off your General Session. And as I explained to the Secretary General and the President of the General Assembly, we are now open, and we're ready, and at any time we can arrange it, we look forward to having—having your heads of state and your foreign ministers here for—for that session.

On September 11th 2001, New York City—the most diverse City in the world—was viciously attacked in an unprovoked act of war. More than five thousand innocent men, women, and children of every race, religion, and ethnicity are lost. Among these were people from 80 different nations. To their representatives here today, I offer my condolences to you as well on behalf of all New Yorkers who share this loss with you. This was the deadliest attack—terrorist attack in history. It claimed more lives than Pearl Harbor or D-Day.

This was not just an attack on the City of New York or on the United States of America. It was an attack on the very idea of a free, inclusive, and civil society. It was a direct assault on the founding prin-ciples of the United Nations itself. The Preamble to the U.N. Charter states that this organization exists "to reaffirm faith in fundamental human rights, in the dignity and worth of the human person. . .to practice tolerance and live together in peace as good neighbors[and] to unite our strength to maintain international peace and security."

Indeed this vicious attack places in jeopardy the whole purpose of the United Nations. Terrorism is based on the persistent and deliberate violation of fundamental human rights. With bullets and bombs, and now with hijacked airplanes, terrorists deny the dignity of human life. Terrorism preys particularly on cultures and communities that practice openness and tolerance. Their targeting of innocent civilians mocks the efforts of those who seek to live together in peace as neighbors. It defies the very notion of being a neighbor.

This massive attack was intended to break our spirit. It has not done that. It's made us stronger, more determined, and more resolved. The bravery of our firefighters, our police officers, our emergency workers, and civilians we may never learn of, in saving over 25,000 lives that day, and carrying out the most effective rescue operation in our history, inspires all of us.

often faulted for failing to understand the local culture and trying to impose solutions that might work well in the United States but not on foreign soil. An additional embarrassment for Giuliani was the indictment of long-time associate and former New York City police commissioner Bernard Kerik. In 2004 Giuliani had recommended Kerik to President Bush for the position of secretary of homeland security. Unfortunately, evidence that Kerik failed to pay taxes for a housekeeper he employed forced him to withdraw his name as a candidate for the position. Shortly thereafter, an investigation into Kerik's ties with organized crime led to his resignation from Giuliani Partners. Giuliani managed to weather these blows to his reputation, however, and planned for a return to public life.

Presidential Campaign

Calls for Giuliani to run for president began surfacing shortly after the September 11 tragedy; however, Giuliani decided to support President Bush, a fellow Republican, in his bid for reelection in 2004. In 2005 a "Draft Giuliani" movement was launched, and by the time Giuliani made a formal announcement of his candidacy in February 2007, he was well ahead of all his rivals in national polls. Throughout that year, polls showed him as the front-runner, although a growing number of more conservative Republicans expressed reservations about his fitness to be the party's standard bearer.

Giuliani was at odds with Republican positions on four important issues. During his career he supported abortion and civil unions for same-sex couples, took a moderate stance on illegal immigration, and pushed for tougher gun-control laws. Many religious leaders felt his personal life (including two divorces and estrangement from his children) made him unfit for the country's top office.

While Giuliani did well in campaign speeches, where he could tout his own record on fighting terrorism, he was less effective in debates and interviews when questioned on controversial topics. His attempts to backtrack on issues such as abortion or gay rights were not viewed as sincere by many potential Republican voters. Anticipating that he would not fare well in strong conservative states such as Iowa or South Carolina, Giuliani set up only skeleton staffs in several states and did little active campaigning there. Instead, he largely concentrated on winning Florida, a state with a substantial number of delegates to the Republican convention, and using that win to generate support in other states with larger numbers of delegates. When caucuses and primaries began in January 2008, the results bore out the expectations of his advisors; Giuliani finished no higher than third in any of the early primaries.

The results in Florida, however, were not what Giuliani anticipated. Though the state was populated with many retirees originally from New York, the former New York City mayor finished a disappointing third, garnering less than 15 percent of the vote. Arizona senator John McCain (36 percent) and former Massachusetts governor Mitt Romney (31 percent) far outdistanced him. Recognizing the inevitability of defeat, on January 30, 2008, Giuliani announced that he was withdrawing from the campaign. At the same time he endorsed the candidacy of McCain, the eventual Republican nominee.

Impact

Rudy Giuliani's actions immediately following the terrorist attack on the World Trade Center became symbolic of America's courage and gave hope to the nation. Across the United States and around the globe people were inspired by his resolve in the face of terrorism. For Giuliani personally, the fame he gained from his visibility as a leader in the nation's response to unprecedented attacks on domestic soil resurrected a flagging political career and was responsible for his early success as a candidate in the 2008 presidential election.

Giuliani's failed bid in the presidential campaign was indicative of a growing trend among the Republican Party. By rejecting him early in the race, Republican voters signaled that they becoming increasingly unwilling to tolerate the moderate positions Giuliani represented. Instead, the party reaffirmed its more hard-line conservative stance on issues such as abortion, immigration, gay marriage, and gun control. As a result, the divide between political parties in the United States became more pronounced, making compromise on virtually any political issue more difficult to achieve.

Further Reading

Barrett, Wayne, and Dan Collins. *Grand Illusion: The Untold Story of Rudy Giuliani and 9/11.* New York: HarperCollins, 2006. Print.

Boyer, Peter. "Mayberry Man." *New Yorker,* 20 August 2007, 44–63. Print.

Mitchell, Katharyne, and Katherine Beckett. "Securing the Global City: Crime, Consulting, Risk, and Ratings in the Production of Urban Space." *Indiana Journal of Global Legal Studies* 15.1 (2008): 75–99. Print.

Popkin, Samuel L. *The Candidate: What It Takes to Win—And Hold—The White House.* New York: Oxford UP, 2012. Print.

Siegel, Fred. *The Prince of the City: Giuliani, New York and the Genius of American Life.* New York: Encounter Books, 2007. Print.

Strober, Deborah Hart, and Gerald S. Strober. *Giuliani: Flawed or Flawless? The Oral Biography.* Hoboken: Wiley, 2007. Print.

Laurence W. Mazzeno

■ *Gladiator*

Identification: Historical epic film about a Roman general who is forced into slavery and later exacts revenge on the emperor by becoming a champion in the gladiatorial arena in Rome

Director: Ridley Scott (b. 1937)

Date: Released on May 5, 2000

Director Ridley Scott's Gladiator *was a great critical and financial success of 2000. The film was applauded for its action and for its examination of the corruption of power and revenge. The film was nominated for twelve Academy Awards and won five, including best picture and best actor.*

The screenplay for *Gladiator* underwent several re-writes before the film went into production in 1999. Screenwriter David Franzoni pitched the film to the production company DreamWorks and wrote the first draft in 1998. Extensive pre-production included the construction of thousands of pieces of armor and the building of a smaller replica of the Roman Colosseum. The filmmakers utilized a great deal of computer graphics as well, especially to depict massive crowds at the Colosseum. Actor Russell Crowe was heavily involved with the development of his character, Maximus Decimus Meridius, even making dialogue suggestions to the screenwriters. Released to great critical praise, much of the film's acclaim emphasized its action sequences and Crowe's performance.

The film revolves around Maximus, a Roman general who is betrayed by Commodus (Joaquin Phoenix), the son of the dying Emperor Marcus Aurelius (Richard Harris). Aurelius wished for Maximus to take power after he died, but when Commodus learned of this he ordered Maximus and his family to be killed. Maximus escapes, but he is unable to save his family. He's picked up by slave traders who sell him to Proximo (Oliver Reed), a gladiator trainer. Maximus, who disguises himself during his battles, uses the gladiator tournaments to eventually get close to Commodus and take his revenge.

Critics who praised the film often mentioned the elaborate action sequences, most notably the opening sequence of the film in which Maximus leads a Roman army against a Germanic tribe. Those who negatively criticized the film often took issue with the lack of character depth in Maximus.

Impact

Gladiator won several film industry awards, including the Academy Awards for best picture and best actor for Russell Crowe, as well as several technical awards. The film also won the Golden Globe award for best motion picture. For those involved with the film, the victories were bittersweet since actor Oliver Reed suffered from a fatal heart attack during filming. The film's success has been attributed to a renaissance in the public's interest in Roman history and a resurgence in historical epic films.

Further Reading

Scott, Ridley, Walter Parkes, and Sharon Black. *Gladiator: The Making of the Ridley Scott Epic (New Market Pictorial Moviebooks)*. New York: Newmarket, 2000. Print.

Winkler, Martin M., ed. *Gladiator: Film and History*. Malden: Blackwell, 2004. Print.

Patrick G. Cooper

■ Gladwell, Malcolm

Identification: British-born Canadian writer
Born: September 3, 1963; Fareham, United Kingdom

Gladwell is renowned for exploring issues related to sociology and human psychology. In addition to his work as a best-selling author, he has served as a staff writer for the New Yorker *since 1996.*

In 2000, *New Yorker* staff writer Malcolm Gladwell published his first book, *The Tipping Point: How Little Things Make a Big Difference*, in which he analyzes how trends and ideas, products, and behaviors spread throughout society and popular culture. Gladwell compares patterns of popularity to infectious diseases, an idea that came to him while covering the AIDS epidemic as a reporter for the *Washington Post*. An instant success, *The Tipping Point* sold millions of copies worldwide and has been translated into twenty-five languages.

Since *The Tipping Point*, Gladwell has published *Blink* (2005) and *Outliers: The Story of Success* (2008), both of which have also become bestsellers. In *Blink* Gladwell looks at why people have a habit of jumping to conclusions so quickly. *Outliers: The Story of Success* (2008) explores how and why some people achieve success and others do not. In his exploration of people from all walks of life—from corporate lawyers to Microsoft CEO Bill Gates—Gladwell argues that it is not the individual we must consider when understanding success but the person's surroundings.

Gladwell finished the decade with the release of yet another bestseller, *What the Dog Saw* (2009), a collection essays that he previously published in the *New Yorker*. Each essay offers a glimpse into the psyche of an individual person and attempts to convey what it would feel like to be that person.

Impact

In 2005, *Time* listed Gladwell as one of the "100 Most Influential People." His articles and books have

Malcolm Gladwell. (Courtesy Pop!Tech/Photograph by Kris Krüg)

Further Reading

Adams, Tim. "The Man Who Can't Stop Thinking." *Guardian* [UK]. Guardian News and Media Ltd., 15 Nov. 2008. Web. 9 July 2012.

Donadio, Rachel. "The Gladwell Effect." *New York Times.* New York Times Co., 5 Feb. 2006. Web. 9 July 2012.

McDonald, Alyssa. "The NS Interview: Malcolm Gladwell." *New Statesman.* New Statesman, 24 May 2010. Web. 9 July 2012.

Cait Caffrey

■ Global warming debate

Definition: A series of international political and social issues regarding the severity, origin, and ultimate result of climate change patterns

The global warming debate is one of the most important issues determining current and future ecological and energy policy and has also raised a variety of questions regarding the relationship between science and politics. Primary issues include whether current climate change is within normal parameters or representative of an unprecedented period of extreme change, and whether or not human activity is one of the major contributing factors to climate change.

helped spark a new style of nonfiction that has been described by Rachel Donadio for the *New York Times* as "a highly contagious hybrid genre . . . one that takes a nonthreatening and counterintuitive look at pop culture and the mysteries of the everyday." With his insightful investigations into society's quirks, and his ability to make inaccessible knowledge accessible, he has turned his unique viewpoints into a highly successful enterprise that continues to illuminate and influence readers.

In July 2012, Gladwell was interviewed, along with others, by Morley Safer for CBS's *60 Minutes* about the phenomenon of kindergarten redshirting, the practice of holding students back for a year before they start elementary school. Gladwell's book *Outliers* influenced redshirting by suggesting to parents that holding the youngest students in a class back a year would enable them to gain what he termed a "cumulative advantage" as the oldest students in the next class.

History of the Debate

The global warming debate centers on the scientific theory that the release of greenhouse gasses—such as carbon dioxide, methane, and nitrous oxide—produced by human industrial activity, can cause warming of the global climate by preventing the escape of solar radiation into space. This theory emerged in the 1950s, fueled by research regarding the effect of burning fossil fuels. By the 1980s, scientific organizations around the world were becoming concerned that human industry could permanently affect global climate in ways that could potentially cause widespread ecological damage.

The Intergovernmental Panel on Climate Change (IPCC), a cooperative research group involving scientists from more than sixty countries, was founded by the United Nations in 1988 to address global warming by creating cooperative international agreements that would reduce greenhouse gas emissions. In 1992, member countries of the United Nations

The remains of a glacier 1,800 meters above the Satsalla River Valley on British Columbia's central coast. (Courtesy Drew Brayshaw)

ratified a treaty known as the United Nations Framework Convention on Climate Change (UNFCCC), signifying the intention to work together to address climate change. The UNFCCC eventually grew to 195 parties.

During the 1990s, a minority group of lobbyists, politicians, and scientists began to question data regarding global warming that was based on the existence of studies providing widely divergent projections from current patterns. Corporations and political organizations threatened by potential restrictions on fossil fuels and other industrial processes utilized this uncertainty in scientific data to argue against those who supported strong regulations to control climate change.

Global Warming Controversy: 2000 to 2004

The 1998 Kyoto Protocol, crafted by the UFNCCC, was the first major attempt to create a set of international policies aimed at reducing greenhouse gas emissions. The protocol required participating countries to reduce emissions by more than 5 percent below 1990 levels between 2005 and 2012. Though the United States ratified the Kyoto Protocol under the Clinton administration, in 2001, under the Bush administration, the United States abandoned the program, becoming the only major world power to decline participation. The Kyoto Protocol became legally binding in 2004, with Russia becoming the nineteenth nation to sign the initiative.

In 2001, the IPCC released its third official report on the state of climate change, revealing that the1990s were the warmest decade on record and that human activity was indicated as a causal factor, though the ultimate effects of current trends were difficult to determine. Threatened by the potential for restrictive regulation, several leading corporations involved in petroleum production cooperated to fund research that called the findings of the IPCC into question, thereby helping to defray public support for greenhouse gas reform. The *New York Times* published an article at the beginning of the 2000s indicating that ExxonMobil contributed more than

$16 million to promote scientific research contradicting the general theory of global warming.

In 2002, the Bush administration established the US Climate Change Science Program (CCSP), an organization aimed at coordinating domestic research into global warming and related phenomena. The program was in part created to satisfy criticisms from environmental organizations, in the wake of the Bush administration's decision to opt out of the Kyoto Protocol.

In 2003, a major heat wave in Europe resulted in temperatures 30 to 40 percent higher than average and led to the death of an estimated 20,000 to 35,000 individuals, according to a study in the French journal *Comptes rendus biologies*. While some scientists contended that the heat wave was the result of global warming, others argued that the event was a result of naturally occurring climate fluctuations unrelated to human activity.

In November of that year, the Commonwealth of Massachusetts led a class action suit against the Environmental Protection Agency (EPA), joined by several other states, in an effort to force the EPA to officially categorize greenhouse gasses as pollutants, thereby requiring regulations. The debate continued until 2007, when the US Supreme Court ruled that the EPA was required to recognize and regulate greenhouse gasses as pollutants.

Global Warming Debate: 2005 to 2010

In 2005, Rick Piltz, a senior member of the CCSP, resigned from the organization claiming that its data had been censored by the Bush administration in an effort to create deliberate ambiguity regarding climate change. The *New York Times* and other newspapers reported on Piltz's accusations, centering on the activities of Philip Cooney, chairman of George W. Bush's Council on Environmental Quality and a former lobbyist for the American Petroleum Institute.

Cooney resigned in the wake of Piltz's accusations and was hired by ExxonMobil the same year. Cooney was asked to testify at hearings before the United States House Committee on Oversight and Government Reform in 2007, and he conceded that he had played a role in censoring information from the CCSP, claiming that he was directed to do so by superiors within the Bush administration.

The El Niño season of 2005 raised significant global warming controversy, especially following the deluge of New Orleans by Hurricane Katrina. While some scientists, including members of the IPCC, contended that increased hurricane activity is related to global warming, a large number of scientists rejected this position, claiming that hurricane formation is a complex phenomenon not immediately tied to human activity.

In the wake of Katrina, opposition groups strengthened their case against the IPCC, aided by a high profile case in which leading scientists accused the IPCC of overstating the case for global warming in response to political pressure. Christopher Landsea, a leading American expert on hurricane development, resigned from the IPCC in 2005, withdrawing his contribution to the IPCC's fourth report on climate change on the basis that the leadership of the organization was promoting research aimed at pushing a political agenda.

In 2006, the Pew Global Attitudes Project reported that the populations of China and the United States—the highest contributors of global greenhouse gasses—had the lowest level of concern about climate change. According to the report, only 20 percent of Americans agreed that global warming was a major concern. The 2006 documentary *An Inconvenient Truth*, focusing on former Vice President Al Gore's effort to raise awareness about climate change, increased popular coverage of the issue and also led to an increase of popular support. The following year, Gore and the IPCC shared the Nobel Peace Prize for their efforts to promote public awareness about the issue.

In 2007, the Heartland Institute, a conservative think tank, released a list of five hundred publications that contradicted the mainstream scientific consensus on climate change. The Heartland Institute's report was widely criticized within the scientific community for misrepresenting existing data, but it served to deepen the lack of public consensus regarding climate change. That same year, the IPCC's *Fourth Assessment Report* was released, containing a wealth of additional data linking the warming of ocean waters, rivers, and the shifting of seasonal patterns to human activity.

In 2009, an anonymous hacker spread stolen confidential e-mails taken from representatives of the Climatic Research Unit (CRU) at Britain's East Anglia University, which were used as evidence by opponents of the IPCC to suggest that the agency was distorting research to promote its agenda. The CRU reported that the e-mails were taken out of context and that members of their organization were not involved in attempting to misrepresent research or data regarding climate change.

In November 2009, the United States attended the United Nations Climate Change Conference in Copenhagen, Denmark, aimed at producing a new global strategy to further progress made under the Kyoto Protocol. The conference was widely considered to be a failure, as heads of state were unable to reach an agreement on future measures or policy recommendations. The conference resulted in the Copenhagen Accord, a document proposed by US representatives that identified global warming as one of the world's most significant current issues, but the accord did not provide any proposals for policy or restriction initiatives.

A report released in April 2011 by the Brookings Institution reported that the number of Americans who believed in the existence of global warming had fallen from 72 percent in 2008 to 58 percent in 2010, with 26 percent of Americans reporting the belief that global warming is not based on solid evidence. However, some analysts pointed out that shrinking concern over global warming may represent the prevalence of other concerns, including economic issues, taking precedence over global warming in the short term.

Though public opinion remained divided on the issue at the end of the 2000s, the vast majority of scientists were in agreement with the IPCC that climate change is a measurable ongoing phenomenon with clear links to human activity. Polls released by the Pew Center in June of 2009 showed that 89 percent of scientists, from a variety of fields, believe that the sharp increase in global warming during the late twentieth and early twenty-first centuries is linked to the burning of fossil fuels and other human activities. Record snowfall across the United States in 2010 was utilized by a number of anti–global warming supporters to argue against the prevailing global warming theory; however, IPCC spokespeople contended that cold winters are in keeping with overall data concerning the variations caused by increasing atmospheric pollutants.

Impact

The global warming debate was one of the most intense political, media, and public policy debates of the 2000s. Strong evidence emerged from a variety of

scientific disciplines indicating that climate change is an ongoing, measurable phenomenon, though the ultimate causes and results of these changes remained an area of intense disagreement. Scientific consensus increased during the decade, as did public consensus in a majority of countries, while the population of the United States was uniquely divided on the issue—with a small majority believing in the human origins of global warming. The prevalence of doubt regarding global warming in the United States is directly related to a variety of factors, including political and corporate efforts to obfuscate data on both sides of the debate in an effort to support political agendas.

A variety of books and documentary films were produced during the decade documenting both the study of global warming and the human connection to climate change, helping to bring the issue to the forefront of public consciousness. Among the issues discussed in the media was the concern that political issues were influencing scientific data produced on both sides of the debate. This led to a meta-examination of the issue within a number of books and articles produced during the decade, investigating the ethics and social responsibility inherent in the relationship between science and politics.

Further Reading

"Background on the UNFCCC: The International Response to Climate Change." *United Nations Framework Convention on Climate Change*. United Nations Framework Convention on Climate Change, 2012. Web. 13 Aug. 2012. Official website of the UNFCCC provides background of the organization and a review of initiatives proposed by the UNFCCC.

Houghton, John Theodore. *Global Warming: The Complete Briefing*. 3rd ed. New York: Cambridge UP, 2004. Print. Textbook written for science students and general readers introducing many of the core concepts in the global warming debate.

Maslin, Mark. *Global Warming: Causes, Effects, and the Future*. Updated ed. St. Paul: MBI, 2007. Print. Information regarding the potential outcomes of climate change on the atmosphere, hydrosphere, and lithosphere of the earth.

Layzer, Judith. "Deep Freeze: How Business Has Shaped the Global Warming Debate in Congress." *Law & Ethics in the Business Environment*. 7th ed. Ed. Terry Halbert and Elaine Ingulli. Mason, Ohio: South-Western, 2012. 210–14. Print. Essay discusses the economic, political, and industrial issues surrounding the global warming debate and the policies related to climate change.

Oberthür, Sebastian, and Hermann E. Ott. *The Kyoto Protocol: International Climate Policy for the 21st Century.* New York: Springer, 2010. Print. Comprehensive analysis of the Kyoto protocols for specialists and general readers to understand the political debates, international issues, and research leading to the Kyoto Protocols.

Micah Issitt

■ Gonzales v. Carhart

The Case: US Supreme Court ruling upholding the constitutionality of the Partial-Birth Abortion Ban Act of 2003

Date: Decided on April 18, 2007

Indicating a shift in its stance on abortion and women's rights, the Supreme Court upheld the Partial-Birth Abortion Ban Act, refuting claims that the law placed "undue burden" on women. Many in the medical profession saw the court's decision as opening the door to government involvement in the health decisions of Americans.

In 2003, US Congress passed the Partial-Birth Abortion Ban Act (PBA ban), the first federal restriction on an abortion procedure since the Supreme Court ruling in *Roe v. Wade* legalized abortion in 1973. Just three years prior to the Act's passing, the Supreme Court struck down a similar ban in Nebraska in *Stenberg v. Carhart* (2000), citing the state law's vague terms and lack of an exception for women's health. Based on the *Stenberg* ruling, two courts of appeals declared the 2003 PBA ban unconstitutional on the same grounds. In response to lower courts' striking down the ban, US Attorney General Alberto Gonzales appealed. Challenging the rulings by the US Court of Appeals for the Eighth and Ninth Circuits, Gonzales claimed the constitutionality of the ban. As the appeals were similar, the Supreme Court's decision in *Gonzales v. Carhart* (which appealed the Eighth Circuit's opinion) also served as a response to *Gonzales v. Planned Parenthood* (which appealed the Ninth Circuit's opinion).

During the hearing, the American Congress of Obstetricians and Gynecologists (ACOG) filed an amicus brief stating its opposition to the PBA ban.

The brief warned against government interference in the doctor/patient relationship, and emphasized the safety advantages of partial-birth abortion, or intact dilation and evacuation, over non-intact dilation and evacuation, in which the fetus is pulled apart within the uterus to allow for its removal. According to the ACOG, the law limits doctors in their ability to provide care.

Despite the precedent set by the *Stenberg* ruling, the Supreme Court upheld the constitutionality of the PBA Ban Act. Anthony Kennedy, delivering the majority opinion, neither refuted nor supported the Court's previous decision in *Stenberg*, as the cases referenced separate bans on partial-birth abortions. Rather, the Supreme Court relied on the federal legislation's specificity, as well as its minimal exceptions for women whose lives were at risk, to deem the ban constitutional.

Impact

Gonzales indicated a shift in the Supreme Court's stance on abortion, with critics also seeing it as a shift away from science. Of the five justices in the majority, all were Catholic. Some believe the categorical Catholic opposition to abortion on religious grounds significantly influenced the ruling. By upholding the Partial-Birth Abortion Ban Act and confirming that fetal life is a state interest, the Supreme Court validated a degree of congressional authority over the medical decisions of pregnant women.

Further Reading

"ACOG Statement on the US Supreme Court Decision Upholding the Partial-Birth Abortion Ban Act of 2003." *American Congress of Obstetricians and Gynecologists.* American Congress of Obstetricians and Gynecologists, 18 Apr. 2007. Web. 6 Sep. 2012.

Harrison, Maureen, and Steve Gilbert, eds. *Landmark Decisions of the United States Supreme Court VII, 2000–2005.* Carlsbad: Excellent Books, 2006. Print.

Leverich, Jean, ed. *Abortion.* Detroit: Greenhaven, 2010. Print.

Lucia Pizzo

■ Gonzales, Alberto

Identification: US Attorney General
Born: August 4, 1955; San Antonio, Texas

Before serving as the eightieth US attorney general, Alberto Gonzales had an extensive career in law, politics, and government. He spent many years in the service of the Republican Party and was a particularly close ally of George W. Bush. In fact, the partnership between Gonzales and Bush began well before the Bush presidency.

During his tenure as governor of Texas, George W. Bush chose Alberto Gonzales as the state's general counsel in 1994. Gonzales subsequently served under Bush as Texas's secretary of state in 1997 and was appointed to the Texas Supreme Court in 1999. Critics of Gonzales claim that he did not properly serve in his role as legal counsel to Governor Bush, given that the state of Texas executed more prisoners than any other US state during his term. Nonetheless, Gonzales was named White House counsel to President Bush in 2001.

In 2004, President Bush nominated Gonzales to succeed departing attorney general John Ashcroft. Bush's nomination of Gonzales to the position resulted in some criticism from Republicans who did not consider him a strong political conservative. The nomination, however, was approved, and Gonzales was sworn in on February 14, 2005. Alberto Gonzales became the first Hispanic attorney general in US history.

In 2006, the Justice Department was investigated by the Office of Professional Responsibility regarding its role in the National Security Agency's (NSA's) domestic spying program. A December 2005 report in the *New York Times* stated that the NSA was conducting surveillance of individuals in the United States without the necessary warrants. President Bush essentially put a halt to the investigation by denying access to the classified information required to conduct it. Although it has been suggested that Bush did this to prevent Gonzales's name from being revealed in relation to the program, White House spokespeople said the move was made under the auspice of executive privilege in order to keep sensitive materials guarded in the name of national security.

Eventually, Gonzales was asked to testify in front of the Senate Judiciary Committee regarding whether or not he knew of any disagreement within the Justice Department over the legality of the wiretapping and surveillance efforts. Although former government officials such as retired Federal Bureau of Investigation director Robert Mueller and former

Alberto Gonzales. (Courtesy Matthew Bradley)

deputy attorney general James B. Comey testified that Gonzales knew that there was a dispute regarding the program's legality, Gonzales himself spoke only generally of the issue. Critics suggested that he did not offer specifics because he did not want to appear as having been complicit in a potentially unconstitutional and legally questionable program.

The dismissal of eight US attorneys brought further scrutiny to Gonzales and the Bush administration.. The majority of the dismissed attorneys had recently received favorable reviews from the Justice Department. A controversy soon arose over allegations that the firings were politically motivated.

Critics claimed that the firings took place because the attorneys had opinions that contradicted the political agenda of the Bush administration. In a press conference, Gonzales denied he had any knowledge of the firings. However, subsequently released Department of Justice records stated that Gonzales himself had authorized the termination of the various attorneys.

Gonzales was eventually forced to give congressional testimony regarding the controversy. In his testimony, Gonzales stated that he could not recall his involvement in the firings because he was attending to many other things at the time.

There was widespread speculation that Bush's appointment of Gonzales to the post of US attorney general was a precursor to Gonzales's eventual nomination to the US Supreme Court. Questions regarding this possibility persisted after Supreme Court justice Sandra Day O'Connor announced her retirement in July 2005. However, it is rumored that Gonzales was not considered a good Supreme Court nominee by members of Bush's conservative base of supporters, and the nomination never occurred.

Gonzales's tenure as US attorney general was controversial and politically charged. Nonetheless, President Bush never wavered in his support of Gonzales despite the tumultuous criticism levied by the media and by both Republicans and Democrats in Congress. Both the domestic surveillance controversy and the controversy surrounding the US attorney firing scandal led to bipartisan calls for Gonzales's resignation. Nonetheless, President Bush continually defended Gonzales.

On August 26, 2007, Gonzales submitted his letter of resignation to President Bush. He did not explain the specific reasons behind his decision to leave, but he did thank President Bush for the opportunity to serve as attorney general. President Bush appeared to regret Gonzales's decision and stated that his departure was a result of political wrangling.

In July 2009, Gonzales was hired as a diversity recruiter by the Texas Tech University system. He also teaches political science at the university.

Impact

Gonzales was the first Hispanic attorney general and the highest-ranking Hispanic government official in US history. He was named by *Time* magazine as one of the most influential Hispanic Americans and received the Distinguished Leadership award in 2006 from Leadership Houston. Despite considerable controversy and court proceeding during his tenure as attorney general and his resignation, Gonzales is recognized for his fight against terrorism and protecting children from sexual predators.

Further Reading
Goldsmith, Jack, *The Terror Presidency: Law and Judgment inside the Bush Administration.* New York: Norton, 2007. Print

Ortner, Jill. *The President's Counselor: The Rise to Power of Alberto Gonzales.* New York: Rayo, 2006. Print

United States Congress Senate Committee. "Confirmation Hearing on the Nomination of Alberto R. Gonzales to Be Attorney General of the United States." Washington, DC: BilioGov, 2010. Print.

■ Google

Definition: An American technology company, specializing mainly in Internet search and online advertising

Incorporated in the late 1990s, Google became one of the leading technology companies by the end of the 2000s. The business started as an Internet search engine and grew rapidly once it monetized its search technology by using innovative models of advertising. With that revenue, the company expanded into numerous other fields such as providing online maps, e-mail services, productivity tools, video sharing, and mobile devices.

Although Google started in 1998 with only three employees at a garage in Menlo Park, California, within two years the company had become the top search engine in the world with more than one billion web pages in its index. By the end of 2000, the company founded by Larry Page and Sergey Brin was available in twenty-six languages and was providing more than sixty million searches each day. Its traffic was growing several thousand percent per year.

The increased popularity of the search engine provided the company with a lucrative market for the launch of its advertising services, such as AdWords. The platform worked by serving context-sensitive text advertisements based on keywords chosen by the advertiser. The cost depended on the popularity of the keyword and the number of people who clicked on the advertisement. The new advertising platform was flexible and affordable enough for small businesses and quickly became highly successful. The format of the advertisements allowed only text, which users preferred over the more obtrusive image advertisements used by competing websites. At the same time, Google was expanding its corporate customer base by offering SiteSearch, a search engine using Google's efficient technology to locally search large organizational websites for relevant information. By the end of 2000, the company had 120 corporate clients in more than thirty countries.

Google exhibit at the American Library Association conference. (Courtesy of OzinOH)

voice-communication service using the Internet, in 2007 and relaunched it as Google Voice. The online video-sharing service YouTube became a notable exception to Google's rebranding strategy when it was acquired in 2006. Instead of being integrated into Google Video, the new asset continued to exist under its original name.

In 2007, Google entered the mobile-device industry with its smartphone operating system, Android. Set to compete against other major players in the sector such as Apple's iOS, Microsoft's Windows Mobile, and Research in Motion's Blackberry OS, Google's new operating system was touted as an open platform, backed by a joint effort of many leading hardware manufacturers and telecommunication companies. By the end of the decade, Android showed tremendous potential, growing more than 1,000 percent in market share in 2009 alone.

Continued Growth and Acquisitions

Google made its initial public offering (IPO) on August 18, 2004. Following its policy of innovation, Google priced the shares by an unusual Dutch auction method. This gave small investors a greater chance to compete with major banks and financial institutions. The IPO managed to secure $1.2 billion for Google, providing the company with much-needed resources for expansion. Shares given to employees and early investors made many people very rich overnight. The IPO also gave Google the leverage needed to acquire smaller companies as its stock valuation reached $29.4 billion.

Google started buying other tech companies in 2001. Company heads often searched out start-ups offering new technologies that they wanted to further develop and integrate with Google's own services. One such case was Deja.com's Usenet discussion service, which found a new place in Google's portfolio of online products rebranded as Google Groups. Keyhole, makers of three-dimensional mapping software, joined the list of acquisitions in 2004 and later resurfaced as Google Earth. In 2005, Urchin, a web analytics company, formed the basis of Google Analytics. Writely, a web-based word-processing software company, later became a part of Google Docs. Google acquired Grand Central, a

Corporate Culture and Social Responsibility

During the 2000s, Google became known for the great environment it created for its employees. The company headquarters in Mountain View, California, included a number of amenities uncommon in corporate offices. The facility featured laundry and dry-cleaning services, gyms, volleyball and basketball courts, medical services, and day care. Indoor climbing walls, bowling alleys, pub-style lounges, and massage rooms ensured that employees had little reason to go far from their work spaces in search of recreation. Food, prepared by professional chefs, was free for employees at the US campus. Because employees remained on-site, productivity was high and workdays were frequently long.

The benefits of working at Google went well beyond gourmet meals and extravagant facilities. Employees enjoyed retirement benefits in which personal savings were matched by the company. Google provided bonuses of up to 30 percent per year. The value of company stock, which all employees received, rose steadily. Yet the most unique perk at Google was the freedom to pursue one's own ideas—rather than assigned projects—for up to 20 percent of the workday.

From Google's inception, Page and Brin prided themselves on the eccentric culture of their company. Playing pranks and breaking conventions were encouraged. Interviews were conducted while roller skating. Aprils Fools' jokes became a part of corporate branding when Google started incorporating them annually in its search engine as early as 2000. Ideas such as inoculating Chechen refugees against cholera as a marketing strategy were seriously entertained.

As profits grew, Google became more involved in charitable initiatives. Google Grants, a program to provide free advertising to nonprofit organizations, was established in 2003. According to a 2009 report, it had secured more than $600 million since its start. Google.org debuted in 2004 as the company's centralized effort to address global philanthropic and ecological challenges. The nonprofit organization sought to improve the quality of life and the environment by leveraging Google's core competencies in the technology field. Google.org concentrated on renewable energy, crisis prediction and prevention, public services, and growth of small businesses.

Another initiative that Google avidly supported was network neutrality. The goal of the movement was to keep the Internet free of government or corporate censorship or control and open to all people. In 2006, Eric Schmidt, CEO of Google at the time, officially stated the company's commitment to the cause of network neutrality in a letter to all Google users. He urged users to oppose any proposed legislation that would limit the freedom of the Internet.

Impact

Growing from a small company to one of the leaders in the field of technology, Google had a significant impact on the lives of many people living in the United States during the 2000s. Apart from providing many businesses and individuals with valuable online tools, the company had a measurable economic impact on the country. A report found that Google created $54 billion of economic activity for American businesses and nonprofit organizations in 2009 alone.

Further Reading

Brin, Sergey, and Lawrence Page. "The Anatomy of a Large-Scale Hypertextual Web Search Engine." *Stanford University InfoLab*. Stanford U, 1998.

Web. 4 Dec. 2012. Provides an explanation of the way the Google search engine works.

Edwards, Douglas. "The Beginning." *Wall Street Journal*. Dow Jones, 16 July 2011. Web. 4 Dec. 2012. An article by a former employee of Google recalling his experience at the company.

Johnson, Claire Hughes. "Google's Economic Impact." *Google*. Google, 2010. Web. 4 Dec. 2012. A report by the vice president of global online sales describing Google's economic impact on the United States in 2009.

Levy, Steven. *In the Plex: How Google Things, Works, and Shapes Our Lives*. New York: Simon, 2011. Print. An in-depth overview of the history of Google and its development of applications and software. Discusses the company's finances and employees, as well as the Googleplex work campus.

Levy, Steven, Brad Stone, and Peter Suciu. "All Eyes on Google." *Newsweek* 29 Mar. 2004: 48–58. Print. Profiles Google and discusses its inception and development, as well as search-engine technology in general.

Lohr, Steve. "At Google, Cube Culture Has New Rules." *New York Times*. New York Times, 5 Dec. 2005. Web. 4 Dec. 2012. Describes the benefits of working at Google.

Lyons, Daniel. "Google This!" *Newsweek* 7 Dec. 2009: 34. Print. Discusses the relationship and competition between Google and Microsoft with reference to Bing, Microsoft's search engine.

Miroslav Farina

■ Gore, Al

Identification: US vice president and environmental activist
Born: March 31, 1948; Washington, DC

Former congressman and forty-fifth vice president of the United States, Al Gore is among the most recognizable political figures of the late twentieth and early twenty-first centuries. His work as vice president was an important factor in the economic prosperity of the United States during the late 1990s, and his role in the controversial presidential election of 2000 has ensured his place in the historical record. His environmental activism led to the production of the film An Inconvenient Truth *(2006), based on his lectures on climate change.*

Al Gore. (World Economic Forum/swiss-image.ch/Photograph by Monika Flueckiger)

Al Gore was inaugurated as the forty-fifth vice president of the United States in January 1993, serving two terms under President Bill Clinton. Gore's vice presidency was marked by his support for conservation and environment-friendly technology as well as his advocacy of the Internet. He was an active proponent for the latter's growth and supported a federal program to provide libraries and public schools with Internet access.

In June 1999, Gore declared his intent to run for president in 2000, hoping that his fifteen years of experience in the federal government would encourage Americans to vote for him. Gore's presidential campaign platform concentrated on education and health care reform. He was in favor of a renewed focus on children's health, promising to increase immunization and prevent smoking among youth.

Early in the campaign, Gore was challenged for the Democratic presidential nomination by former senator Bill Bradley, who withdrew from the race in March 2000 after failing to win any primary elections. In an effort both to appease moderate voters and to ward off criticism of his campaign-finance tactics, Gore selected Senator Joe Lieberman as his running mate. Known for his socially conservative voting record in the Senate, Lieberman was a boost for the Gore campaign and became the first ever Jewish candidate to run on a major national ticket.

After a heated campaign season, the election made history as the closest and most disputed US presidential election ever. Throughout the election, Gore led Bush in popular votes, but the race hinged on the twenty-five electoral votes at stake in Florida. Although the media declared both Bush and Gore the winner at various stages in the process, when election day was over, there was no clear victor.

Complicated legal disputes over irregularities in the way the Florida election was run left the presidency undecided for more than a month. In December 2000, a 5–4 Supreme Court ruling halted the recounting of votes in Florida, and Bush was declared the winner by a controversial and slim margin of 537 votes. Gore officially ended his campaign and urged voters to put the scandal behind them and recognize Bush as the legitimate president.

After the election, Gore concentrated on writing and teaching. He accepted positions as a visiting professor at Fisk University, Middle Tennessee State University, Columbia University Graduate School of Journalism, and the University of California, Los Angeles. He continued to make numerous speeches on the environment, the US war in Iraq, and the Democratic Party.

In addition to teaching and speaking engagements, Gore remained an active businessman. In 2001, he became a senior advisor to Google and vice chairman of Metropolitan West Financial LLC. In 2003, he was invited to become a member of the board of directors for Apple. In 2004, Gore launched the investment firm Generation Investment Management. Gore has also advised President Bush on numerous matters and criticized some of Bush's policies publicly.

In 2004, Gore began a partnership with Joel Hyatt to create a television channel named Current. The channel targeted an eighteen-to-twenty-four-year-old demographic in an effort to educate about politics and world events. Gore described the channel as a "combination of CNN and MTV." The station debuted in 2005.

The 2006 film *An Inconvenient Truth*, for which Gore wrote the teleplay and which was based on his lectures on climate change, brought the issue of global warming to the forefront of popular culture and won two Academy Awards, including one for best documentary.

Impact

Despite his controversial loss in the 2000 presidential election, Gore continues to be an important political force in the American government. He is celebrated for spreading public awareness about environmental issues. The film *An Inconvenient Truth* helped raise awareness about climate change and may significantly impact the environmental health of the world, as it has begun to be adopted in academic curriculum. Gore is also the recipient of the prestigious Nobel Peace Prize for his work on climate change.

Further Reading

Gore, Al. *An Inconvenient Truth: The Planetary Emergency of Global Warming and What We Can Do about It.* New York: Rodale, 2006. Print.

___. *Our Choice: A Plan to Solve the Climate Crisis.* New York: Penguin, 2009. Print.

Maraniss, David. *The Prince of Tennessee: Al Gore Meets His Fate.* New York: Schuster, 2000. Print.

Turque, Bill. *Inventing Al Gore.* Boston: Houghton, 2000. Print.

■ GPS navigation systems and tracking

Definition: Receivers that use Global Positioning System (GPS) satellites to provide real-time location and time data

On June 26, 1993, the US Department of Defense launched its twenty-fourth Navstar satellite into orbit, thus completing the network of two dozen satellites known as the Global Positioning System. The system was initially reserved for military use, but in May 2000, the US government ended its practice of intentionally degrading the system's capabilities for civilian use. Immediately, civilian navigation devices become nearly ten times more accurate and consumer demand for GPS devices exploded.

In the United States, Global Positioning System receivers rely on the government's system of two-dozen satellites, which provide the user with real-time positioning, navigation, and timing (PNT) data. GPS devices intended for consumer use became widely available after May 1, 2000, when the US government ended its practice of providing "selective availability" for civilian signals, thereby dramatically improving the accuracy of nonmilitary GPS devices. With increased precision, receivers became more valuable for vehicular navigation.

GPS navigation systems were soon adopted for many recreational uses, including hiking and cycling, and spawned an entirely new recreational activity known as "geocaching." Over the course of the decade, GPS devices became increasingly sophisticated, with advancements in digital mapping software to provide point-of-interest and real-time traffic data. Car and boat manufacturers began offering these navigation systems as standard accessories. GPS became a popular application for smartphones and was even adopted for some digital cameras. As technological advancements allowed for smaller devices, some were designed to be worn as wristwatches, especially convenient for jogging. Small receivers could be attached to pet collars or worn as pendants by children or senior citizens so caregivers could keep tabs on their whereabouts. When imbedded in a fleet of trucks or taxicabs, GPS receivers could provide real-time tracking, or the data could be collected and analyzed later on a computer. Just as GPS technology was becoming ubiquitous, its stability was challenged when, on December 6, 2006, a solar flare created an

GPS devices. (Courtesy Karl Baron)

unexpected solar radio burst, which distorted GPS signals or jammed devices.

Impact

GPS technology has greatly enhanced scientific research, and the devices have been used to track bird migrations and to monitor the slight movements of tectonic plates, among other applications. The devices have also enhanced public safety by providing the location of callers to emergency dispatchers. GPS has made travel in vehicles safer and obtaining directions much less time consuming. By the end of the decade, several other GPS satellite networks were in development, including the European Union's Galileo system and China's Beidou system.

GPS has also been implicated in illegal uses, often over the invasion of privacy. As the decade came to a close, courts were divided over the issue of tracking suspects without a warrant; in 2012, the US Supreme Court ruled that the warrantless use of GPS to track suspects represented a violation of the Fourth Amendment. Other cases have challenged the legality of requiring cell phone providers to share location and date data logged by users' cell phones.

Further Reading

"GPS at Ground Zero: Tracking World Trade Center Recovery." *GPS World* 13.9 (2002): 16–26. Print.

Waxer, Cindy. "Navigating Privacy Concerns to Equip Workers with GPS." *Workforce Management* 84.8 (2005): 71. Print.

Sally Driscoll

■ Green business (sustainable business)

Definition: A business that is environmentally friendly in its practices, processes, and products and/or services, seeks to treat suppliers, employees, customers, and community members fairly and ethically, and strives for profitability

As more people realized the dangers of global climate change and the necessity of taking steps to protect the environment, the number of businesses that strove to become more "green," or sustainable, greatly increased during the 2000s. While many of these businesses focused on green issues for environmental reasons, many also did so to make money. Because of this, the green movement saw a huge increase of businesses promoting environmental awareness, products, and practices during this time.

As the green movement exploded in the 2000s, many businesses took action to protect the environment. They started small, taking such steps as printing on both sides of paper, turning off computers and lights, and recycling products ranging from electronics to ink cartridges. Once businesses realized the savings, they were often motivated to take more steps to reduce waste and save energy. Many installed solar panels and energy-efficient lighting, traded old electronics, and upgraded heating systems. Businesses not only saw the green movement as a way to protect the environment, but also as a way to improve their bottom line through thrift.

When large corporations saw how much money they could save through green practices, many joined the movement. In 2005, Walmart announced a plan to reduce energy use at its stores. The chain, long criticized for poor labor practices, was praised for its efforts to save energy. Numerous other corporations followed suit, improving their images and incomes as well.

Although green companies such as Tom's of Maine and Burt's Bees had been around for decades, new companies such as Method cleaning products were developed to meet new demand for green products in the 2000s. Existing companies also began rolling out an abundance of green products during this time. Japanese car companies such as Toyota and Honda introduced hybrid vehicles early in the decade, and American manufacturers Ford, Chrysler, and General Motors began following suit around the mid-2000s. In 2008, Clorox introduced Green Works, its line of naturally derived cleaning products. Businesses also changed the way they made their products in the name of saving the environment, focusing on such efforts as improving products' energy efficiency. Products such as Frito-Lays' SunChips began to be packaged in biodegradable and recyclable materials. Major mainstream manufacturers also acquired green companies and marketed them more widely, as with Colgate-Palmolive's 2006 acquisition of Tom's of Maine and Clorox's 2007 acquisition of Burt's Bees.

Impact

The boom in new green businesses and existing companies adopting green practices demonstrates that going green can be as good for business as it is for the planet. Not only are the green business practices affecting the environment by reducing energy consumption and cutting down on the amount of chemicals released, they also make and save businesses money. For instance, while recycling cuts down on waste, which saves money and reduces the amount of material sent to landfills, it also appeals to a market that is growing ever more conscious of environmental issues.

Further Reading

Brookins, Miranda. "Reasons Businesses Go Green." *Houston Chronicle*. Hearst Communications, Inc. Web. 27 Nov. 2012.

Levine, David. "You Are the Policy Leaders We Have Been Waiting For." *GreenBiz.com*. GreenBiz Group Inc. 27 Nov. 2012. Web. 27 Nov. 2012.

Linn, Allison. "Corporations Find Business Case for Going Green." *MSNBC*. NBCNews.com. 18 Apr. 2007. Web. 27 Nov. 2012.

Angela Harmon

■ Green technology

Definition: The application of scientific knowledge to create more efficient machines and methods that will minimize or eliminate the negative impact human beings can have on the environment

Growing concerns about the world reaching peak oil production, as well as the environmental impact of greenhouse gases in the atmosphere from the burning of fossil fuels, have prompted many individuals and industries to look toward green technologies. In 2008, worldwide investments in renewable energy technologies surpassed fossil fuel technology investments for the first time. At the same time, more environmentally friendly technologies have been decreasing in price, making them more desirable to consumers.

For several decades, scientists and environmentalists have issued warnings about the way the global climate has been changing since the beginning of the Industrial Revolution in the 1700s. Since that time, more and more fossil-based fuels like coal and oil have been burned in order to produce the goods and services people expect to have in the modern world. Although the climate has always changed due to natural phenomena like plate tectonics, solar radiation, and volcanic eruptions, scientists and environmen-

talists have come to believe that the burning of fossil fuels over the last few centuries has also greatly contributed to climate change. They argue that technology must be improved to be less wasteful, more efficient, and less harmful to the environment. They believe the way to do this is to invest in renewable energy sources that would ultimately end the dependence on fossil-based fuels. In the last decade, business leaders have also begun investing in green technologies, as many of them believe that the world is entering a period in which peak oil production—the point at which oil extraction would hit its height before going into permanent decline— is approaching and these alternative energy technologies are becoming cheaper, more practical, and necessary.

Advances in Renewable Energy

Renewable energy is energy that is derived from natural resources such as sunlight, geothermal heat, wind, and water. Unlike energy produced from the burning of fossil fuels, which is finite because those sources will ultimately be depleted, energy from natural resources is continually replenished. Although the technology to harness renewable energy has been around for decades (as with solar panels) or even centuries (as with wind or hydropower), advances in renewable energy technology in the first decade of the twenty-first century have allowed them to be seen as a more viable alternative to burning oil or gas. Specific fields that have seen considerable technological advancement include solar energy, wind energy, biomass power, biofuels, geothermal power, and ocean tidal power.

For several decades, solar power, harnessed by solar panels on rooftops, was popularly seen as being both inefficient and very expensive, despite the nearly limitless energy resource the sun provides. For many years, most solar panels were made of the chemical element silicon, but as demand for silicon has increased, alternatives have been sought. In the last decade, scientists at Ben-Gurion University in Israel have developed solar cells composed of gallium arsenide, a compound used in numerous electronic products that has also proven to be more efficient in collecting solar energy. Another advancement in solar energy is the development of spherical solar cells, which, unlike their rectangular predecessors, allow sunlight to be collected from every angle. Finally, the creation of paint-on solar cells, which can be applied to flexible plastic sheets, enables researchers to collect solar energy from areas and surfaces previously unimagined.

Wind energy is among the most popular green energy technologies in the United States; in 2007, the use of wind grew by 57 percent in the state of Texas and by 43 percent in the country as a whole. Concerns about the growing chains of giant wind farms, which are comprised of noisy turbines that can kill birds and bats, prompted researchers to produce better wind collectors, including turbines on higher towers that would both increase their output and boost efficiency by 20 percent. Another development is the bladeless turbine, based on a 1913 patent by famed inventor Nicola Tesla, which has its complete machinery hidden inside its housing and works almost silently via a turbine of rotating metal plates supported by magnetic bearings.

Unlike wind energy, which is becoming cheaper as the technology improves, biomass power has great promise but is still more costly than drilling for oil. Biomass power is clean energy produced from burning algae, a single-celled organism comprised of 50 percent oil. Burning algae, however, does not add the greenhouse gas carbon to the air because it takes the same amount of carbon from the atmosphere as it burns through photosynthesis, which converts light energy into chemical energy.

Another popular green energy in the 2000s has been biofuel production, notably ethanol created from crops like sugarcane and corn. These prototype biofuels, however, proved less than ideal because they raised the prices of food products while at the same time competed ineffectively against traditional gasoline. Inedible crops like jatropha oil and switchgrass have shown more potential, as they both are not competitive with food products and can compete financially with gasoline, provided the infrastructure and technology are in place.

Geothermal power is power derived from Earth's heat. Researchers believe that this source of energy has enormous potential. In recent years, the natural gas industry has learned how to extract gas from remote places through a combination of horizontal drilling and hydraulic fracturing (also known as fracking), a process that involves drilling a hole, pressuring the hole, and pumping water into the hole to release the gas. Researchers believe a similar process, known as enhanced geothermal systems (EGS), would be able to extract the earth's heat in a similar manner by pumping cold water down and

allowing it to heat up underground. One estimate from a 2006 report funded by the US Department of Energy concluded that EGS could provide the country with its total yearly energy use 140,000 times over.

Like geothermal power, ocean tidal power boasts enormous potential, particularly in the United States where the areas off the northeastern Atlantic Ocean and the northwestern Pacific Ocean are ripe for development. The process involves harnessing the energy produced from the tidal differences between the daily periods of low and high each day. In order for this process to work most effectively, there must be a difference of sixteen feet between low and high tide, but there are about forty such sites on Earth where ocean tidal power could be employed.

Popular Commercial Products

Perhaps the greatest boon to green technology has come through the growing popularity of more environmentally friendly products, most notably hybrid gas and electric cars that burn less gasoline and compact fluorescent light bulbs (CFLs), which are more energy efficient than their incandescent counterparts. Hybrid cars received a huge boost in 2001 when Toyota began selling the Prius, the world's first mass-produced hybrid vehicle. Sold in more than seventy nations, it gained great popularity in both the United States and Japan during the previous decade. In 2008, more than one million Priuses had been sold and millions more have been sold since that time. The success of this vehicle was considered a watershed moment in the automobile industry, with every major manufacturer producing its own variant of the hybrid car. Some of the most notable hybrids include the Nissan Leaf, the Chevy Volt, the Ford Fusion Hybrid and the Toyota Camry Hybrid, among others. Each of these vehicles boasts excellent fuel economy through electric batteries that minimize the amount of gasoline needed to run it.

Compact fluorescent light (CFL) bulbs have been around since the 1890s, almost as long as the incandescent variety, but it was not until the last decade that they began to become competitive. Although the typical CFL uses approximately 75 to 80 percent less energy than an incandescent bulb, they were not widely used by consumers for a number of reasons: they were more expensive than incandescent bulbs, could not be used with a dimmer, tended to flicker when warming up and emitted a harsher, less warm light. Improvements in the technology that have eliminated many of these concerns, combined with the willingness of bulb manufacturers to ramp up production of CFLs, has lowered their costs somewhat and made them more appealing to consumers. Although CFLs remain more costly than incandescent bulbs, their energy efficiency provides greater savings on electric bills over the life of the bulbs, which has made individuals, companies, and even governments take a second look at them. For example, Australia, Canada, and the European Union began the process of banning the sale of incandescent bulbs in 2009.

Many researchers, however, foresee a day on the horizon when CFLs are replaced with light emitting diodes (LEDs), which, unlike fluorescent and incandescent bulbs, do not use heat to produce light, but rather semiconductors that increase their output by *removing* heat. At present LEDs are good for colored lighting in spotlight applications like floodlights or car headlights but are not efficient enough for emitting the kind of diffuse white light needed in most living spaces and commercial areas.

Impact

Many energy industry observers see green technology as a growing part of the global economy, not as a fad that may be abandoned at some point in the future. According to the International Energy Agency, power capacity from renewable energy sources came to 280,000 megawatts in 2008, three times what nuclear power plants in the United States were generating in the same year. As of 2012, roughly 16 percent of global energy consumption was derived from renewable energy resources and this number is expected to grow as more nations seek to become greener. Concerns about reaching peak oil and fears over climate change are prompting governments worldwide to find alternative sources of energy and more efficient ways to use the traditional fuel sources they currently employ. Coupled with these concerns are many nations' needs to keep down costs since the global economy entered a severe recession in late 2007.

The future of green technology will depend as much on the willingness of governments and corporations to invest in it, as it does on consumers' desire to use the goods that derive from it in their homes. The growing calls for more efficient cars, lighting, and other power-driven goods, both in the United States and abroad, suggests that average people are

willing to make the change to green technology, provided there is economic incentive for them to do so.

Further Reading

Madrigal, Alexis. *Powering the Dream: The History and Promise of Green Technology.* Cambridge: Da Capo, 2011. Print. Provides a narrative history of environmental technology and outlines where it might be going in the near future.

Pernick, Ron, and Clint Wilder. *The Clean Tech Revolution: Discover the Top Trends, Technologies, and Companies to Watch.* New York: Collins, 2008. Print. Argues that green technology is here to stay because major corporations all over the world are now funding it.

Shariff, Jamil. *50 Green Projects for the Evil Genius.* New York: McGraw, 2009. Print. Details simple ways individuals can help to create a more efficient, healthier, and more sustainable environment.

Sobha, Geeta. *Green Technology: Earth-Friendly Innovations.* New York: Rosen, 2008. Print. Provides a concise overview of the issues related to environmental technology in general and how alternative sources of energy are being studied. Aimed toward young adults.

Zehner, Ozzie. *Green Illusions: The Dirty Secrets of Clean Energy and the Future of Environmentalism.* Lincoln: U of Nebraska P, 2012. Print. Suggests that alternative energy technologies like wind and solar power come with their own downsides and limitations. The author argues that the problem humans face is not finding new and better sources of energy, but reducing consumption by changing the wasteful aspects of modern society.

Christopher Mari

■ Greenspan, Alan

Identification: Chairman of the Federal Reserve, 1987–2006
Born: March 6, 1926; New York, New York

As the second-longest serving chairman of the Federal Reserve, Greenspan was credited with the ability to calm the stock market and to guide the economy along a path of low inflation and low unemployment.

A former chairman of the Council of Economic Advisers under President Gerald Ford, Alan Greenspan

Donald Rumsfeld presents Alan Greenspan (left) with the Department of Defense Medal for Distinguished Public Service, January 2006. (U.S. Department of Defense/National Archives/6702037/Photograph by Petty Officer First Class Chad J. McNeeley)

returned to government in 1980, as an outside advisor to the Reagan administration. Greenspan's career-defining opportunity came in 1987 when President Reagan selected him to replace Paul Volcker as chairman of the Federal Reserve Board, the group responsible for US monetary policy. With his years of experience analyzing the economy and working with the government, Greenspan seemed well-suited for the position.

The first major test that Greenspan faced as chairman came within months of his start, with the collapse of the stock market on October 19, 1987, often referred to as Black Monday. On that day, the Dow Jones Industrial Average dropped 22.61 percent, the largest single-day percentage drop in its history. While not responsible for the stock market, the Federal Reserve is responsible for the soundness of the banking system. Recognizing the potential danger to credit markets and, ultimately, the economy, the Federal Reserve responded, under the guidance of Greenspan, by issuing a statement the next day to assure markets that the Federal Reserve would support the financial system. Greenspan backed up that statement with actions to restore confidence in the banking system. By taking decisive action, Greenspan is often credited with averting what could have turned into a severe recession. This event increased his credibility with markets and contributed to his reputation as a calm leader.

Greenspan served as Federal Reserve chairman for more than eighteen years; he was reappointed four times for four-year terms and served under four presidents. At home in the halls of power and at the A-list Washington, DC, parties he often attended with his second wife, television journalist Andrea Mitchell, Greenspan came to personify the Federal Reserve.

During his time as chairman, Greenspan displayed the same pragmatism seen at his confirmation hearing and did what the circumstances seemed to require. His steady approach to the job saw the United States through such events as the stock market crash in October 1987; two recessions, 1990–91 and 2001; the Asian financial collapse in 1997; and the demise of the hedge fund Long-Term Capital Management, which, it was feared, would destabilize markets around the world. Greenspan is often credited with guiding the US economy through these perils with only modest levels of inflation and unemployment and with solid economic growth. Since his retirement in 2006, he has continued to speak about the dangers the economy faces and to defend his record against criticism that his policies may have led to the financial crisis beginning in 2007.

Impact

During Greenspan's tenure as chairman of the Federal Reserve—from 1987 to 2006—he guided the United States through a myriad of economic hurdles, including the Black Monday stock crash and the short-lived recession that followed the Gulf War. He is known for dismantling high mortgages and unfair lending practices over the course of his extensive career. Although critics have implicated his policies in the subprime mortgage crisis and housing crash that began in 2007, a year after he retired from the Federal Reserve, he was also pivotal in rebuilding the American economy in its wake.

Further Reading

Fleckenstein, William A. *Greenspan's Bubbles: The Age of Ignorance at the Federal Reserve*. New York: McGraw, 2008. Print.

Greenspan, Alan. *The Age of Turbulence: Adventures in a New World*. New York: Penguin, 2007. Print.

Overveldt, Johan van. *Bernanke's Test: Ben Bernanke, Alan Greenspan, and the Drama of the Central Banker*. Chicago: Agate, 2009. Print.

Randall Hannum

■ Growth of megachurches

Definition: Megachurches are usually Protestant churches with weekly attendance rates of two thousand or more. During the 2000s, the number and size of many megachurches increased significantly.

Though institutions often took decades to reach megachurch numbers, many achieved this status in the early twenty-first century. Most were located near cities in areas experiencing growth. Many built fitness centers, bookstores, and other facilities for their congregations and offered multilingual services.

Most megachurches grew in newer suburbs of growing cities during the 2000s. The majority were located in southern states, with 14 percent of the total located in Texas by 2010. The number of megachurches doubled between 2001 and 2006, from about six hundred to over 1200. Most megachurches drew the majority of their congregants from other churches.

These institutions were predominantly multiethnic and engaged in contemporary forms of worship, such as modern music and light shows. Many added buildings and facilities, creating a campus or a city within a city. Though megachurches have often been thought to feature arenas or stadiums filled with worshipers, many times members attended various smaller services—they could choose from an average of five a weekend by 2008. A few churches offered as many as twenty-four services a weekend. In 2009, for example, the Second Baptist Church of Houston in Texas welcomed 24,000 people to its five campuses and various services.

During the mid-2000s, many megachurches changed the way they operated, focusing on small groups, eliminating television broadcasts, and widely using the Internet. Tremendous growth in creating satellite campuses began around 2003. Many megachurches prepared for transitions in the pulpit by increasing training for clergy.

Megachurches became as well known for their finances as for their size. The average income of a megachurch in 2008 was $6.5 million. About half of the income paid for salaries, about 25 percent was used for buildings, and much of the rest was devoted to missions and programs.

Impact

Though growth was the norm for many megachurches, at least one of the most prestigious faltered late in the decade. Crystal Cathedral Ministries in California, widely known for its *Hour of Power* television program and elaborate live pageants with animals, lost 29 percent of its revenue in 2009 and teetered toward bankruptcy.

Megachurches were credited with bringing some Americans back to worship—in a 2010 survey by the Hartford Institute for Religion Research, about a fourth of new attendees reported that they had not attended another church recently. The real basis of participation, however, seemed to be in fostering a sense of community. More than half of the congregants surveyed volunteered at their church, while about 60 percent participated in the churches' small groups. Greater interest and participation in political and social causes held promise to further increase megachurches' relevance and reach.

Further Reading

Lampman, Jane. "Megachurches' Way of Worship Is on the Rise." *Christian Science Monitor.* Christian Science Monitor, 6 Feb. 2006. Web. 27 Dec. 2012.

Saurage-Altenloh, Susan. "Factistics: Megachurches." *Houston Chronicle.* Hearst Communications, 30 July 2010. Web. 27 Dec. 2012.

Thumma, Scott, and Warren Bird. "Changes in American Megachurches: Tracing Eight Years of Growth and Innovation in the Nation's Largest-Attendance Congregations." *Hartford Institute for Religion Research.* Hartford Seminary, 12 Sept. 2008. Web. 27 Dec. 2012.

Josephine Campbell

■ *Grutter v. Bollinger*

The Case: United States Supreme Court ruling in favor of the University of Michigan's affirmative action policy

Date: Decided on June 23, 2003

In Grutter v. Bollinger, *the US Supreme Court upheld the University of Michigan's affirmative action policy, stating that the policy was constitutional because it treated race as only one of many factors that determined whether a student was eligible for acceptance into the university.*

Since its inception, the concept of affirmative action has been controversial. The term refers to a method of policy making in which college admissions or business hiring practices are specifically designed to help increase the number of participating minorities. While affirmative action policies are generally intended to foster cultural diversity, some believe that their implementation results in discrimination against white people.

In 1996, Barbara Grutter, a white woman, applied for admission to the University of Michigan's law school. Upon receiving a rejection notice, Grutter learned that there were minority applicants who had been selected over her even though they had lower admission scores. Grutter subsequently filed a lawsuit against the school. She won her initial case in US District Court in 2001. After that ruling was overturned by an appeals court, the case went to the US Supreme Court in 2003.

Grutter alleged that the school was discriminating against white applicants by placing an unjust emphasis on race in its admissions decisions. The Supreme Court, in a five-to-four decision, ruled that the University of Michigan's admittance policy was constitutional because its process was sufficiently individualized and tailored closely enough to each applicant to be legally satisfactory. The court stated that its opinion was based on the fact that the university's selection process did not include a quota system and only regarded race as one of many factors involved in determining whether an applicant is adequately qualified for admittance.

Impact

In *Grutter v. Bollinger*, the Supreme Court not only reaffirmed its landmark decision in *Regents of the University of California v. Bakke* (1978), the first major case regarding collegiate admissions and affirmative action, but also further refined that decision. Through its ruling, the court clearly established that an affirmative action program is constitutional only if the program is sufficiently individualized, if it considers race only as one of many factors, and if it is specifically designed to maintain an adequate level of diversity within an institution. Most importantly, the ruling meant that the court's decision in *Grutter v. Bollinger* upheld and supported the concept of affirmative action itself.

Further Reading

Grutter v. Bollinger. 539 U.S. 306. Supreme Court of the United States. 2003. *Supreme Court Collection.* Legal Information Inst., Cornell University Law School, n.d. Web. 11 Oct. 2012.

"Grutter v. Bollinger and Gratz v. Bollinger (2003)."
PBS. Educational Broadcasting Corporation, 2007.
Web. 11 Oct. 2012.

Smolla, Rodney A. *The Constitution Goes to College: Five
Constitutional Ideas That Have Shaped the American
University.* New York: NYU P, 2011. Print.

Jack Lasky

■ Guantánamo Bay detention camp

Definition: A detention camp at the US naval base in
Guantánamo Bay, Cuba, designed as a detainment
center for suspected terrorists

*Following the terrorist attacks of September 11, 2001, and
the American invasion of Iraq and Afghanistan, the Guantánamo Bay detention camp was established at the US
Naval Station at Guantánamo Bay in Cuba to hold suspected terrorists. Since its founding, the camp has been subject to numerous allegations of mistreatment of detainees,
and its potential closure has been hotly debated.*

As a result of the September 11, 2001, terrorist attacks, the United States launched a widespread anti-
terrorism campaign that led to the armed invasion of
Iraq and Afghanistan, two countries thought to be
playing a central role in al-Qaeda's operations. Simultaneously, US government officials also established the Guantánamo Bay detention camp in
Guantánamo Bay, Cuba, as a location for detaining
terrorism suspects and potentially dangerous prisoners of war. In a strategic move to avoid following
the international legal requirements pertaining to
the handling of prisoners of war, the administration
of US President George W. Bush labeled these detainees "unlawful enemy combatants." This special
designation meant that Guantánamo inmates would
not be protected by the Geneva Convention's rules
regarding prisoners of war.

Since its opening in January 2002, the Guantánamo Bay detention camp has held nearly 800 detainees. These detainees generally fall into one of
three categories: nonpenal enemy combatants,
held to prevent their return to the battlefield; prisoners facing or expected to face criminal charges;
and prisoners cleared for transfer or release to another country, but who are still being held due to
concerns about threats to their well-being after
transfer. Under normal conditions, according to
the Geneva Convention, nonpenal detainees must
legally be freed when hostilities come to a close,
but, given the nature of the ongoing conflict with
al-Qaeda, it may be possible for them to be detained indefinitely.

Controversies

The US policies justifying the detainment of prisoners at Guantánamo have been a subject of controversy since the camp was opened. Opponents of the
camp argue that applying the legal status of unlawful
enemy combatants to detainees is a violation of their
basic human rights. Specifically, as a result of this designation, detainees are often denied access to a fair
trial or any trial at all. The methods by which some
Guantánamo detainees have been tried have often
been sharply criticized. In many cases, detainees were
given little or no choice in selecting their legal representation and were often denied full access to the evidence against them.

Additionally, these trials were sometimes argued
using evidence procured through interrogation
techniques that some regard as torture. These interrogation techniques have been the most controversial aspect of the Guantánamo operation. According
to leaked internal documents and the claims of
former detainees, officials at Guantánamo regularly
made use of interrogation techniques such as sleep
deprivation, stress positions, and waterboarding.
The latter, which is a form of simulated drowning,
was the most publicized and highly criticized of
these techniques.

The revelation of alleged torture at Guantánamo
has raised many questions about the effectiveness
of the facility. While these questions have primarily
focused on the ethics of using such brutal interrogation techniques, opponents have also argued that the
legal validity of any confession or other information
obtained through torture may be doubtful. Supporters of the policies used at Guantánamo argue
that the circumstances of the US-led War on Terrorism make it necessary to rely on techniques that
might normally be considered unacceptable to obtain crucial information that would likely never be
divulged otherwise.

Potential Closure

Guantánamo Bay became one of the leading issues
of the 2008 presidential election, as Democratic

Army Specialist Anthony Berkowitz, a chaplain's assistant, gives religious items to a detainee in Camp Delta, Joint Task Force Guantanamo. (Courtesy Joint Task Force Guantanamo)

presidential nominee Barack Obama made closing the facility one of his principal campaign promises. Within days of taking office, Obama announced that Guantánamo would close within a year. He initiated a comprehensive review to determine how best to transfer detainees out of the base and hold them for future questioning in other locations. Obama's executive orders on the matter also included a mandate suspending all military trials at the base in anticipation of their transfer into the federal court system.

However, President Obama's plan to close Guantánamo Bay encountered considerable opposition from Republicans and others. Those who were against the closure of Guantánamo argued that bringing suspected terrorists into the United States to be tried and housing them in US prisons would be too dangerous. Initial opposition made the Obama administration's original plan to close Guantánamo by January of 2010 impossible, and additional developments further decreased the chances of the facility being closed in subsequent years.

Impact

Despite the setbacks, plans to close Guantánamo were still being developed by the end of the decade. While many believe that Guantánamo's original purpose was justified by the events of September 11, 2001, and the ensuing Iraq and Afghanistan wars, the

facility's history of dubious legality and alleged torture have become an indelible part of its legacy. As a result, its role in the War on Terrorism is likely to continue to be regarded as controversial.

Further Reading

"Guantánamo Bay." *Jurist.* Jurist Legal News and Research Services, 8 July 2012. Web. 27 Dec. 2012. An overview of Guantánamo Bay presented by an online legal news service based at the University of Pittsburgh School of Law.

"Guantánamo Bay Naval Base (Cuba)." *New York Times.* New York Times Co., 17 Oct. 2012. Web. 27 Dec. 2012. A New York Times–produced overview of Guantánamo Bay

Hannaford, Alex. "Inside Guantánamo." *Esquire.* July 2010: 52–57. Print. A British journalist's account of his experience visiting Guantánamo Bay.

Leigh, David, James Ball, Ian Cobain, and Jason Burke. "Guantánamo Leaks Lift Lid on World's Controversial Prison." *Guardian.* Guardian News and Media, 24 Apr. 2011. Web. 27 Dec. 2012. An article detailing the contents of leaked US military files, obtained by the New York Times and the Guardian, pertaining to Guantánamo detainees.

Masters, Jonathan. "Closing Guantánamo?" *Council on Foreign Relations.* Council on Foreign Relations, 9 Nov. 2011. Web. 27 Dec. 2012. A backgrounder discussing the issue of the Guantánamo Bay camp as it related to the 2012 election.

Pfeifer, William L., Jr. "The Evolution of Guantánamo Bay." *The Politicus.* The Politicus, 2 Feb. 2009. Web. 27 Dec. 2012. An overview of Guantánamo Bay and President Barack Obama's attempts to close it.

Jack Lasky

■ Gun control

Definition: Any effort to limit sale, possession, or use of firearms among individuals, often through background checks, waiting periods between buying and owning weapons, and banning certain types of weapons

The issue of gun control has been at the center of the culture wars in the United States, attracting vociferous supporters and opponents. Gun shows are prevalent across the United States, and the right to bear arms is central to the democratic identity of gun enthusiasts. Still, Americans are divided over whether guns perpetuate or deter violence.

Historically, gun control has divided American culture. It was initially used to bar slaves from possession. In the 2000s, the issue of gun control still reflected regional concerns. Where hunting is a part of life and leisure, as it is in the South and Northwest and in rural areas, guns are cherished. In contrast, the Northeast and urban settings tend to favor gun control. While these regional divides greatly overshadow partisan divisions, Democrats are viewed more often as pro-gun control, and Republicans are seen as pro-gun.

In the twenty-first century, these divisions have solidified into groups that lobby Congress and march for their causes. The largest gun-control proponent is the Brady Campaign to Prevent Gun Violence. In 2001, this group merged with the Million Moms March, which marched on Washington, DC, to demand stronger gun laws. Vastly larger than these organizations, the National Rifle Association (NRA) grew throughout the 2000s to the 4-million-member mark, enabling the group to be the most powerful lobby in Washington, DC.

The NRA and Elected Officials

The 2000 election, in which Republican George W. Bush defeated Democrat Al Gore, can be viewed as a victory for gun rights. Gore pushed gun control as a topic in the debates and while he campaigned. Partly because of a fear that Gore would diminish their gun rights, Americans elected Bush.

Meanwhile, the NRA gained prominence. In 2003, senator Larry Craig introduced what would become the Protection of Lawful Commerce in Arms Act, which the NRA supported. However, when amendments were added to the act to renew the Federal Assault Weapons Ban of 1994 (set to expire in 2005) and to require background checks for buyers at gun shows, the NRA rescinded their approval. As a result, the legislation was voted down.

After Bush was reelected in 2004 and Congress gained representatives in favor of the NRA, the act was reintroduced, passing in 2005 without the amendments. The act's journey revealed just how powerful the NRA had become.

District of Columbia v. Heller

In 2008, the Supreme Court of the United States heard the case *District of Columbia v. Heller*, which challenged a Washington, DC, ban on handguns, the strictest gun-control law in the country. As the Supreme Court rarely ruled on Second Amendment cases, the hearing was significant. The Second Amendment states, "A well regulated militia, being necessary to the security of a free State, the right of the people to keep and bear Arms, shall not be infringed." While gun proponents interpret the amendment as a protection of the individual right to own weapons, precluding gun control, those opposed focus on the right of states to keep militias and to supply those defenders, not individuals, with guns.

Justice Antonin Scalia gave the majority opinion, affirming individual rights to gun ownership and dismissing the handgun ban in Washington, DC, as unconstitutional. This occasion was the first time the court ruled that a ban on firearms could violate the Constitution. Still, Scalia acknowledged the importance of some gun control laws, like those that withheld guns from criminals and the mentally ill, restricted weapon types (like machine guns), and limited where guns could be carried. The decision has largely been viewed as a triumph of the Originalist approach to constitutional interpretation, as both the majority opinion and those dissenting relied on the historical circumstances that impelled the Second Amendment to defend their positions.

Impact

Throughout the 2000s, American attitudes toward gun control grew increasingly lax. Across states, restrictions on conceal and carry laws were lifted. States enacted "stand your ground" laws and Castle Doctrines that expanded the notion of self-defense, verging on encouraging violent encounters. Americans questioned the effectiveness of gun-control laws. Some wondered both if fewer guns really result in reduced crime, especially crimes of passion, and if gun-control laws empower criminals who obtain weapons on the black market. Some also wondered if limiting gun availability would just cause people with violent impulses to use other weapons.

Violence in the United States is high, particularly when compared to other industrialized nations. The frequency of mass shootings was just as common in the 2000s as in other decades. Still reeling from the shooting at Columbine High School in 1999, Americans were shocked and saddened by a shooting at Virginia Tech in 2007, in which a student killed thirty-two people, and a shooting at the Fort Hood military base, where an army psychologist killed thirteen people. Those who favor gun control point to these tragedies as confirmation of their cause. Those supporting gun rights tend to blame the individuals involved rather than the weapons that enabled them.

Further Reading

Bloomberg, Michael R., et al. "Lawyers, Guns and Mayors." *New York Times: Opinion.* New York Times Co., 24 Feb. 2004. Web. 27 Dec. 2012. Offers opinions on the Protection of Lawful Commerce in Arms Act from prominent mayors.

Burbick, Joan. *Gun Show Nation: Gun Culture and American Democracy.* New York: New P, 2006. Print. Examines the intersection of gun ownership, democracy, and American identity.

Tushnet, Mark V. *Out of Range: Why the Constitution Can't End the Battle over Guns.* New York: Oxford UP, 2007. Print. Provides a legal framework for understanding the Second Amendment, relying on various interpretations of the Constitution.

Wilson, Harry L. *Guns, Gun Control, and Elections: The Politics and Policy of Firearms.* New York: Rowman, 2007. Print. Presents gun control from a political perspective, focusing on policies, how they are created and shaped, and their public reception.

Winkler, Adam. *Gun Fight: The Battle over the Right to Bear Arms in America.* New York: Norton, 2011. Print. Outlines the history of gun use in the United States, particularly through the lens of constitutional disputes over the Second Amendment.

Lucia Pizzo

H1N1 flu pandemic of 2009

The Event: Global outbreak of a new strain of influenza, the H1N1 virus
Date: March 2009–May 2010

During the spring of 2009 a new strain of influenza virus appeared which was similar to the 1918 influenza outbreak that had killed tens of millions of people. The initial concern was that large percent of the population might be at similar risk of severe infection.

Early in the spring of 2009 an outbreak of influenza began in Vera Cruz, Mexico, in which the causative agent was identified as the H1N1 strain of the Influenza A virus. A similar strain was associated with the 1918 outbreak (known as the Spanish flu) which resulted in an estimated fifty million deaths worldwide. The H1N1 had briefly reappeared during the late 1970s in Fort Dix, New Jersey, and in northern China, but was locally confined. The rapid spread in 2009 within the Mexican population and beyond—the first cases in the United States were reported in California in April—gave rise to fears that a worldwide pandemic similar to that of 1918 might occur.

The 2009 virus appears to have been the result of a triple recombinant of human, bird, and pig influenza viruses, hence the popular designation as the "swine flu." Responses by health authorities were rapid, including recommendations to limit travel to Mexico or other areas in which the virus appeared. In some instances the response by authorities to the swine flu bordered on panic; several countries banned the importation of pork products and Egypt ordered the slaughter of all domestic pigs.

The virus proved difficult to grow in the laboratory, so vaccines were in short supply during the first months of the outbreak. While the virus readily passed from human to human—by November an estimated 15 to 20 percent of the American population had been infected—it proved to be significantly less lethal than originally feared. The precise number of persons eventually infected worldwide is difficult to estimate because many people did not exhibit influenza-like symptoms and statistics were incomplete. The Centers for Disease Control and Prevention has estimated approximately 60 million were infected in 74 countries, with some 12,000 fatalities.

Impact

The level of mortality due to influenza as a result of the 2009 outbreak was no higher than that during normal flu seasons, and proved significantly lower than had originally been feared. In addition, the demographics of severe infection were different from the yearly outbreaks. The 2009 pandemic was largely confined to persons under the age of eighteen; few cases were reported among those over age sixty. Epidemiologists attributed these findings to significant immunity among older adults, the result of having been previously exposed.

Since the young were considered at greater risk, among the recommendations was that any vaccination program should give priority to those under the age of eighteen.

Further Reading

Barry, John M.. *The Great Influenza: The Story of the Deadliest Pandemic in History.* New York: Penguin, 2005. Print.

Dehner, George. *Influenza: A Century of Science and Public Health Response.* Pittsburgh: U of Pittsburgh P, 2012. Print.

Khiabanian, Hossein, et al. "Differences in Patient Age Distribution between Influenza A Subtypes" *PLoS ONE* 4.8 (2009): 1–5. Print.

Richard Adler, PhD

■ *Halo* franchise

Definition: Console-based series of first-person shooter (FPS) video games developed by Bungie, Inc.

First released for Microsoft's Xbox game console in 2001, the Halo *games repopularized the FPS genre of video games and are considered Microsoft's flagship video game titles. As a launch title,* Halo: Combat Evolved *validated the Xbox and was pivotal in its success. The* Halo *games were instrumental in opening video games up to a broader audience. The series also created a large fan base and culture with adaptations into other media, such as novels.*

In the *Halo* games, players assume the role of the main character—Master Chief, a cybernetically enhanced human—as he fights a hostile alien alliance called the Covenant. The franchise is comprised of the original trilogy *Halo: Combat Evolved* (2001), *Halo 2* (2004), and *Halo 3* (2007), along with spinoff titles *Halo Wars* (2009) and *Halo 3: ODST* (2009). *Halo Wars* was developed by Ensemble Studios and, unlike the others, is a real-time strategy game. The series' plot focuses on a war between humans and the Covenant, with environments that range from the tight interiors of spaceships to wide-open alien landscapes. Players have a host of human and alien weapons to choose from, as well as several air- and land-based vehicles. The name of the series is based on planetary ring installations called Halos, which play a key role in the overarching plot. The trilogy has received some of the highest video game ratings, with Metacritic ratings of 97, 95, and 94, respectively.

   Halo: Combat Evolved pioneered the local area network (LAN) configuration setup for Xbox, allowing up to sixteen players to connect to each other with Ethernet cables. This contributed to a rise in popularity of social gatherings called "LAN parties" in which players brought their console and televisions to play with others. *Halo 2* improved the experience by adding online play via Xbox Live, effectively bringing the LAN experience to anyone with an internet connection. *Halo 3* improved further by adding the Forge, a feature which let players create and share custom maps.

Impact

Halo: Combat Evolved ensured the success of Microsoft's Xbox and sold more than six million copies in the ten years following its release. *Halo 2* and *Halo 3* set and broke records for launch day and pre-order sales, with the latter generating $170 million on its first day. The franchise established a canon that generated adaptations in novels, graphic novels, comic books, and even a machinima (video created from edited in-game footage) series named "Red vs. Blue." *Halo 2* is also credited with popularizing alternate reality games with its *I Love Bees* marketing campaign. New games continue to borrow from the successes and innovations that Halo first established, from network infrastructure to user-interface design.

Further Reading

Buckell, Tobias. *Halo Encyclopedia: The Definitive Guide to the Halo Universe.* New York: DK, 2011. Print.
Nutt, Christian. "Bungie in 2008: Reflecting on *Halo 3*, Moving Beyond." *Gamasutra.* UBM TechWeb, 2 June 2008. Web. 28 June 2012.
Parker, Seb. "Halo: A Sales History." *VGChartz.* VGChartz, 1 July 2011. Web. 27 June 2012.

Andrew Maul

■ *Hamdan v. Rumsfeld*

The Case: US Supreme Court ruling on the legality of military commissions created by the Bush administration
Date: Decided on June 29, 2006

In deference to the international laws of war established by the Geneva Conventions, the Supreme Court found illegal the Bush administration's military commissions set up to try detainees held at Guantánamo Bay. Though hailed by some as a win for detainees' rights and a commitment to humane treatment of prisoners of war, the court left open the possibility that military commissions could be legally utilized in future situations.

Before his capture in 2001 and transfer to the US military's Guantánamo Bay detention center, Salim Ahmed Hamdan was a driver for Osama bin Laden. In 2004, a US military commission attempted to try him for terrorist conspiracies. Questioning the commission's legitimacy, Hamdan filed for a writ of habeas corpus. The administration of US President George W. Bush had classified him as an "enemy combatant" and claimed that, because international law did not recognize this classification, the military commission need not abide by international law to try him. Responding to Hamdan, the US District

Court for the District of Columbia accepted his petition, asserting that Hamdan's status as an enemy combatant was invalid because it had been determined solely by the president, who was not himself a "competent tribunal." In 2005, the US Circuit Court of Appeals for the District of Columbia reversed the ruling of the district court and supported trial by military commission. In November, the Supreme Court agreed to hear Hamdan's case, in which Secretary of Defense Donald Rumsfeld was the main defendant.

Supporting Hamdan, the Center for Justice and Accountability (CJA) filed a brief that exposed violations of the Geneva Conventions. While the case was heard, Congress passed the Detainee Treatment Act of 2005 (DTA), which barred US courts from hearing habeas petitions from Guantánamo detainees. Supporting the defense, Senators Jon Kyl and Lindsey Graham submitted a brief claiming that the DTA prevented the court from hearing Hamdan's case.

Asserting its jurisdiction, the Supreme Court ruled in the petitioner's favor. The court charged that the Bush administration was not authorized to create military commissions without prior permission from Congress. They criticized the commission for violating the Uniform Code of Military Justice by withholding evidence from the defendant, including confessions obtained through torture, and restricting appeals to the executive branch. The commission had also violated the Geneva Conventions by failing to ensure trial by a "regularly constituted court." While the court criticized President Bush for overstepping his wartime powers, it also emphasized the potential legality of future commissions, assuming they comport with military and international law.

Impact

In 2006, Congress passed the Military Commissions Act (MCA), making the DTA retroactive and nullifying *Hamdan*. However, as Hamdan was classified an enemy combatant and as the MCA only pertained to "unlawful enemy combatants," all charges were dropped against him in 2007. In December, he was reclassified as unlawful, found guilty of terrorism, and in 2008 was sentenced to sixty-six months imprisonment, most of which he was credited with already having served; he was subsequently transferred to Yemen and released in 2009.

Highlighting the importance of terminology in military law, the *Hamdan* ruling checked executive power. Although the military commission eventually tried him, the case challenged the extent of presidential powers in war.

Further Reading

Hansen, Jonathan M. *Guantánamo: An American History*. New York: Farrar, 2011. Print.

Schading, Barbara. *The Civilian's Guide to the US Military*. Cincinnati: Writer's Digest, 2007. Print.

Lucia Pizzo

■ Hanks, Tom

Identification: American film actor, producer, and director
Born: July 9, 1956; Concord, California

Hanks has long been a box office draw for film audiences worldwide. His mass appeal can be credited to his "average Joe" likeability, and his ability to deliver both comedic and dramatic performances. In addition to his work as an actor, Hanks is also a successful film and television producer.

In 2000, Tom Hanks collaborated with *Forrest Gump* (1994) director Robert Zemeckis for *Castaway*, in which Hanks plays a FedEx employee who becomes stranded on a remote island after a plane crash. Audiences and critics praised the film. Hanks's performance earned him his fifth Academy Award nomination.

Hanks took time off from his acting career in 2001 to produce the HBO television miniseries *Band of Brothers*, which chronicles the experiences of a regiment of soldiers during World War II. He directed one episode of the series, and was awarded an Emmy for his work.

Returning to film work in 2002, Hanks enjoyed many successes. In *Road to Perdition*, Hanks plays a hit man who must protect his son after the youngster witnesses his father kill a man. In *Catch Me If You Can* (2002), he portrays FBI agent Carl Hanratty. Based on a true story, the movie chronicles the pursuit of a teenage con artist, played by Leonardo DiCaprio. Critics commended Hanks for his role as the straitlaced Hanratty. That same year, Hanks became the youngest actor to receive the American Film Institute's Life Achievement Award.

Tom Hanks. (©iStockphoto.com/Jason Merritt)

Hanks worked with some noteworthy filmmakers in 2004, including the Coen Brothers in *The Lady Killers* and Steven Spielberg in *The Terminal.* Computer-generated imagery also allowed Hanks to play several different characters in Zemeckis's animated film *The Polar Express.* The actor starred in the film adaptation of novelist Dan Brown's bestseller *The Da Vinci Code* in 2006. In *The Da Vinci Code,* Hanks portrays a professor who uncovers a vast conspiracy following a murder at the Louvre. Although critics gave it mostly negative reviews, the film earned more than $200 million in the United States.

Hanks next appeared with Julia Roberts in *Charlie Wilson's War* (2007), based on a book about Wilson, a US congressman from Texas, his involvement in a covert operation in Afghanistan, and his unusual antics. Hanks, who also served as a producer on the film, earned a Golden Globe nomination for his role. As producer of the HBO

biographical miniseries *John Adams*, Hanks was awarded an Emmy for Outstanding Miniseries in 2008. He received a Producers Guild of America Award in 2009. He next produced an adaptation of the popular children's book *Where the Wild Things Are* (2009), which was directed by Spike Jonze. His final acting project of the decade was *Angels and Demons* (2009), the sequel to *The Da Vinci Code.*

Impact

Hanks's performances have won him many fans as well as many awards. The 2000s were a particularly successful decade for the actor. His many talents as an actor, producer, and director have established him as one of the most successful and versatile professionals in the entertainment industry.

Further Reading

Gardner, David. *The Tom Hanks Enigma: The Biography of the World's Most Intriguing Movie Star.* London: Blake, 2007. Print.

Mytnick, Colleen. "Life According to Tom Hanks." *Cleveland Magazine.* Great Lakes, Oct. 2009. Web. 9 July 2012.

"Tom Hanks." *Biography Today* (2010): 1. *Biography Reference Center.* Web. 27 Aug. 2012.

Cait Caffrey

■ Hanssen, Robert Philip

Identification: American FBI agent and convicted spy

Born: April 18, 1944; Evergreen Park, Illinois

Robert Philip Hanssen was a former FBI agent who is currently serving a life sentence at the United States Penitentiary in Florence, Colorado. He was convicted of espionage for aiding Russia and the Soviet Union for twenty-two years, from 1979 to 2001. In addition to selling American intelligence, Hanssen also stole over $1.4 million for the Soviet Union.

Over the years, Robert Philip Hanssen's duties at the Federal Bureau of Investigation gave him access to a variety of highly classified information. Hanssen's first bureau assignment was to the Gary, Indiana, office in 1976, but subsequent assignments moved him back and forth between New York City and Washington, DC. He acted as liaison to the State Department Office of Foreign Missions and was responsible for tracking espionage agents working in the United States under diplomatic cover. He was also the liaison to the State Department's Bureau of Intelligence and Research. Nevertheless, he quickly grew disillusioned with the FBI, which he felt underestimated his talents.

Hanssen functioned as a "mole," or embedded double agent, for the KGB, trading yet more secrets for cash, diamonds, and deposits in a Russian bank account. He utilized a system known as the "dead drop," which allowed him to leave documents and agents to leave payment at a prearranged site without the need for face-to-face meetings. In his communications, Hanssen identified himself variously as "B," "Ramon," and "Ramon Garcia."

Although Hanssen eventually collected as much as $1.4 million for his work, monetary gain does not seem to have been his primary motive. Instead, he seems to have delighted in deceiving those closest to him. Moreover, despite being a seemingly devoted family man, a Roman Catholic, and a member of the conservative Catholic organization Opus Dei, Hanssen was obsessed with sex and pornography. Sworn to uphold the ideals of the FBI and the United States, he nevertheless sold his country's secrets with no apparent compunction.

The FBI was finally able to identify Hanssen through information provided by a former KGB officer in return for seven million dollars. Hanssen was reassigned to the Washington office, where he could be kept under closer observation, and was arrested on February 18, 2001, at one of his customary dead drop sites. In order to avoid the death penalty, he pleaded guilty on July 6, 2001, to fifteen counts of spying and conspiracy. He was sentenced to life in prison without parole on May 10, 2002. His actions have been documented in books and film, including the 2007 documentary, *Superspy: The Man Who Betrayed the West.*

Impact

Robert Philip Hanssen is regarded as one of the most damaging spies in American history. By the time he was arrested, he had passed on some six thousand pages of documents and twenty-seven computer disks of highly sensitive information to the Russians. The information he sold came from the FBI, the Central Intelligence Agency (CIA), the

Pentagon, and the National Security Agency (NSA), the last of which probably suffered the most damage.

Among many other secrets, Hanssen revealed the names of Soviet agents actually working for the United States (several of whom were then executed by the Soviets); US estimates of Soviet missile strength; specific American plans for retaliation in case of war and for protecting top US officials; and details of electronic eavesdropping and surveillance techniques. He also provided the Soviets with software used to track intelligence cases—software that, in turn, a Russian agent may have sold to the terrorist organization al-Qaeda. Intelligence officials realized after the fact that they should have recognized signs of danger in Hanssen's often erratic behavior and work habits and consequently tightened their procedures.

Further Reading

Cherkashin, Victor and Gregory Feifer. *Spy Handler: Memoir of a KGB Officer—The True Story of the Man Who Recruited Robert Hanssen and Aldrich Ames.* New York: Basic, 2005. Print.

Havill, Adrian. *The Spy Who Stayed Out in the Cold.* New York: St. Martin's, 2001. Print.

Schiller, Lawrence. *Into the Mirror: The Life of Master Spy Robert P. Hanssen.* New York: Harper, 2002. Print.

Vise, David A. *The Bureau and the Mole: The Unmasking of Robert Philip Hanssen, the Most Dangerous Double Agent in FBI History.* New York: Atlantic, 2002. Print.

Wise, David. *Spy: The Inside Story of How the FBI's Robert Hanssen Betrayed America.* New York: Random, 2002. Print.

Grove Koger

■ Harper, Stephen

Identification: Twenty-second prime minister of Canada
Born: April 30, 1959; Toronto, Canada

Stephen Harper is the twenty-second prime minister of Canada. He first took office on February 6, 2006, and has since governed during difficult times of economic instability. His Conservative Party is now the dominant force in Canadian politics, commanding a majority in Parliament.

Stephen Harper. (Courtesy Prime Minister's Office)

In 1993, Stephen Harper was elected to the House of Commons as the Reform Party's candidate for the Calgary West riding, or electoral district. In 1997 he left Parliament in order to become the vice president of the advocacy group the National Citizens Coalition. He would later become the coalition's president. In 2002, Harper returned to the House of Commons as a member of the Canadian Alliance and as the minister representing Calgary Southwest. In 2003, Harper cofounded the Conservative Party of Canada, merging the Progressive Conservatives and his own Canadian Alliance. The new party selected him as its leader. Only one year after his ascension to the party's leadership, he led the Conservatives to secure an additional twenty-five seats in the House of Commons. In January 2006, he led his party to win 124 seats. On February 6, 2006, he was sworn in as the twenty-second Prime Minister of Canada.

In late 2007, the United States was entering into a recession. Harper's budget for 2008 included a number of provisions designed not just to help Canadian taxpayers weather what could be a major storm, but to help much of Canada avoid recession altogether. Before talk of recession reached a fever pitch, the Tory budget featured $12.3 billion in business and personal tax cuts. In early 2008, Harper announced the creation of a $1 billion fund to protect the communities that rely on industries that have been hardest hit over the years, such as forestry. Following the resulting worldwide economic downturn, taxpayer and municipal relief became a major issue for the Harper leadership.

One of Harper's greatest challenges has been Canada's failing infrastructure. A 2008 study by the Federation of Canadian Municipalities estimated that $123 billion is needed to address Canada's infrastructure issues, far more than the government is able to offer. Harper's approach to supplying these funds has been to target provinces rather than municipalities. For example, he provided $2.2 billion to British Columbia, which in turn used the funds to improve the ports and infrastructure along the coast. He has also worked with premiers in Nova Scotia and British Columbia to establish frameworks by which they might repair their own municipal roadways and systems. For example, for a province to obtain funds from the Building Canada program, it must demonstrate that the funds will be used to satisfy one or more of fifteen "principles," including transit, highways, wastewater treatment, and tourism. Harper's federalist approach has prompted premiers to seek his attention and work together within certain agreed-upon guidelines. His approach has been successful in building closer working relationships and accessibility between premiers and the federal government.

The Fortieth Canadian General Election was held on October 14, 2008. Prime Minister Harper's Conservative Party gained enough votes to retain its minority government in the Canadian House of Commons. Six weeks after the election, opposition parties sought to defeat the Conservative government with a motion of non-confidence. Harper requested and was granted a prorogation, or postponement, of the non-confidence vote, which then never came to pass.

Impact

Harper's administration has governed during dire economic times, but managed to instigate much needed improvements to Canada's infrastructure, and reshaped the relationship between provincial governments and the federal establishment. On May 2, 2011, Harper's Conservative Party won a parliamentary majority for the first time during his tenure as prime minister. Many analysts expect that Harper, after working with a majority opposition for his entire career as prime minister, could begin to enact sweeping policy changes as result of having finally gained a majority mandate.

Further Reading

Cody, Howard. "Minority Government in Canada: The Stephen Harper Experience." *American Review of Canadian Studies* 38.1 (2008): 27–42. Print.

Kukucha, Christopher J. "Dismembering Canada? Stephen Harper and the Foreign Relations of Canadian Provinces." *Review of Constitutional Studies* 14.1 (2009): 21–52. Print.

Wells, Paul, and John Geddes. "What You Don't Know about Stephen Harper. (Cover Story)." *Maclean's* 124.4 (2011): 14–27. Print.

Michael Auerbach

■ Harry Potter films

Definition: Eight blockbuster movie adaptations of J. K. Rowling's Harry Potter fantasy series

The Harry Potter movies brought the spirit of J. K. Rowling's best-selling fantasy series to the big screen with impressive special effects, award-winning acting, and medieval settings that sparked the imagination. Each film set records at the box office and earned nominations for numerous awards throughout the world. Most importantly, the films were viewed as a huge success by many Potter fans, a tribute to the strong collaboration between Rowling and the film directors.

Warner Brothers released the highly anticipated movie adaptation of the first Harry Potter book, *Harry Potter and the Philosopher's Stone* (renamed *Harry Potter and the Sorcerer's Stone* in the United States), in late November 2001, while British author J. K. Rowling was busy at work completing the fourth book in the series. The film, directed by Chris Columbus with a budget of $125 million, brought to life the Hogwarts School of Witchcraft and Wizardry and its sundry characters in a thrilling adaptation that was a hit with Potter readers and nonreaders alike. Much of the success of the film series was due to the tight controls that Rowling had placed on production when she sold the movie rights, insisting on British actors and settings.

The children who were cast in the lead roles, eleven-year-old Daniel Radcliffe (Harry Potter), ten-year-old Emma Watson (Hermione Granger), and eleven-year-old Rupert Grint (Ron Weasley), ended up performing throughout the entire series and thus offered cohesion for the films while maturing with the characters as they aged from movie to movie. The sequels consisted of *Harry Potter and the Chamber of Secrets* (2002), also directed by Chris Columbus; *Harry Potter and the Prisoner of Azkaban* (2004), directed by

Alfonso Cuarón; *Harry Potter and the Goblet of Fire* (2005), directed by Mike Newell; *Harry Potter and the Order of the Phoenix* (2007), directed by David Yates; and *Harry Potter and the Half-Blood Prince* (2009), also directed by David Yates. Filming was done at Alnwick Castle, Bodleian Library, Gloucester Cathedral, and other historic and culturally important locations. Beginning with *Azkaban*, IMAX versions of the films were also released. By the end of the decade, the first six movies had grossed over $5 billion worldwide. The final book in the series, *Harry Potter and the Deathly Hallows*, was split into two separate film installments, directed by David Yates and released in 2010 and 2011.

Impact

The eight films of the Harry Potter series grossed more than $7.7 billion, and the movies offered some of the best escape entertainment of the decade. The most critical Potter fans, however, often found the movies much less satisfying than the books. The films allowed nonreaders to join in the "Pottermania" frenzy. They also sparked an interest in British culture and history, and several sightseeing tours have been established that bring

Left to right: Daniel Radcliffe, Rupert Grint, author J. K. Rowling, and Emma Watson at the London premiere of The Prisoner of Azkaban, *May 2004. (Mike Marsland/WireImage/Getty Images)*

visitors to a number of Harry Potter film sites across the United Kingdom.

Further Reading

McCabe, Bob. *Harry Potter: Page to Screen, the Complete Filmmaking Journey*. New York: Harper, 2011. Print.

Sibley, Brian. *Harry Potter Film Wizardry*. New York: Harper, 2010. Print.

Sally Driscoll

■ Hate crimes

Definition: Physical, verbal, and/or psychological assaults on individuals based on race, ethnicity, gender, religion, disability, and/or sexual orientation

Hate crimes remained a difficult legal, social, and political issue during the 2000s. The terrorist attacks of September 11, 2001, and the push for legalized same-sex marriage led hate criminals to launch physical, verbal, and psychological attacks on people of various sociological backgrounds.

Although law enforcement agencies have combated hate crimes for decades, the 2000s were a period in which a significant number of high-profile hate crimes took center stage. These crimes took a wide range of forms, from written and verbal threats to graffiti, demonstrations, and acts of physical violence. At the same time, however, federal and state governments took steps to more effectively prosecute those who commit hate crimes in the United States. Among the many issues that inspired hate crimes during the 2000s were the terrorist attacks of September 11, 2001, and the push for the legalization of same-sex marriage.

Terrorist Attacks of September 11, 2001

In some cases, hate crimes are committed by people who link their victims to the actions of others. In other words, they might hold their victims "responsible" for the crimes committed by people of the same race, ethnic group, or religious faith as their victims. The terrorist attacks of September 11, 2001, which resulted in thousands of deaths in New York City, Pennsylvania, and Washington, DC, provide an example of this type of hate crime. Those attacks were perpetrated by members of al-Qaeda, a group of Islamic extremist terrorists, many of whom were of Arab descent. Once that fact had been established publicly (coupled with the fact that the media provided extensive coverage of the people who comprised al-Qaeda's leadership), many Americans acted out against those whom they believed could have ties to al-Qaeda's brand of terrorism.

Many of the crimes committed against people of Arab ethnicity or Islamic faith were based on a knee-jerk, paranoid reaction to the trauma of that day. For example, within hours of the attacks, an Islamic cultural center in Eugene, Oregon, began receiving death threats. In New York, a Bangladeshi taxi driver was viciously assaulted by his passenger, who thought he was a Muslim. Even those who, in the minds of the perpetrators, resembled Arabs or Muslims were victimized—there were hundreds of September 11–fueled hate crimes committed during the 2000s against Sikhs (who do not practice Islam but who wear long beards and robes and, to ignorant observers, resemble Arabs and Muslims). In the one-year period following the September 11 terrorist attacks, anti-Arab and anti-Muslim hate crimes spiked a staggering 1,600 percent.

Over time, the passions that inspired this spike in hate crimes diminished. This fact was in no small part the result of the activism of federal, state, and local governments and a wide range of religious- and social issue–oriented organizations conducting public outreach programs designed to reduce paranoia and inform the public on the differences between true Islam and the radical forms practiced by the terrorists. In New York City and Washington, DC, where the attacks were focused, the number of hate crimes dropped to negligible numbers. Some observers have cited the efforts of President George W. Bush and Congress to unify Americans against al-Qaeda and its sponsors as fearmongering that could have restarted crimes against Muslims and Arabs. Then again, as more people became educated on the nature of radical Islamic terrorism, statistics show that this type of hate crime slowly diminished in the latter part of the 2000s.

Same-Sex Marriage

The 2000s were a pivotal period for gay rights advocates. At the beginning of the decade, Vermont became the first state to allow "civil unions," enabling same-sex couples to enjoy benefits given to legally married heterosexual couples. The law touched off a firestorm of controversy in other states and in the federal government. Meanwhile, courts across the country, including the US Supreme Court, began to hear cases that called for equal protections, including marriage, under the law for homosexual men and women. In 2004, the Massachusetts Supreme Judicial Court ruled that nothing in the state's constitution prohibited gay couples from marrying and that the state should therefore sanction same-sex marriage. Following the Massachusetts decision, several other states also moved to allow homosexual men and women to marry. At the same time, an increasing number of legislatures were addressing employee benefits for same-sex couples. Meanwhile, gay men and lesbians began to be portrayed more sympathetically in popular culture, with television programs and films presenting homosexuality in a mainstream light.

As the gay- and lesbian-rights agenda moved forward in the 2000s, social conservatives angrily denounced the trend. Many people acted in violent fashion. In 2003, a sixteen-year-old lesbian in Massachusetts was brutally attacked a day after she attended an event that promoted tolerance for the gay community. During that same year, a woman in New Jersey was fatally stabbed after it was revealed that she was a lesbian.

In fact, in 2003, there was a significant increase in antigay hate crimes. Following the US Supreme Court's ruling that struck down a Texas law outlawing sodomy, there was a 24 percent rise in hate crimes against gay men and women in the United States. In New York City, antigay crimes rose 43 percent in the second half of 2003 when compared to the same period in 2002.

During the 2000s, each victory for the gay rights agenda seemed to trigger a violent backlash in the form of antigay hate crimes. Representatives of federal, state, and local governments spoke out against such violence and discrimination and preached tolerance. However, creating effective awareness campaigns has proven difficult, as it has been a challenge to calculate precisely the number of such crimes committed (hate crime reporting has been highly flawed). By the middle of the 2000s, according to one study, gay men and women were the target of hate crimes approximately six times more than the Federal Bureau of Investigation (FBI) reported.

Impact

Hate crimes significantly increased during the 2000s, in large part because of the September 11 terrorist attacks and the advancement of the gay rights agenda. However, the two issue areas—anti-Muslim/anti-Arab and anti-gay sentiment—have seen decidedly different outcomes. In the case of the former, violence against Muslims and Arabs (as well as those who appear to be members of either of those communities) decreased in the year after the terrorist attacks, a result of effective public outreach programs. In the latter, however, hate crime rates seemed to spike each time the gay community achieved a victory in the courts or the legislatures.

The high rate of occurrence of hate crimes in the United States during the 2000s fostered calls for better reporting of such activity as well as increased awareness campaigns and law enforcement practices. Legislatures were increasingly empowering law enforcement officials to understand the nature of hate crimes and to act appropriately against the perpetrators. The FBI increased its effort to better compile and distribute information and statistics on hate crimes in the United States. This data can help law enforcement target susceptible areas and more effectively prosecute offenders.

Further Reading

Disha, Ilir, James C. Cavendish, and Ryan D. King. "Historical Events and Spaces of Hate: Hate Crimes against Arabs and Muslims in Post-9/11 America." *Social Problems* 58.1 (2011): 21–46. Print. Explores the roots of anti-Muslim and anti-Arab hate crimes in the period following the September 11 attacks.

Healy, Christopher. "Marriage's Bloody Backlash." *Advocate* 913 (2004): 38–40. Print. Focuses on the rising number of antigay hate crimes seemingly linked to the legalization of same-sex marriage.

Gerstenfeld, Phyllis B. *Hate Crimes: Causes, Controls, and Controversies.* Thousand Oaks: Sage, 2010. Print. Reviews a number of high-profile hate crimes that were given coverage in American media and the legislative initiatives that were triggered by these events.

Swigonski, Mary E., Robin Mama, and Kelly Ward. *From Hate Crimes to Human Rights: A Tribute to Matthew Shepard.* New York: Routledge, 2001. Print. Describes how the gay rights movement has suffered a wide range of hate crimes and harsh discrimination, which led to a number of initiatives during the 2000s to protect the civil rights of gay and lesbian citizens.

Welch, Michael. *Scapegoats of September 11: Hate Crimes and State Crimes in the War on Terror.* New Brunswick: Rutgers UP, 2006. Print. Discusses how the public's response to the radical Islamic terrorist attacks, coupled with the federal government's efforts to unify Americans against such organizations, contributed to the type of scapegoating that lead to many hate crimes against Muslims and Arabs.

Wright, Ellen. "The Gaying of America: 2003 in Review." *Lesbian News* 29.6 (2004): 21. Print. Describes some of the early 2000s victories in the gay rights movements in parallel to a number of high-profile gay rights–related hate crimes.

Michael P. Auerbach

■ Health care

Definition: Assistance provided by doctors, nurses, or other certified professionals for the maintenance of well-being and the prevention, diagnosis, and treatment of illness and disease

The cost of health care was a major concern in the United States in the 2000s. Health care coverage continued to rise, in no small part because of the rising cost of medical procedures. This issue proved extremely complex and politically divisive, with leaders attempting to address citizens' health care needs without endangering employers.

One of the major issues facing presidential candidates during the 2000 election campaign was the cost and quality of the American health care system. The issue itself was complex, but on the minds of both private citizens and employers was the high cost of insurance premiums. The proposed solutions were myriad, ranging from comprehensive reforms (such as universal health care) to smaller and more focused reforms. As the debate continued throughout that campaign and the decade, more people went without quality health coverage, adding to the severity of the situation.

The High Cost of Health Care

From 2000 through 2004, the cost of employers' health insurance premiums increased by double digits annually. The rates of increase were five times the rate of both inflation and the increase in employee wages. There were a number of major factors contributing to this staggering rate of increase. One

of the reasons was that many hospitals and their doctors frequently ordered comprehensive medical procedures, tests, and treatments for their patients. This practice helped doctors avoid lawsuits but was also expensive. With insurance companies paying for these extra procedures, the additional costs were transferred to the customers.

Another factor contributing to these costs was the price of managing customer accounts. According to one study, one-third of US health care expenditures go to the administration of health insurance. This area includes paying insurance company staff, managing paperwork, and paying out claims. During the 2000s, a great deal of effort was expended to cut down on paperwork and thus save costs, but the high price of providing coverage to thousands of clients continued to contribute to the large price tag on health coverage.

The health insurance industry has long been driven by market forces. In other words, when one insurer raises its premium rates, it is likely that others will follow suit. This fact contributed to the health care issue, as the rates of all private insurance companies seemed to be close to one another. The similar prices of insurance packages led to the continued use of health maintenance organizations (HMOs), which are managed care plans that involve networks of participating doctors. These programs are not as expensive as preferred provider organizations (PPOs) offered by large insurance companies, but they can limit the types of procedures covered and the quantity of available physicians.

Still another contributing factor to the health care issue is government programs such as Medicaid and Medicare. These programs give health care coverage to the nation's poorest citizens (Medicaid) and senior and disabled citizens (Medicare). Frequently, people who lack full coverage go to the hospital for emergency treatment. Medicaid and Medicare reimburse the hospital for treating these people, but the reimbursement rate is only a fraction of what procedures costs. Therefore, hospitals must increase prices for the same procedures for patients with full coverage, which results in higher premiums across the board. Adding to this issue is that so many people do not have health insurance or primary care physicians (they use the emergency room as issues arise). Thus, because an increasing number of people have been without insurance, hospital

Life Expectancy in the United States at 65 Years, 2000 and 2009

Country	Gender	2000	2009
United States	Male	16.0	17.6
	Female	19.0	20.3
Canada	Male	16.5	18.5
	Female	20.2	21.6
Median of 30 other countries	Male	15.55	17.45
	Female	19.1	20.8

Source: Center for Disease Control and Prevention

resources have become strained and costs have been driven further upward.

Solutions

Policymakers debated this oft-contentious issue throughout the 2000s. Some of the reform attempts offered by Congress addressed parts of the overall issue. For example, in 2003, the George W. Bush presidential administration passed a measure creating a prescription drug benefit for Medicare recipients, helping seniors purchase much needed medications. (The high cost of health insurance coverage has been a major factor in the price of prescription medications, as insurance typically mitigates the high costs of these drugs). Other solutions were more comprehensive. For example, in 2001, the Democratic Congress attempted to pass a Patient's Bill of Rights, which would, among other initiatives, allow people to sue their HMOs if they were denied coverage or otherwise allowed to suffer under the plans. Many of the reforms offered in Congress, particularly the larger initiatives, failed largely because of their overwhelming price tags.

In 2006, Massachusetts became the first state to successfully craft a comprehensive health care reform act. The law was crafted by the Democratic majority in the state legislature and signed into law by Republican governor Mitt Romney. One of the law's main elements was a mandate, or requirement, that all citizens in Massachusetts have health insurance, a status they would need to report on

their state income tax return. Employers would be required to provide access to one or more health insurance plans, or else face an annual fine for each employee without such access. The law would be funded by eliminating a fund that compensated hospitals for treating uninsured patients and by the aforementioned fines. The state also established a network whereby the state's unemployed and impoverished residents could obtain affordable health coverage despite their financial status. The goal of this far-reaching law was to provide coverage to all Massachusetts residents with minimal cost to the state's general fund, the source of the state's annual budget.

The Massachusetts law gave inspiration to federal lawmakers who had been vexed by the costs and partisanship involved in reforming the health care system. In 2008, presidential candidate Barack Obama pledged to pass universal health care (health care for all Americans) in some form, while Congress renewed efforts to reform the existing health care system. Meanwhile, other states introduced reforms of their own. By the end of the decade, five states (Minnesota, New Jersey, Connecticut, Utah, and Florida) had passed comprehensive health care reform laws, and more than half of the states were examining reform legislation. In 2010, Congress and President Obama passed into law another reform law, the Patient Protection and Affordable Care Act (PPACA), which used the Massachusetts model as its inspiration and added rules that prohibited insurers from denying coverage to people with preexisting conditions.

Impact

The factors contributing to the issue of affordable health care in the United States are myriad, as have been attempts to reform the system. The prevalence of so many uninsured citizens, the high cost of premiums, and the expensive price tags associated with hospital treatment are among the wide range of mitigating factors that lawmakers have sought to address. Lawmakers have taken both incremental and comprehensive approaches to reform. However, one of the main issues preventing any successful implementation of reforms has been the costs involved.

The 2000s saw a series of significant steps taken toward passage of effective reforms. Massachusetts led the way in the latter 2000s, with other states and the federal government following suit by the end of the decade. The Massachusetts law did see an uptick in the number of insured residents, although many reports at the end of the decade revealed that health premium rates continued to rise despite the law's efforts to rein in those costs.

Further Reading

Cohn, Jonathan. *Sick: The Untold Story of America's Health Care Crisis—And the People Who Pay the Price.* New York: Harper, 2008. Print. Analyzes the causes of the problems in the US health care system, including the costs of hospital care and rising insurance rates.

Hackmann, Martin B., Jonathan T. Kolstad, and Amanda E. Kowalski. "Health Reform, Health Insurance, and Selection." *American Economic Review* 102.3 (2012): 498–501. Print. Describes how the 2006 Massachusetts reform law increased enrollment in health insurance plans.

Harrington, Charlene, and Carroll L. Estes. *Health Policy: Crisis and Reform in the US Health Care Delivery System.* 5th ed. Sudbury: Jones, 2007. Print. Provides a basic overview of health care–oriented public policy and the federal legislative process.

Hussain, Aftab, and Patrick A. Rivers. "Policy Challenges in US Health Care System Reform." *Journal of Health Care Finance* 36.3 (2010): 34–46. Print. Describes the political forces at work in the effort to reform the American health care system.

Reid, T. R. *The Healing of America: A Global Quest for Better, Cheaper, and Fairer Health Care.* New York: Penguin, 2010. Print. Provides a description of the US health care system in comparison to those of other countries, including those with universal health care systems.

Venkatesh, Arjun K., et al. "Use of Observation Care in US Emergency Departments, 2001 to 2008." *PLoS ONE*, 6.9 (2011): 1–10. Print. Describes an important component of emergency care—treatment without admission, a contributor to the costs associated with hospital care.

Michael P. Auerbach

■ Hilton, Paris

Identification: American heiress, actress, model, and celebrity
Born: February 17, 1981; New York City, New York

Hilton, an heiress to the hotel chain that bears her surname, became a pop-culture phenomenon with the debut of her reality show The Simple Life *in 2003. She was soon the most well known modern "celebutante"—a person primarily famous for being wealthy. Hilton branded perfumes, jewelry, and nightclubs with her name. Legal troubles and time in jail curtailed her career late in the decade.*

Socialite Paris Hilton drew attention throughout the 2000s for her reality television antics, and her involvement in an infamous sex tape. A former boyfriend, actor and producer Rick Salomon, videotaped an intimate encounter the couple shared in 2001, which was later uploaded to the Internet. The Salomon video surfaced a few weeks before *The Simple Life*, the reality television series starring Hilton and her best friend, Nicole Richie, debuted in 2003. Thirteen million viewers tuned in to the FOX series, which featured the young, wealthy women doing menial chores on a farm in rural Arkansas. Although critics denounced *The Simple Life*, the show was renewed for several seasons.

In 2004, Hilton released an autobiography, *Confessions of an Heiress*. That same year, she became the namesake of the Club Paris nightspots, and made millions from the venture before being fired in 2007 for missing appearances. Hilton again made headlines in 2005 when her cell phone was hacked, and the contact information of her famous friends was posted online. She released an album, *Paris*, to poor reviews in August 2006. A month later, Hilton was arrested for driving under the influence. She accepted a plea agreement and received probation. After feuding for some time, Hilton and Richie reconciled and returned for a fifth season of *The Simple Life* in late 2006.

In January 2007, Hilton pleaded no contest to alcohol-related reckless driving, but violated her probation by driving with a suspended license the following month. Hilton was sentenced to forty-five days in jail. She was incarcerated for several days, and served the remainder of her sentence under house arrest.

Paris Hilton (right) performing community service with the Hollywood Beautification Team. (©iStockphoto.com/Kevork Djansezian)

Impact

Hilton and Richie's reality series and subsequent fame increased the public's appetite for news about celebrities and socialites. Although other reality shows have since featured other celebutantes, *The Simple Life* was the most successful and enduring. Hilton received less media attention as the global recession developed and deepened late in the decade. However, new shows about wealthy individuals like Hilton, such as *Real Housewives of Beverly Hills*, remain popular.

Further Reading

Associated Press. "Economy's Cultural Impact Tough to Gauge." *Newsday.* Newsday, 27 Sept. 2009. Web. 9 July 2012.

CNN. "Paris Hilton Out of Jail." *CNN.* Cable News Network, 7 June 2007. Web. 6 July 2012.

Ebner, Mark. *Six Degrees of Paris Hilton: Inside the Sex Tapes, Scandals, and Shakedowns of the New Hollywood.* New York: Gallery, 2009. Print.

Hilton, Paris. *Confessions of an Heiress.* New York: Touchstone, 2004. Print.

"Paris Hilton Biography." *People.* Time Inc., 2012. Web. 6 July 2012.

Josephine Campbell

■ HIV/AIDS

Definition: The human immunodeficiency virusin (HIV) is the etiological agent for acquired immune deficiency syndrome (AIDS).

Since AIDS was first recognized in 1981 approximately thirty million persons have died from the disease. While no vaccine was developed to prevent the disease during the first decade of the twenty-first century, improved programs for treatment and the institution of preventive measures resulted in a decrease in mortality of nearly 25 percent.

HIV is the virus class known as retroviruses, of which the genome is ribonucleic acid (RNA) and which replicate through a deoxyribonucleic acid (DNA) intermediate. The agent uses a viral enzyme, reverse transcriptase, to copy the genome into DNA, which integrates into the host chromosome. The specific cell infected and killed is the T lymphocyte, a cell that regulates the immune response. The virus requires two proteins on the surface of the cell for infection; the CD4 protein allows attachment of the virus, while a hormone (chemokine) receptor is necessary for entry. Mutations in either prevent infection. Once the virus is replicating it requires another enzyme, a protease that cleaves a viral protein that constitutes part of its structure, for maturation and release. Antiviral therapy has largely targeted either the reverse transcriptase or protease.

Depletion of CD4+ cells, the T lymphocytes, below 1000 per microliter of blood places a person at risk for any of a large number of opportunistic infections. AIDS is identified when the person is HIV positive and has been diagnosed with any of these infections.

Incidence and Prevalence of AIDS

While no vaccine has proven effective in protecting against AIDS, preventive measures have reduced the likelihood of infection. A 2006 study demonstrated that male circumcision significantly reduced the risk of infection; diaphragm usage by women however, demonstrated no reduction in risk.

Estimates are that 68 million persons worldwide are infected (as of 2012), most in underdeveloped countries. In the United States total AIDS cases are estimated at 1.3 million. While the yearly incidence of AIDS in the United States had declined by 2001, numbers increased after 2002. African Americans and Latinos represented 75 percent of new cases. In part, this was the result of poor education addressing the risk of infection; a significant number of people have shown indifference to their risk of contracting the disease or falsely believe there is a cure. Many of the cases are among gay men (defined as "men who have sex with men"); a 2007 study found nearly half of gay African Americans may be HIV positive. Many of these men were initially unaware they were HIV positive.

Prospective Treatments for AIDS in the Near Future

Antiretroviral therapy is generally started when the number of CD4+ cells drops below 350 per microliter of blood. Beginning in 2011, a worldwide study known as START has tested if the initiation of antiretroviral therapy when CD4+ numbers drop to 500 is more useful in reducing the level of virus than when the number drops to 350. The theory is that earlier treatment may both prove more beneficial and decrease the risk of transmission to an HIV-negative partner. Early results using some eleven different drugs targeting both the viral reverse transcriptase and viral protease demonstrated more than a 90 percent reduction in transmission to previously uninfected partners.

Another approach addressed the question of whether pre-exposure prophylaxis (PrEP) may actually prevent infection in men who refuse to practice safe sex. Clinical trials began in 2007 among HIV-negative gay men in six countries. They were given the drug Truvada, an inhibitor of reverse transcriptase. A 2011 report suggested a reduction in infection of more than 75 percent in men who maintained the recommended schedule in use of the drug.

Since the chemokine protein CCR5 on the surface of CD4+ cells is necessary for entry of the virus, scientists are testing whether genetically engineered cells that lack the protein may render the person resistant to the disease. The initial test case was an HIV-positive individual who developed leukemia. Following eradication of bone-marrow cells to treat the leukemia, the patient received a transplant from an individual whose cells lacked the CCR5 protein. After five years the patient showed no evidence of AIDS. Further research has taken place to test the usefulness of the approach in other HIV-infected persons.

Impact

The use of combinations of drugs, referred to as drug "cocktails," for treatment of AIDS, highly active antiretroviral therapy (HAART) originated in 1996 and represented the first long-term effective treatment of the disease. The cost of manufacturing the drugs, as well as the accessibility of treatment in poor countries, has resulted in limited availability in much of the world. Political changes in countries such as those in southern Africa, the site for much of the increase in HIV incidence, have allowed an increased awareness of how the virus is transmitted. Attempts to reduce prostitution and to educate the populations about the use of condoms have met with only limited success.

HAART therapy has proven much more successful in developed countries. The transmission of HIV from infected women to children has been reduced from 25 percent to nearly 1 percent; the goal is to eliminate such transmission by 2015. Early treatment of infected persons, or pre-exposure prophylaxis, has significantly extended the prospective life span of patients and has shown strong evidence that risk of transmission to an uninfected partner is also reduced.

Further Reading

Harden, Victoria. *AIDS at Thirty: A History.* Washington, DC: Potomac, 2012. Print. Thorough overview of the disease, its discovery, and development and failures of methods of treatment. Included are numerous references from both popular media and scientific works.

June, Carl, and Bruce Levine. "Blocking AIDS Attack." *Scientific American* 306.3 (2012): 54–59. Print. Review of the mechanism of immunodeficiency following infection. Describes new methods of treatment.

Montagnier, Luc. *Virus: The Co-Discoverer of HIV Tracks Its Rampage and Charts the Future.* New York: Norton, 2000. Print. Autobiography of the scientist who, along with Robert Gallo, discovered HIV and its role in AIDS. Description of the science behind the discovery.

Stine, Gerald. *AIDS Update 2012.* New York: McGraw, 2012. Print. Complete overview of advances in AIDS research during 2011. Includes the history of the disease, the likely origins, and prospective treatments.

Timberg, Craig, and Daniel Halperin. *Tinderbox.* New York: Penguin, 2012. Print. Account of both how HIV jumped from nonhuman primates to humans and the role of the West in the development and spread of the disease. The authors suggest realistic mechanisms for its control.

Richard Adler

Philip Seymour Hoffman. (©iStockphoto.com/Sean Gallup)

■ Hoffman, Philip Seymour

Identification: American actor and director
Born: July 23, 1967, Fairport, New York

Philip Seymour Hoffman appeared in several critically acclaimed films in the 2000s. In 2005, he won the Academy Award for Best Actor for his portrayal of author Truman Capote. In addition to his work in film, Hoffman is a stage actor and director.

During the 1990s and early 2000s, Philip Seymour Hoffman appeared in several television and supporting film roles before getting his first starring role as a widower in the film *Love Liza* in 2002. The following year, he starred as a gambling addict in the film *Owning Mahoney* (2003).

The year 2005 marked a high point in Hoffman's acting career. Not only did he receive an Emmy Award nomination for his role as Charlie Mayne in the miniseries *Empire Falls* (2005), but he also won the Academy Award for Best Actor in a Leading Role for his portrayal of author Truman Capote in the film *Capote* (2005). For that role, Hoffman also won a Golden Globe Award, a Screen Actors Guild Award, as well as awards from several different film critics associations. Hoffman stated that playing Capote was the most difficult role of his career, and that he practiced the author's distinctively high-pitched voice for five months prior to shooting.

Hoffman received critical acclaim again for his supporting role in the film *Charlie Wilson's War* (2007), in which he portrayed a US Central Intelligence Agency officer. The role earned him an Academy Award nomination for best supporting actor. Hoffman was again nominated for the award in 2008 for his role as a priest accused of sexually abusing a student in the film *Doubt*. That same year, he starred in the film *Synecdoche, New York* (2008), which in 2009 film critic Robert Ebert called the best film of the decade.

Hoffman has received critical acclaim for his stage acting and directing as well. In 2000, he received a Drama Desk nomination for best actor for his role in the Off-Broadway play *The Author's Voice* and a Tony Award nomination for his role in the play *True West*. Hoffman received another Tony Award nomination for his role in the 2003 production of *Long Day's Journey Into the Night*. He was nominated for Drama Desk awards for his directing of the plays *Jesus Hopped the 'A' Train* in 2001 and *Our Lady of 121st Street* in 2003. Hoffman continued to act in the theater in the 2000s as a member of the Off-Broadway LAByrinth Theater Company, based in New York City.

Impact

Hoffman has become one of the most sought-after actors in film and theater. He made his debut as a film director in 2010 with the film *Jack Goes Boating*.

Further Reading

Hill, Derek. *Charlie Kaufman and Hollywood's Merry Band of Pranksters, Fabulists and Dreams: An Excursion Into the American New Wave*. Harpenden: Kamera, 2008. Print.

Hirschberg, Lynn. "A Higher Calling." *New York Times*. New York Times Co., 28 Dec. 2008. Web. 26 Jul. 2012.

Patrick G. Cooper

■ Homosexuality and gay rights

Definition: Major political, social, and cultural developments related to the movement toward equal rights for gay, lesbian, bisexual, and transgender individuals

The first decade of the twenty-first century was a time of profound social and cultural progress for gay, lesbian, bisexual, and transgender (GLBT) people throughout the United States. In addition to gaining the right to marry in several states, GLBT individuals filled prominent roles in popular culture and were elected to political offices in defiance of the

widespread prejudices that had been an obstacle in previous decades.

Throughout the 2000s, the movement toward equal rights for GLBT individuals became a significant facet of American politics, media, and culture. A number of major developments occurred during the decade, particularly in the area of same-sex marriage, though the GLBT community faced some setbacks as well.

Landmark Legislation

The decade began with landmark legislation by the Vermont state legislature with regard to the legal acknowledgement of same-sex couples. In 2000, Vermont became the first US state to recognize same-sex couples who joined in civil union. While the decision stopped short of specifically referring to same-sex unions as marriages, the law did declare that those in civil unions would be granted the same rights, privileges, and benefits as married spouses with regard to areas such as tax status and health care. New Jersey followed suit with similar legislation in 2006.

In November of 2003, the debate over same-sex marriage took center stage in Massachusetts when the Massachusetts Supreme Judicial Court ruled in *Goodridge v. Department of Public Health* that any legislation banning same-sex couples from marriage would violate the state constitution, as it would treat GLBT individuals as second-class citizens. The landmark ruling was made despite the vocal opposition of conservative religious groups as well as some politicians. Massachusetts marriage licenses began to be issued to same-sex couples in May of 2004.

By the end of the decade, Connecticut, Iowa, Vermont, and the District of Columbia had followed Massachusetts's example, though the same-sex marriages performed in those areas of the country remained unrecognized on the federal level. California legalized same-sex marriage in 2008; however, this legalization ended only months later when Proposition 8 amended the state constitution to prohibit non-heterosexual marriage.

In addition to the *Goodridge* ruling, the year 2003 included a landmark US Supreme Court ruling regarding sodomy laws in the United States. The court ruled in *Lawrence v. Texas* that state antisodomy laws were unconstitutional. In its decision, the high court decreed that all US citizens had a right to privacy and liberty concerning consensual intimate conduct.

Float at the Christopher Street Day ("Gay Pride Parade") in New York City. (Courtesy Soffimoffi)

Not all court rulings regarding GLBT rights during the 2000s found in favor of GLBT individuals or organizations. In 2000, a Supreme Court decision upheld the rights of all private organizations to set membership rules, in keeping with the right to freedom of association guaranteed by the First Amendment, thereby granting organizations the right to refuse entry to GLBT people. This ruling followed legislative action against the Boy Scouts of America, which in the wake of the ruling continued to deny membership to homosexuals.

Political Victories

During the 2000s, a number of openly GLBT individuals were elected to positions in state legislatures across the United States. More than 130 gay, lesbian, bisexual, and transgender political candidates were on US ballots during the 2001–2 election cycle, a number that increased to more than 160 the following year. In 2000, Democrat Ed Flanagan of Vermont became the first openly gay man to be nominated as a major-party candidate for the United States Senate, while Vermont Republican Karen Kerin became the first transgender individual to be a major party nominee.

By 2007, issues important to GLBT citizens received national attention in the US political sphere. That year, the Human Rights Campaign sponsored the first US presidential forum focusing specifically on GLBT issues, extending invitations to each presidential candidate in every major American political party. While six Democratic presidential candidates opted to participate in the discussion, including future secretary of state Hillary Clinton and future president Barack Obama, all Republican candidates declined. The absence of Republican candidates symbolized a decade-long disconnect between the GLBT community and one of the United States' most prominent political parties.

Popular Culture

Changing societal perceptions of GLBT individuals led to an increased visibility of GLBT-themed storylines and characters in American popular media. Cable television programs focusing on GLBT characters included *Queer as Folk* and *The L Word*, while the channel Logo, established in 2005, aired a variety of programming targeted toward gay, lesbian, bisexual, and transgender viewers.

No longer deemed overtly provocative by television audiences or critics, coming-out narratives were featured prominently in widely popular cable and network television shows throughout the 2000s, notably on shows such as *ER, Buffy the Vampire Slayer*, and *Six Feet Under*. The 2005 Ang Lee–directed film *Brokeback Mountain*, centered on the decades-long romantic relationship between two men, was nominated for eight Academy Awards including the award for best picture. The film has since been considered a watershed moment for the depiction of bisexuality in major American cinema.

Prominent GLBT musicians such as Ani DiFranco, Ricky Martin, Michael Stipe, Rufus Wainwright, Lady Gaga, and Kaki King all received widespread commercial and critical acclaim throughout the 2000s. The decade was also a pivotal time for GLBT athletes in both amateur and professional sports. Seven openly gay athletes participated in the 2000 summer games in Sydney, Australia, including US men's diving team captain David Pichler. In addition, several retired American professional athletes, notably NFL player Esera Tuaolo, NBA player John Amaechi, WBNA player Sheryl Swoopes, and golfer Rosie Jones, publically came out as gay in the hope of laying the groundwork for widespread acceptance of future GLBT athletes in the major American sporting leagues.

Impact

By the early 2000s, landmark legal cases, medical and psychological discoveries, and widespread exposure in popular media had led to an increase in the acceptance of homosexuality, bisexuality, and transgenderism in the United States. The significant contributions made by GLBT individuals across all spectrums of society throughout the decade would only help aid the continued integration and acceptance of all people in North American society, regardless of their race, sex, gender identity, creed, or sexual orientation, into the next decade.

Further Reading

Carlson, Darren. "Acceptance of Homosexuality: A Youth Movement." *Gallup.* Gallup, 19 Feb. 2002. Web. 14 Nov. 2012. Discusses the increasing acceptance of homosexuality among young people in the 2000s.

Fejes, Fred. *Gay Rights and Moral Panic: The Origins of America's Debate on Homosexuality.* New York: Macmillan, 2008. Print. Chronicles the development of the gay rights movement in the United States, providing historical context for the events of the 2000s.

Snyder, R. Claire. *Gay Marriage and Democracy: Equality for All.* Lanham: Rowman, 2006. Print. Provides an overview of the issues surrounding same-sex marriage and argues that its legalization is consistent with the principles of democracy.

Stone, Amy L. *Gay Rights at the Ballot Box.* Minneapolis: U of Minnesota P, 2012. Print. Discusses the various anti-GLBT ballot initiatives that have hindered the gay rights movement in the United States and their effects.

"Timeline: Milestones in the American Gay Rights Movement." *PBS.org.* WGBH Educational Foundation, n.d. Web. 14 Nov. 2012. Provides information about many of the key events in the gay rights movement in the United States.

John Pritchard

■ Honeybee colony collapse disorder

The Event: Sudden, unexplained decrease in bee colonies in the United States, Europe, and the Middle East

Date: Syndrome first discovered during fall 2006

Colony collapse disorder (CCD) is the mysterious disappearance of adult honeybees during the latter half of the decade, thought to be the result of multiple causes.

In 2006 the sudden disappearance of adult honeybees from colonies throughout the United States, Europe, and the Middle East became a crisis of international concern. Humans are highly dependent on bees not only for honey production, but, more importantly, for the pollination of dozens of varieties of fruits and vegetables, as well as almonds, hay, cotton, and other crops. Beekeepers first noticed the syndrome during the fall and winter season in 2006 and 2007, when adult worker bees were disappearing from their hives without any trace, leaving behind only the young bees, the queen, and the honey they had already produced. Without worker bees, the hives died off completely.

The phenomenon was named colony collapse disorder (CCD) and there were many opinions and theories about the probable causes of the syndrome. Speculation regarding the probable cause or causes included cell phone radiation, a brand new disease, toxic pesticides, invasive mites, fungal infections, poor nutrition, drought, and stress incurred by the bees as pollination services moved their beehives from farm to farm. The United States Department of Agriculture (USDA) established the CCD Steering Committee, which set in place an action plan to collect data, analyze bee samples, conduct research, and formulate preventive measures, while teams of entomologists from research universities also began studying the phenomenon. Israeli acute paralysis virus (IAPV) and the *Varroa* mite, one of the most destructive pests to honeybees during the twentieth century, have been of particular interest to researchers. Another prime suspect has been neonicotinoids, a class of systemic insecticides used to coat seeds. Neonicotinoids are known to interfere with the ability of bees to find their way back to their hives and were banned in France, Germany, and other countries after being implicated in colony collapse disorder.

Impact

Until the presence of colony collapse disorder, beekeepers averaged annual losses of about 15–20 percent due to *Varroa* mites, fungi, and other known factors. CCD was responsible for increasing losses to 30 percent or more, a potentially disastrous increase as humans depend on bees to pollinate roughly one-third of the world's food supply. Specific concerns have included the possibility of a shortage of honey and other foods, as well as increased food prices as the agricultural industry pays more for pollination services. At the end of the decade, scientists remained unable to pinpoint the causes of CCD, but many conclude that a combination of factors is probably responsible.

Further Reading

Cox-Foster, Diana and Dennis vanEngelsdorp. "Saving the Honeybee." *Scientific American* 300.4 (2009): 40–47. Print.

Kaplan, J. Kim. "A Complex Buzz." *Agricultural Research* 56.5 (2008): 8–11. Print.

Schacker, Michael. *A Spring Without Bees: How Colony Collapse Disorder Has Endangered Our Food Supply.* Guilford: Lyons, 2008. Print.

Sally Driscoll

■ Hosseini, Khaled

Identification: American author
Born: March 4, 1965; Kabul, Afghanistan

Khaled Hosseini is an Afghan-born American author known for his best-selling novels The Kite Runner *(2003) and* A Thousand Splendid Suns *(2007). His sensitive portrayals of daily life and culture in Afghanistan resonated with American audiences in the 2000s while the War in Afghanistan was still ongoing.*

Khaled Hosseini was born in Kabul, Afghanistan. His father was a diplomat with the Afghan Foreign Ministry and his mother was a high school teacher. To avoid the fallout from the 1978 overthrow of the Afghan government, the family settled in San Jose, California, in 1980. Though Hosseini had written stories since childhood, he never seriously considered becoming a writer, choosing a more lucrative career in medicine because of the poverty his family had endured during their first years in the United States. In 1999, he began expanding one of his short stories into what would become *The Kite Runner*. The novel, eventually published in May 2003, was a sleeper hit—after a slow start in hardcover, it had sold four million copies by 2007 and spent two years on the New York Times Best Sellers list for paperback trade fiction.

With renewed American interest in Afghanistan following the US invasion of that country in 2001, the novel was poised to become a success. Though critics occasionally regarded some passages as overly sentimental or melodramatic, book clubs embraced the novel for its humanizing portrayal of an unfamiliar culture. With the paperback release, it quickly became a word-of-mouth best seller.

In preparation for his next novel, Hosseini returned to Afghanistan in March 2003 for the first time in twenty-seven years. He toured what remained of Kabul after the Soviet invasion, the Taliban regime, and the US invasion had decimated the city. He developed all that he learned while visiting relatives and talking to people in the streets into his second novel, *A Thousand Splendid Suns*.

A Thousand Splendid Suns is set in Kabul during the thirty years spanning the Soviet invasion to the reconstruction efforts following the Taliban rule. The novel concerns two young Afghan women, Mariam and Laila, who were forced into marriage with a brutish cobbler, Rasheed. Critics acknowledged that *A Thousand Splendid Suns* was a better effort than *The Kite Runner*, though they still pointed out its tendencies toward sentimentality and melodrama. In May 2007, the novel debuted at the top of *Publishers Weekly*'s best seller list.

Reception of Hosseini's works has been mostly positive within Afghanistan, though the author admits that some readers have objected to his treatment of ethnic issues. Wali Ahmadi, a professor of Afghan literature at the University of California, Berkeley, contends that Hosseini's novels oversimplify the culture's ethnic strife, and that, in reality, the Pashtun-Hazara divide is less antagonistic than the author's fictional portrayals.

A film adaptation of *The Kite Runner* was released in December 2007, and Columbia Pictures has purchased the movie rights for *A Thousand Splendid Suns*. Hosseini took a sabbatical from his medical career in 2004. In 2006, he became a goodwill envoy for the United Nations High Commissioner for Refugees. As an envoy, he visited Sudanese refugee camps in Chad in hope of raising awareness regarding the Darfur crisis.

Impact

Hosseini has enjoyed attention and acclaim thanks to the quality and timeliness of his novels. At a time when focus on Afghan life and culture was at a fever pitch, Hosseini's novels gave American audiences a glimpse into the lives of a people they were constantly confronted with on the evening news, but knew little about.

Further Reading

Bush, Laura. "Khaled Hosseini." *Time* 171.19 (2008): 104–105. Print.

Duffey, Keenan. "Author Tackles Afghan Refugee Crisis." *Washington Report on Middle East Affairs* (2012): 56. Print.

Kirschling, Gregory. "Khaled Hosseini [THE STORY-TELLER]." *Entertainment Weekly* 941/942 (2007): 94–96. Print.

■ Hostages in Iraq

Definition: Americans and other individuals who were taken captive by terrorists or insurgents during the Iraq War

In the years following the US invasion of Iraq in 2003, a number of Americans, other foreigners, and Iraqis were taken hostage by terrorists or other groups seeking to end the foreign military presence. Some were released, while others were killed by their captors. This trend added an element of danger particularly for foreign civilians such as journalists and aid workers.

Following the United States–led invasion of Iraq in 2003, troops on the ground were faced with the daunting challenge of engaging forces loyal to deposed leader Saddam Hussein as well as foreign terrorists. During the campaign, a large number of foreign civilians were also in Iraq, some providing logistical support to US forces and others providing consultative services to the new government or humanitarian aid to the people of Iraq. Although they were not directly involved in the military conflict, these civilians faced the risk of being kidnapped by terrorist groups and other insurgents. Over the course of the decade, a number of Americans, citizens of allied nations, and Iraqis were abducted and held as hostages by such groups. Some of the individuals who were taken hostage were eventually released, while others were killed. There was no single motivation for hostage taking; rather, there were many, ranging from the political or ideological to the financial.

Terrorism

Hostage taking was a common tool for Iraqi and foreign terrorists alike during the conflict. Such groups, particularly those loyal to Jordanian terrorist Abu Musab al-Zarqawi, were motivated by the desire to frighten and intimidate the Western forces in Iraq. When Zarqawi and his associates abducted American Nicholas Berg in 2004, the hostage takers sought no ransom; instead, they videotaped a statement and beheaded Berg on-camera, later broadcasting the video on the Internet. In another incident that year, Zarqawi's group captured British citizen Kenneth Bigley. Despite efforts from countries such as Great Britain, Ireland, and even Libya, Bigley was held in captivity for several weeks and eventually killed. In both cases, the international media contributed to the terrorists' visibility by reporting on and broadcasting their messages.

The brutality of these and similar incidents was in many cases effective. When three Japanese citizens were captured by a terrorist group demanding that Japan withdraw its 550 troops from Iraq, the Japanese government refused. However, this event as well as the unpopularity of the Iraq War in Japan led the Japanese government to withdraw its troops from Iraq only two years later. A Turkish trucking association similarly pulled its operations out of Iraq when its workers were taken hostage.

Ransom

After Hussein's regime was removed and a new government and infrastructure began to be established, a cottage industry of kidnapping arose in areas of Iraq that lacked security. Kidnappers took advantage of the near-lawlessness in such areas to take foreign contractors, journalists, and aid workers hostage and hold them for ransom. According to some accounts, Westerners were the most popular targets; kidnappers generally sought ransoms in the thousands of dollars for Iraqi hostages but demanded hundreds of thousands or even millions of dollars for Western hostages.

The US government and many of its allies made it clear that they would not pay any ransom or negotiate with terrorists, but some governments were not as rigid. Italian authorities were reported to have raised $1 million to secure the release of Simona Pari and Simona Torretta, two Italian aid workers who were abducted from their office in Baghdad in broad daylight in 2004. A Jordanian businessman was also held hostage but was released after his family paid his ransom.

The fates of hostages such as Berg and Bigley, whose experiences were shared by the terrorists via the Internet, encouraged many individuals and governments to negotiate with hostage takers and pay the necessary ransoms. Since there was no way to know if the kidnappers were of the same mindset as the terrorists who killed Berg and others, some felt it was necessary to err on the side of caution.

Impact

Although several major terrorist leaders operating in Iraq, including Zarqawi, were killed by the end of the 2000s, the region remained a hazardous one for civilians. Some groups continued to take hostages, seeking money or the withdrawal of US and other forces from the country. In late 2011 the US government withdrew its military forces from Iraq, officially ending the war, although fighting between insurgents and Iraqi forces continued.

Further Reading

Cronin, Richard P. *Japan's Self-Defense Forces in Iraq: Motivations, Constraints, and Implications for US-Japan Alliance Cooperation.* Washington: Congressional Information Service, 2004. Print. Describes the effects of the 2004 abduction of several Japanese citizens on the long-standing military partnership between the United States and Japan.

Hallums, Roy. *Buried Alive: The True Story of Kidnapping, Captivity, and a Dramatic Rescue.* Nashville: Nelson, 2010. Print. Chronicles the personal experiences of Roy Hallums, an American civilian contractor taken hostage in Iraq in 2004.

Kember, Norman. *Hostage in Iraq.* Toronto: Lorimer, 2007. Print. Provides the account of several missionaries who were taken hostage in 2005 during the Iraq conflict.

Tinnes, Judith. "Counting Lives in a Theater of Terror—An Analysis of Media-Oriented Hostage Takings in Iraq, Afghanistan, Pakistan and Saudi Arabia." *Perspectives on Terrorism* 4.5 (2010). Web. 4 Nov. 2012.

Ware, Michael, Timothy J. Burger, and Mark Thompson. "The Enemy with Many Faces." *Time*, 19 Sept. 2004: 42–45. Print. Discusses the added dimension of danger presented by the trend of terrorists capturing civilians.

Michael P. Auerbach

■ Housing market in the United States

Definition: The sector of the US economy that deals with the building, renovating, buying and selling of residential real estate—everything from co-op apartments and condominiums to single- and multifamily houses

In the past decade, American homeowners watched as the values of their homes hit record heights before depreciating considerably in the recession that began in late 2007. After mortgage brokers relaxed credit qualifications for first-time buyers beginning in the late 1990s, more Americans than ever before became homeowners in the first decade of this century. Many of these same buyers, however, lost their homes when the real estate bubble burst. They could no longer afford to pay mortgages that were "underwater"—meaning that the homeowners owed more on their mortgages than the homes were worth.

Owning a home of one's own has long been seen as a source of wealth generation and upward mobility in the United States. Yet a majority of Americans did not own their own homes until after World War II (1939–1945). In 1940, owner-occupied housing units accounted for just 44 percent of the national total, but this changed considerably in the postwar period. With the infrastructure of much of Europe and Asia recovering from a war that had left the mainland United States unscathed, the U.S. economy boomed by selling goods both domestically and overseas. This booming postwar economy also fueled a great surge in homeownership. Returning veterans, who had easier access to lines of credit, wanted to own their own homes. The housing industry responded by building large urban and suburban developments across the United States. By 1960, 61.9 percent of US housing units were owner-occupied. Between 1960 and the late 1990s, the rate of home ownership in the country hovered steadily between 62 and 65 percent.

Increasing Homeownership

About 66 percent of the population owned their own homes in 2000. This figure surged up to 69.2 percent in 2004. The sudden increase in homeownership, after being largely unchanged for so many decades, was due in large part to banks and other mortgage lenders easing their credit standards during the late

Foreclosure signs became an all-too-common sight during the US recession that began in 2008. (Courtesy Jeffrey Turner)

1990s and into the first half of the next decade. The administrations of President Bill Clinton (1993–2001) and President George W. Bush (2001–9) greatly encouraged this increase in home ownership. As mortgages became more available to people previously ineligible for them, the US Federal Reserve, which as the central banking system controls monetary policy in the United States, expanded lending further by lowering the base borrowing rate. With such low interest rates at their fingertips, Americans sought mortgages as never before. In turn, most banks—believing they could reap substantial profits by selling mortgage-backed securities to their investors—became very willing to lend to almost anyone, including those with little in savings and low income. The justification for selling such mortgage-backed securities to investors was that home prices would continue to rise and homeowners could be counted on to pay their mortgages.

Rampant speculation in the US housing market, including builders and homeowners who believed they could turn a substantial profit by buying a property, giving it a quick makeover and selling it to a new owner (also known as "flipping"), caused average home prices to more than double in a seven-year period. Interestingly, this rise in home values occurred at a time when average salaries were either flat or barely rising when adjusted for inflation. Historically, housing expenditures have been roughly 30 percent of a homeowner's income, but this changed during the real estate boom, as rising home prices caused more and more buyers to sink an increasing chunk of their incomes into their mortgages. Despite this troubling phenomenon, Americans, more than ever, saw their homes as the key to their future financial security.

The Bubble Bursts

In mid-2006, average national home prices began to drop, after rising across the nation through the first half of the decade. This decline sped up as the global economy entered a severe recession late the next year. The real estate boom that had been helping to sustain the US economy had turned out to be just a bubble.

Housing bubbles are not uncommon in the United States. Home prices had hit all-time highs in 1979 and 1989 before crashing, but this most recent bubble was particularly severe. When the US economy entered a recession in 2001, the Federal Reserve expanded liquidity in the credit market instead of restricting it. This allowed greater numbers of less-than-qualified borrowers to get home loans from banks and other lending institutions that were eager to give them out. And although every age group saw an expansion in borrowing, individuals younger than age thirty were the largest beneficiaries of these relaxed restrictions. Unfortunately, they were also the ones most likely to take additional risks by signing up for more exotic loans like adjustable rate mortgages (ARMs), which have a low initial interest rate that varies (and thus can increase significantly) after a specific period of time . Younger Americans were also more likely to take out loans with little to no money handed over as a down payment. Those who took out such mortgages were typically more likely to default on their mortgages, particularly at a time when wages were not keeping up with home prices and adjustable mortgage rates. (According to one recent study, homeownership in the United States would have actually decreased between 2000 and 2005, instead of rising as it did because of relaxed mortgage qualifications.)

With the collapse of the housing market, homeownership in the United States began to dwindle, declining to 66.6 percent in 2008 and to 66.4 percent in the first quarter of 2011. Foreclosures—in which the bank or lender takes the property from the borrower for failure of payment—hit record levels in the third quarter of 2009, a period in which fully one in every 136 housing units in the nation had received a foreclosure filing. In response to this wave of foreclosures, banks and other lenders, who were still reeling from the poor investments they had made in the lead-up to the recession, tightened credit qualifications again.

Unequal Homeownership Declines

While homeownership declined across the board in the United States, minority homeowners were more likely to lose their homes than white homeowners during this period. This was due in part to the fact that minority homeowners, particularly Hispanics and African Americans, were more likely than whites to have taken out riskier mortgages and were therefore more susceptible to defaulting on them. While mortgage refinancing or other loan modifications became widely available following the collapse of the real estate market, minority homeowners were often denied such new loans because their communities had endured higher unemployment rates during the recession. In October 2009, approximately 16 million people were officially unemployed in the nation and the unemployment rate stood above 10 percent. The unemployment rate was notably higher during this same period among African Americans (15.4 percent) and Latinos (12.7 percent).

Home prices also suffered a steeper decline among many minority homeowners than whites, dropping 11 percent for Latinos, 5 percent for Asian Americans and 1 percent for African Americans. By comparison, white homeowners saw their home values drop by 2 percent on average. Housing market researchers credit the steep drop in home prices among Latinos to the fact that the three states that saw the biggest decline in prices, Florida (down 16 percent), California (down 16 percent) and Nevada (down 9 percent), are home to large numbers of Hispanic homeowners.

In 2008, some twenty-two states experienced very large declines in home values. In these states it was far more likely that homeowners would find themselves holding mortgages that were worth more than the current value of their homes. The housing market, however, was also buoyed in 2008 by home price increases in seven states: North

Carolina, Oregon, Pennsylvania, Tennessee, Texas, Utah, and Wyoming .

Impact

Economists and housing industry experts have faulted both lenders and borrowers for the real estate bubble and subsequent collapse. Lenders have been criticized for giving mortgages to borrowers who they knew could not afford them; borrowers have been criticized for believing they could use their homes as a quick way to make a buck. Government policymakers have also been faulted for the collapse of the housing market. Following the recession in 2001, many policymakers and analysts believed that the housing market could provide a tremendous economic stimulus to the nation, and by and large, it did so. New loans helped to fund everything from sales at big box stores like The Home Depot to construction jobs to interior decoration in this period, but it all came at a price—a weakened housing market that has prolonged an economic malaise that began with the recession of the late-2000s.

Most housing industry observers, including people like famed investor Warren Buffett, the editorial of the *Wall Street Journal* and the International Monetary Fund (IMF), believe that conditions in the housing market will have to improve considerably in order for the US economy to recover enough to spur sustained job creation. As of 2012, there are some signs suggesting that a bottom may have been reached in the housing market, but many economists admit it will likely take several more years to clear the glut of foreclosed and unsold houses off the market before a national revival in new home construction can take hold.

Further Reading

Allen, Franklin, James R. Barth, and Glenn Yago. *Fixing the Housing Market: Financial Innovations for the Future.* Upper Saddle River: FT, 2012. The authors use a historical framework to describe the current housing conditions in the United States and offer ways to prevent another crisis in the future.

Immergluck, Daniel. *Foreclosed: High-Risk Lending, Deregulation, and the Undermining of America's Mortgage Market.* Ithaca: Cornell UP, 2011. In this book, a mortgage expert explains how the current housing crisis in the United States was created through a combination of bank deregulation and risky lending practices and looks at how various communities across the country have been impacted by recent events.

King, Peter. Housing *Boom and Bust: Owner Occupation, Government Regulation and the Credit Crunch.* London; New York: Routledge, 2010. This concise volume, intended for students, provides a comprehensive explanation of how bubbles in the housing market have formed and how, using historic precedent, they can be mitigated in the future.

Sowell, Thomas. *The Housing Boom and Bust.* New York: Basic, 2009. The author of this book details how mortgage-backed securities led to the current economic and housing crisis and faults politicians in both major political parties for helping to bring it about.

Wessel, David. *In Fed We Trust: Ben Bernanke's War on the Great Panic.* New York: Three Rivers, 2010. This highly praised volume by the economics editor of the Wall Street Journal describes how Ben Bernanke, the Federal Reserve chairman, responded to the worst economic downturn since the Great Depression of the 1930s: the recent collapse in the US housing market and the financial crisis that resulted from it.

Christopher Mari

Arianna Huffington. (Courtesy World Economic Forum/ swiss-image.ch/Photograph by Michael Wuertenberg)

■ Huffington, Arianna

Identification: Greek American author, news columnist, editor, and media executive
Born: July 15, 1950; Athens, Greece

Arianna Huffington is a Greek American author, news columnist, and media executive who is best known as the editor in chief of the news and pop-culture website the Huffington Post, *which she cofounded in 2005. Huffington came to prominence in 2003, when she ran as an independent candidate in the California gubernatorial recall election.*

Arianna Huffington garnered significant national attention as a staunch conservative during her husband's 1992 campaign for Congress. Huffington and her husband separated in 1997; following their divorce, Huffington's political stance became increasingly liberal. In 2003, she ran as an independent candidate in California's gubernatorial recall election of Democratic governor Gray Davis. She lost by a large margin, earning less than 1 percent of the vote and placing fifth out of 135 candidates. Republican Arnold Schwarzenegger won the election and replaced Davis as governor.

In 2005, Huffington cofounded the *Huffington Post*, an online news website and content aggregator, and serves as the president and editor in chief of the Huffington Post Media Group. The site began as a group blog featuring the contributions of 250 prominent Americans, including anchorman Walter Cronkite, actress Diane Keaton, and author Nora Ephron. However, many of the initial contributors did not maintain their blogs and, in 2006, Huffington recruited former *Newsweek* journalist Melinda Henneberger to assemble a team of staff writers and journalists to develop original content for the *Post*. The site's tremendous popularity has made Huffington a major force in American media. Though critics would accuse the site of liberal leanings, Huffington remained insistent that the site's purpose was to "move beyond" conventional conceptions of American political viewpoints.

Impact

The *Huffington Post* became one of the world's most popular political websites of the decade. Though the *Post* drew criticism for its aggressive content-aggregation and search-optimization practices, by the end of the decade, it was attracting twenty-six million unique visitors each month. In 2009, *Time* magazine named the site one of its "25 Best Blogs." Huffington's reimmersion into political writing, notably her 2008 work *Right Is Wrong: How the Lunatic Fringe Hijacked America, Shredded the Constitution, and Made Us All Less Safe*, would establish her as an outspoken proponent for the liberal political movement in the United States. In July 2009, Huffington was named one of the "Most Influential Women in Media" by *Forbes* magazine.

Further Reading

Blakeley, Kiri. "The Most Influential Women in Media." *Forbes*. Forbes.com LCC, 14 July 2012. Web. 9 Aug. 2012.

Bustamante, Cruz. "Huffington Withdraws from Recall Race." *CNN.com*. Cable News Network, 30 Sept. 2003. Web. 12 Aug. 2012.

Goldman, Andrew. "Arianna Huffington's Next Move." *New York Times*. New York Times Co., 1 Apr. 2011. Web. 10 Aug. 2012.

John Pritchard

■ Hulu

Definition: Hulu is a website that provides on-demand streaming videos of television shows, movies, and other programs from several networks and distributors.

Launched in 2007, Hulu has revolutionized the way consumers watch television by moving audiences to an online platform. Hulu's on-demand and paid subscription service provides users with programming from major networks such as NBC, Fox, and Nickelodeon, as well as movies and content produced specifically for Hulu. Hulu is available on computers, televisions, smartphones, and tablets.

Hulu was created in 2007, when NBC Universal and News Corporation announced a deal with AOL, MSN, Myspace, and Yahoo! to create an online video service for providing access to full episodes and clips of television shows, as well as movies. Jeff Zucker,

President and CEO of NBC Universal, explained that it would also allow advertisers to reach a larger audience. In June 2007, NBC named Jason Kilar CEO of Hulu. Kilar was formerly an executive at the retail website Amazon. The site debuted in beta form in October 2007, and went live to the public in March 2008. By fall of that year, Hulu had over one hundred content providers. The website was listed fourth on *Time* magazine's "50 Best Inventions of 2008" list. Hulu was named 2008 "Website of the Year" by the Associated Press.

The Walt Disney Company became an equity owner of Hulu in 2009, joining NBC Universal, News Corporation, and Providence Equity Partners. Many industry experts saw Hulu as a threat to cable service providers, fearing that advertisers and consumers would gradually drop their service for online content. Hulu made it easier for advertisers to target specific audiences by utilizing detailed market analysis.

While Hulu continued to grow in users and the services they provided throughout the decade, television remained the number one way consumers watched programming. A survey conducted in 2009 found that only 10 percent of households who pay for cable would consider dropping their service in favor of online programming. In October 2009, News Corporation Deputy Chairman Chase Carey announced that NBC would begin offering a premium Hulu service, for a fee, in 2010.

Impact

The success of Hulu demonstrated the power of online on-demand programming, and shows what is possible when a commercial broadcasting television network such as NBC embraces this platform. While Hulu did not lead to a sharp decline of cable service providers like DirecTV and Comcast, it has forced these providers to rethink their approach to advertising and monthly fees.

Further Reading

Kramer, Staci D. "It's Official: Disney Joins News Corp., NBCU In Hulu; Deal Includes Some Cable Nets." *Washington Post*. 30 Apr. 2009. Web. 13 Oct. 2012.

Morgan, Sarah. "Will Hulu Be the Death of TV?" *SmartMoney*. 13 May 2010. Web. 13 Oct. 2012.

Sandoval, Greg. "Hulu Unveils $9.99 Premium Service." *CNET*. 29 June 2010. Web. 13 Oct. 2012.

Patrick G. Cooper

■ Human Genome Project

Definition: A scientific research initiative with the goal of identifying all of the 20,000 to 25,000 genes in human deoxyribonucleic acid (DNA)

The US Department of Energy and the National Institutes of Health coordinated the Human Genome Project, which officially began in October 1990. Researchers examined the genetic makeup of different nonhuman organisms to identify all of the estimated genes in human DNA, while also addressing the ethical, legal, and social issues (ELSI) involved with this research.

The Human Genome Project (HGP) began in 1990 and was led by Aristides Patrinos, director of the Office of Biological and Environmental Research of the US Department of Energy. The group had several goals, including identifying all of the genes in human DNA, sequencing the three billion chemical base pairs in human DNA, and addressing the ELSI brought forth by such research. Initially, the project was scheduled to take fifteen years, but thanks in part to new developments in technology, researchers were able to complete a draft of the human genome in 2000 and a more detailed sequence in 2003.

The First Draft of the Human Book of Life

On June 26, 2000, the following remarks by President Bill Clinton and British Prime Minister Tony Blair, the director of the National Human Genome Research Institute, Dr. Francis Collins, announced that a "first draft" of the human genome had been completed:

Science is a voyage of exploration into the unknown. We are here today to celebrate a milestone along a truly unprecedented voyage, this one into ourselves. Alexander Pope wrote, "Know then thyself. Presume not God to scan. The proper study of mankind is man." What more powerful form of study of mankind could there be than to read our own instruction book?

I've been privileged over the last seven years to lead an international team of more than a thousand of some of the best and brightest scientists of our current generation, some of them here in this room, who have been truly dedicated to this goal. Today, we celebrate the revelation of the first draft of the human book of life. . . .

Surely, the human genome is our shared inheritance, and it is fitting and proper that we are all working on it together. Now, thus far, every milestone set by the International Human Genome Project has been met—on schedule or, in some cases, ahead of schedule.

Today, we deliver, ahead of schedule again, the most visible and spectacular milestone of all. Most of the sequencing of the human genome by this international consortium has been done in just the last 15 months. During that time, this consortium has developed the capacity to sequence 1,000 letters of the DNA code per second, seven days a week, 24 hours a day. We have developed a map of overlapping fragments that includes 97 percent of the human genome, and we have sequenced 85 percent of this.

The sequence data is of higher quality than expected with half of it in finished or near-finished form. And all of this information has been placed in public databases every 24 hours, where any scientist with an Internet connection can use it to help unravel the mysteries of human biology. Already, more than a dozen genes, responsible for diseases from deafness to kidney disease to cancer, have been identified using this resource just in the last year. . . .

I think I speak for all of us in this room, and for the millions of others who have come to believe in the remarkable promise of biomedical research, that we must redouble our efforts to speed the application of these profound and fundamental observations about the human genome to the cure of disease. That most desirable of all outcomes will only come about with a continued powerful and dedicated partnership between basic science investigators and academia, and their colleagues in the biotechnology and pharmaceutical industries.

To help reach these findings, researchers examined the genetics of different nonhuman organisms including fruit flies and laboratory mice. Researchers looked at areas of the genome where variations were commonly found. The theory behind this was that because many diseases are common to nonhuman animals and humans, so too would be the genetic variations that cause them. The HGP's aim was to map and identify the genetic variants that increase the risk of diseases such as cancer and diabetes, leading to more focused diagnoses and treatments. Research findings were also applied to problems in health care, energy production, and agriculture.

Approximately 3 to 5 percent of the project's budget went to studying the related ELSI, making it the largest bioethics program in the world. One of the primary aspects of the ELSI research was fairness in the use of genetic information. Researchers questioned who should have access to personal genetic information, how it should be used, and who should claim ownership to this information. They questioned how an individual's personal genetic information affects society's perceptions of the individual. Other topics covered by ELSI research include reproductive issues, clinical issues, and conceptual implications.

During the project, the Department of Energy and the National Institutes of Health awarded grants for innovative research and the HGP licensed its newly developed technologies to private companies. The federal government did this to propel the development of new medical applications and to promote the biotechnology industry in the United States. Although the project released their findings in 2003, researchers continue to conduct genetic research.

Impact

The Human Genome Project is one of the largest research projects in contemporary science. Researchers have gained valuable insight into human DNA that will lead to new advances in medicine and biotechnology. Before the project's initial findings in 2000 and 2003 were even published, breakthroughs were made in the administration of genetic tests for examining an individual's predisposition to a variety of diseases. The project has also led to advances in the study of evolution, human biology, and the diagnosis and possible prevention of certain illnesses.

Further Reading

McElheny, Victor K. *Drawing the Map of Life: Inside the Human Genome Project.* New York: Basic Books, 2012. Print.

Palladino, Michael A. *Understanding the Human Genome Project.* 2d ed. Upper Saddle River: Benjamin Cummings, 2005. Print.

Patrick G. Cooper

■ Hurricane Ike

The Event: Category 4 hurricane that caused significant damage to Texas, Louisiana, and Arkansas, as well as parts of the Caribbean
Date: September 1–14, 2008
Place: Gulf Coast of the United States and the Caribbean

Hurricane Ike was one of the most destructive natural disasters in US history. Ike was responsible for more than one hundred deaths across the Caribbean and the United States. Its landfall on the US Gulf Coast created one of the costliest disasters the United States had ever experienced.

Hurricane Ike began forming over the ocean off the west coast of Africa in late August, and was categorized as a tropical storm on September 1. As the storm made its way through the Caribbean, it strengthened to a category 4 hurricane, causing serious damage in Cuba. Ike then moved along the southern coast of the United States through the Gulf of Mexico. The storm weakened after its landfall in Cuba, but the extent of hurricane-force winds spread as Ike passed over the Gulf Coast. The storm became so large that its winds spanned six hundred miles and gusted at speeds up to 110 miles per hour, making the waters of the Gulf of Mexico extremely turbulent. By the time Ike reached Texas, the storm surge had reached ten to fifteen feet in height. On September 13, the storm made landfall along the northern end of Galveston Island, Texas, and most of the homes on nearby Bolivar Peninsula and many on Galveston Island were completely razed by the surge.

Throughout Texas, Louisiana, and Arkansas, eighty-four people died as a result of Hurricane Ike. In Texas and Louisiana, nearly three million people were left without power. Ike's winds were so strong in

FEMA Urban Search and Rescue team Indiana Task Force 1 searches a neighborhood in Sabine Pass, TX, in the aftermath of Hurricane Ike. (FEMA/Photograph by Jocelyn Augustino)

Houston, Texas, that part of the roof of Reliant Stadium was ripped off. The storm also caused significant damage and twenty-eight deaths throughout the Ohio River Valley as it pulled to the north. The total estimated damage of Ike in the United States was valued at more than $24.9 billion, making it the third-costliest US hurricane following Katrina (2005) and Andrew (1992).

Impact

Hurricane Ike caused more than half a million gallons of crude oil to spill into the Gulf of Mexico and the waters surrounding Texas and Louisiana. More than three thousand pollution reports tracked the influx of hazardous materials into nearby communities. Many people also complained about the way the Federal Emergency Management Agency (FEMA) handled the aftermath of the storm. Texas in particular criticized FEMA for its unpreparedness and slow response. Hurricane Ike inspired Houston politicians to recommend the construction of the "Ike Dike," a proposed barrier wall that would stretch sixty miles along the coast to protect the city from future hurricanes, although no formal action has yet been taken on the idea.

Further Reading

Berg, Robbie. *Tropical Cyclone Report Hurricane Ike (AL092008) 1–14 September 2008.* National Hurricane Center. National Oceanic and Atmospheric Administration, 3 May 2010. PDF file.

Drye, Willie. "'Freak' Hurricane Ike Will Cost $22 Billion." *National Geographic.* National Geographic Society, 15 Sept. 2008. Web. 7 Aug. 2012.

Federal Emergency Management Agency. *Mitigation Assessment Team Report: Hurricane Ike in Texas and Louisiana: Building Performance Observations, Recommendations, and Technical Guidance.* FEMA, Apr. 2009. PDF file.

Krauss, Clifford. "Hurricane Damage Extensive in Texas." *New York Times.* New York Times, 13 Sept. 2008. Web. 7 Aug. 2012.

Cait Caffrey

▪ Hurricane Katrina

The Event: Category 3 hurricane that struck east of
New Orleans, causing massive damage to the city
Date: August 29, 2005
Place: Southeast Louisiana, Mississippi, and Alabama
Gulf coast

*Hurricane Katrina struck the Gulf coast just east of New
Orleans, Louisiana, causing levee breaches within the city
and surrounding communities. Massive flooding destroyed
much of city's residential and commercial areas; destruction along the Mississippi and Alabama coastline was also
catastrophic. More than eighteen hundred lives were lost.
Damage estimates exceeded $125 billion, making the event
the costliest natural disaster in the history of the United
States.*

Katrina, the eleventh storm of the 2005 hurricane
season, formed on August 23 in the Atlantic Ocean
as a tropical depression and reached hurricane
strength the next day. After passing over the
southern tip of Florida, the hurricane entered the
Gulf of Mexico and quickly rose in intensity to category 5, the highest level on the Saffir-Simpson scale.
Its predicted track took it straight up the delta of the
Mississippi River toward New Orleans. Government
officials at every level feared Katrina would bring catastrophe to the city, much of which sits below sea
level between the Mississippi River and Lake Pontchartrain. The city's mayor, Ray Nagin, vacillated
for some time about issuing a mandatory evacuation
order but finally did so the day before the storm hit.
Nagin designated the Superdome, a massive football
stadium and entertainment complex in the central
business district, as an emergency evacuation center
for those unable or unwilling to leave. While approximately 1.2 million people left the region ahead of
the storm, more than one hundred thousand people
remained inside New Orleans when Katrina passed
through.

Storm Damage

Just before Katrina came ashore on August 29, its ve-
locity subsided to category 3, suggesting that it would
be a dangerous storm but not necessarily as deadly as
Hurricane Betsy, which flooded 20 percent of New
Orleans in 1965, or Hurricane Camille, which destroyed most of the structures along the Mississippi
Gulf coast in 1969. Katrina made landfall in extreme

southeast Louisiana then veered slightly eastward to
strike the Mississippi Gulf coast.

The storm surge, which exceeded twenty-five
feet in some places, obliterated structures along
the coastline from Mississippi to Florida, destroying
nearly all buildings within a mile of the coast. Initially New Orleans was spared the worst of the
storm, because winds in the city were high but not
excessive. Unfortunately, the storm surge that came
up from the Mississippi Delta and westward across
Lake Borgne and Lake Pontchartrain placed inor-
dinate stress on the complex levee system that
guards much of the Greater New Orleans area from
flood damage.

The massive earthen levees along the Mississippi
River worked effectively; however, levees and flood
walls lining the drainage canals that crisscross the city
were breached in several places. Large steel retaining
walls collapsed, allowing waters from three major canals to swirl unimpeded into residential neighborhoods and commercial areas. Within hours, 80 percent of the city was flooded; water depth in some
places reached twenty feet. Nearly half of the thirty-
five hundred miles of levees protecting the area were
damaged or destroyed. On the east bank of the Mississippi, only those sections of New Orleans built
close to the river and along the Metairie and Gentilly
ridges, the only areas of the city above sea level, escaped total devastation.

Thousands of individuals who had decided to remain home or who lacked transportation to evacuate were forced to seek refuge in attics or on rooftops or to flee to higher ground. Many were trapped
in their homes and did not survive. Virtually every
roadway in the city was under water. Flooding was
indiscriminate, as both working-class neighborhoods
such as the city's Lower Ninth Ward and the affluent
subdivision of Lakeview were inundated and made
uninhabitable.

Failure of Emergency Response

Despite years of planning for a hurricane disaster
such as Katrina, rescue and relief efforts were woe-
fully inadequate. Much of the communications
equipment normally used for coordinating police,
fire, and rescue operations was under water for days,
as were police, fire, and rescue vehicles; agencies outside the city had a difficult time bringing in replacement equipment. Many local police and fire department personnel had evacuated with their families,

FEMA Urban Search and Rescue task forces assist New Orleans residents whose neighborhood was flooded by Hurricane Katrina, August 31, 2005. (FEMA/Photograph by Jocelyn Augustino)

and those who remained could not carry out their responsibilities. Hospitals could not get emergency supplies because most roads were impassable, and helicopters were allocated for rescue efforts. The situation would have been even worse had it not been for the heroic efforts of both the US Coast Guard, which evacuated people from precarious locations, and the "Cajun flotilla," a hastily organized group of small boats from southwest Louisiana that entered the city and collected stranded residents.

Compounding problems for first-line responders was a failure of leadership at the executive level. Federal officials outside the city, especially in Washington, DC, refused to accept on-scene reports as accurate; few wanted to believe the extent of the disaster. President George W. Bush, vacationing in Texas, seemed unaware of, or unconcerned about, the magnitude of the disaster. Louisiana governor Kathleen Blanco seemed unable to exert sufficient leadership to muster state resources. Blanco and Bush argued over command of the National Guard

in the area, further delaying effective response from a group equipped and trained to deal with catastrophes of this magnitude. Consequently, supplies arrived slowly and a coordinated effort to evacuate storm victims took a full week.

Federal officials on site, especially those at the Federal Emergency Management Agency (FEMA), were overwhelmed and unable to coordinate any rescue or resupply efforts. FEMA director Michael Brown, who had traveled to Louisiana ahead of the storm, was unable to get government agencies to respond to emergency requests for resources needed to conduct rescue operations or to care for the people who were congregated at the Superdome or on the elevated interstate highway and overpasses in the city. Within forty-eight hours, he asked the Department of Defense to take over federal responsibility for managing disaster relief. Ironically, television crews, unfettered by the bureaucratic red tape that kept officials from getting out to survey the disaster or deliver relief, broadcast a steady stream of images showing people trapped on rooftops or milling about on the few spots of dry ground awaiting rescue.

Conditions worsened during the first seventy-two hours after the storm hit. The evacuee population at the Superdome quickly exceeded twenty-five thousand; the crowd had insufficient food and water, and restroom facilities became inoperative. Word of problems at the Superdome caused many residents fleeing their homes to congregate at the New Orleans Convention Center; within days approximately twenty thousand were housed there. This facility also had no food, water, or bedding for evacuees. Rumors that armed gangs were committing various crimes within the facility made rescue personnel hesitant to enter. Similar rumors hampered rescue efforts within the city, where police reported looting and even sniper fire. The situation deteriorated to the point that officials authorized the military to restore order.

Relief efforts were hampered because, despite prior planning, requests from designated agencies never reached federal supply centers or neighboring states. Notwithstanding this bureaucratic failure, some states acted immediately. Both Florida and Texas mobilized their emergency response crews to help Alabama, Mississippi, and Louisiana, sending relief supplies and opening evacuation shelters. The assistance provided by Texas for those displaced in Louisiana was particularly important, since many who escaped Katrina were unable to return home for months. Temporary lodging in places such as Houston and Austin often turned into semipermanent residences as federal and state officials were unable to offer immediate help to those wishing to return to New Orleans.

Systemic Problems Exposed

Hurricane Katrina exposed the long-term failure of the US Army Corps of Engineers to provide adequate flood protection for the city of New Orleans and surrounding areas. Over the years, more expensive construction was avoided as the Corps experienced budget cuts, and relatively cheap but questionable construction methods were adopted. Compounding the problem was the requirement that the Corps coordinate with the New Orleans Levee District and the Sewerage and Water Board when designing new levees or upgrading existing ones; these political bodies often placed development interests ahead of flood protection. For ex-

ample, pressures on the Corps to limit the footprint of protective structures running through the city caused engineers to construct flood walls that were insufficient to withstand even modest surges; swirling waters ate away the supporting earthworks that held up steel retaining walls.

The storm also revealed the failure of government and social-service agencies to address the long-standing problems of racial and economic injustices in New Orleans. Evacuation plans failed to provide guaranteed transportation for thousands of poor who had no personal vehicles. When the city began rebuilding, assistance programs were targeted almost exclusively at homeowners; renters, who were predominantly poor and African American, received virtually no financial assistance to rebuild their lives.

Housing projects in the city, also occupied mostly by African Americans, were torn down and replaced with new neighborhoods where rental payments were beyond the means of most who had lived in the projects. In fact, repopulating New Orleans became a major problem because the city lacked sufficient housing. FEMA attempted to alleviate the problem by providing trailers, but many took months to arrive, and some never made it out of staging areas hundreds of miles away. Ironically, wages for service industry jobs increased as businesses tried to attract workers, but at the same time, rates skyrocketed on available rental properties, making it impossible for the poorest residents to find affordable accommodations. Some viewed the actions of government agencies and local businesses as a systematic attempt to keep African Americans from returning to New Orleans.

Impact

More than eighteen hundred people lost their lives during Hurricane Katrina and the chaos that ensued in its aftermath. Exact statistics are hard to determine, however, because more than 1.5 million people were forced to evacuate from regions in Louisiana, Mississippi, and Alabama that were affected by the storm. Catastrophic damage and the presence of floodwaters that remained inside New Orleans for weeks prevented many from returning to their homes for as long as a year or more. Some chose not to return, permanently reducing the city's population. The African American community in New Orleans, disproportionately affected by neighborhood flooding, made up a large percentage of semipermanent or permanent refugees. In cities such as Baton Rouge and Houston, rising crime rates were blamed on the refugees, causing further hardships for this population.

The economic impact on the region and the nation was also significant. The city's transportation, water, sewer, electric, gas, and communications systems were ravaged. Federal, state, and local agencies spent billions of dollars to restore homes, businesses, and infrastructure. Total damages exceeded $125 billion, making Katrina the costliest storm in American history. During the following seven years, the federal government allocated nearly $15 billion to construct or upgrade a levee system to protect New Orleans from future storm surges.

Reputations were affected as well. The image of the Corps of Engineers was permanently damaged. FEMA director Brown resigned within weeks of Katrina. Although Mayor Nagin won reelection in May 2006, Governor Blanco gave up her bid for a second term. President Bush was blamed for federal inaction after the storm. His political influence and legacy were both weakened considerably by the catastrophe. In 2006, Democrats used Katrina as a rallying cry to win a majority of seats in Congress.

Further Reading

Angel, Roger, et al. *Community Lost: The State, Civil Society, and Displaced Survivors of Hurricane Katrina.* New York: Cambridge UP, 2012. Print. Discusses the importance of government services in assisting people displaced by the storm.

Bergal, Jenni, et al. *City Adrift: New Orleans before and after Katrina.* Baton Rouge: Louisiana State UP, 2007. Print. Essay collection examining the multiple effects of Hurricane Katrina on New Orleans.

Cooper, Christopher, and Robert Block. *Disaster: Hurricane Katrina and the Failure of Homeland Security.* New York: Times, 2006. Print. Focuses on the failure of federal agencies to provide adequate support to relief efforts in New Orleans during the days immediately after Katrina struck the region.

Freudenberg, William R., et al. *Catastrophe in the Making: The Engineering of Katrina and the Disasters of Tomorrow.* Washington, DC: Shearwater, 2009. Print. Explores causes for New Orleans's vulnerability to hurricanes like Katrina and evaluates the government's poor performance before, during, and after the storm.

Johnson, Cedric, ed. *The Neoliberal Deluge: Hurricane Katrina, Late Capitalism, and the Remaking of New Orleans.* Minneapolis: U of Minnesota P, 2011. Print. Scholars explore the underlying causes for the failure of national disaster plans and efforts to rebuild New Orleans after Hurricane Katrina.

Levitt, Jeremy I., and Matthew C. Whitaker, eds. *Hurricane Katrina: America's Unnatural Disaster.* Lincoln: U of Nebraska P, 2009. Print. Essays focusing on the human costs of Katrina, explaining how the storm highlighted and exacerbated racial and economic problems in New Orleans.

McQuaid, John, and Mark Schleifstein. *Path of Destruction: The Devastation of New Orleans and the Coming Age of Superstorms.* New York: Little, 2006. Print. Explains how geography, meteorology, and political decisions contributed to problems caused by the storm; describes events during the first five days after Katrina passed through New Orleans.

Laurence W. Mazzeno

■ Hurricane Rita

The Event: Category 5 hurricane that caused significant damage to the US Gulf Coast
Date: September 18–26, 2005
Place: Florida, Louisiana, and Texas

Hurricane Rita caused extensive damage to many areas of the US Gulf Coast that were still recovering from the destruction caused by Hurricane Katrina just a month earlier. Parts of Florida saw minor flooding and power outages, while the Louisiana/Texas border region received heavy flooding.

Just a few weeks after Hurricane Katrina flooded large areas of the US Gulf Coast in August 2005, another hurricane threatened the same region. On September 18, 2005, Tropical Storm Rita formed in the Atlantic Ocean, becoming a category 1 hurricane two days later. The hurricane neared the Florida Keys on September 20, with winds of more than 76 miles per hour. This caused minor flooding and power outages in Florida. Rita then traveled westward across the Gulf of Mexico, becoming a category 5 hurricane. Hurricane Rita marked the third time that two category 5 storms formed in the Atlantic Ocean during the same season. It was also one of the strongest storms on record, with winds reaching 175 miles per hour. By the time Rita reached the Texas/Louisiana border on September 24, it was downgraded to a category 3 hurricane, with wind speeds of nearly 120 miles per hour. The strong winds traveled about 150 miles inland and significantly affected the coastal regions of Louisiana and Texas.

Parts of Texas and Louisiana suffered substantial damages, particularly in areas near the state line. The flooding destroyed thousands of homes and buildings, and heavy rains caused crop damage to thousands of acres of farmland. Millions of residents near the Texas/Louisiana state line experienced power outages that lasted for weeks. Rita also damaged two oil refineries near Port Arthur, Texas, and caused the temporary shutdown of sixteen additional refineries. Wind gusts brought down numerous trees that blocked roadways and interstates along the Gulf Coast, making it difficult for evacuees to return home.

Impact

Hurricane Rita prompted the largest evacuation in US history, with an estimated two million people evacuating from areas of Texas as the storm approached. In New Orleans, Rita further aggravated the earlier effects of Hurricane Katrina. Entire communities were devastated and desolate, filled with damaged and abandoned properties. Seven people died directly from the effects of the hurricane and 112 more indirect deaths were attributed to Rita. Damages from the storm were estimated at $10 billion.

Further Reading

Associated Press. "In Receding Floodwaters, More Damage Found." *NBCNews.com*. NBCNews.com, 27 Sep. 2005. Web. 7 Aug. 2012.

National Climate Data Center. "Hurricane Rita: Overview." *National Climate Data Center*. NOAA Satellite and Information Service, 22 Sep. 2005. Web. 7 Aug. 2012.

Sylvester, Judith. *The Media and Hurricanes Katrina and Rita: Lost and Found*. New York: Palgrave Macmillan, 2008. Print.

Angela Harmon

■ *The Hurt Locker*

Identification: A film that follows the work of a reckless bomb technician and his bomb squad as they locate and dismantle bombs in Baghdad during the Iraq War.
Director: Kathryn Bigelow (b. 1951)
Date: Premiered in Hollywood on June 5, 2009, after appearing at several international film festivals in 2008.

The Hurt Locker was one of the most critically acclaimed films of the 2000s. It was the first film about the Iraq War to focus on the psychology of the individuals who risked their lives in the conflict, while also depicting the war as a psychological battlefield. It was the first Academy Award for a female director. The film also won best picture and best screenplay.

The screenplay for *The Hurt Locker* was written by reporter Mark Boal, who worked as an embedded journalist during the Iraq War with US Army Explosive Ordnance Disposal (EOD) squad. His fictional treatment of the dangers faced by the men as they sought out and dismantled bombs set by insurgent militias caught the attention of director Kathryn Bigelow. Bigelow had established herself as a director of suspenseful television and action movies, such as *K-19: The Widowmaker* (2002) and *The Weight of Water* (2000). For *The Hurt Locker,* she cast Jeremy Renner in the leading role of Staff Sgt. William James, a cocky master technician, and selected Anthony Mackie and Brian Geraghty to play his war-weary subordinates.

The Hurt Locker takes place during a time of peak violence and bombings in Baghdad. After an EOD technician dies in a bomb explosion, James is requested to return to Iraq for another volunteer tour of duty as his replacement. The decision to return is easy, as James's life in the civilian world is wrought with disappointment, and his state of mind remains heavily influenced by his war experiences. The job of a bomb technician requires tremendous discipline, precision, and a sense of heightened intuition. The heavily armored protective suit worn by technicians, known as "the hurt locker," is where the film gets its name. Throughout the film, James eschews the rules and commonsense and does things his own way. The result is a tension-filled, action-packed movie.

The Hurt Locker was nominated for nine Academy Awards and won six, including best actor, best original screenplay, best director, and best picture. Bigelow was the first woman director to win best director, and the film was the lowest-grossing movie to ever to win best picture. It was made on a budget of $11 million, unlike most blockbuster movies, which commonly cost ten to twenty times that amount to produce.

Impact

The Hurt Locker successfully portrayed the realities of urban warfare experienced by members of the military during the Iraq War. Danger lurked in every neighborhood, where neither children nor the elderly could be completely trusted, and where a bomb could turn up in such innocuous places as piles of trash or animal carcasses. Rather than making a political commentary on the war, the film raises questions about the nature of war in general, and depicts the psychological impact of armed conflict on military service members.

Further Reading

Barker, Martin. *A 'Toxic Genre': The Iraq War Films.* London: Pluto, 2011. Print.

Ebert, Roger. "*The Hurt Locker*" *RogerEbert.com.* Roger Ebert.com, July 8, 2009. Web. 28 Aug. 2012.

Taubin, Amy. "Hard Wired." *Film Comment* 45.3 (2009): 30–35.

Sally Driscoll

■ Hybrid automobiles

Definition: Hybrid automobiles are vehicles fueled by a combination of gasoline and electricity. They typically offer better fuel efficiency and are more environmentally friendly than traditional gasoline-powered vehicles.

Hybrid automobiles became more popular during the 2000s due to technological advances, increasing consumer desire for fuel-efficient vehicles, and fuel-economy regulations. Economic and environmental factors also contributed to increased hybrid development and adoption during the 2000s.

Of the hybrid cars available in the 2000s, the hybrid electric vehicle (HEV) made the greatest strides with consumers. HEVs typically include both an internal combustion engine (ICE) that runs on gasoline and an electric motor capable of powering the vehicle without burning fuel. Some HEVs have distinctive features, such as regenerative braking, which allows the electric motor to absorb energy from the vehicle as it slows down, and the ability to shut off the gasoline engine while idling.

The electric motor in an HEV can power the car independently at low speeds, but its primary purpose is to act as a generator, converting energy from the ICE into power that can be stored in the vehicle's battery for later use. The motor also boosts power when passing or accelerating. Storing extra energy in the battery makes it a critical component of the vehicle, increasing the importance of having a long-lasting, reliable battery capable of storing large quantities of energy. HEV batteries are typically made from nickel metal hydride but may also be made from lithium ion, which is more lightweight but also more expensive to manufacture.

Plug-in hybrid electric vehicles (PHEVs) have batteries that must be recharged by being plugged into an electricity source, providing an additional way to gather energy. PHEVs may require 40 percent to 60 percent less petroleum than vehicles with ICEs.

In addition to hybrid vehicles, electric vehicles (EVs), hydrogen fuel cell vehicles, and compressed natural gas vehicles (CNGs) have been produced for purposes of fuel efficiency.

Production and Sales

In the early 2000s, electric vehicles may have seemed like a futuristic notion to consumers accustomed to nearly a century of gasoline-powered vehicles, but many of the first automobiles were electric. When the Baker Electric Car, for example, was developed in 1900, nearly 30 percent of passenger vehicles were electric. Because their driving range was limited, electric vehicles were eventually overtaken by gasoline-powered cars.

The Toyota Prius was the first mass-produced hybrid vehicle available to the public. Released in Japan in 1997 before wide release in the United States in 2001, the first Prius was a gasoline-electric hybrid vehicle capable of achieving forty-one miles per gallon (mpg). The Honda Insight, another HEV, was the first hybrid vehicle available in the United States. Released in 1999, it could achieve forty-seven to fifty-three mpg.

Engine for the Ram Plug-in Hybrid Electric Vehicle (PHEV). (Courtesy Chrysler Group)

Toyota and Honda dominated the US hybrid market for the first half of the 2000s, but other automakers eventually followed. Ford released the Ford Escape Hybrid in 2004 and the Mercury Mariner Hybrid in 2005. Ford's focus on bringing hybrid technology to the compact sport utility vehicle (SUV) segment reflected a conflict between the SUV's popularity and poor fuel economy. Lexus, Nissan, Mazda, Chrysler, and General Motors all released hybrid vehicles by 2008. Rising gas prices and the financial crisis of 2008 helped lead consumers toward fuel efficiency.

Despite the increasing frequency with which other automakers released hybrids, Toyota's early mover advantage and aggressive marketing gave it a dominant market position. By August 2009, Toyota had sold more than 2 million hybrids worldwide, and the Prius represented about 50 percent of US hybrid sales through the 2000s. Hybrids represented about 1 percent of all US vehicle sales during the 2000s.

Government Programs

In addition to changing consumer sentiment, government regulations and incentives regarding fuel economy helped broaden support for hybrids. The US Department of Energy (DOE) provided tax credits of up to $3400 to those who purchased HEVs after December 31, 2005. The promotion was valid for the earlier of either sixty thousand vehicles sold

or an expiration date of December 31, 2010. A similar promotion for PHEVs provided a credit of up to $7500.

The Corporate Average Fuel Economy (CAFE) standard, which is calculated for a full fleet of vehicles, did not change from 2000 to 2009, remaining steady at 27.5 mpg. Critics have noted that CAFE standards allow automakers to produce many fuel-inefficient vehicles balanced out by a few very efficient vehicles, such as hybrids.

In addition to setting CAFE standards, the US Environmental Protection Agency (EPA) regulates city, highway, and combined city/highway mileage. Vehicles also receive a greenhouse gas score that measures carbon dioxide (CO_2) and other greenhouse gases that are thought to affect climate. Superior fuel economy creates a higher greenhouse gas score, meaning that the vehicle emits fewer greenhouse gases. The EPA Air Pollution Score uses a scale of zero to ten, with ten indicating the vehicle with the fewest emissions.

Problems

Some consumers hesitated to purchase early hybrids for fear that the battery would have to be replaced at a high cost within a short timeframe. In addition, environmental groups were concerned about the safety of battery manufacturing and disposal. A lesser-known problem with batteries centered on the patent for the nickel metal hydride battery, which was part owned by oil company Chevron. The patent dispute and oil company interests allegedly delayed hybrid production, but Chevron's claim was bought out in 2009. Despite battery concerns, perhaps the most serious safety issue with hybrids in the 2000s concerned braking glitches in the 2010 Prius, which ultimately led to a recall.

Limited driving range and charging concerns prevented widespread hybrid adoption. Most batteries could not store enough energy for drives longer than fifty to one hundred miles, necessitating the use of the ICE. Because few vehicle-charging stations existed in the 2000s, PHEV owners found it difficult to recharge on long trips. Even for drivers able to find stations, charging took time: a "fast" direct current (DC) charge could take twenty minutes to add sixty or eighty additional miles of range.

Generating electricity to recharge PHEVs or EVs was seen as potentially detrimental as well. That is, if the electricity being used to power and recharge electric vehicles was produced by coal-fired power plants, the emissions produced by those plants might be more environmentally damaging than the emissions that a gasoline-powered vehicle would have produced.

Impact

At the end of the 2000s, challenges such as vehicle safety, battery life, limited driving range, and the environmental impacts of battery and electricity production remained obstacles to widespread adoption of hybrid cars. Nevertheless, technological advances and social factors increased their popularity throughout the decade, setting the stage for improved fuel economy and environmental awareness by drivers and automakers.

Further Reading

Alternative Fuels Data Center: Electricity. US Dept. of Energy, 30 July 2012. Web. 11 Oct. 2012. Provides cost-benefit information, statistics, geographical data, and legal resources relating to electric and hybrid vehicles.

Anderson, Curtis D., and Judy Anderson. *Electric and Hybrid Cars: A History.* Jefferson: McFarland, 2004. Print. A history of electric and hybrid vehicles from the early days of the automobile to the early twenty-first century.

Boschert, Sherry. *Plug-In Hybrids: The Cars That Will Recharge America.* Gabriola Island: New Soc., 2006. Print. Offers an optimistic take on the potential for PHEVs to transform personal transportation.

Motavalli, Jim. *High Voltage: The Fast Track to Plug In the Auto Industry.* Emmaus: Rodale, 2011. Print. A consumer-friendly exploration of the evolution of electric and hybrid vehicles. Particularly focuses on modern cars such as the Nissan Leaf and Chevy Volt.

Yost, Nick. *The Essential Hybrid Car Handbook: A Buyer's Guide.* Guilford: Lyons, 2006. Print. Focused on purchasing but provides a thorough overview of hybrid automobile technology and development.

Kerry Skemp

■ Illinois v. Wardlow

The Case: US Supreme Court ruling on what constitutes reasonable suspicion precipitating search and seizure

Date: Decided on January 12, 2000

In deference to typical human behavior in response to sighting a police officer, the Supreme Court ruled that fleeing from an officer, particularly in a high crime area, establishes reasonable suspicion. The court also ruled that consequent search and seizure of the suspicious individual is legally permissible.

While on patrol in a high-crime area in Chicago, Illinois, police officers noticed a man fleeing in an area of the city infamous for narcotics trafficking. This man, William "Sam" Wardlow, was seen holding a bag. After his capture, officers searched for a weapon and found a gun. Such a search, known as a Terry stop, is allowable if officers can articulate reasonable suspicion, as determined in *Terry v. Ohio* (1968). Unlike the process for obtaining a search warrant, which requires probable cause, a Terry stop relies solely on an officer's own evaluation of a situation.

Pending trial, Wardlow submitted a petition, claiming that the discovery of his gun should not be used against him since it was illegally seized. He relied on the Fourth Amendment's protection against unreasonable searches and seizures. While an Illinois trial court disagreed with Wardlow's petition, the Illinois Appellate Court and Illinois Supreme Court reversed the lower court's decision. In response, the US Supreme Court determined that running from the police in a high-crime area creates reasonable suspicion of illicit behavior and warrants search and seizure.

Chief Justice William Rehnquist delivered the majority opinion for the sharply divided court. The majority contended that while unprovoked flight from police officers could be construed as innocent, the possibility of innocence does not rule out suspicion. They acknowledged that by upholding Terry stops in Wardlow's situation, innocent people would likely be searched under this broad interpretation of reasonable suspicion. The court's dissenting justices emphasized the many innocent reasons for flight, claiming that such an array of possibilities could not support wide use of the Terry stop. The justices also cited the case's tenuous usage of the terms "high-crime area" and "flight" as irresponsibly vague.

Impact

The court's decision in *Illinois v. Wardlow* empowered police officers over individual freedoms. The effects have been most severely felt among minority populations. Since the Wardlow decision, a number of policies have been implemented that broadly interpret reasonable suspicion. The New York Police Department's Stop-and-Frisk policy relies on stopping and searching people in high crime areas in order to deter crime. This policy has been shown to disproportionately target minorities who often live in these areas. Similarly, Arizona's immigration policy, which uses routine traffic stops to uncover illegal immigrants, has been accused of racial profiling. The decision's reliance on a police officer's subjective interpretation of a situation has allowed personal bias and racial profiling to undermine justice, driving a wedge between communities and those employed to protect them.

Further Reading

Del Carmen, Rolando V. and Craig Hemmens, eds. *Criminal Procedure and the Supreme Court: A Guide to the Major Decisions on Search and Seizure, Privacy, and Individual Rights.* Lanham: Rowman & Littlefield, 2010. E-book.

Kappeler, Victor E. *Critical Issues in Police Civil Liability.* 4th ed. Long Grove: Waveland P, 2006. Print.

Lucia Pizzo

■ IMAX

Definition: A motion picture format larger than traditional cinema projection that was utilized in feature films and movie theaters in the 2000s

Although IMAX films could initially be found strictly in museums and science centers—where mostly educational and specialty films were shown—the large format has since been embraced by the motion picture industry. The technology, which utilizes a higher resolution rate via a larger film size, was developed by the IMAX Corporation based out of Canada. Several major films are released in the IMAX format every year.

IMAX films could be seen exclusively in science centers and museums throughout the 2000s in the United States. These largely documentary films were much shorter than feature films and it was not until Walt Disney Studio's *Fantasia 2000* (1999) that the potential for IMAX technology in the motion picture industry was realized. Various branches of IMAX technology have been developed including IMAX 3-D and the IMAX digital camera, which has become widely used in major motion picture productions.

More than one hundred IMAX films were produced in the 2000s. These films covered a range of educational topics such as dinosaurs and ocean life. By 2009, more than five hundred IMAX theaters had been built in more than forty countries. IMAX theaters feature a large rectangular screen that is commonly sixteen meters high by twenty-two meters wide (approximately fifty-three feet high by seventy-two feet wide).

Some IMAX theaters are built inside a dome, commonly thirty meters (ninety-eight feet) in diameter, that project films on a hemispherical screen. Before high-definition IMAX cameras were introduced, IMAX films were shot on 70mm film, which required the use of large platters rather than standard film reels and required a special projector to run the film through horizontally rather than vertically. IMAX digital projectors and IMAX screens were introduced in several movie theater chains, including AMC Theatres.

After releasing *Fantasia 2000*, Disney rereleased *Beauty and the Beast* (1991) and *The Lion King* (1994) in IMAX with new high-resolution negatives. In 2002 Disney released *Treasure Planet* in both IMAX and regular theaters, making it the first film to be released simultaneously in both formats. In 2002,

IMAX introduced their Digital Media Remastering technology that converted film to the IMAX format. Warner Bros. Pictures followed suit in 2003 and released two sequels to *The Matrix* (1999) in IMAX theaters. Several filmmakers have partially shot their feature films using IMAX cameras. The 2008 film *The Dark Knight* features six sequences shot in IMAX, for example. Due to several technical difficulties such as heavy cameras and short film loads, no feature-length film has yet to be shot entirely in IMAX.

Impact

IMAX technology helped create a more immersive experience for moviegoers. The IMAX Corporation advanced film technology in a variety of ways including audio and high-definition visuals. IMAX films shown at museums and science centers have increased the attendance at these institutions, and its use in feature films has expanded the scope a director can work with. As the technology further develops, IMAX will continue to increase what is possible with film.

Further Reading

Fuchs, Andreas. "IMAXimum Impact: Studio Movies Go Big with Large-Format Reader." *Film Journal International.* Film Journal International, 15 May 2012. Web. 5 Aug. 2012.

Griffiths, Alison. *Shivers Down Your Sping: Cinema, Museums, and the Immersive View.* New York: Columbia UP, 2012. Print.

Jannarone, John. "IMAX's Headroom for Growth Should Lure Movie Investors." *Wall Street Journal* 9 Jan. 2012: C8. Print.

Patrick G. Cooper

■ Immigration to the United States

Definition: The process of traveling to live permanently in a country other than an individual's native country; the processes and procedures required to obtain legal residence in a foreign country

Immigration was one of the most politically contentious issues of the 2000s after the September 11, 2001, terrorist attacks against the United States created widespread concern over the potential for immigrant involvement in terrorist activities. Immigration forms an important source of labor

for many US industries and plays a major role in patterns of population growth and diversification. In addition, immigration became a major economic issue in the 2000s, especially in terms of the ongoing debate over the cost of immigration control programs and the economic impact of immigrants on native employment.

Immigration and Population

Immigration to the United States reached its highest levels during the decade from 1990 to 2000, peaking in 1999 with 1.5 million immigrants arriving in the country. According to Brookings Institution research, more than 8.8 million immigrants arrived in the United States between 2000 and 2010. The Census Bureau estimated the foreign born population in 2010 at over 39.95 million, constituting roughly 12.9 percent of the more than 308 million people in the United States as a whole. Immigration has decreased substantially from peak levels in the 1990s, when the foreign born population constituted more than 14 percent of the populace. More than eleven million immigrants, many of whom arrived in the country in the 1990s, obtained permanent legal residence during the 2000s.

Fertility rates in the United States have decreased from their peak in the 1950s of 3.7 children per woman to approximately 2.0 children per woman in 2010. Despite falling fertility levels, analysts believe that the US population will continue to increase even without the annual influx of immigrants. However, population growth has slowed overall from a peak in the 1990s of 13 percent per year, to a 2010 estimate of 9.7 percent annually.

While the foreign-born population was distributed across the United States, more than 50 percent of foreign-born residents lived in one of four US states at the end of the decade: California, New York, Texas, and Florida. More than one in four residents of California were foreign-born and more than 25 percent of arriving immigrants settled in California during the decade. More than 20 percent of New York residents were foreign born, though New York City, the historic primary hub for US immigration, experienced significant reductions in immigrant arrivals during the decade.

Changes in Immigration Patterns during the 2000s

Immigration patterns changed substantially in post–September 11 America, due in part to more stringent

Immigration reform rally, Lexington, KY, April 10, 2006. (Courtesy of Britt Selvitelle)

restrictions and requirements placed on potential immigrants. The Patriot Act of 2001 and the creation of the Department of Homeland Security in 2002 restructured the governmental processes involved in immigration policy and substantially altered the process of applying for and obtaining legal entry to the United States. The Enhanced Border Security and Visa Entry Reform Act of 2002 placed further restrictions on immigrants and required certain classes of immigrants to submit to investigation and to commit to annual renewals of visitor permits. The last major attempt to reform immigration policy came with the REAL ID act of 2005, which placed additional requirements on the identification needed to get a state-issued identification card or a driver's license.

Post–September 11 immigration reform and restructuring played an important role in declining levels of legal immigration throughout the rest of the decade. More stringent guidelines for citizenship requests and policy changes to application procedures were among the factors affecting this aspect of the immigration process. Legal immigration was reduced more sharply than illegal migration and by 2010 the greatest reduction to immigration numbers came from fewer legal immigrants obtaining entrance to the country.

In 2010, the Pew Research Center released data suggesting that illegal immigration had decreased by one- to two-thirds between 2005 and 2009, largely due to increased border regulations and the economic recession in the United States from 2007 to 2009. In March of 2009, the number of illegal immigrants living in the nation was estimated at 11.1 million. Further, the Pew report indicated that the most significant reductions in illegal immigration affected immigrants from Latin American countries other than Mexico. Mexico remained the largest source of illegal migrants to the United States, contributing an average of seven million illegal migrants annually.

Another notable change in immigration during the decade was the tendency for immigrants to settle in areas other than the nation's primary metropolitan regions. New York, Miami, Los Angeles, Houston, and Chicago housed 43 percent of the nation's immigrants in 2000, but only housed 38 percent of immigrants in 2010. In addition, more immigrants decided to settle in suburban rather than metropolitan areas. The number of immigrants living in the suburbs of major metropolitan areas increased from 48 percent in 2000 to 51 percent in 2010.

Characteristics of the Foreign-Born Population

Legal permanent residents are individuals that have received permission to live and work in the United States on a permanent basis. The permanent legal resident card is often informally known as a "green card," because the resident cards were green in color from the 1940s to the mid-1960s.

During the 2000s, more than eleven million individuals became permanent residents of the United States. Of those obtaining permanent residency, 4.4 million were from the Americas (Canada, Mexico, the Caribbean, Central America, and South America), 3.4 million were from Asia, 1.3 million were from Europe, and more than 759,000 were from Africa. More than one million individuals achieve permanent resident status each year, with the exception of 2003 and 2004, which were the two years of the decade with the lowest number of individuals achieving resident status. The creation of the Department of Homeland Security in 2002 and an overall restructuring of im-

migration guidelines reduced the numbers of individuals achieving legal permanent resident status for this two-year period.

In 1970, nearly 80 percent of immigrants were non-Hispanic whites from Canada and Europe and only 6 percent were Asian or Hispanic/Latino. This trend has seen a complete reversal during the 1990s and 2000s. During these two decades, most of the immigrants arriving in the United States came from Asia, Mexico, and Central America. Between 2000 and 2009, more than 34 percent of immigrants were from Asia and 41 percent were from Latin American countries.

A number of groups opposed to immigration have expressed concern that rising numbers of foreign-born residents may threaten the status of English as the primary language of the United States. Census Bureau research indicates that more than 50 percent of foreign-born individuals speak English as a primary language or speak English "very well." Approximately 10 percent of the foreign born population did not speak English at all.

Census Bureau analyses also indicate that the foreign-born population were more likely than the native-born population to remain employed and to work in the labor force. More than 67 percent of foreign-born individuals participated in the labor force, as opposed to 63 percent of the native-born. However, despite high employment rates, foreign-born individuals are less likely to achieve financial stability. Foreign-born individuals earn less than half of native-born individuals in terms of median income and only 66 percent of foreign-born individuals received some form of health insurance, as compared to 83 percent of the native-born population. In addition, more than 19 percent of foreign-born individuals lived below the poverty line, as compared with 15 percent of the native-born population.

Economic Impact of Immigration

A variety of studies have attempted to investigate the overall economic impact of immigration in the United States. Some contend that adding immigrant laborers to the workforce should depress wages for American workers, or at least reduce the rate at which wage increases are distributed. Analyses of employment and wage rates have failed to demonstrate clear evidence that immigration contributes to wage depression, however. In a 1995 report published by the Cato Institute, researchers contend that wage increases and reductions appear to be unrelated to immigration and that immigration has no overall impact on economic well being for the native-born workforce.

A variety of studies have shown that in some cases, foreign-born workers may cause depressions in local job availability, while in other cases, foreign-born workers may increase productivity and wages within an industry because the influx of workers increases demand and availability of new projects. Economic analyses from a variety of sources indicate that immigration boosts economic prosperity in the long term, though it may lead to wage reductions for some workers over the short term.

Impact

Overall, immigration during the 2000s was lower than in previous decades, though it still played an important role in the 2.7 percent growth recorded for the US population as a whole. Following the September 11, 2001, terrorist attacks, immigration and immigrant rights became a major issue in American politics and the many changes implemented to immigration policy during the decade resulted in reduced rates of both legal and illegal immigration.

The primary legislative change to immigration policy developed during the decade was the REAL ID Act of 2005, which sought to impose mandatory requirements on the documentation needed to obtain state-issued identification. The REAL ID Act was controversial and was approved partially because the legislation was linked to other high priority economic initiatives. By 2012, the federal government had not yet begun enforcing the statutes contained within the REAL ID Act. Some political analysts have opposed the act on the basis that the federally mandated identification requirements could allegedly be used to restrict certain rights, including the right to vote.

Further Reading

Bernstein, Nina. "Study Finds Immigration in U.S. Peaked in 2000." *New York Times*. New York Times, 28 Sept. 2005. Web. 15 Nov. 2012. Article written mid-decade explains changing immigration trends in the United States and discusses potential future patterns in immigration.

Martin, Philip, and Elizabeth Midgley. "Population Bulletin Update: Immigration in America 2010." *Population Reference Bureau*. Population Reference Bureau, June 2010. Web. 15 Nov. 2012. Provides an analysis of current and past population trends

with regard to immigration patterns. Also covers the economic impact of immigration.

Varsanyi, Monica. *Taking Local Control: Immigration Policy Activism in U.S. Cities and States*. Palo Alto: Stanford UP, 2010. Print. Overview of the legal actions regarding immigration leading up to the 2000s and the response from the populace in terms of activism and organized protest.

West, Darrel M. *Brain Gain: Rethinking U.S. Immigration Policy*. Washington, D.C.: Brookings Inst., 2010. Print. Provides an analysis of US immigration policy and a history of immigration statutes leading through the first decade of the twenty-first century.

Wilson, Jill H., and Audrey Singer. "Immigrants in 2010 Metropolitan America: A Decade of Change." *Brookings*. Brookings Inst., 13 Oct. 2011. Web. 15 Nov. 2012. Discusses immigration patterns during the 2000s with a focus on changes in immigration statistics in comparison to the 1990s.

Micah L. Issitt

■ Income and wages in the United States

Definition: The money that an individual earns on a regular basis from an employer or through investments in items such as real estate, stocks, or bonds

During the 2000s, the vast majority of Americans saw their paycheck wages either stagnate or shrink when adjusted for inflation. This financial difficulty came at a time when investment incomes also underperformed. US income stagnation in the 2000s was driven by growing income inequality and weak economic growth. Income inequality occurs when top earners receive a greater share of the nation's total income than lower and middle-class earners.

Stagnation has been the chief defining characteristic of income and wages in the United States during the first decade of the twenty-first century. The root causes of this phenomenon are poor economic conditions and growing income inequality. The US economy endured two economic recessions during the 2000s, the first coming in 2001 and lasting about eight months; the second in December 2007 and ending in September 2009. Economic growth in the US has remained anemic. The 2001 recession resulted from the collapse of stock values in the information technology market. This collapse is also referred to as the bursting of the Internet or dot-com bubble. The US economy suffered further as a result of the September 11, 2001, terrorist attacks.

The late-2000s recession occurred after the collapse of the US housing market, which was overinflated by loose lending practices on the part of the banking industry, and by customers seeking to purchase homes on easy credit. Both recessions, as well as the impact of globalization on the US economy, kept American wages and incomes stagnant throughout the 2000s.

Poor Economic Conditions

Although economists considered the 2001 recession relatively mild, the recovery that followed it was very weak. Between the end of the first recession and the beginning of the second, the US economy grew at an annual rate of 2.7 percent. During the preceding two decades, US economic growth exceeded 3.5 percent annually. The weak recovery that followed the 2001 recession was met with a severe second recession in 2008 that not only wiped out the economic gains of that recovery, but caused the income of the average US family to decrease to 1996 levels, when adjusted for inflation. Even before the recession of the late 2000s, also known as the Great Recession, the US economy was growing at the slowest rate of any decade since World War II (1939–45).

Many economists consider the Great Recession to be the worst economic downturn in more than fifty years. In its wake, poor and middle-class Americans have been unable to make up lost ground, a phenomenon last seen in the Great Depression of the 1930s. By the end of 2000s, many Americans feared that they and their children would not do as well as their parents and grandparents had. Economic data bore their fears out. Households that supported themselves on wages from one or more salaried positions did not keep up with inflation. In 2000, the median family income, adjusted for inflation, peaked at $64,232. For the first time since the Great Depression, income declined in every tax bracket. Wealthier households, which generally have investment portfolios comprised of stocks, bonds, and real estate, also saw their earnings dwindle.

A Generational Problem

The Great Recession caused average US household incomes to fall for three consecutive years between 2009 and 2011. This declining income highlighted a

Average Weekly Earnings by Industry, 2000 and 2010

Sector	2000	2010
Natural resources and mining	$735	$1217
Construction	$686	$957
Manufacturing	$591	$948
Trade, transport, and utilities	$450	$684
Information	$701	$1142
Finance	$537	$1020
Professional and business services	$535	$975
Education and health	$449	$761
Leisure and hospitality	$217	$339
Other services	$413	$645

Source: United States Department of Labor Bureau of Labor Statistics

growing trend of income inequality in the United States. In addition to declining wages, lower-income and middle-class Americans were squeezed by rising expenses and stagnant wages during the 2000s. US families felt the strain of higher prices for health insurance, schooling, childcare, transportation, housing and other expenses against their inflation-adjusted stagnant wages and incomes.

In 1980, the top 1 percent of earners made 8 percent of national income; by 2011, they were earning 16 percent of it. Households in the top 1/1000 of income (earning $1.5 million in 2010) have seen a 100 percent (inflation-adjusted) increase in income since 1980. By comparison, households in the middle of the income spectrum saw just an 11 percent increase in their income over the same period. The bottom 99 percent of US incomes grew by just 6.8 percent between 2002 and 2007. That same group had seen an income increase of 20 percent between 1993 and 2000.

The last time such large disparity existed between the income of wealthy Americans and everyone else was 1929, the year of the stock market crash that sparked the Great Depression. During

the Depression, reforms enacted to protect investments, restrict financial speculation, and stabilize
banks helped to shrink income inequality. Following World War II, the US economy boomed, further shrinking the gap between rich and poor
during the 1950s and 1960s. Beginning in the 1970s,
however, income inequality began to reemerge, due
in large part to globalization and establishment of
the finance, insurance, and real estate ("FIRE")
economy; and government policies that allowed for
growth in the financial sector.

Globalization—the process by which goods and
services are bought, sold, manufactured, and distributed internationally—has changed the US economy
tremendously. Capitalism has always sought to produce the best products at the lowest costs, but in a
globalized economy, the drive toward lower costs
sent production activity overseas, to less expensive,
non-unionized workforces. US manufacturing jobs
with good wages and benefits could not compete
with cheaper labor overseas that could produce the
same products at much lower costs. The result was
fewer competitive-wage jobs in the United States.

As manufacturing moved overseas, the US economy came to rely more on its service industry, including its finance, insurance, and real estate sectors. The FIRE economy's growth was aided by the
easing of financial regulations in the 1970s. As the
finance-based aspects of the US economy earned
more profit, investors began pulling their money
out manufacturing and putting it into services. For
example, auto manufacturers were beginning to
make more money selling loans to customers than
what they actually made in building their vehicles.
In 2006, just before the housing bubble burst, the
finance and banking sector was making 45 percent
of all US corporate profits. In earlier decades, this
sector represented just 6 percent of corporate
profits.

As the US economy shifted from being manufacturing based to being oriented toward the service
sector, changes in US government regulations facilitated and encouraged riskier financial speculation in
order to increase profits and tax revenues. This
riskier investment activity—which included everything from hedge funds, to the dot-com boom, to the
housing market—was deemed safe enough for the
middle class to invest in, which they did in great numbers. Therefore, when the bubbles in these markets
burst, the losses were felt across America by those

who used these riskier investments to increase household incomes suppressed by flat wages and rising expenses. The collapse of the housing market was devastating for the average American. Historically, most
US wealth accumulation and investment has been
based in home mortgages. By comparison, the vast
majority of Americans have far less invested in stocks,
bonds, or retirement accounts.

Impact
Declining economic mobility and growing income
inequality remain significant problems in the United
States. One of the bedrock principles of American
life is that anyone—whether native-born or natural-
ized citizen—has the opportunity to succeed, regardless of background or economic status. In the
2000s, the toll the weak economy had on average income and wages in the nation threatened this ideal.
Weaker earnings led to higher poverty rates, and an
inability for younger and less affluent Americans to
get ahead.

Many younger Americans, unable to earn a living
wage, have come to realize that they will not be able
to afford the same standard of living that their parents enjoyed. Moreover, weaker wages for Americans
of all ages means less disposable income for the purchase of goods and services—a particularly dire
problem for the US economy going forward. This is a
vicious cycle. If weaker wages and incomes lead to
less spending, as most economists believe it does,
then it will take even longer for the US economy to
begin creating the kinds of jobs that will end income
stagnation, improve income inequality, and create a
robust American economy.

Further Reading
Barlett, Donald L., and James B. Steele. *The Betrayal of
the American Dream.* New York: PublicAffairs, 2012.
Print. Argues that policies benefiting the wealthy
have hurt the American middle class. Covers the
impact of tax policy, pension elimination, free
trade, and deregulation.

Johnston, David Cay. *Free Lunch: How the Wealthiest
Americans Enrich Themselves at Government Expense
(and Stick You with the Bill).* New York: Penguin,
2007. Print. Looks at regulations implemented
during the 2000s and their impact on American
taxpayers.

Kelly, Nathan J. *The Politics of Income Inequality in the
United States.* Cambridge; New York: Cambridge

UP, 2009. Print. Analyzes data from income surveys and other sources to see whether and how political dynamics influence the distribution of incomes in the United States.

Noah, Timothy. *The Great Divergence: America's Growing Inequality Crisis and What We Can Do About It.* New York: Bloomsbury, 2012. Print. A nonpartisan investigation of the causes of the income gap in the United States.

Stiglitz, Joseph E. *Freefall: America, Free Markets, and the Sinking of the World Economy.* New York: Norton, 2010. Print. A comprehensive look at the Great Recession by a leading expert on market failure.

Christopher Mari

■ *An Inconvenient Truth*

Identification: A documentary detailing Al Gore's efforts to draw attention to the issue of global warming
Director: Davis Guggenheim (b. 1963)
Date: Released January 24, 2006

The Oscar-winning documentary An Inconvenient Truth *polarized much of the country. Though many believed its message about the threat of global warming, others, including some scientists, declared global warming a myth. Though the scientific community largely acknowledged the changes in the earth's climate, their causes were the subject of much debate.*

An Inconvenient Truth grew out of Al Gore's personal and professional experiences. He first wrote about climate change in his 1992 book *Earth in the Balance: Ecology and the Human Spirit.* During that time, he created a slide show about global warming. Later, while serving as vice president of the United States from 1993 to 2000, he and President Bill Clinton worked to protect the environment, though they faced opposition from Republicans in Congress.

In 2000, Gore ran for president but lost. Later, he believed the environmental progress that had been made under Clinton was being eroded under President George W. Bush. Gore began traveling and speaking about environmental issues, using his slide show to illustrate his points.

The basic premise of global warming is that some of the sun's light waves are trapped by the earth's atmosphere, keeping the planet warm enough to support life—a phenomenon known as the greenhouse effect. Human activity, including the use of carbon fuels, increases greenhouse gases, which thicken the atmosphere. If too much of the sun's heat is trapped in the atmosphere, the earth's temperature rises. Gore's presentation detailed various environmental trends that indicate this is what is happening in the world today.

In the decade after he first created the environmental slide show, Gore added more information and made improvements. His wife, Tipper, encouraged him to write another book using elements of the slide show. Gore introduced his data in a Power-Point presentation at locations around the country, speaking to several hundred people at a time. Film producer Laurie David attended one of these events. She and producer Lawrence Bender spoke to Gore about creating a film based on his slideshow presentation to bring his message to a wider audience. David and Bender recruited Jeffrey Skoll, founder of Participant Productions, and Davis Guggenheim, a director, to help persuade Gore to do the project.

The data presented in *An Inconvenient Truth* draws connections between subjects without stipulating causal relationships. Though scientists speculate that such things as changes in the prevalence of mosquito-borne diseases have been caused by climate change, no clear relationships have been proven. However, while some scientists quibbled with details, overall, most agreed that climate change was an issue that must be addressed.

Controversy and Criticism

A number of individuals and organizations challenged Gore's information and conclusions. Global warming was argued on many fronts, including as a scientific, an economic, and a political issue. Even among those who agreed that climate change was a concern, there was often disagreement about what should be done to address it.

In the United Kingdom, where the film was added to the science curriculum of primary schools, a legal challenge resulted in a 2007 British High Court ruling that the film contains scientific errors. The nine errors cited included attribution of snowcap melting on Mount Kilimanjaro to human-induced global warming. The court ruled that the film could still be shown to students but must be accompanied by guidance notes.

Prospects for Change

Gore has cited a number of factors that have allowed global warming to continue, in particular population growth, technology, and human shortsightedness. He has noted that his message is one of warning but also of opportunity, because the dangers of global warming present new prospects in industry and employment.

Despite the serious nature of his data, Gore remained optimistic about fostering change. He advocated small changes individuals can make, such as lowering thermostats in their homes, driving less, and recycling. Gore donated all profits from the book and the film to efforts to combat global warming.

Impact

The documentary served to open widespread debate and discussion of climate change. Increased interest encouraged a number of organizations and programs to address global warming. Perhaps more important, the film generated discussion of environmental issues among the general public. Many programs were launched to help individuals and families chart the environmental impact of their actions. More effort was made to develop alternative energy sources. Such products as hybrid cars and solar panels became more readily available, and businesses to serve these markets developed.

Government action following the release of *An Inconvenient Truth* included the establishment by Congress of the Select Committee on Energy Independence and Global Warming and passage of a climate-change bill, the Waxman-Markey Bill, in 2009. Elsewhere, *An Inconvenient Truth* was incorporated into school curricula in five countries, including England and New Zealand.

Further Reading

Archer, David. *Global Warming: Understanding the Forecast.* 2nd ed. Hoboken, NJ: Wiley, 2011. Print. Textbook that outlines the science and policy of the issue of global warming.

Freedland, Jonathan. "Born Again." *Guardian.* Guardian News and Media, 30 May 2006. Web. 6 Aug. 2012. Interview with Gore about the film, environmental issues, and American politics.

Gore, Al. *An Inconvenient Truth: The Planetary Emergency of Global Warming and What We Can Do about It.* New York: Rodale, 2006. Print. Contains much

of Gore's environmental presentation information.

—. *Our Choice: A Plan to Solve the Climate Crisis.* New York: Rodale, 2009. Print. Gore suggests solutions to climate-change issues, including developments in harnessing renewable energy sources.

Intergovernmental Panel on Climate Change. *Climate Change 2007: The Physical Science Basis: Working Group I Contribution to the Fourth Assessment Report of the Intergovernmental Panel on Climate Change, 2007.* New York: Cambridge UP, 2007. Print. Report on climate change science, including future projections, by the United Nations' Intergovernmental Panel on Climate Change (IPCC).

Peck, Sally. "Al Gore's 'Nine Inconvenient Untruths.'" *Telegraph.* Telegraph Media Group, 11 Oct. 2007. Web. 6 Aug. 2012. British High Court singles out nine claims as scientific errors and rules that the predictions made in the film were political.

Josephine Campbell

■ Indian Ocean earthquake and tsunami

The Event: An undersea earthquake in the Indian Ocean that caused a devastating tsunami

Date: December 26, 2004

Place: Indian Ocean coastal countries, including Indonesia, Sri Lanka, India, Thailand, Somalia, Maldives, Malaysia, Myanmar, Tanzania, Bangladesh, and Kenya

In December 2004, a massive earthquake occurred under the Indian Ocean, triggering the most destructive tsunami in history. Without warning, the tsunami quickly reached countries on the Indian Ocean coast, causing widespread death and destruction. Many nations, including the United States, pledged aid to help rebuild the affected countries and to establish a tsunami warning system.

On December 26, 2004, a megathrust earthquake with a magnitude of 9.0 or greater (the US Geological Survey reports a magnitude of 9.1) occurred under the Indian Ocean about 150 miles off the west coast of the island of Sumatra, Indonesia. Known as the Sumatra-Andaman earthquake, the shaking lasted for more than eight minutes in Indonesia, and people in Thailand and the Maldives felt the quake more than 1,500 miles from its epicenter. By the time seismologists issued a tsunami warning, it was too late. The earthquake triggered a tsunami that reached several coastal countries on the Indian Ocean, with Sumatra being one of the first areas hit by the waves. The waves, which reached as high as fifty feet in some places, caused hundreds of thousands of deaths and destroyed numerous cities and island communities.

According to the US Geological Survey (USGS), the Sumatra-Andaman earthquake had at the time the fourth-highest death toll of any earthquake (it was pushed into fifth place by the 2010 Haiti earthquake), and it caused the most destructive tsunami in history. It also was the largest-magnitude earthquake in more than forty years. USGS said the earthquake's destruction was comparable to the release of twenty-three thousand Hiroshima-type atomic bombs.

The earthquake occurred at the subduction zone between the India and Burma tectonic plates. The India plate had been sliding under the Burma plate for more than two centuries without a major quake. When the fault ruptured, the Burma plate suddenly slipped upward, uplifting a large area of the seafloor underneath the Indian Ocean by several meters. The movement activated a series of shocks that sent waves of water in every direction. The tsunami traveled at the speed of a jetliner for more than three thousand miles, reaching the shores of several countries within thirty minutes and killing people in thirteen different countries, including Indonesia, Sri Lanka, India, and Kenya.

Warning Signs

The USGS reports that most tsunamis occur in the Pacific Ocean and are rare in the Indian Ocean. Tsunamis typically happen in surges that may be minutes or hours apart. The waves often occur in cycles, and the first ones may not always be the largest. A receding ocean is the first sign of a tsunami. Survivors of the Indian Ocean tsunami later reported that they had seen the ocean retreat hundreds of meters, leaving fish and coral reefs exposed. Experts warn that when this happens people may have as little as five minutes to get to higher ground for safety.

In Thailand, a student told newspapers that she remembered this detail from her geography class and used it to save herself and her family. A man in

Survivors gather to receive food and supplies during humanitarian relief operations on Sumatra. (U.S. Navy/Photograph by Airman Patrick M. Bonafede)

India said he saw this fact on a television report and alerted his village of the impending danger. Survivors in many of the affected countries reported that they saw animals moving to higher ground and birds flying away from the ocean minutes before the tsunami occurred.

Aftermath

Over 230,000 people are estimated to have been killed by the tsunami. About nine thousand people were tourists from many parts of the world, including the United States and Europe. More than two million people were displaced. Entire towns and villages were destroyed. Buildings, roadways, and bridges no longer existed. Farmland was ruined by the saltwater of the ocean, and thousands of miles of the Indian Ocean coastline were obliterated. Huge waves overtopped small, inhabited islands such as Kandholhudhoo in the Maldives. The province of Aceh, Indonesia, was one of the hardest hit areas: Approximately 170,000 people were swept away within minutes. Ground motions too slight to be felt without instrumentation occurred at every point on the globe following the earthquake, as the seismic waves spread outward from the epicenter. The earthquake was so powerful that it increased the tilt of Earth's axis by an estimated 2.5 centimeters.

Impact

More than two hundred thousand people lost their lives because of the Indian Ocean tsunami. This was attributed to the lack of an effective tsunami warning system in the Indian Ocean. In 2004, six experimental tsunami-monitoring buoys were being tested, but these were not sufficient to detect a threat. Since the tsunami, the United Nations Educational, Scientific and Cultural Organization's (UNESCO's) Intergovernmental Oceanographic Commission established an Indian Ocean Tsunami Warning System to help save lives in the event of another tsunami. In addition, many nations around the world pledged help to those affected by the tsunami. Among them, the US government sent military assistance and committed $350 million in relief aid. Private donations in the United States accounted for more than $200 million.

Further Reading

Beaumont, Peter, et al. "After the 2004 Tsunami: Rebuilding Lives, Salvaging Communities." *Guardian.* Guardian News and Media, 23 Dec. 2009. Web. 8 Aug. 2012. A newspaper article looking back at the communities affected by the 2004 Indian Ocean tsunami.

"The Deadliest Tsunami in History?" *National Geographic.* National Geographic Society, 7 Jan. 2005. Web. 7 Aug. 2012. *National Geographic* report about the tsunami.

Intergovernmental Oceanographic Commission. "Indian Ocean Tsunami Warning System Performed Well, Detailed Assessment Underway." *Intergovernmental Oceanographic Commission.* UNESCO, 13 Apr. 2012. Web. 8 Aug. 2012. A UNESCO report on the early performance of the Indian Ocean Tsunami Warning System.

Jaffe, Bruce, Eric Geist, and Helen Gibbons. "Indian Ocean Earthquake Triggers Deadly Tsunami." *Sound Waves.* US Geological Survey, Dec. 2004/Jan. 2005. Web. 8 Aug. 2012. A newsletter reporting USGS scientists' findings about the Indian Ocean earthquake.

Lace, William W. *The Indian Ocean Tsunami of 2004.* New York: Chelsea House, 2008. Print. An account of the 2004 Indian Ocean tsunami, discussing how more people could have been saved.

Angela Harmon

■ Indoor smoking bans

Definition: Bans enacted to curb indoor smoking throughout the United States

Prior to 2000, most Americans were free to smoke in public and private establishments such as workplaces, restaurants, and bars. Throughout the 2000s, however, many US cities and states began enacting indoor smoking bans. By the end of the decade, twenty-two states had put indoor smoking bans into place, while dozens of other cities and states had limits on where a person was allowed to smoke.

A handful of states began enacting smoking bans throughout the 1990s. San Luis Obispo, California, became the first city in the world to ban smoking in bars in 1990. The states of California, Utah, and Massachusetts then enacted smoking restrictions that made it illegal to smoke in most public places. Some exemptions allowed people to smoke in specially designated areas.

The first statewide indoor smoking ban came in 2002, when Delaware banned smoking in public and private establishments, workplaces, restaurants, and bars. The following year, New York adopted a ban. Massachusetts followed suit in 2004, as did Rhode Island and Washington in 2005. The following year, New Jersey, Colorado, Hawaii, Ohio, and the District of Columbia enacted similar smoking bans. These bans were catching on rapidly, and more states began enacting similar laws.

The Centers for Disease Control and Prevention (CDC) concluded that several factors contributed to the spike in states enacting smoke-free laws. The public was made increasingly aware of the dangers of secondhand smoke and requested stricter measures to protect public health. In 2006, the Surgeon General released a report detailing the risks associated with exposure to secondhand smoke. This report influenced many state and local officials to enact smoking bans in their jurisdictions. By 2007 Arizona, New Mexico, Minnesota, Illinois, and Maryland were all smoke-free states. Iowa and Oregon enacted indoor smoking bans in 2008, with Utah, Nebraska, Vermont, Maine, and Montana not far behind in 2009. By the end of the decade, smoke-free places went from being rare to being the norm; twenty-two states were completely smoke-free indoors, and many other cities and states were considering smoking bans and restrictions.

Impact

Many organizations began conducting studies on the effects of the smoking bans. Several of these reports found a decrease in heart disease and heart attacks. An Institute of Medicine report found a link between smoking bans and reduced rates of heart disease. A CDC report confirmed these findings. While the number of states that enacted smoking bans decreased after 2009, the CDC's Office on Smoking and Health predicted that comprehensive smoking bans could impact all states by 2020.

Further Reading

Jones, Charisse. "Ban Ignites Smoking Wars in New York City." *USA Today*. Gannett, 1 July 2003. Web. 4 Dec. 2012.

Song, Sora. "Half of US States Have Enacted Indoor Smoking Bans Since 2000." *Time*. Time, 21 Apr. 2011. Web. 4 Dec. 2012.

"State Smoke-Free Laws for Worksites, Restaurants, and Bars—United States, 2000–2010." Centers for Disease Control and Prevention, 22 Apr. 2011. Web. 4 Dec. 2012.

Angela Harmon

■ Intelligent design

Definition: The belief that some biological systems are so complex that they must have been designed

Proponents of intelligent design argue some biological structures are so complex that evolution cannot explain their origin. Despite the implication of intelligent design as a religious alternative, some state boards of education have attempted to allow teaching intelligent design.

The premise of intelligent design is that some characteristics of life, including cell components such as flagella and mitochondria or blood-clotting pathways, are so complex they could not have developed through natural selection. The implication is that science cannot explain their formation. Because creationism is clearly a religious doctrine, intelligent-design proponents on some school boards have attempted to include the teaching of intelligent design in schools under the umbrella "controversial theories."

During spring 2005, the Kansas State Board of Education held a series of hearings to develop a science curriculum in which alternative theories to evolution could be included. The premise was that "intelligent design is science based," while "evolution has been proven false." Proponents of science boycotted the

hearings, allowing creationist organizations such as the Discovery Institute to dominate the meetings. Composed primarily of religious conservatives, the board voted to include references to intelligent design in the science curriculum. However in the 2006 elections, most of the supporters of the alternative measures were voted out of office; the new board returned the curriculum to one that was science-based.

In 2008, the state of Louisiana passed the Louisiana Science Education Act, which allowed teachers to teach "controversial theories," including intelligent-design alternatives to evolution, using materials not specifically proscribed within the curriculum. Such materials could include books authored by proponents of intelligent design. In response to complaints by scientists (and some educators) that endorsing intelligent design in the classroom promoted religion, the board noted that the language in the bill prevented any promotion of religious doctrine. Despite the board's contention that the purpose of the bill was to "foster critical thinking" among students about issues in addition to evolution, such as global warming, opponents of the bill maintain that it clearly represented an attempt to insert a loophole in the curriculum to misrepresent evidence supporting evolution.

Impact

In 2005, *Kitzmiller v. Dover Area School District* clearly established that teaching intelligent design as an alternative to evolutionary "theory" was a violation of the Establishment Clause of the Constitution. School boards in several states have attempted to argue that allowing the teaching of "controversies" while also including language in such bills that religious doctrine cannot be promoted addresses the separation of religion and state.

By the end of the decade, courts had not conclusively rule on the constitutionality of the process. In the absence of such guidance some secondary school teachers have altogether eliminated the teaching of evolution beyond the simplest concepts in order to avoid controversy, either from the school boards or from parents who do not want their children to hear such ideas.

Further Reading

Dembski, William, and Jonathan Witt. *Intelligent Design Uncensored: An Easy-to-Understand Guide to the Controversy*. Downers Grove: InterVarsity, 2010. Print.

Lebo, Lauri. *The Devil in Dover: An Insider's Story of Dogma v. Darwin in Small-Town America.* New York: New, 2008. Print.

Shermer, Michael. *Why Darwin Matters: The Case against Intelligent Design.* New York: Holt, 2006. Print.

Richard Adler, PhD

■ Internet marketing

Definition: Internet marketing is the process of using online tools and resources to find and attract a target audience for an organization's product or service.

Internet technologies transformed marketing from a one-way "push" broadcast endeavor to a two-way "pull" relationship using compelling content to engage consumers with brands. Search engines, e-mail, and social media played major roles in making marketing measurable, cost-effective, and consumer-oriented throughout the 2000s.

Search Engine Optimization and Marketing

Search engine optimization (SEO) and search engine marketing (SEM) efforts became critical to the business world in the 2000s. Marketers began using SEO techniques to improve their website's ranking in search results by focusing on targeted keywords, and attracting links from other web pages. Marketers also began paying search engines such as Google and Yahoo! to run advertisements next to search results for particular keywords or phrases. Pay-per-click (PPC) ads charged advertisers only when consumers actually clicked.

The top search engine marketplaces in the 2000s were Google AdWords (released in 2000), Yahoo! Search Marketing (formerly Overture, acquired by Yahoo! in 2003), and Microsoft adCenter (founded 2006). By 2008, online advertisers were spending $13.5 billion annually on search engine marketing.

Online Advertising

During the 2000s, online advertisers recognized the Internet's potential for tracking and understanding user behavior, and developed sophisticated platforms for targeting advertisements that continue to be used. Popular online advertising companies included Google's Ad Sense (founded in 2003), DoubleClick (acquired by Google in 2007), Yahoo!, Microsoft Network, AOL, Zedo (founded 1999), and AdBrite (founded in 2002).

Some common ad types were the banner ad, a wide visual advertisement, typically at the top or bottom of a site; the pop-up ad, which "popped up" or appeared in a new browser window; and interstitials, which displayed as sites loaded. As Internet speeds and technologies evolved during the 2000s, multimedia ads with animations and video grew popular. Some publishers offered "site takeovers," allowing a single advertiser to use all ad space on a given website. The content and format of multimedia web marketing continues to evolve.

Internet-based affiliate marketing also grew in popularity during the 2000s. This type of marketing allowed publishers to be paid in exchange for running embedded ad material. For example, a website discussing new eyewear trends could make money if visitors used special affiliate links on the site to purchase glasses. Affiliate payments were rendered only when a product was purchased, making it a cost-effective technique.

Online advertising grew annually from 2002 through 2008, declining in 2009, due in part to the global financial crisis. Online video ads, however, grew rapidly in 2009, posting a 40 percent improvement, indicating increased consumer engagement with multimedia content. Total online ad spending was $22.4 billion in 2009, with approximately 48.2 percent of that spent on search, 21.3 percent on banner ads, 9.9 percent on classified ads, 6.8 percent on lead generation, 6.7 percent on rich media (digital interactive media that includes dynamic motion), and 4.6 percent on video. The $22.4 billion total in 2009 was up over 275 percent from $8.1 billion in 2000.

Metrics and Targeting

Internet marketing represented an opportunity for companies to collect information not only about their target audience, but also about the effectiveness of their ads. While the effectiveness of print ads was difficult to measure, advertisers were able to easily track whether online ads were garnering a response. Vital metrics included impressions (how often ads were displayed), clicks (how often consumers clicked on an ad), and conversions (how often consumers made a purchase after clicking an ad). Online ads were tracked using "cookies," small pieces of data stored on users' computers.

Cookies were also used to track consumer behavior across the Internet, and many advertising platforms developed the ability to target advertisements on one website by using information about user behavior on another website, a function known as behavioral targeting. For example, if a user searched for a particular brand of running shoes on a retail website, advertising platforms could then display an ad for that shoe on a website that the user viewed later. Geotargeting similarly allowed advertisers to target messages about offers based on a user's geographic location.

Social Media Marketing

The advent of social media in the 2000s represented an unprecedented channel of communication for companies seeking to connect with customers and understanding their customer's needs. The most popular platforms for social media marketing included Facebook (founded 2004), Twitter (2006), LinkedIn (2003), and YouTube (2005). Each platform attracted slightly different types of users and supported slightly different marketing techniques.

On social media, brands shared information such as new product release schedules, or compelling stories of consumers using their products. Companies were able to offer special discounts to their social media followers. The ability to share purchases, review products, or discuss brands became ubiquitous. Social news sites such as Digg (2004) and Reddit (2005) allowed users to post links to specific stories and vote on them, providing another source of social media traffic. Ratings services also provided user-generated content that marketers used to promote products and services.

Blogging was another critical component of social media marketing. Easy-to-use blogging tools made it possible for consumers and marketers alike to create online content about products and services. Some marketers targeted amateur bloggers for promotions, offering free products in exchange for reviews. Businesses and marketers created Facebook pages and other blogs for their brands, posting updates and encouraging users to interact and share. This type of content creation, which included video and music work, was considered a type of "inbound marketing," designed to pull in users with interesting content.

The phenomenon of "going viral" involved online content spreading rapidly, primarily through social media. Beginning in the early 2000s, going viral became a goal for many companies. However, attempts to create "viral" videos for advertising purposes often failed, because it was often hard to produce or predict exactly what would resonate with the public enough to attain mass popularity. One successful corporate viral video series was *Will It Blend?*, wherein the blender company Blendtec portrayed its product blending everything from a cell phone to a football.

The detailed information that social media users shared about themselves helped advertisers direct ads more accurately than ever before. Social media also provided ways for ads to look less like ads. "Sponsored Tweets" looked similar to non-ad content shared on Twitter, as did "promoted posts" on Facebook.

Mobile and Local Marketing

In the late 2000s, smartphones with location-based services enabled by global positioning software (GPS) began to open up additional channels for online marketing. Marketers developed campaigns targeted for display on mobile devices, and sent local offers to consumers in a specific geographic location. Although only about 20 percent of the United States had smartphones at the end of 2009, the adoption rate is growing quickly and mobile is poised to become a big marketing channel.

Impact

During the 2000s, internet marketing, and social media in particular, transformed marketing into a conversation with customers, and provided marketers with an unprecedented amount of data about their audience that is now used to target, test, and evaluate multimedia marketing messages across online platforms.

Kerry Skemp, MA

Further Reading

Blanchard, Olivier. *Social Media ROI: Managing and Measuring Social Media Efforts in Your Organization.* Indianapolis: Que, 2011. Print. Describes how to manage and measure social marketing campaigns for organizations and businesses.

Fox, Scott. *Click Millionaires: Work Less, Live More with an Internet Business You Love.* New York: AMACOM, 2012. Print. A guide for entrepreneurs interested in setting up their own e-commerce businesses.

Kabani, Shama Hyder. *The Zen of Social Media Marketing: An Easier Way to Build Credibility, Generate Buzz, and Increase Revenue.* Dallas: BenBella, 2012. Print. Explains how to use social media platforms to connect to customers and clients.

Kerpen, David. *Likeable Social Media: How to Delight Your Customers, Create an Irresistable Brand, and Be Generally Amazing on Facebook (and Other Social Networks).* New York: McGraw, 2011. Print. Instructions for using word-of-mouth marketing to promote businesses.

Li, Charlene and Josh Bernoff. *Groundswell, Expanded and Revised Edition: Winning in a World Transformed by Social Technologies.* Cambridge: Harvard Business Rev. P, 2011. Print. An instructive and current social media how-to manual. Includes case studies and graphic charts.

■ Internet memes

Definition: An idea or image, commonly consisting of humorous photos or phrases, that spreads rapidly across the Internet

Evolutionary biologist Richard Dawkins first coined the term meme *in 1976. He used it to describe an idea that organically reproduces and spreads throughout a society. Through the Internet, memes are able to spread quickly and reach millions of online users within hours. There is seemingly no limit to what a meme can be. Videos, websites, parodies, phrases, photos, and other online items are all considered Internet memes. Marketing agencies quickly began utilizing memes to promote various products, shows, and films.*

Online Origins and Popular Memes

Internet memes began as websites that were made popular through word of mouth and online sharing. One of the earliest examples of a meme website is the Hamster Dance, which debuted in 1998 and featured graphics interchange formats (GIFs) of animated hamsters dancing to a looped song. The first website meme to become massively popular in the 2000s was the website Hot or Not, which launched in October 2000. The website allows users to upload their photos and have other users rate their attractiveness. Within a week, Hot or Not was receiving nearly two million hits a day.

One of the first Internet memes that was not a website is the flash animation "Peanut Butter Jelly Time!" The video became hugely popular in 2002 and featured a cartoon banana dancing to a song of the same name. In March 2001, the phrase "All Your Base Are Belong to Us" became the next big Internet meme. This phrase was taken from a Japanese video game that was produced in the 1990s in which a character speaks the poorly translated phrase. The phrase was accompanied by a brief video and was quickly embraced by online humorists and video game enthusiasts.

In 2005 the video sharing website YouTube was launched, allowing for video memes to spread even faster through email, blogs, and social media. YouTube also led to meme comedy series, which were ongoing memes in the form of short films. One of the first of these popular memes was Ask a Ninja. This series featured a ninja, portrayed by cocreator Douglas Sarine, who answered questions. Another video meme series that was popular on YouTube was *lonelygirl15*. This series premiered in June 2006 and ran until August 2008. The series featured a fictional teenage girl named Bree who was played by actress Jessica Lee Rose. The show was presented as Bree's video blog and it was not until September 2006 that the series was revealed to be fictional. The series received over 110 million combined views and was applauded for being one of the first online drama series.

LOLCats

Possibly the most successful and influential meme of the 2000s was the phenomenon of LOLCats. A LOLCat is an image of a cat with humorous text attached to it. The text, known as LOLSpeak, is written in a misspelled, quirky manner, as if a cat were the one writing it. The name comes from the online acronym *LOL*, for "laughing out loud." While the term LOLCat first surfaced on the Internet in 2005, the memes did not become immensely popular until January 2007 when the website I Can Has Cheezburger was launched to aggregate these images.

After its launch, the website, created by Hawaiian bloggers Eric Nakagawa and Kari Unebasami, was quickly receiving over one million views per day. It is credited with creating the popular animal-based memes that use LOLSpeak. According to its owners, by July 2007 the website was receiving nearly five hundred submissions per day. In September 2007 the website was acquired by investors for $2 million. The popularity of LOLCats and other animal photos with LOLSpeak continued strong through the end of the decade.

Marketing through Memes

Marketing experts utilized memes throughout the decade to advertise a variety of products, media, TV shows, films, and more. Memes created to market a product can spread organically through social media and other online outlets at no cost to the advertiser. Other advertisers adopted memes that were already popular online to incorporate the image or phrase into more traditional advertisements. As the meme becomes more popular, the source website will increasingly come up on Internet search engines such as Google, making whatever product or service the meme is advertising more popular. All of these reasons made Internet memes a very popular tool in the 2000s.

Some of the more successful advertising memes of the 2000s were the commercials created for FreeCreditReport, a personal credit score website. The commercial featured a band singing humorous songs about their poor credit. The advertising began in October 2007 and the commercials quickly spread online. Several parodies of the commercials were uploaded soon after.

Another successful meme marketing campaign is *Will It Blend?*, a series of humorous infomercials created by blender manufacturer Blendtec. The first infomercial was uploaded to YouTube on October 30, 2006 and became an instant success. The series stars creator Tom Dickson; in each episode Dickson attempts to blend an item consumers would not normally put into a blender in order to demonstrate his product's strength. These items include golf balls, marbles, and cell phones. Dickson went on to make national television appearances and the *Will It Blend?* series has received tens of millions of views.

Impact

Internet memes continually helped shape popular culture and marketing in the 2000s. Although many memes were spread through the Internet solely for comedic purposes, many of them were embraced by advertisers as inexpensive promotional tools for branding and marketing. Memes helped make ordinary people into overnight celeb-rities and, in the case of LOLCats, millionaires. There is no exact science to making a meme popular, but those creative and lucky enough were able to make their mark on popular culture.

Further Reading

Pogue, David. "Internet Memes 101: A Guide to Online Wackiness." *Pogue's Posts.* New York Times Co., 8 Sept. 2011. Web. 9 Nov. 2012. This article looks at popular Internet memes from the 2000s to 2011.

Sax, David. "The Growing Power of the Meme." *Bloomberg Businessweek.* Bloomberg LP, 14 June 2012. Web. 9 Nov. 2012. This article looks at advertising through memes and various meme campaigns.

Sternbergh, Adam. "Hey There, Lonelygirl." *New York Magazine.* New York Media LLC, 20 Aug. 2006. Web. 9 Nov. 2012. This article examines the phenomenon of the *lonelygirl15* meme series and its impact on popular culture.

Tozzi, John. "Bloggers Bring in the Big Bucks." *Bloomberg Businessweek.* Bloomberg LP, 13 July 2007. Web. 9 Nov. 2012. This article talks about the financial success of the creators of I Can Has Cheezburger website.

Wortham, Jenna. "Behind the Memes: Kickin' It With the I Can Has Cheezburger? Kids." *Wired Magazine.* Condé Nast, 25 Apr. 2008. Web. 9 Nov. 2012. This article presents an interview with the creators of the "I Can Has Cheezburger" meme.

Patrick G. Cooper

■ Inventions

Definition: A device or process created through experiment and research that often results in the development of consumer products, while others impact scientific or medical investigation and discovery

Inventions can dramatically shape the development of human culture in new and novel ways. During the 2000s, the development of Internet technology and personal electronics had a major impact on commerce, education, and communication across the world. Other inventions of the decade substantively altered fields such as medicine, transportation, and the scientific understanding of the universe.

Internet and Personal Technology

During the 1990s, the Internet morphed from a communications network used largely by computer science professionals and institutions into a global communications phenomenon used by millions around the globe. Contributing to the rapid spread and dominant importance of the Internet as a tool for communication and commerce were a number of key inventions that attracted a growing number of users to the online community.

Social networking was not invented during the 2000s, but online social networks created during the decade transformed social networking from a niche interest into a major global form of communications with numbers of users rivaling email and cellular telephone communication. The invention of the social networking site Friendster in 2000, followed by MySpace in 2001 and Facebook in 2004 attracted thousands of new users to the Internet. Personal networking sites allowed users to communicate with friends, but also became a powerful marketing tool for businesses and entrepreneurs looking to promote new products or ideas. By the end of the decade, Facebook was the largest social networking site in the world with more than 500 million users.

The invention of YouTube, a video-sharing website that allows users to post videos and to comment on videos posted by other users, was another of the major Internet inventions of the 2000s. Created by three independent engineers in 2005, the popularity of YouTube expanded rapidly during the year and the site was hailed as one of the leading technological innovations of the year by *Time* magazine. In 2006, Google Inc. purchased YouTube for more than $1.5 billion and has since operated the site as a subsidiary company.

The Apple iPhone. (Courtesy Biz Stone)

During the course of the decade, YouTube grew far beyond its initial function as a site for social interaction and became a powerful tool for education and marketing. By the end of the decade, YouTube was used by a variety of companies to promote products, music, films, and political issues. The website was successfully used for advertising in the 2008 campaign of President Barack Obama, whose videos reached millions of Internet users.

Another major Internet innovation of the decade was Wikipedia—an online, user-generated encyclopedia—which debuted in 2001 and has since compiled millions of entries covering a wealth of human knowledge. Wikipedia has largely supplanted traditional encyclopedias as standard popular reference for a variety of topics, though the information offered through Wikipedia has not been sufficiently edited or verified such that the online encyclopedia can be considered a reliable source. Despite some uncertainty regarding the information offered through the site, Wikipedia represents a novel innovation, allowing users to both submit information and to edit and criticize each other's additions to the database, thereby providing a built-in system for correction fueled by a collective interest in creating a reliable database for free information.

Recording and film production companies started experimenting with digital audio and video in the 1970s and the use of digital film and audio expanded in the 1980s. In the 1990s audio engineers developed the MP3 format for audio files, which opened the door to a new era in music storage and transfer, allowing individuals to store and enjoy their music from digital storage modules built into MP3 players and home computers rather than storing music on external media, like compact discs (CDs).

Though personal digital music players became available in the 1990s, it was not until the debut of the iPod, from Apple Inc., in 2001 that personal digital music players gained widespread acceptance. Thanks largely to the marketing created by Apple for the iPod, interest in digital music grew rapidly during the decade and a number of prominent music purveyors adopted digital downloads to their basic sales format. In 2011, sales of digital music in the United States eclipsed compact disk and vinyl sales for the first time and, while industry experts believed that CD sales would remain an important part of the market for the next decade, most believe that digital downloads will eventually make CD technology obsolete.

Another major innovation of the decade was the invention of the smartphone, a device that combines personal computing technology with cellular phone capabilities. The first device available in the United States was the Kyocera 6035, which debuted in 2001. Other devices followed, including the open source Android platform released in 2003 and supported by funding from Google Inc. The release of Apple's iPhone in 2007 changed the market for smartphones considerably, as Apple's success in marketing and their popular interface helped to make Apple's iPhone the most popular smartphone on the market. By the end of the decade, smartphones were becoming the standard in cellular technology and most of the new phones released by major manufacturers were able to handle limited data and web browsing in addition to cellular and text communication.

Medicine and Personal Health

Medical research contributes new and groundbreaking inventions each year though few of the innovations emerging from medical technology become well known publicly. Within each decade, a select few medical innovations gain widespread recognition for their overall impact on health care.

Among the more notable medical innovations of the 2000s was the AbioCor artificial heart, which was implanted in the first human patient in 2001. The Massachusetts-based AbioCor company spent more than thirty years in development and testing before the first artificial heart was deemed safe for implant. The AbioCor artificial heart was the first self-contained artificial heart on the market and symbolized, for many in the medical profession, a new age of medical engineering, which could eventually lead to permanent artificial replacements for key organs.

Another invention that gained widespread popularity during the decade was the contraceptive patch Ortho Evra from Ortho-McNeil Pharmaceuticals in 2002. The Ortho Evra patch requires weekly application and was the first contraceptive alternative proven to be as effective as birth control pills, but without daily application. Millions of users switched to the birth control patch during the decade. The patch was advertised as being as safe as the birth control pill, however, in 2009 research revealed that, because the patch exposes users to higher levels of estrogen than birth control pills, users suffer from increased risk of blood clots. The overall importance of the birth control patch may also be in the future potential for topical medical treatment as an alternative to medicines ingested through the digestive system.

Vehicular and Automotive Technology

Automotive giant Toyota permanently altered the automotive industry with the introduction of the first hybrid fuel cell car in 2000, the Toyota Prius. The Prius uses a dual electric/fuel propulsion system, which allows the driver to run the engine using an electric battery, and then to switch to utilizing fuel as the battery power diminishes. The car can also be plugged into an outlet to charge the battery. Electric hybrid cars provide better gas mileage and produce fewer emissions than standard automobiles and represent an initial effort on the part of the automobile industry to address growing environmental concerns over automobile emissions and the cost of petroleum.

Hybrid cars gained acceptance during the decade, and Toyota remained one of the most popular companies offering hybrid vehicles, with several additional iterations of the Prius following the company's initial release. By 2012, Toyota had sold more than 2.5 million units to the general public. Other automobile companies including Honda, Dodge, Ford, and Cadillac also began offering hybrid vehicles to consumers during the decade. Though hybrid vehicles have been advertised as an "environmentally friendly" alternative to standard automobiles, some environmentalists contend that hybrid cars still produce high levels of pollution and argue that the automotive industry should shift toward dedicated, all-electric designs.

The Segway was an innovative two-wheeled, battery-powered vehicle released to the public in 2001 from inventor Dean Kamen. Utilizing innovative self-balancing technology in addition to battery power, the Segway provides a transportation alternative unlike any other product and became popular as a touring device for companies offering guided Segway tours through popular tourist spots. Philadelphia, New York, and San Francisco are three of many cities that have Segway tour companies operating within city limits.

Though Segway inventor Dean Kamen and allied organizations have lobbied for the Segway to be listed as a vehicular aid for persons with disabilities, the device was not approved as such by the Food and Drug Administration (FDA) by the end of the decade. In addition, some states and municipalities across the United States banned Segways on public sidewalks for safety concerns, though the devices can be used on bike lanes and along slow moving roads within most states. In 2010, James W. Heselden, owner of Segway Inc., died in an accident while riding a Segway, raising further questions about the safety concerns associated with the vehicle.

Science Exploration

In 2004, NASA engineers and scientists began working on what would become the next generation of space flight technology. The result of this research program was the new Ares rocket system, which was unveiled to the public in 2009 with an unmanned test flight. The Ares rocket utilizes a substantially different design than the rockets used to power Space Shuttle missions in previous decades, with upgraded sensors, engines, and fuel containment technology to make the new generation of rockets safer and more powerful than any previously utilized for space travel. In recognition of the technological advancements used in the design of the rocket, *Time* magazine named the Ares rocket the best invention of 2009.

While NASA is working on the next generation of shuttles to carry astronauts into space, research and development continues on the Ares rocket system, which is intended to make it possible for NASA to conduct the first manned trip to Mars, though tentative dates for this exploratory mission are far from being determined. At present, NASA intends to use Ares rockets to send astronauts to the moon by 2021, though an earlier date is possible. Industry analysts say that the Ares system represents a major advancement in space flight technology and is the first in what will likely become the future of propulsion systems for decades.

Impact

Though Internet and information technology expanded rapidly in the 1990s, the first decade of the 2000s saw many of the major innovations that transformed the Internet into the most important technological innovation of the era. During the course of the decade, Internet sites like YouTube, Facebook, and Wikipedia helped to transform the Internet into the most important and wide-reaching global platform for communication and information. During this same period, technological inventions including smartphones facilitated access to Internet data and information and contributed to a rapid expansion of information technology during the decade. These inventions and innovations were the cornerstones of a new global technology market that became one of the dominant facets of global consumerism.

While innovations in personal and communication technology will likely leave the most lasting mark in the history of the decade, inventions from a variety of other fields also had major impacts on human life, including a number of key medical breakthroughs and scientific discoveries. Research into the nature and sequence of the human genome, though not representative of any single invention during the decade, was one of the most significant scientific discoveries of the period and contributed to a variety of further developments in both medicine and science technology. Human genetics research is likely to lead to many more technological innovations in the next decade as scientists and physicians utilize genetics to refine and develop new treatments and genetic technologies.

Further Reading

"Best Inventions of 2001." *Time*. Time, 19 Nov. 2001. Web. 16 Nov. 2012. Brief articles from *Time* magazine that discuss the best inventions of 2001 and include a discussion of the AbioCor artificial heart and a variety of other key 2001 inventions.

Heussner, Ki Mae. "The Top 10 Innovations of the Decade." *ABC News*. ABC News Network, 1 Dec. 2009. Web. 4 Dec. 2012. Discusses ten inventions from the 2000s and their effect on daily life, including GPS devices, text messaging, and Google.

Kluger, Jeffrey. "The Best Inventions of the Year: NASA's Ares Rockets." *Time*. Time, 12 Nov. 2009. Web. 16 Nov. 2012. Presents some of the basic facets of NASA's Ares rocket system and discusses the significance of the system for future space travel technology.

Long, K. F. *Deep Space Propulsion: A Roadmap to Interstellar Flight*, New York: Springer, 2012. Print. Covers the future of space travel and space technology, including the design and future plants for the Ares rocket system.

Rosenweig, Roy, and Anthony Grafton. *Clio Wired: The Future of the Past in the Digital Age*. New York: Columbia UP, 2011. Print. Covers the history and potential future developments in Internet

technology as well as mobile, Internet accessible devices.

Wei, James. *Great Inventions that Changed the World*. Hoboken: Wiley, 2012. Print. Includes a discussion about the historical processes leading to some of the most important inventions of the twentieth and twenty-first centuries. Also discusses aspects involved in the process of invention.

Micah L. Issit

■ iPhone

Definition: A popular smartphone designed by Apple that offers Internet access and the ability to download mobile applications developed by users

The iPhone transformed wireless communications and brought smartphone usage to the mainstream, all while securing record profits for Apple. In many ways, the iPhone set industry standards for smartphones throughout the 2000s, although Apple nevertheless drew criticism for its aggressive patenting and marketing practices.

The iPhone was announced by Apple in January 2007 and made available for sale in June of that year. Its appealing design, aggressive marketing, and ease of use made the iPhone the first smartphone to gain widespread consumer adoption. The iPod, an MP3 player released by Apple in 2001, had already attracted many consumers to use Apple products, setting the stage for the iPhone's popularity. After a failed collaboration with Motorola on the ROKR E1 music phone in 2005, Apple decided to design its own phone internally. The project started in 2005 and reportedly cost $150 million to develop.

Notable iPhone features included a glass touch screen (most phones at the time had plastic screens), unprecedented support for multitouch interactions and gestures, aluminum backing, 2.0-megapixel camera, an accelerometer to adjust orientation, web browsing, visual voicemail, and a music player that integrated with iTunes, Apple's online music store. The iPhone was billed as a phone, web browser, and iPod all in one. The first iPhone offered GSM/EDGE cellular network access, Bluetooth wireless connectivity, and Wi-Fi, and could initially be purchased with 4 or 8 gigabytes of memory for $499 or $599 respectively (a pricier 16-gigabyte model was added later).

The iPhone was initially available only on the AT&T cellular network, frustrating consumers under contract with other providers. Apple arranged a revenue-sharing agreement with AT&T for a cut of every customer's monthly plan, and the iPhone's popularity empowered cell phone manufacturers in negotiating deals with wireless carriers. The original iPhone was an immediate and sustained success. Consumers waited in long lines on release day, and the phone sold rapidly, moving nearly two million units by the end of 2007. By the fourth quarter of 2008, Apple was selling nearly seven million iPhones each quarter, and twenty-one million iPhones had been sold internationally by the end of 2009.

Later models of the iPhone include the iPhone 3G, which was released in June 2008 with 3G, third generation telecommunications technology, and assisted global positioning system (A-GPS) capabilities. The iPhone 3 GS came out in June 2009, adding a compass, 3.2-megapixel video camera, and improved processing speeds. Some have criticized Apple for building "planned obsolescence" into devices with its frequent new releases. Apple also drew criticism after several companies that manufactured iPhone components, most notably Foxconn in China, were investigated for deplorable working conditions.

Impact

The iPhone transformed consumer expectations regarding mobile communications devices, disrupted the wireless industry, and opened up mobile application development. *Time* magazine named the iPhone the invention of the year in 2007. By the end of 2009, Apple had captured approximately 15 percent of the global smartphone market, and nearly 50 percent of the profits thanks to the device's relatively high price.

Further Reading

Edson, John. *Design Like Apple: Seven Principles For Creating Insanely Great Products, Services, and Experiences.* Hoboken: Wiley, 2012. Print.

Pogue, David. *iPhone: The Missing Manual.* Sebastopol: O'Reilly, 2012. Print.

Wooldridge, Dave, and Michael Schneider. *The Business of iPhone and iPad App Development: Making and Marketing Apps that Succeed.* New York: Apress, 2011. Print.

Kerry Skemp, MA

■ iPod

Definition: A line of digital media players manufactured by Apple

The iPod, one of the most innovative products in history, has been more than a convenient tool used for entertainment. It not only became the symbol of the digital music revolution, of personal success, and of corporate loyalty, but also an icon for an entire generation and their file-sharing habits, legal or otherwise.

Apple introduced its first iPod in October 2001, when the portable digital music player industry was still in its infancy. At the time, players had tiny storage capacities of just ten or fifteen songs, were compatible only with Microsoft Windows, and had either retained the same round shape of the portable CD player (Creative Nomad Jukebox) or the clunky rectangular shape associated with the antiquated Sony Walkman (Sensory Sciences Rave MP 2200). On the other hand, the iPod had been designed exclusively for Macintosh users. It was about the size of a deck of cards, with a pioneering scroll wheel for navigation and two-inch LCD screen that displayed the song and artist. Sleek, futuristic looking, and intuitive, its five gigabytes could hold one thousand songs—a mind-boggling feat at the time. While the cost of $399 was prohibitive for many consumers, the first iPod and the ten-gigabyte model that came out a few months later generated so much interest that Apple continued to refine its design.

Apple iPods. (Courtesy redjar)

From then on, a new model, or "generation," appeared on the market each year, featuring more storage capacity, a new color palette, enhanced navigation design, and other upgrades. Apple began offering new models as well: the iPod mini (January 2004), iPod photo (October 2004), iPod shuffle (January 2005), iPod nano (September 2005), and the iPod touch (September 2007). As is common with guitars or tennis rackets, Apple also released special edition iPods, endorsed by music artists U2, Madonna, and Elton John, among others. Much of Apple's success was tied to their iTunes Music Store, launched in April 2003, with songs available only in the newer, higher quality M4A files. As only Apple products could play M4A files at the time, Apple's proprietary decision caused some divisiveness among audio enthusiasts and antagonism toward the corporation. Still, with little competition, Apple cornered the market and continued to dominate it even after Microsoft introduced the Zune in September 2006. In April 2007, Apple announced the sale of the one hundred millionth iPod.

Impact

The iPod's design immediately became the standard for portable audio players and was widely copied by other manufacturers. Even though the Zune, SanDisk's Sansa Fuze, and other models were comparable in quality and considered better buys for the budget-minded consumer, none came close to the popularity of the iPod. By then, the iPod had come to represent an entire generation, accompanying the millenials as they walked across campus, worked out at fitness centers, or traveled in airplanes—while also symbolizing the sometimes-illegal file-sharing habits that had shaken the music industry. In addition, the iPod had revolutionized an entire industry with audio products and accessories that did not exist before 2001.

Further Reading

Buckley, Peter. *The Rough Guide to iPods & iTunes*. 6th ed. London: Rough Guides, 2009. Print.

Levy, Steven. "iPod Nation." *Newsweek*. Newsweek/ Daily Beast Company, 25 July 2004. Web. 11 Sept. 2012.

Sally Driscoll

■ Iraq and Afghanistan War veterans

Definition: Veterans from any branch of the military who took part in the conflicts in Iraq and Afghanistan, which were spurred by the September 11, 2001, terrorist attacks on the United States

Regardless whether they suffer physical or emotional trauma from their service, Iraq and Afghanistan War veterans confront numerous challenges when returning to civilian life, including obtaining employment and finding housing. Public response to veterans' needs in the 2000s indicates a shift from the widespread anti-troop sentiment expressed during and after late twentieth-century conflicts.

On September 11, 2001, Islamic extremists from the fundamentalist group al-Qaeda hijacked four planes and attacked several buildings in the United States, destroying the World Trade Center towers in New York City, damaging the Pentagon, and killing almost three thousand American civilians. On September 18, US president George W. Bush signed a joint resolution permitting the use of force in order to combat terrorism; this led to the bombing of Afghanistan to target the Taliban government, which was protecting al-Qaeda. After the initial destabilization of the Afghan government, the United Nations set up a provisional government and established the International Security Assistance Force (ISAF) in December 2001. In 2002, ground forces were sent into Afghanistan to try to locate terrorist cells in the mountain caves. The War on Terror, as it came to be known, was accompanied by the 2003 invasion of Iraq, in which Iraqi dictator Saddam Hussein was ousted. Hussein was alleged to have had connections to several terrorist organizations, including al-Qaeda, and have possessed weapons of mass destruction. Both claims were later disproved.

President Bush and Secretary of Defense Donald Rumsfeld declared that "major combat" was over in Afghanistan and Iraq by May 2003, but troops remained in order to rebuild infrastructure and support the government and local security forces. Violence continued to escalate through 2000s, especially in the form of suicide bombings. Thus, in 2009, newly elected US president Barack Obama promised to rededicate and reorganize efforts overseas. With an increased amount of monetary aid heading to Pakistan, new commanders in Afghanistan, and five thousand additional NATO troops, a new "focused counterinsurgency strategy" was implemented in the region. In December 2009, President Obama declared that thirty thousand more troops would be sent to Afghanistan (in addition to the sixty-eight thousand already there), with the intent of training Afghan security more effectively and creating the conditions that would allow the United States to begin pulling out troops in July 2011.

Problems Facing Returning Veterans

While most veterans leave the service and return to civilian life without too many lasting detriments from their time overseas, they have unique challenges that most of the population do not understand. The 2.4 million veterans who served in Iraq and/or Afghanistan make up only about 1 percent of the total population.

One of the largest and most difficult problems that troops face after deployment is post-traumatic stress disorder (PTSD), which can vary in intensity from mild to extreme cases in which the sufferer has difficulty distinguishing friend from foe. A 2011 Pew Research Center poll reported that 37 percent of Iraq and Afghanistan veterans, who may or may not have received formal diagnoses, had suffered PTSD symptoms. According to a 2009 study by Michael P. Atkinson, Adam Guetz, and Lawrence M. Wein, risk of developing PTSD increased significantly for service members who were deployed multiple times. The determination of whether a soldier has the condition varies, depending on several factors such as when they are examined. Because symptoms do not always appear immediately or present in the same manner, diagnosing the condition can be difficult. Other factors such as combat fatigue and separation from family are among other issues that service members face, both before and after deployment, and can lead to a very fragile mental state.

Traumatic brain injuries (TBIs) also became common during these wars. Many former service members were left with speech, memory, and/or motor impairment, as well as emotional problems, due to TBIs. TBIs and PTSD were frequently blamed for the increase in suicide among both active-duty and discharged service members; between 2005 and 2010, one service member committed suicide every thirty-six hours.

Abuse of opiates and narcotics has been a particular problem among service members and veterans

of the Iraq and Afghanistan wars, including those who have incurred severe injuries and those with PTSD. Between 2005 and 2010, over fifteen thousand veterans had been prescribed opiates for pain, among them nearly three thousand PTSD sufferers and over eighteen hundred with non-PTSD mental health concerns. Untreated withdrawal from these and other battlefield prescriptions has led a significant number of veterans to seek out drugs illegally upon their return to civilian life and to committing petty crimes. A program known as the Veterans Court has begun in Philadelphia to stem the rise in crime committed by veterans, many of whom are addicted to drugs or alcohol and have untreated mental health issues. Through probation, community service with veterans' support groups, and rehabilitation or counseling for offenders, the Veterans Court is helping reduce recidivism.

Sexual violence against female service members is a newer wartime phenomenon, and it places female veterans at increased risk of self-harm. In 2010, nearly a third of female service members said they had been victims of assault during their term of service, though far fewer had reported it to officials. This, along with emotional strain and higher incidence of PTSD, likely contributes to the statistic showing that the risk of suicide among female veterans is threefold higher than that for female civilians.

Despite Department of Veterans Affairs' home loans and housing assistance, homelessness has long plagued returning service members, and Iraq and Afghanistan war veterans are joining the ranks of the homeless in large numbers. By 2011, veterans made up 16 percent of the total adult homeless population, and of these, young veterans were far more likely to be homeless than their counterparts in the greater communities. Between 2006 and 2010, the number of women veterans who were homeless soared, rising by 141 percent.

Support Networks

Even the service members who return home and are able to deal with their experiences without severe negative impacts on their lives face issues that make reintegration into civilian society difficult; more than 40 percent of recent veterans report difficulty with reentry. Especially with the economic crisis of the last part of the decade, veterans have trouble finding work, and nearly a third are unemployed. Veteran support groups, such as the Iraq and Afghanistan

Veterans of America (IAVA) and Veterans for Common Sense, assist veterans with finding jobs, obtaining health insurance, and pursuing higher education. The IAVA, established in 2004, is not only committed to helping veterans build a community for themselves when they return home, but also connecting them to other veterans who have had similar experiences. While healthy service members previously had little organized support once they left the military, these types of support groups keep growing in number and influence.

Service members who are seriously injured or mentally unstable used to face a similar position upon discharge from the military and from whichever hospital they recuperated in. After returning home, most veterans could only receive help from the Department of Veterans Affairs offices and medical centers, which were often underfunded and located far from veterans' homes. New programs, such as the Wounded Warriors Project, which was founded in 2003, are filling in the gaps by providing rehabilitation services, higher education, employment training and placement assistance, and peer mentoring for veterans who have serious physical or mental issues. Like the IAVA, the Wounded Warriors Project also advocates for pro-veteran government policies and aims to raise public awareness of veterans' issues and funds for support services. By creating an atmosphere of support and teaching veterans how to aid one another, these programs help service members grow and relearn their strength and independence.

Impact
The increase in public support for returning service members may be a direct result from disrespect and lack of compassion often shown veterans from other conflicts, namely the Vietnam War. In the 2000s, those who did not agree with US involvement in the Middle East were more likely to distinguish between the wars and the troops fighting them. Even those who supported the wars themselves were glad to see troops withdrawn from Iraq; about three-quarters of those polled by the Pew Research Center supported the move. Over 90 percent of survey respondents also indicated they felt proud of the troops, and 75 percent had thanked service members for their efforts.

Despite the warm feelings the American public had for its troops, veterans and civilians alike recog-

nized the disparities between themselves. Over 80 percent of recent veterans polled said that the public does not understand their challenges, making the public-awareness campaigns of veterans' support groups all the more important. Government and military officials have also increased efforts to address the problems of active-duty service members and veterans. Among these are better screening for and treatment of psychological problems, facilitating reporting and prosecution of sexual violence within the military, cracking down on for-profit educational institutions that mislead veterans about employment prospects, and giving incentives to companies that hire veterans.

Further Reading
The 9/11 Commission Report: Final Report of the National Commission on Terrorist Attacks upon the United States. Washington: GPO, July 2004. PDF file. The official US governmental report on the terrorist attacks that prompted US involvement in the Middle East.

Iraq and Afghanistan Veterans of America. IAVA.org, 2011. Web. 5 Dec. 2012. Website of one of the support groups for returning veterans, detailing their mission and activities.

"Mission." *Wounded Warriors Project.* Wounded Warriors Project, Inc., 2011. Web. 5 Dec. 2012. Explains the purpose and mission of Wounded Warrior Project and how they seek to help injured service members.

"Obama's Address to the Nation on the Way Forward in Afghanistan and Pakistan December 2009." *Council on Foreign Relations.* Council on Foreign Relations, 1 Dec. 2009. Web. 5 Dec. 2012. A transcript of President Obama's speech to the nation outlining his goals and actions concerning troop deployment in the Middle East.

"US War in Afghanistan: Tracking a War (1999–Present)." *Council on Foreign Relations.* Council on Foreign Relations, 2012. Web. 5 Dec. 2012. A timeline showing events leading up to the war and during the decade.

"War and Sacrifice in the Post-9/11 Era: The Military-Civilian Gap." *Pew Social & Demographic Trends.* Pew Research Center, 5 Oct. 2011. Web. 5 Dec. 2012. A survey of service members, veterans, and civilians regarding various aspects of the post–September 11 wars and military service.

Anna Accettola, MA

■ Iraq Resolution (2002)

The Law: Federal legislation authorizing the use of military force against Iraq
Date: Enacted on October 16, 2002
Also known as: Authorization for Use of Military Force against Iraq Resolution of 2002

The Iraq Resolution gave President George W. Bush authority to use military force against Iraq to enforce United Nations sanctions and to remove the threat to the United States posed by Iraq's weapons of mass destruction.

Almost immediately after terrorist attacks against American targets on September 11, 2001, President George W. Bush and his administration initiated a campaign to link Iraq's repressive dictator Saddam Hussein with terrorist groups and to convince the American public that regime change in Iraq was necessary for the continuing security of the United States. Playing on the American public's fears of another attack on US soil, senior administration officials laid out a scenario in which the country appeared vulnerable if immediate action against Iraq were not taken. Although the United Nations had already passed a series of resolutions to punish Iraq for repeated violations of treaties and basic human rights, President Bush insisted that only armed intervention would relieve the imminent threat posed by Saddam Hussein. Under the 1973 War Powers Act, however, use of military force required congressional approval. Hence, during the spring and summer of 2002, the Bush administration made public its rationale for seeking a resolution authorizing the president to employ armed forces against Iraq.

Convincing Congress to Act
During the summer of 2002, the Bush administration began making serious charges about the threat Iraq posed to the safety of the United States, principally because of Saddam Hussein's aggressive pursuit of weapons of mass destruction. Administration officials, led by Vice President Richard Cheney and Secretary of Defense Donald Rumsfeld, vigorously argued that Iraq had consistently ignored UN sanctions imposed after the Gulf War of 1991. Furthermore, they claimed that Saddam Hussein was providing significant aid to terrorist organizations such as the one that had attacked the United States in September 2001. President Bush made his case for armed intervention in Iraq before the UN General Assembly on September 12, 2002, but even before that informed Congress that he wished to obtain authority to use force against Iraq if he deemed such action necessary.

A week after addressing the United Nations, President Bush sent congressional leaders a draft resolution that would grant him authority to employ military force throughout the Middle East. Neither the House nor the Senate agreed to give the president such wide authority; instead, revisions limited the scope of any military action to Iraq. Although some in Congress, particularly Democratic Senator Robert Byrd, thought more time was needed to consider the measure, the resolution was brought up for vote in the Senate on September 26 and in the House on October 2. After debating several additional amendments, on October 10 the House voted 296 to 133 in favor of the resolution; the next day the Senate adopted it by a margin of 77 to 23.

Elements of the Resolution
The Joint Resolution to Authorize the Use of United States Armed Forces against Iraq cites several reasons as the primary justification for action: Saddam Hussein's government had repeatedly violated the United Nations cease-fire agreement, which it had signed to end the first Iraq conflict; it had thwarted efforts of UN inspectors to verify the destruction of its weapons of mass destruction; it had continued to repress its own people; and it harbored international terrorists. Furthermore, Saddam Hussein had displayed aggressive behavior toward the United States by attempting to assassinate President George H. W. Bush in 1993, and he had demonstrated willingness to use weapons of mass destruction in a previous war against Iran. Citing the many UN resolutions calling for action to restrain Iraq's bellicose intentions and the possibility that Iraq could launch an attack on the United States at any moment, the resolution authorized the president to "use the Armed Forces of the United States as he determines to be necessary and appropriate" to defend the nation against threats from Iraq, and to "enforce all relevant UN Security Council resolutions regarding Iraq." The resolution required the president to report periodically to Congress on his actions; in return, Congress acknowledged that it was granting the president authority under the War Powers Resolution of 1973 to declare war whenever he thought appropriate.

Impact

The immediate result of the passage of the Iraq Resolution was to free President Bush to pursue war against Iraq without having to obtain further authority from Congress. Although some in the United States and overseas urged the president to seek UN approval for an invasion, over the next six months the Bush administration built up military forces and continued its public relations campaign to convince Americans that war was both inevitable and justified. Nevertheless, even as preparations for war were being made and the invasion launched in March 2003, information became public that some of the intelligence used to justify war against Iraq was either unreliable or incorrect. Many in Congress and across the country began suggesting that hardliners in President Bush's inner circle had ignored warnings from the intelligence community about the tenuous nature of some claims about Iraq's capabilities or intentions. As a result, several investigations were launched into the administration's conduct in negotiating passage of the resolution. Calls for the president's impeachment were raised, although no action was taken before President Bush left office in 2008.

Further Reading

Bonn, Scott A. *Mass Deception: Moral Panic and the US War on Iraq.* New Brunswick: Rutgers UP, 2010. Print. Harsh critique of the Bush administration's campaign to create panic among Americans as a means of justifying war with Iraq.

Grimmett, Richard F. *The War Powers Resolution: After Thirty Years.* Ed. Gerald M. Perkins. Washington, DC: Congressional Research Service, 2004. Print. Examines elements of the Iraq War Resolution and explains its relation to the War Powers Resolution of 1973.

Harvey, Frank P. *Explaining the Iraq War.* Cambridge: Cambridge UP, 2012. Print. Challenges arguments that the Bush administration ran roughshod over Congress and duped the American people in its rush to wage war with Iraq.

Pfiffner, James P. *Intelligence and National Security Policymaking on Iraq: British and American Perspectives.* College Station: Texas A&M UP, 2008. Print. Contains lengthy analysis of the arguments made by the Bush administration to convince Congress and the public that war with Iraq was in the interests of national security.

Pillar, Paul R. "Intelligence, Policy, and the War in Iraq." *Foreign Affairs* 85.2 (2006): 15–27. Print. Former intelligence analyst explains how the Bush administration manipulated evidence to justify the need for the Iraq War Resolution and convince Americans that war with Iraq was necessary.

Laurence W. Mazzeno

■ Iraq War

Definition: Military conflict between Iraq and the United States following a United States–led allied invasion of that nation in March 2003

The Iraq War, also known as the Second Gulf War, was a military conflict initiated by the United States to remove the dictatorial regime of Iraqi President Saddam Hussein. The war began when the United States led a global coalition force in a military invasion of Iraq in March of 2003, after several years of international diplomatic efforts to assess Iraq's weapons programs had failed due to a lack of cooperation by the Hussein regime.

Allegations of Weapons of Mass Destruction

Following the culmination of the first Gulf War (1990–91) and the Hussein regime's failed invasion of neighboring Kuwait, Iraq was forbidden by the United Nations to purchase, manufacture, or store weapons of mass destruction. The Hussein regime was forced to comply with a UN Security Council resolution mandating that an international group of weapons inspectors be allowed to continually survey all Iraqi military operations for any evidence of such weapons. Iraq begrudgingly maintained compliance with UN weapons inspectors through 2002, when the nation's cooperation began to wane due to the regime's frustration with long-standing UN economic sanctions against it and its perceived threat of neighboring Iran.

In his January 2003 State of the Union Address, President George W. Bush went public with a report from British intelligence sources that claimed Iraq's dismissal of weapons inspectors was part of a large plan to accumulate material to build a nuclear weapon. In his speech, Bush also vaguely alluded to an association between the Hussein regime and unnamed terrorist entities. This accusation was particularly significant in the aftermath of the September 11,

Senior Airman Josh Reddick, a life support technician, reviews maps and search-and-recovery techniques with Capt. Jason Cobb at Al Asad Airfield, Iraq. (U.S. Air Force/Photograph by Captain Shannon Collins)

2001, terrorist attacks in the United States. Despite protests from key NATO allies such as Canada, France, and Germany, leaders in the United States and in Great Britain, notably Prime Minister Tony Blair, were eager to proceed with invasion plans and vanquish Saddam Hussein.

In February of 2003, United States Secretary of State Colin Powell gave a speech before the United Nations assembly in which he presented the case for international military action against Iraq. In his presentation, Powell claimed that several Iraqi defectors had informed the US Central Intelligence Agency (CIA) of an elaborate chemical and biological weapons system operated by the Hussein regime. Powell referred to evidence illustrating that Iraq was in possession of mobile chemical weapons laboratories, as well as large stockpiles of chemical and biological weapons.

Powell's assertions did not quell continued calls for diplomacy. Former US president Bill Clinton,

Bush's Army Chief of Staff Eric Shinseki, and French foreign minister Dominique de Villepin were some of the most prominent statesmen who spoke out publicly against the potential perils of an invasion of Iraq. Most notable of their concerns was the potential for violent clashes among Iraq's historically opposed Shiite and Sunni Muslim majorities in the absence of the Hussein regime.

Yet the Bush and Blair administrations stood fast on their assertion that Iraq posed a threat to the United States, the United Kingdom, and the entire international community. The Bush administration rationalized a military invasion of the country not only due to accumulating weapons evidence, but under the aggressive antiterrorist foreign policy measures enacted by the United States in the wake of the September 11 attacks. This conglomeration of legislation, military strategy, and foreign policy principles would eventually become known as the Bush Doctrine.

Invasion and Iraqi Defense

In a public address on March 17, 2003, President Bush issued an ultimatum demanding that Saddam Hussein relinquish control of Iraq and depart the country within forty-eight hours or face a United States–led invasion. Hussein refused the demand. On March 20, the United States and allied forces commenced the invasion of Iraq, staged from US bases in neighboring Kuwait and aircraft carriers in the Persian Gulf.

The Iraqi capital of Baghdad was heavily bombarded by airstrikes in the early hours of the war, during the US military operation dubbed Shock and Awe. These initial air strikes destroyed key Iraqi military communication apparatus and almost completely destroyed its already inferior air force. Shock and Awe was also later revealed to have targeted Hussein himself, his sons, and senior members of Iraqi military leadership—although much of the Iraqi power structure, though weakened, would survive.

Continued widespread US airstrikes on Iraqi defense systems and weapons caches severely limited the strength of opposition forces in the war's opening weeks. Convincingly outmanned and operating at the discretion of a swiftly deteriorating leadership, the majority of the Iraqi army was overwhelmed by allied forces approximately three weeks after the invasion began. Hussein's malnourished and poorly equipped army surrendered in droves.

Allied invasion forces faced more formidable resistance in pockets of major Iraqi cities from Hussein's Republican Guard, a contingent of the regime's most loyal troops. Some of the war's most ferocious fighting took place in the southern city of Nasiriyah and the central Iraqi city of Fallujah.

On May 1, 2003, less than two months after the beginning of the invasion, President Bush gave a public address on the deck of the aircraft carrier USS *Abraham Lincoln*, declaring an end to major combat operations in Iraq. With both of Saddam Hussein's sons killed by allied attacks and the Iraqi army officially disbanded, the remaining lawlessness and smattering of violence propagated by anti-American forces were deemed by Bush and officials within his administration, including Defense Secretary Donald Rumsfeld, as the last desperate actions of a defeated force.

Despite the declaration of victory, the Hussein regime's weapons stockpiles and manufacturing facilities that were so paramount in the US justification of the invasion would never materialize. A 2005 Presidential Commission on Iraq's weapons capability determined that none of the prewar Iraqi weapons intelligence utilized by Great Britain and the United States was factually accurate.

Capture of Hussein

Saddam Hussein's sons Uday and Qusay Hussein, key figures in the dictatorship throughout their father's decades in power, were killed in an allied ambush in the northern Iraq city of Mosul in June of 2003. Yet Saddam himself managed to elude capture for several months after the invasion.

With an upsurge in violence against American and UN targets in Iraq throughout the summer of that year, many military and media analysts considered the plausibility that Hussein was leading the insurgency while in hiding. Yet with his country overthrown, his sons dead, and most of his inner circle gone, including close family members acting in cooperation with allied forces, the prevailing assumption was that Hussein's resources, mobility, and influence were in rapid decline.

Post-Invasion Insurgency

US military commanders were significantly caught off guard by the ferocity and magnitude of the anti-American sentiment in the years following the toppling of the Hussein regime. The anti-American forces in Iraq were comprised of a diverse mix of those loyal to Hussein's Ba'athist political party, Iraqi nationals who disputed the notion of resisting to a new American-backed government after years of oppression. Sunni Muslim religious tribes also comprised a large contingent of the insurgents; they had a long history of sectarian violence with Shi'a Muslim tribes who summarily aligned with the United States and allied forces.

The violence between the two warring factions reached such heights that by 2008, many analysts considered Iraq to be in the throes of a civil war. The insurgency stretched US and allied forces to a point at which they could rarely be called upon to perform routine security—border and street patrols necessary to protect Iraqi civilians, US leadership, and pro-Western Iraqi politicians eager to begin construction on a new government.

The result was a heavy American reliance on private military contractors and commercial security services, organizations that would come to be utilized more during the Iraq War than in any other military conflicts in history. The US government would spend over $100 billion on private security firms throughout the war. Numerous incidents of cultural insensitivity and aggressive posturing by private contractors would weaken the reputation of allied forces throughout the conflict.

The Iraq War at Decade's End

International opinion of the United States and allied invasion force withstood a significant blow in 2004, after human rights violations by US soldiers against detained Iraqi soldiers in the Abu Ghraib prison complex came to light. Leaked photographs outlined systematic torture, rape, and psychological abuse of Iraqi prisoners at the hands of US soldiers. The Abu Ghraib scandal would eventually shed light on the widespread use of torture by the Bush administration in the wake of the September 11 attacks, both in Iraq and in US military installations throughout the world.

The 2005 investigation surrounding the Downing Street Memo, an outline of a 2002 British government meeting stating that US officials had fixed intelligence and facts regarding Hussein's weapons stockpiles and military capability to justify the war, fueled widespread American and international dissatisfaction with the genesis and strategy surrounding the conflict. In an attempt to quell civic dissatisfaction with the war and regain control over continually recalcitrant insurgent forces, President Bush announced a plan to deploy nearly twenty-five thousand additional American troops into Iraq in his January 2007 State of the Union Address.

The Surge, as it would come to be known, would be a pivotal topic in the run-up to the 2008 US presidential campaign, which pitted Republican senator John McCain against Democratic senator Barack Obama. Obama's pledge to end the Iraq War was a major part of his platform, and American dissatisfaction with the conflict was one of the major factors to which his substantial victory over McCain was attributed.

The quelling of the major violence in Iraq by the end of the 2000s was largely attributed to the US troop surge of 2007, along with increased compromise and the dwindling military capabilities of Iraqi insurgent leaders. By 2009, the Obama administration had begun the long process of withdrawing American forces in Iraq, leaving in its place a new, allied-trained Iraqi army.

The Iraq left behind by invading forces was far from the peaceful, democratic nation the leaders of the United States and Great Britain had envisioned would remain following the invasion at the war's outset. Iraq and its diverse population would continue to grapple with the vast, long-standing cultural and ethnic conflicts and often violent power struggles that rapidly transformed their country after the fall of Saddam Hussein.

The United States military officially completed its departure of Iraq in December 2011.

Impact

The human toll and exorbitant financial cost of the Iraq War notwithstanding, the conflict also served as a sea change in the American perception of military conflict. The majority of US military action since the Vietnam War had been supported by the American public as a necessary evil with which to uphold the values of Western democracy. However, the Iraq War was made far less palpable in terms of public perception, due to its questionable genesis, rampant media coverage, and ghastly guerrilla-style violence. Never before had the vulnerability of the US Armed Forces been made so readily apparent.

The Bush administration's flawed reasoning surrounding the invasion of Iraq also reopened the debate on the power of the executive branch over the armed services, the role of Congress in formal declarations of war, and the future role of the United States military as the global defender of those living under oppressed regimes. The war also brought to bear questions regarding the aging notion of the United States as a global superpower, and if traditionally powerful military forces such as those of the United States and Great Britain were equipped to handle a large-scale guerilla insurgency.

Further Reading

Anderson, Jon Lee. *The Fall of Baghdad.* New York: Penguin, 2004. Print. An eyewitness account of the invasion of Baghdad. Chronicles what it was like for Iraqis in living under Saddam Hussein's regime and afterward, as well as during the war. Also focuses on journalists covering the war.

Cerf, Christopher, and Micah L. Sifry, eds. *The Iraq War Reader.* New York: Touchstone, 2003. E-book. In-depth discussion of the Iraq War from various perspectives, essays, and documents. Focuses particularly on the political policies and history that led to the war, as well as future challenges.

Murphy, Dan. "Siege of Fallujah Polarizing Iraqis." *Christian Science Monitor.* Christian Science Monitor, 15 Apr. 2004. Web. 8 Oct. 2012. Discusses how the fighting in Fallujah changed the opinions of many Iraqis about the war.

Silberman, Laurence H., et al. *Commission on the Intelligence Capabilities of the United States Regarding Weapons of Mass Destruction.* Washington, DC: Federation of American Scientists, 31 Mar. 2005. PDF. Presents the results of an investigation into the validity of the claim that Iraq possessed weapons of mass destruction. Focuses on the errors made by the Intelligence Community and recommends changes to that organization.

Singal, Jesse, Christine Lim, and M. J. Stephey. "Seven Years in Iraq: An Iraq War Timeline." *TIME.* Time Inc., 19 Mar. 2010. Web. 8 Oct. 2012. A timeline of the Iraq War, from March 2003 to March 2010.

John Pritchard

■ Israel and the United States

Definition: Political relationship between the United States and the state of Israel

The relationship between Israel and the United States maintained its status as one of the most conspicuous in the arena of international relations throughout the 2000s. In addition to the United States' continued diplomatic support of Israel in its ongoing conflict with the Palestinian Arabs, the importance of the US-Israeli alliance was often a major factor in the course of American foreign policy in the Middle East throughout the decade.

Israel and the Clinton Administration

The years 2000 and 2001 marked the last period of Bill Clinton's presidency of the United States. Clinton was a staunch advocate of Israeli interests throughout his entire eight-year term as president. He successfully brokered a peace treaty between Israel and Jordan in 1994, establishing peace, mutual recognition of sovereignty, and security cooperation between the two nations after nearly fifty years

of conflict. The president entered the waning years of his term with hopes of similarly reigniting efforts to end the long-running Israeli-Palestinian conflict, simmering with varying degrees of intensity since the violent establishment of Israel in 1948 displaced hundreds of thousands of Palestinian Arabs who fled to surrounding countries and the Israeli-occupied territories known as the West Bank and Gaza Strip.

Clinton hosted the third and final summit of his presidency between Israel and Palestine in Shepherdstown, West Virginia, in July of 2001. The talks failed to produce any significant progress in the decades-old issues at the center the conflict, which continued to be the major cause of violent conflict between the two peoples. These issues included Palestinian sovereignty, land ownership rights in the city of Jerusalem, the status of Palestinian refugees, and the establishment of permanent borders separating the two parties. The failure of Clinton's final summit to set forth any definitive plan for resolution was further damaged by continued violence between Israeli and Palestinian forces throughout the summer of 2001.

The Quartet and Bush's "Road Map" for Peace

The United States' support for Israel and the Middle East peace process would continue following the inauguration of George W. Bush in 2001. In the wake of the September 11, 2001, terrorist attacks, Bush issued several public statements decrying terrorist violence in the Middle East, a tactic utilized by both pro-Israeli and pro-Palestinian forces for decades.

Bush also urged Israel to offer support in the international manhunt for al-Qaeda terrorist leader Osama bin Laden, who remained at large. Debate regarding the United States' influence in the region among Middle Eastern leaders and their populace reached an all-time high during the US-led invasion of Iraq in March 2003, an action that was never publically supported or objected to by Israeli state officials.

Bush's 2003 peace plan, which would come to be known as the "road map for peace," was constructed by the United States in concert with the European Union, the United Nations, and Russia, a collaboration that came to be known as the Quartet on the Middle East, or simply the Quartet.

Bush traveled to the Middle East in May of 2003 to discuss the measures of the peace plan with

Israeli and Palestinian leadership. The ambitious, three-phase proposal addressed the conflict in diplomatic, geographic, and military terms. Most notably, the plan called for the establishment of an independent Palestinian state and for the creation of commercial, environmental, defense, and border agreements between this newly sovereign Palestine and Israel.

The Israeli government agreed to the stipulations set forth in the road map only after offering fourteen concessions to accompany the plan, including their desire for a demilitarized Palestinian state and ultimate authority over the security of its borders. The road map also called for the appointment of a Palestinian prime minister to help negotiate the peace process; however, both the United States and Israel stipulated that longtime Palestinian Liberation Organization leader Yasser Arafat would be unqualified for the post given his long-running involvement in military action against Israel.

Despite the ambitious nature of the road map proposal and the positivity surrounding its conception and development, the possibility of implementing the plan was short-lived. In the weeks following the departure of Bush and other world leaders at the closure of the diplomatic negotiations, new eruptions of violence between the opposing factions once again put a halt to the peace process.

The Palestinian Authority, which governs the West Bank and Gaza, and four of the main pro-Palestinian military factions under its influence agreed to a tentative cease-fire at the end of June 2003. This fragile peace was marked by more US-led meetings between the two parties, this time helmed by US National Security Advisor Condoleezza Rice.

American domestic support for a US-led solution to the Israeli-Palestinian peace effort did not waver, despite Bush's wavering approval ratings. However, by the end of 2003, the first phase of the road map continued to stall, due largely to the failure of the cease-fire. Terrorist violence against Israel continued from pro-Palestinian factions, and Israel refused to consider any negotiations that required the state to wholly abandon its settlements in the territory of Gaza.

Yet, following a series of letters between President Bush and Israeli Prime Minister Ariel Sharon over the winter of 2004, Israel began to back off its hard-line stance on Gaza and other territorial disputes.

US-Israeli Response to New Hamas Majority

Hope for the road map was born anew in August of 2005, when Israel, under joint agreement with Palestinian officials, began abandoning settlements in the Gaza Strip. However, when the Palestinian Islamist group Hamas, classified by the United States and many other countries as a terrorist organization, won majority control of the Palestinian Legislative Council in the beginning of 2006, talks once again stalled, as Israeli officials refused to negotiate with the new Palestinian majority.

In 2006, the Quartet outlined three rules that they required of the newly Hamas-led Palestinian Authority in order for Israel and the international community to return to the negotiating table. These included formal diplomatic recognition of the state of Israel, an immediate stop to all military action against Israeli interests, and formal acknowledgement of all previous treaties, among them the road map for peace. The Hamas-led Palestinian Authority rejected each condition, which resulted in the formal suspension of US negotiations with the group.

By the conclusion of Bush's tenure in office, he spoke publically about the political and geographic concessions both Israel and the Palestinians would have to make in order to form a lasting peace in the region. Bush's prediction that a signed peace treaty between Israel and Palestine would be in place prior to his departure from the presidency never came true.

Following his election in 2008, President Barack Obama offered overtures to both the Israeli and Palestinian people in a landmark 2009 speech in Cairo, Egypt, less than a year after his inauguration. Obama's speech made international headlines, primarily for its particularly empathetic overtures toward Palestinians, a tone rarely, if ever, taken by a sitting US president. Obama also insisted that the United States would continue to refute the legitimacy of Israeli settlements in the West Bank.

Economics, Defense, and Tourism

The 2000s marked a continuation of strong economic and cultural ties between the United States and Israel. Israel remained the biggest recipient of US foreign aid throughout the decade, a status it had maintained since its formation.

American financial aid to Israel in the 2000s was brokered in nearly every facet of industry, from economic and infrastructure development aid, to scientific and medical research, to defense and security purchases. In 2007, the Bush administration and the Israeli government agreed to a ten-year military aid package between the two countries worth approximately $30 billion, the largest such military agreement between the United States and any non-NATO ally.

In 2008, the United States opened a radar facility in the Negev Desert in southern Israel. The facility's opening marked the first permanent foreign military base on Israeli soil. The US outpost was constructed to enhance the radar capability of the Israeli Defense Forces, giving it advance notice of any incoming long-range missiles, as well as to provide additional American military intelligence in the region.

The year 2007 was also marked by significant growth the American-Israeli Cultural Foundation (AICF), which added ten thousand new members that year. The AICF remained a major advocate of Israeli music, art, dance, and film in the United States throughout the decade, raising funds for a variety of scholarships and charitable interests in both nations.

American tourists continued to comprise the majority of visitors to Israel throughout the 2000s, despite the nation's fragile tourist infrastructure. A record half a million Americans visited Israel in 2007. Over a third of these visitors were American Christians visiting the country's numerous religious landmarks, such as the Jordan River, the Sea of Galilee, and other historical and archeological sites related to Christianity.

Impact

The diplomatic, political, and economic ties that make up the strong allegiance between the United States and Israel were strengthened in the 2000s. Israel remained a key foothold of the Western-style democratic tradition in a Middle East region continually battered by political upheaval, religious conflict, and anti-American sentiment. The 2000s marked a subtle change in the United States' strategy toward the Israeli-Palestinian peace process: For the first time, as voiced by both Presidents Bush and Obama, the United States publically recognized that Israeli concessions would need to mirror those of

the Palestinians if a lasting peace were to ever be achieved.

Further Reading

Butcher, Tim. "George Bush Predicts Deal on Palestinian State." *Telegraph* [London]. Telegraph Media Group, 11 Jan. 2008. Web. 14 Aug. 2012. A report about Bush's desire for a Palestinian state before he left office.

"Israel's Response to the Road Map." *The Knesset.* State of Israel, 25 May 2003. Web. 14 Aug. 2012. A list covering Israel's concessions to Bush's road map for peace.

"Joint Statement: US-Israel Joint Economic Development Group Joint Statement." *US Department of State.* US Dept. of State, 20 June 2003. Web. 14 Aug. 2012. Discusses the plan for United States aid for Israeli economic growth.

Mark, Clyde R. "Israeli–United States Relations." *Federation of American Scientists.* Congressional Research Service, 9 Nov. 2004. Web. 14 Aug. 2012. History and current status of relations between the United States and Israel, including work toward brokering peace between Israel and the Palestinians.

Mearsheimer, John J., and Stephen M. Walt. *The Israel Lobby and US Foreign Policy.* New York: Farrar, 2007. E-book. Web. 14 Aug. 2012. A discussion of the impact of the Israel lobby on US foreign policy, including how it has affected America's relationship with the rest of the Middle East. The authors argue, controversially, that the United States' immense support of Israel is neither in Israel's nor the United States' long-term interests.

Sharp, Jeremy M. "US Foreign Aid to Israel." *Federation of American Scientists.* Congressional Research Service, 12 Mar. 2012. Web. 14 Aug. 2012. A specialist report on US foreign aid to Israel, covering past support and support up to the date of the report, as well as an analysis of the issues involved.

Zeleny, Jeff, and Alan Cowell. "Addressing Muslims, Obama Pushes Mideast Peace." *New York Times.* New York Times, 4 June 2009. Web. 14 Aug. 2012. Covers Obama's 2009 speech to Israel and Palestine.

John Pritchard

J

■ Jackson, Michael

Identification: American recording artist
Born: August 29, 1958; Gary, IN
Died: June 25, 2009; Los Angeles, CA

Jackson paved the way for many modern recording artists. He was a musical pioneer who set records for best-selling albums and concert tours, awards, and charitable contributions. He was dubbed the "King of Pop" because his work could not be compared to that of any other artist.

Michael Joseph Jackson, known as the "King of Pop" was the most commercially successful recording artist of the 1980s whose tours broke world records for attendance and total gross ticket sales. Jackson's success continued until 1993, when he was accused of molesting a thirteen-year-old boy who frequently visited Jackson at his Neverland ranch. Jackson and the accuser's family settled out of court. Jackson married Lisa Marie Presley, the daughter of Elvis Presley, in 1994, but the two divorced in 1996. Later that year, Jackson married his pregnant nurse, Debbie Rowe. Jackson and Rowe's first child, Prince Michael Jackson, Jr., was born in 1997. Jackson's second child, Paris Michael Katherine Jackson, was born in 1998. In 1999, Jackson and Rowe divorced; Rowe granted Jackson full custody of their children.

The 2000 edition of *The Guinness Book of World Records* names Jackson as record holder for the Most Charities Supported by a Pop Star, at approximately forty organizations. *Invincible,* Jackson's tenth album, was released in October, 2001, despite a contract dispute between Jackson and Sony Music Entertainment. Although the album went double platinum in the United States, sales for the album were low compared to Jackson's past albums.

Prince Michael Jackson II, Jackson's second son, was born in early 2002. Jackson caused an outcry in

Michael Jackson. (Dave Hogan/Getty Images Entertainment/Getty Images)

November 2002 when he dangled his baby son, nicknamed "Blanket," over the railing of a hotel balcony in Berlin, Germany. The star later apologized for the incident.

In 2003, Jackson faced child molestation accusations from another thirteen-year-old boy and his family. Criminal charges were filed in Santa Barbara County and the case went to trial in January of 2005. Jackson was acquitted five months later.

After years of rumors of a comeback tour, in March of 2009, Jackson held a press conference and announced he would perform a series of concerts at London's O2 Arena. Ten concerts were initially scheduled, but the number increased to fifty after record-breaking ticket sales. On June 25, 2009, less than three weeks before the initial show, dubbed *This Is It*, Jackson died suddenly of cardiac arrest. After being treated by paramedics at his rented home, he was pronounced dead at Ronald Reagan Medical Center at the University of California, Los Angeles. Jackson was buried on September 3, 2009. On February 8, 2010, Jackson's personal physician, Conrad Murray, was charged with involuntary manslaughter in the singer's death. Murray was accused of administering the anesthetic propofol, in addition to other medications, to Jackson, who reportedly suffered from insomnia.

Impact

Jackson's talent, showmanship, and creativity made him a singular entertainer. *Thriller* (1982), Jackson's second collaboration with producer Quincy Jones, was groundbreaking and solidified Jackson's status as the ultimate crossover recording artist. Before *Thriller* was released, cable channel MTV (Music Television) lacked diversity in its music-video programming. The success of *Thriller* paved the way for other African American artists, not only on MTV but everywhere. Jackson was recognized as having elevated the music video from a mere promotional tool to an art form He was a trendsetter and international icon. Posthumously, he continued to be a top-selling artist. The film *This Is It*, released in October of 2009, documents Jackson's rehearsals for his This Is It concerts. The film, which debuted at number one at the box office, showcases Jackson's artistry and work ethic, and the timeless appeal of his music.

Further Reading

Bennett, Joy T. "Michael Jackson: Then and Now" *Ebony* 63.2 (2007): 80–90. Print.

Grant, Adrian. *Michael Jackson: A Visual Documentary, 1958-2009—The Official Tribute Edition.* London: Omnibus, 2009. 'Print.

Jackson, Michael. "An Ebony Interview: Michael Jackson in His Own Words." Interview by Bryan Monroe. *Ebony* 63.2 (2007): 94–109. Print.'

—. *Moonwalk.* 1988. Reprint. New York: Harmony, 2009. Print.

Taraborelli, J. Randy. *Michael Jackson: The Magic, the Madness, the Whole Story, 1958–2009.* New York: Grand Central, 2009. Print.

Kassundra Miller

■ James, LeBron

Identification: American professional basketball player
Born: December 30, 1984; Akron, Ohio

James's agility and skill on the court has often drawn comparisons to the athleticism of basketball legend Michael Jordan. James, who has also competed as an Olympic athlete, also oversees the LeBron James Family Foundation. The organization focuses on assisting single parents and their children.

LeBron James's skill on the basketball court drew attention early in his life. As a high school junior, he considered a move to the National Basketball Association (NBA), but decided instead to complete his high school education. During his senior year, James averaged 31.6 points per game. By the time he graduated high school, he had accumulated 2,657 points, 892 rebounds, and 523 assists.

The Cleveland Cavaliers selected James with their first overall pick in the 2003 NBA draft. He averaged twenty points per game during his rookie season. At the conclusion of the 2003 season, James was named NBA Rookie of the Year. He was the youngest player in NBA history to receive the honor, and the in Cavaliers franchise history. James's success also earned him several lucrative endorsement deals. During his first year in the NBA, he signed a $90 million contract with Nike.

In 2004, James was a member of the US Olympic men's basketball team, which competed at the Summer Olympics in Athens, Greece. The Americans beat Lithuania to earn a bronze medal in the games. Soon after, James's girlfriend, Savannah Brinson, gave birth to a son, LeBron Jr.

In 2005, James increased his average points per game to more than twenty-seven. That same year, James renewed his contract with the Cavaliers. In 2007, Brinson and James had their second son, Bryce Maximus. James again played for the US

LeBron James. (©iStockphoto.com/EdStock)

Olympic team in 2008, earning a gold medal against Spain. After becoming a free agent in 2010, James signed a new contract with the Miami Heat. His departure from the Cavaliers resulted in negative publicity in Cleveland, where he had been revered as a hometown hero. In 2012, James won his first NBA championship as a member of the Heat, who defeated the Oklahoma City Thunder. He was named series MVP.

Impact

James remains one of the most dominant and widely known players in professional sports. In addition to his success on the court, he has served as a philanthropist and a positive role model for many. He is a member of Hoop Heroes, a group that pairs NBA players with corporate sponsors to support the After-School All-Stars program. The initiative provides academic support, enrichment opportunities, and fitness activities for middle school students across America. The LeBron James Family Foundation is noted for programs such as the Playground Build Initiative, which provides playgrounds for children in urban areas such as New Orleans, Phoenix, and Dallas.

Further Reading

Christopher, Matt. *On the Court with LeBron James.* New York: Little, 2008. Print.

Morgan Jr., David Lee. *LeBron James: The Rise of a Star.* Cleveland: Grey, 2003. Print.

Gina Kutcha

■ Jay-Z

Identification: American rapper and record producer
Born: December 4, 1969; New York, NY

Jay-Z (a.k.a. Shawn Corey Carter) helped shape hip-hop music in the wake of the East Coast–West Coast gangsta rap rivalry. Through his role as a record executive, both at Roc-A-Fella Records and Def Jam Records, Jay-Z has discovered and fostered a number of successful artists.

New York rapper and producer Jay-Z's first album of the 2000s was *The Blueprint* (2001), which was received well both critically and commercially. The album managed to maintain street credibility while appealing to mainstream audiences, partly because it sampled vintage soul music. Unlike other Jay-Z albums, *The Blueprint* has only one featured guest artist, Eminem, although it features a number of producers, including Kanye West, Timbaland, Just Blaze, and Bink. Included on the album is the song "Takeover," which samples the Doors' "Five to One," and KRS-ONE's "Sound of da Police." "Izzo (H.O.V.A.)" was the first, and most successful, single released from the album, and it features a sample of "I Want You Back" by the Jackson Five. The song addresses, among other topics, his struggles with the music industry.

Jay-Z continued to release albums until 2003, when he announced his retirement from recording and performing in order to focus on business ventures. Though retired, Jay-Z continued to work on side

Jay-Z. (©iStockphoto.com/Kevin Winter)

projects, such as his 2004 collaboration with rock group Linkin Park, *Collision Course*. In addition, in 2004 Jay-Z was named president and chief executive officer of Def Jam Records, which finalized his split from Dash and Burke. Jay-Z officially ended his retirement in 2005, and he released his next album the following year. In addition to his activities as an artist and record executive, Jay-Z has his own clothing line, Rocawear, which specializes in hip-hop fashion, and he is co-owner of the New Jersey Nets basketball team. In April, 2008, Jay-Z married singer Beyoncé Knowles.

Impact

By filling the void left in the New York rap world after the death of the Notorious B.I.G. in 1997, Jay-Z helped shape the future direction of rap. He demonstrated how a rap artist could appeal to a mainstream audience while maintaining street credibility, sustaining his core base of fans while appealing to new ones. Jay-Z has also helped propel the careers of numerous artists both through collaborations on his solo albums and through his activities as a record executive. Last, Jay-Z has demonstrated how a rap artist can be a successful entrepreneur and serve as a trend-setter for hip-hop culture and fashion.

Further Reading

Brown, Jake. *Jay-Z and the Roc-A-Fella Dynasty*. New York: Colossus, 2005. Print.

Bryan, Carmen. *It's No Secret: From Nas to Jay-Z, from Seduction to Scandal, a Hip-Hop Helen of Troy Tells All.* New York: VH1, 2006. Print.

Clements, Car. "Musical Interchange Between Indian Music and Hip-Hop." In *Critical Minded: New Approaches to Hip-Hop Studies*, edited by Ellie M. Hisama and Ruth Crawford. Brooklyn: Inst. for Studies in American Music, 2005. Print.

Oliver, Richard, and Tim Leffel. *Hip-Hop, Inc.: Success Strategies of the Rap Moguls*. New York: Thunder's Mouth, 2006. Print.

Wang, Oliver, ed. *Classic Material: The Hip-Hop Album Guide*. Toronto: ECW, 2003. Print.

Matthew Mihalka

■ Jeffs, Warren

Identification: President of the Fundamentalist Church of Jesus Christ of Latter-Day Saints
Born: December 3, 1955; San Francisco, California

Warren Jeffs is the leader of the polygamous Fundamentalist Church of Jesus Christ of Latter Day Saints (FLDS), an isolated offshoot of the more mainstream Church of Jesus Christ of Latter-Day Saints which does not sanction polygamy. When Jeffs was arrested in 2006, he was on the FBI's most wanted list for his role in FLDS's illegal practice of forcing underage girls to marry much older men.

Warren Steed Jeffs, a former school principal, took over leadership of FLDS in Hilldale, Utah, after the death of his father, Rulon Jeffs in September 2002. At the time, Hilldale and Colorado City, Arizona were twin towns that spanned the border and were populated by FLDS families. This twin city settlement was a clever one, chosen so that sect members could retreat across the state line whenever a raid was conducted by one state or another.

It was alleged by other FLDS members that one of Jeffs's first moves as prophet was to take over all but two of his father's many wives, including his own mother. He continued this power grab by assuming control of a trust that held all the land and buildings in the twin communities and excommunicating, or throwing out of the church, some one hundred men. When Jeffs did this, he separated them from their wives and children, effectively exiling them from the community, and gave their families to other men loyal to him. Jeffs soon stood out from other prophets by his enthusiasm for arranging marriages for young girls, many under the legal age. Although church lawyers advised against the practice, Jeffs ignored the advice and continued, even taking a twelve-year-old wife himself. Trouble began for Jeffs in 2002 when one of his followers was charged with bigamy and unlawful sex with a minor, because of his unofficial polygamous marriage to a sixteen-year-old in 1998.

Wanting to move to a more secure location, Jeffs directed his followers to start buying land and building in Pringle, South Dakota, and Mancos, Colorado. The largest new compound was built was in Eldorado, Texas. Known as the Yearning for Zion ranch, the 1,700-acre compound included a dairy, a cheese factory, meeting hall, family homes, barracks, and a massive temple. It is estimated that between 150 and 600 people live in the compound.

By 2005, Jeffs faced a variety of charges issued by Utah and Arizona, including a charge by one of his nephews, Brent Jeffs, of sexual abuse when he was principal of Alta Academy. He also faced charges of conspiracy to commit sexual conduct with a minor, and sexual conduct with a minor and rape as an accomplice. Not trusting the legal and judicial system, Jeffs tried to ignore the charges. When that became impossible, he ran, and became a fugitive. He was added to the list as one of the FBI's ten most wanted criminals in May 2006.

Finances for the FLDS had always been suspect, and they ran most of them through an organization called the United Effort Plan (UEP) Trust. In 2005, a judge assumed control of the trust amid charges that the church leaders were abusing their control of it. There was more trouble for Jeffs in April 2007 when authorities found that the Pentagon had contracts worth $1.7 million with companies owned by FLDS leaders. Through these contracts, it was estimated some $200,000 per month was being channeled to FLDS.

Jeffs was finally arrested in Las Vegas, Nevada, on August 29, 2006, when the car he was traveling in was pulled over by a state trooper on a routine stop. He had with him $53,000 in cash, wigs, credit cards, cell phones, and laptops. He was tried and convicted on of being an accomplice to rape in Utah in 2007, where he was sentenced to ten years to life. The Utah Supreme Court overturned Jeffs's conviction in July 2010 due to incorrect jury instructions and ordered a new trial.

In January 2008, according to unsealed court documents, Jeffs tried to hang himself in his prison cell after refusing to eat for a month. In July 2008, Jeffs was taken from his prison cell to the hospital, as he was suffering from fevers, shaking, and convulsions. He was released a few days later and returned to prison.

New charges against Jeffs were filed after Texas authorities raided the Yearning for Zion ranch in 2008. In August 2011, Jeffs was sentenced to life in prison for two counts of sexual assault on a child. Jeffs is serving his sentence in Texas. He will not be eligible for parole until 2056.

Impact

Warren Jeffs is a self-proclaimed prophet and the President of the Fundamentalist Church of Jesus Christ of Latter-Day Saints (FLDS). He was on the FBI's ten most wanted list until his highly publicized arrest on August 28, 2006 and would faced two first-degree felony charges of accomplice rape. His arrest and time spent as the leader of the FLDS has been represented in nonfiction book and film documentaries, including Carolyn Jessop's book, *Escape* (2007), and *Damned to Heaven* (2008) by Pawel Gula and Tom Elliott.

Further Reading

Brower, Sarah and Jon Krakauer. *Prophet's Prey: My Seven-Year Investigation into Warren Jeffs and the Fundamentalist Church of Latter-Day Saints.* New York, NY: Bloomsbury, 2011. Print.

Stephen Singular. *When Men Become Gods: Mormon Polygamist Warren Jeffs, His Cult of Fear, and the Women Who Fought Back.* New York, NY. Macmillan. Print.

Weyermann, Debra. *Answer Them Nothing: Bringing Down the Polygamous Empire of Warren Jeffs.* Chicago, IL: Chicago review P, 2011. Print.

Lee Tunstall

■ Job Creation and Worker Assistance Act of 2002

The Law: Federal legislation that provided an economic stimulus for businesses
Date: Signed on March 9, 2002

In response to the economic downturn of the early 2000s, the Job Creation and Worker Assistance Act of 2002 (JCWAA) attempted to promote economic recovery by reducing taxes on businesses. By providing businesses with this economic stimulus, Congress aimed to facilitate job creation.

Characterized as an economic stimulus plan, the JCWAA primarily assisted businesses through increased tax deductions. To increase business deductions, JCWAA offered a first-year, 30 percent bonus depreciation. This deduction could be used in addition to standard first-year deductions and could be applied toward any business property acquired between September 10, 2001, and September 11, 2004, excluding real estate. This provision sought to encourage small business creation and attempted to boost new businesses that were struggling.

JCWAA also expanded business deductions by increasing the carryback period for net operating losses (NOLs) by three additional years. NOLs occur when a business's expenses exceed its profits. This provision temporarily allowed businesses to carry back NOLs from 2001 or 2002 and apply them as a deduction to the previous five years. Typically, NOLs may only be applied to the previous two years. By applying NOLs from one year as a deduction to profits from another year, businesses could lessen their tax liability. And by reducing a business's taxable profits, JCWAA also reduced the amount due in taxes, thereby creating a stimulus.

In addition to providing tax incentives for businesses, JCWAA addressed other recovery needs. The act allocated funds to New York City to assist in the recovery from the terrorist attacks of September 11, 2001. It also offered incentives for clean energy use and production by extending tax deductions and credits for renewable energy that would have otherwise lapsed. While the act recognized the necessity of job creation, it also acknowledged an interim need to assist the vast number of unemployed Americans. To do so, JCWAA extended unemployment assistance eligibility by thirteen weeks, allowing states to opt in to this provision. JCWAA also sought to assist families. The act also renewed funding for the Temporary Assistance for Needy Families program.

Impact

Opinions on the lasting impact of the Job Creation and Worker Assistance Act of 2002 vary based on the analyst. Those who support tax cuts for businesses as a means to job creation view the act as a success. Alternatively, others consider tax cuts for businesses to be little more than a handout to the wealthy. Either way, it is difficult to quantify the jobs created by any one act of Congress. The most visible impact of JCWAA was that it further reinforced the partisan divide in Congress over differing approaches to economic improvement.

Further Reading

Bartlett, Bruce. *The Benefit and the Burden: Tax Reform—Why We Need it and What it Will Take.* New York: Simon, 2012. Print.

Smith, Allen W. *The Big Lie: How Our Government Hoodwinked the Public, Emptied the S.S. Trust Fund and Caused the Great Economic Collapse.* Winter Haven: Ironwood, 2009. Print.

Lucia Pizzo

■ Jobs and Growth Tax Relief Reconciliation Act of 2003

The Law: Federal legislation that reconfigured the tax code
Date: Signed on May 28, 2003
Also known as: Bush tax cuts

In an effort to promote job creation and economic growth, Congress passed the Jobs and Growth Tax Relief Reconciliation Act (JGTRRA) in 2003. Those in favor of the act believed that lowering taxes would invigorate the jobs market and consumer spending, thereby encouraging economic prosperity.

Sponsored by Representative Bill Thomas of California, the JGTRRA built upon the Economic Growth and Tax Relief Reconciliation Act of 2001 (EGTRRA). Together, these laws became known as the Bush tax cuts. Primarily, JGTRRA reconfigured the tax code. Across all tax brackets, the act lowered individual income tax rates, primarily by accelerating reductions initially scheduled to become effective in

2004 and 2006 by the EGTRRA. It also revised tax brackets, so that taxpayers who were previously on the lower edge of a tax bracket became those on the higher edge of the next lower tax bracket. These edge groups reaped the greatest benefits in tax rate reductions. Reductions were also made to the tax rates on capital gains and dividends.

In addition to tax cuts, the JGTRRA addressed deductions and state financial woes. The act increased deductions for joint filers of taxes and increased the child tax credit to support families. It also allocated $10 billion in direct grants to the state and local levels and gave $10 billion to Medicaid, the government program that provides health insurance for low-income Americans.

As shown by its reception among members of Congress, the JGTRRA was highly partisan. Among senators, the act received only two votes from Democrats, and only seven Democrats in the House of Representatives voted for it. This divided response resonated with the American public. Those who supported the act thought that lower tax rates would give businesses more money to spend on hiring and would give consumers more money to spend on goods and services. Those opposed to the act claimed that it disproportionately favored wealthy Americans through its reduction of tax rates and its focus on cuts to capital gains and dividends tax rates, which affect those in higher income brackets more than others.

Impact
Although the Bush tax cuts were intended, in part, as a means of job creation, many have criticized the cuts and their minimal results as ineffective. The cuts largely contributed to the federal budget deficit created during the administration of President George W. Bush and have been identified as a precursor to the Great Recession of 2008. Still, while many of the cuts were set to expire in 2010, they were renewed under President Barack Obama to alleviate the tax burden on Americans while the country recovered from recession.

Further Reading
Bartlett, Bruce. *The Benefit and the Burden: Tax Reform—Why We Need It and What It Will Take*. New York : Simon, 2012. Print.
Bush, George W. *Decision Points*. New York: Broadway, 2011. Print.

Lucia Pizzo

■ Jobs, Steve

Identification: American entrepreneur and co-founder and CEO of Apple Inc.
Born: February 24, 1955; San Francisco, CA
Died: October 5, 2011; Palo Alto, CA

Steve Jobs was one of the leading innovators of the information age. As chief executive officer (CEO) of both Apple Computer and Pixar Animation Studios, he consistently raised the bar on industry standards in computing and digital media throughout his career, which began in 1976. Jobs's quest for innovation was coupled with his desire to create rather than follow trends, a tendency which earned him the respect of competitors and consumers alike. Regarded as exceedingly charismatic, Jobs's ability to convince others of the importance of his ideas was a vital factor in the success of his companies, despite occasional setbacks.

Steve Jobs was born to an American mother and a Lebanese college professor on February 24, 1955 in San Francisco, California. Jobs showed an interest in machines very early in his life, and as a high school student he attended lectures at Hewlett-Packard, then a small company in Silicon Valley. There, he met his friend and longtime partner, Steve Wozniak, who would provide the technological expertise Jobs needed to start Apple Computer Incorporated.

Jobs and Wozniak were part of a group of computer enthusiasts whose focus was building homemade computers and computer chips. It was Wozniak who was more involved with building hardware, but Jobs saw the marketing potential of the group's inventions. He and Wozniak managed to sell one hundred homemade computers to a local computer store, and Apple Computers was born.

Apple Computer became a publicly-traded company in 1980. Jobs hired former PepsiCo executive John Sculley to run business operations, and the company expanded further. With Sculley's help, Apple established its reputation as a unique innovator, initiating the Macintosh line of computers in 1984 after nearly four years of development.

However, Jobs became involved in conflicts with Sculley and eventually he was forced to leave the company. Jobs's ouster from Apple occurred because the company changed its focus from home computing to the small business market. Jobs was

Steve Jobs. (©iStockphoto.com/ Justin Sullivan)

also obsessed with perfecting hardware technology, which made the computers he designed expensive compared to other companies, particularly that of IBM, Apple's primary competitor at the time.

Jobs was reappointed CEO of Apple in 1997. He immediately restructured the company's focus, scrapping a number of projects, including the Newton line that included personal digital assistants (PDAs) and mini-keyboards intended to be used in education. With Apple in serious trouble, it became clear to Jobs that he needed to make radical changes to the company, and consider new technologies to market. Turning away from its focus on perfecting hardware, Apple introduced its first and most famous software release in January 2001: iTunes, a digital music converter and player. This was followed in October of that year by the iPod, a handheld digital music player that revolutionized portable music technology.

The iPod, when first released, was only compatible with Macintosh computers, which also helped to revive public interest in the Macintosh. This was not enough to sustain the success of the iPod, however, and Apple began to release PC versions of the iPod in 2002, which caused sales to explode. Apple went on to control over 90 percent of the market share for digital music players.

In 2003, the iTunes Music Store was introduced, selling more than one million songs over the Internet for about a dollar each. Subsequent generations of iPods, such as the iPhoto and iPod Mini, further boosted Apple's reputation as a digital media giant. The success of Apple's digital media division in turn led to more vigorous sales of Apple computers, and its retail franchise, the Apple Store, was inaugurated to distribute the company's now-famous digital media hardware, as well as computers and peripherals.

In January 2006, Steve Jobs sold Pixar to the Walt Disney Company for $4.7 billion, earning a seat on Disney's board as a major shareholder. A number of business analysts were surprised by the turn of events, given Pixar's commercial success in comparison to Disney's in computer animation.

In 2007, Jobs introduced the iPhone. The handheld camera, cell phone, video camera, and media player with a built-in web browser also ran countless software applications or "apps" that were made available on iTunes. A global success, the iPhone revolutionized the concept of the smartphone. Subsequent products including the ultra-thin MacBook Air laptop computer and the iPad tablet computer further solidified Apple's reputation as a manufacturer of revolutionary technological products.

Jobs was diagnosed with a rare form of pancreatic cancer in 2004. Because he had a less aggressive type of cancer, his condition was treated fairly quickly. However, during his absence, Apple executive Timothy Cook temporarily replaced Jobs. In 2009, Jobs had a liver transplant after suffering for several years with a hormone imbalance. He took another leave of absence from the company in January 2011, citing unspecified concerns regarding his health. It was reported, however, that Jobs was continuing to suffer from complications related to pancreatic cancer. Cook was again named as Jobs's replacement during his leave of absence.

On August 25, 2011, Jobs officially stepped down from his post as Apple's CEO, citing health concerns. The company's Chief Operating Officer (COO), Tim Cook, was named as Job's replacement. Jobs remained chairman of Apple's board of directors. Jobs died on October 5, 2011, at the age of fifty-six. Upon news of his death, President Barack Obama hailed Jobs as a visionary and as one of the greatest American inventors.

Impact

Steve Jobs's influence not only includes the invention of computer software and technology—he has revolutionized the way we communicate in today's society. He was a visionary whose fiery personality and extreme self-confidence often left employees and colleagues fearful as well as awestruck. Some said that Jobs's approach to business was more based on his personal mission to the world than a desire to be a major financial player in the technology sector. His work with Apple has produced a number of products that have made him one of the most important inventors of modern times.

Further Reading

Blumenthal, Karen. *Steve Jobs: The Man Who Thought Different.* Harrisonburg: Donnelley, 2012. Print.

Isaacson, Walter. *Steve Jobs.* New York: Schuster, 2011. Print.

Ziller, Amanda. *Steve Jobs: American Genius.* New York, NY: Harper, 2011. Print.

Pilar Quezzaire

■ Johnson, Denis

Identification: American author
Born: 1949; Munich, West Germany

Johnson impressed critics early in his career with his collection of stories, Jesus' Son. *Though he prefers to avoid publicity, Johnson's work throughout the decade has drawn critical and commercial acclaim. He is the recipient of numerous literary awards. In addition to short stories, poems, and novels, Johnson also writes plays and nonfiction articles.*

Born in Germany and raised in Thailand, Tokyo, and Washington, DC, Johnson struggled with drug and alcohol addiction throughout the 1960s and 1970s. *Angels,* his first critically acclaimed novel, was published in 1983, but it was the publication and subsequent praise for *Jesus' Son* in 1992 that seemed to propel Johnson toward the 2000s, when Johnson published across multiple genres and garnered

multiple awards and widespread recognition for his work.

After watching the stage performances of two of his short stories in 1999 at the San Francisco theater company Campo Santo at Intersection for the Arts, Johnson began collaborating with the company, and from 2000 to 2010 he wrote six plays as the company's playwright in residence.

Johnson's sixth novel, *The Name of the World,* was published in 2000. That same year he also published the play, *Hellhound on My Trail.* The collection of essays, *Seek: Reports from the Edges of America & Beyond* (2001) records Johnson's travels throughout the United States, Africa, and the Middle East. The following year brought *Shoppers: Two Plays* as well as the novel *Train Dreams,* which would bring national recognition to Johnson ten years later.

In 2007, Johnson won the National Book Award for his Vietnam-era novel, *Tree of Smoke.* His third wife, Cindy, accepted the award on his behalf while he was on assignment in northern Iraq. When he returned, the National Book Foundation celebrated his win with a reading in Greenwich Village, New York. (The work from which he read was later serialized in *Playboy* magazine and then published as the noir crime novel *Nobody Move* in 2009.) *Tree of Smoke* was then a 2008 finalist for the Pulitzer Prize in Fiction.

Impact

Johnson has had an enduring relationship with Campo Santo. He and the troupe collaborated annually to create socially relevant plays. Among these were *Soul of a Whore* (2003), which addresses controversial issues such as capital punishment and hypocrisy, and *Purvis* (2006), which explores the world of organized crime in the early twentieth century and the lure of power. Both plays were published together in book form in 2012. That same year, Johnson was again a finalist for the Pulitzer Prize for fiction for his 2002 novel *Train Dreams,* which had been reprinted in 2011.

Further Reading

Cowles, Gregory. "Onstage with Denis Johnson." *Arts Beat.* New York Times Co., 21 Apr. 2008. Web. 16 Oct. 2012.

Maury, Laurel. "Hard-Edged Noir Jewel from Denis Johnson." *NPR Books.* NPR, 27 Apr. 2009. Web. 16 Oct. 2012.

Moore, Michael Scott. "Poet of the Fallen World." *SF Weekly News.* SF Weekly LP, 19 Feb. 2003. Web. 16 Oct. 2012.

Josephine Campbell

◼ Johnson, Jimmie

Identification: American NASCAR race car driver
Born: September 17, 1975; El Cajon, CA

Jimmie Johnson is an American race car driver who quickly sped to fame after he began his career in the NASCAR Cup Series in 2001. Johnson has since made several remarkable accomplishments, including becoming the first rookie driver to lead in point standings and the only driver to win at least three races in each of his first seven seasons. Johnson further solidified his standing in racing history in 2008 when he became only the second driver in NASCAR history to win three consecutive Sprint Cup Series championships. Heading into the 2009 racing season, Johnson's forty career wins are the most of any driver since his rookie season.

Jimmie Johnson's racing career began on two wheels instead of four. In fact, before debuting in the NASCAR Cup series in 2001, Johnson didn't even have one hundred starts in stock car racing. However, Johnson was already accustomed to winning, and had won his first motorcycle racing championship at the age of eight. His success continued during his time at the Mickey Thompson Entertainment Group (MTEG) stadium series, where he won three straight stadium motocross championships.

Johnson finally made the move to pavement racing in 1998 when Fishel put him behind the wheel of a race car in the national American Speed Association (ASA), earning him the title of Rookie of the Year. Johnson also debuted in the NASCAR Busch Series, and by 2000, he was racing full-time as a Busch Series driver for Herzog Motorsports, officially rounding the corner towards premiere stock car racing.

After Herzog Motorsports lost their official sponsor, Johnson made the switch to Hendrick Motorsports, home of fellow NASCAR driver Jeff Gordon. (Incidentally, it was Gordon's recommendation that earned Johnson his developmental deal.) On October 7, 2001, Johnson started his first NASCAR Cup series race for Hendrick Motorsports,

Jimmie Johnson. (Courtesy Kim Phillips)

seated behind the wheel of the #48 Lowe's Chevrolet.

Johnson's official rookie season was 2002, and he shifted to racing in the NASCAR Nextel Cup Series (the sponsor would later change to Sprint). As a full-time driver for Hendrick Motorsports that year, he would finish fifth in the overall standings and capture his first career victory, but would ultimately fall short of earning NASCAR Rookie of the Year honors. Johnson's racing career took one more step during the 2003 season, as he posted three additional victories and managed to stay within the top-ten standings throughout the season.

The following season, Johnson finished second overall in the Nextel cup standings. He also swept the two races held at three individual raceways—Lowe's Motor Speedway, Pocono Raceway, and Darlington Raceway. He would continue to add to his career victories during the 2005 season, including another sweep at Lowe's Motor Speedway. However, Johnson slipped to fifth overall in the final championship standings after a cut tire limited him in the final race. Johnson's success on the racetrack reached new heights during the 2006 season, which included his first Daytona 500 victory. (However, Johnson's crew chief, Chad Knaus, would be penalized for illegal modifications made to Johnson's race car during qualifications.) At the conclusion of the season, and with five more career victories under his belt, Johnson secured his first NASCAR Cup Series championship.

Johnson's 2007 season did not include the smooth start his previous season did—he was unable to finish the race at Daytona. Nonetheless, he headed toward the final stretch in a race with teammate Jeff Gordon for first place in the standings, collecting six wins in the first half of the season. At one point during the latter half of the season, Johnson scored four consecutive victories to pull away from Gordon, bringing his season total to ten. By season's end, Johnson had asserted his dominance on the race course, edging Gordon by seventy-seven points to retain his Cup Series championship.

Johnson opened the 2008 season with three top-five finishes in his first seven races, but he couldn't secure a win in the months of May and June. However, Johnson and his crew soon shifted into a higher gear, and the results were obvious by mid-summer. By the end of the summer, Johnson found himself only forty points out of first place in the championship standings. He then earned four victories during a five-race stretch. When Johnson sped into the victory lane following the Checker O'Reilly Auto Parts 500, the second-to-last race of the season, a third consecutive NASCAR championship seemed inevitable. In the season-ending event, the Ford 400, Johnson cushioned his lead with a fifteenth-place finish. He then claimed his third championship title, becoming only the second driver to accomplish the feat in NASCAR's sixty-year history.

While Johnson has certainly come a long way since his early days racing motorcycles in the California desert, a large part of his success stems from the dominance of Hendrick Motorsports and the ingenuity of his crew team. Nonetheless, it is Johnson's drive and skill, and his crew's ability to deliver a refined race car as the final stage of the season unfolds, that have earned Johnson and Hendrick Motorsports a place in NASCAR history.

Impact

Johnson was the first race car driver to be named the Male Athlete of the Year by the Associated Press. But he has also increased his visibility off the racetrack as well. In November 2009, Johnson became the first NASCAR driver in history to win four consecutive championships. In 2010, he continued his remarkable run of race victories, earning wins at the Gatorade Duel in Daytona Beach, Florida, and at the Shelby American in Las Vegas, Nevada, among others. In 2006, along with his wife Chandra, Johnson established the Jimmie Johnson Foundation, which raises funds and supports a number of organizations such as Habitat for Humanity. Johnson has also hosted his own golf tournament in San Diego, raising money for local charitable causes.

Further Reading

Doeden, Matt. *Jimmie Johnson.* North Mankota: Capstone, 2008. Print.

LeMasters, Ron Jr. *Jimmie Johnson: A Desert Rat's Race to NASCAR Stardom.* St. Paul: MBI, 2004. Print.

Tieck, Sarah. *Jimmie Johnson: NASCAR Champion.* Minneapolis: ABDO, 2009. Print

Bill Rickards

■ Jones, Norah

Identification: American singer and songwriter
Born: March 30, 1979; New York City, New York

Jones's debut album, Come Away with Me *(2002), was a tremendous success. The album sold more than twenty million copies worldwide, and captured a number of Grammy Awards. Jones continues to perform and record music that blends jazz and country. In addition to her career in music, Jones has also worked as an actor.*

Norah Jones spent most of her childhood and adolescence in Texas, but returned to her native New York City in 1999. In New York, the singer and songwriter was surrounded by new music, and various musical influences. She began performing with a funk-fusion band called Wax Poetic. In December 1999, she formed her own group.

In October 2000, Jones and her friends Jesse Harris, Lee Alexander, and Dan Rieser recorded a demo for Blue Note Records. The label signed her at the start of 2001, and by May she was at work on an

Jude Law and Norah Jones. (©iStockphoto.com/Pascal Le Segretain)

album. The resulting work, *Come Away with Me*, was released on the Blue Note label in 2002. In 2003, Jones and the album took home five Grammy Awards, including album of the year, best new artist, and record of the year.

Jones released her next album, *Feels Like Home*, in 2004. The album *Not Too Late* followed in 2007. Though these records did not earn the massive sales figures of Jones's first album, both reached number one on the Billboard Top 200 chart. In 2009, the singer released *The Fall*, with producer Angelo Petraglia. Jones, who wrote most of the songs on the record, described the work as a breakup album, because much of what she wrote pertained to the end of her eight-year relationship with Lee Alexander. Jones released the compilation album . . . *Featuring Norah Jones* in 2010 on the EMI Music label.

Jones appears in director Kar Wai Wong's 2007 film *My Blueberry Nights.* The art-house film also features Jude Law, Natalie Portman, and Rachel Weisz. Jones also appears in the 2009 film *Wah Do Dem,* directed by Ben Chace.

Impact

Jones's unique combination of popular music and jazz made her debut album *Come Away with Me* a commercial and critical success. She remains one of the most well-known and popular performers in the music industry. In 2012, she released her fifth studio album, *Little Broken Hearts.*

Further Reading

Caramanica, Jon. "From a Cooing Voice, New Moods and Knots." *New York Times.* New York Times. 28 Mar. 2010. Web. 6 July 2012.

Dye, David. "Norah Jones: Sultry, Jazzy and Real." *NPR.* NPR. 21 Sept. 2007. Web. 6 July 2012.

McLean, Craig. "Norah Jones Interview." *Telegraph.* Telegraph Media Group, 9 Feb. 2010. Web. 6 July 2012.

Josephine Campbell

K

■ Kennedy, Ted

Identification: US senator from Massachusetts
Born: February 22, 1932; Brookline, Massachusetts
Died: August 25, 2009; Hyannis Port, Massachusetts

Edward Moore "Ted" Kennedy represented Massachusetts in the US Senate beginning in 1962, when he was elected to finish the term of his brother and newly elected president, John F. Kennedy. He steadily gained influence and won perpetual re-election, remaining a senator until his death in 2009.

Edward Moore Kennedy was elected to President John F. Kennedy's former Senate seat in 1962, and was re-elected to a full term in 1964. He won despite breaking his back in a near-fatal plane crash that June, leaving him incapacitated throughout the campaign. As a junior senator, he took liberal positions on domestic issues and supported most of President Lyndon B. Johnson's foreign policies.

Some of the greatest achievements of Kennedy's career came during a period of Republican control in the Senate, proving that he is capable of political cooperation and bipartisanship. He pushed to enact a minimum wage increase and compromised with Republicans to achieve the Health Insurance Portability and Accountability Act of 1996, which makes it easier for those who change or lose jobs to keep their health insurance. Another significant healthcare victory was the Children's Health Act of 1997, which makes health insurance more widely available to children through age eighteen in all fifty states. Kennedy also worked to enact the Patients' Bill of Rights in 2001, which greater protection for patients and physicians in dealing with insurance companies. Although the bill ultimately failed to pass Congress, Kennedy was cited in 2002 as one of the most influential people involved in health care legislation and reform.

As President George W. Bush undertook what he termed as the "War on Terrorism" in 2001, Kennedy became a strong voice against the idea of a US

Ted Kennedy. (Courtesy Fenton Ayres)

invasion of Iraq. He maintained, along with many other politicians from both parties, that the president had not made a convincing case that war was a necessary or even legal alternative for dealing with Iraq's violation of United Nations resolutions regarding disarmament. Kennedy also criticized Bush for his failure to obtain international support for the invasion.

Kennedy continued to voice his disagreement with Bush's policy in Iraq in 2007. He was the first legislator in Congress to propose legislation that opposed Bush's plan to initiate an increase in US troop levels. Though troop levels in Iraq were increased by the Bush administration, Kennedy remained an opponent of the war.

In the Senate, Kennedy served as chairman of the Labor and Human Resources Committee, and served on the Judiciary Committee and the Armed Services Committee. He was primarily concerned with the issues of civil rights, education reform, fair wages, workers' rights, environmental protection, and maintaining Social Security and Medicare for senior citizens. He was a supporter of same sex marriage, increased gun control initiatives, and abortion rights.

Kennedy suffered a seizure on May 17, 2008, while at home in Hyannis Port, Massachusetts. It was announced on May 20, 2008, that he had been diagnosed as having a malignant brain tumor. Both Democratic and Republican members of Congress made emotional statements in support of Kennedy. After the diagnosis, a Kennedy spokesperson stated that the senator was not considering retirement.

On June 2, 2008, Kennedy underwent brain surgery in North Carolina. Doctors removed as much of Kennedy's brain tumor as possible. Following the operation, Kennedy returned to Hyannis Port on Cape Cod, making a statement that he was feeling well. Kennedy began a regime of targeted radiation and chemotherapy upon his return to Massachusetts.

In January 2009, Kennedy attended the inauguration ceremony of US President Barack Obama. However, following the inauguration, Kennedy suffered another stroke. Nonetheless, Kennedy continued to champion the health care reform initiatives proposed by President Obama early in his administration.

Kennedy passed away on August 25, 2009. His legislative achievements and political legacy were celebrated nationwide. President Obama offered a public statement, calling Kennedy the most effective legislator in modern history.

Impact

As the fourth longest serving member of the United States Senate, Edward Kennedy had a breadth of influence and impact near unrivaled in the nation's history. The assassinations of his brothers Jack and Robert put a family's worth of expectations on the younger Kennedy, but he went on to become the most legislatively effective member of the storied political dynasty, championing healthcare reform, and serving as the elder statesman of liberalism in the Senate.

Further Reading

Cohen, Richard. "The Last Kennedy/Edward Kennedy And The Camelot Legacy/Senator Ted Kennedy." *New Republic* 175.4 (1976): 26–28. Print.

Gabler, Neal. "The Liberal Lion." *Newsweek* 154. (2009): 48–55. Print.

Nexon, David. "Senator Edward M. Kennedy: The Master Legislative Craftsman." *Health Affairs* 28.6 (2009): w1040–w1048. Print.

Wendy Evans

■ Kerry, John

Identification: American politician and US presidential candidate in 2004
Born: December 11, 1943, Denver, Colorado

Democrat John Kerry is the senior US Senator from Massachusetts, having served since 1985. In 2003, Kerry entered the crowded field of Democrats vying for the party's nomination to unseat incumbent President George W. Bush.

John Forbes Kerry earned his law degree from Boston College in 1976, and worked as an assistant district attorney in Middlesex County, Massachusetts for three years. He was elected lieutenant governor of Massachusetts in 1982, and two years later Kerry was first elected to the US Senate.

In his third term as senator, Kerry concentrated on environmental issues, and was a leading opponent of the Bush administration's efforts to open the Arctic National Wildlife Refuge (ANWR) to oil drilling. The Energy Act of 2001 included the Kerry Amendment, which prevented oil and gas drilling on federally protected land.

In the weeks following the September 2001 terrorist strikes against the US, Kerry proposed a concerted energy-conservation campaign to develop renewable sources of energy and eliminating US dependence on foreign oil, and criticized President Bush for missing an opportunity to call the nation to a cause of "energy independence."

Reelected to a fourth term in November 2002, Kerry became the ranking Democratic member of the Committee on Small Business and Entrepreneurship. He also served on the Commerce, Finance and Foreign Relations Committees and is ranking member of the Hispanic Task Force. Through 2002 he chaired the Senate Democratic Leadership Steering and Coordination Committee.

On the issue of the controversial US-led invasion of Iraq in early 2003, Kerry supported the use-of-force resolution President Bush sought in order to declare war. However, when it became apparent that Bush intended to proceed with his war plan even in the face of overwhelming international opposition, Kerry became more vocal in his criticism of the administration's lackluster foreign policy performance.

In 2003, Kerry officially declared his candidacy in the 2004 presidential election. Although he was painted as an early favorite to win the Democratic nomination, by late 2003 some polls showed him lagging behind former Vermont Governor Howard Dean and retired General Wesley Clark in the crowded Democratic field. Kerry prevailed and won the nomination, and later named Senator John Edwards of North Carolina as his running mate. Kerry lost the 2004 election to President George W. Bush.

In late January of 2007, Kerry announced that he would not mount a campaign for the 2008 US Presidential election. The announcement followed a scandal that erupted after Kerry made what he called a "botched joke" while giving a speech to college students in California. Kerry stated that students who don't do well in school "get stuck in Iraq." He apologized for the remark, stating that he was criticizing Bush's "broken policy" related to the Iraq war. Following the death of Senator Ted Kennedy in 2009, Kerry became the senior senator from Massachusetts.

Impact

Kerry, in his nearly forty years as a United States senator, has played a part in many historically important legislative and political battles. He has worked to reform public education, address children's issues, strengthen the economy, protect the environment and advance America's foreign policy interests around the globe. He has voted in favor of gun control, abortion rights, welfare reform, gay rights and free trade. He opposes the death penalty and school voucher programs.

His role in the groundbreaking investigations into the Iran Contra affair helped establish him as a voice on foreign policy and military strategy, and his push on pro-environment legislation in the early 2000s

marked him as an ally of the conservation movement. Since cofounding Vietnam Veterans of America, Kerry has been a vocal senate proponent of veteran's rights, and continues to make veterans outreach a focus of his day-to-day work.

Further Reading

Cottle, Michelle. "The Pakistan Whisperer." *Newsweek* 157.21/22 (2011): 48–49. Print.
Heilemann, John. "True Compass." *New York* 43.25 (2010): 16–19. Print.
Zengerle, Jason. "Swift Return." *New Republic* 239.4 (2008): 14–17. Print.

Wendy Evans

■ Keys, Alicia

Identification: American singer, songwriter, and actress
Born: January 25, 1981; New York City, New York

Keys is one of the best-known R&B singers and songwriters in the world. Known as a pianist, she also plays guitar and cello. In addition to her work as a musician, Keys has also appeared in several films.

Industry executives began to realize Alicia Keys's talent early on. After taking notice of a song she cowrote for the soundtrack of the film *Men in Black* (1997), J Records executive Clive Davis offered her a recording deal, and together they worked on her debut album. *Songs in A Minor*, released in 2001, was a worldwide success. The record went platinum in ten countries, and earned five Grammy Awards, including best new artist and best R&B album. *Rolling Stone* magazine named Keys its new artist of the year.

Her next album, *The Diary of Alicia Keys* (2003), enjoyed similar success and won four Grammys. In 2004, she published a book of poetry and lyrics titled *Tears for Water*. Keys released a live CD/DVD package titled *Unplugged* in 2005. The album reached the top of the Billboard 200 chart and was certified platinum.

Keys made her acting debut in the 2007 film *Smokin' Aces*, playing an assassin. She also played the best friend of Scarlett Johansson's character in *The Nanny Diaries* (2007). Neither film garnered much success at the box office, but the acting experience

Alicia Keys. (©iStockphoto.com/Frederick M. Brown)

inspired Keys to start her own television production company, Big Pita/Little Pita.

Also in 2007, Keys released her third album, *As I Am*. The single "No One" topped the Billboard pop and R&B charts. However, this success came at a price. Keys suffered a mental breakdown during the album's production. After a break, Keys recovered. *As I Am* went platinum three times and earned her two additional Grammy Awards.

In the 2008 film adaptation of *The Secret Life of Bees*, Keys plays one of three African American sisters who take in a teenage runaway in 1960s North Carolina.

Her fourth album of the decade, *The Element of Freedom*, was released in 2009. Although it reached number two on the Billboard 200 chart, it was Keys's first album to reach number one on international charts. The album features a collaboration with rap artist Jay-Z, and was certified platinum in its first month of release.

Impact

Keys's talents as a musician and actor have brought her great success in the entertainment industry. In 2003, Keys cofounded Keep a Child Alive, an organization dedicated to assisting families in developing countries affected by HIV and AIDS. The singer continues to work to raise money for AIDS awareness and treatment research.

Further Reading

"Alicia Keys." *Allmusic.* Rovi, 2012. Web. 10 Sep. 2012.

Iley, Chrissy. "I was Just Waiting for My Time." Interview. *Guardian.* Guardian News and Media, 7 Jan. 2007. Web. 10 Sep. 2012.

Pareles, Jon. "A Neo-Soul Star as She Is: Nurturing Her Inner Rebel." *New York Times.* New York Times, 9 Sep. 2007. Web. 10 Sep. 2012.

Cait Caffrey

■ Kilpatrick, Kwame

Identification: Mayor of Detroit, 2002–8
Born: June 8, 1970, Detroit, Michigan

Kwame Kilpatrick was the sixty-eighth mayor of Detroit, Michigan. His career was marred by scandal and accusations of corruption. He resigned in 2008 after pleading guilty to obstruction of justice.

Kwame Kilpatrick, a lawyer and former teacher from Detroit, ran for the state House seat representing Michigan's Ninth District in 1996, after his mother, Carolyn Kilpatrick, declined to run for reelection to the position, instead launching her first campaign for the US House. Both mother and son won their respective elections that year, and Kwame Kilpatrick would serve two terms in the Michigan House of Representatives, through 2001.

He became the leader of the Democratic Caucus, a first for an African American, and was selected to speak at the 2000 Democratic National Convention in Los Angeles, California.

When Dennis Archer declined to run for reelection as mayor of Detroit in 2001, Kilpatrick threw his hat into the ring. In the nonpartisan primary election, he and fellow Democrat Gill Hill drew the highest number of votes and the right to make a run

Kwame Kilpatrick. (©iStockphoto.com/Bill Pugliano)

for the seat. Foreshadowing the results in the general election, Kilpatrick took 51 percent of the primary vote. In the general election, Kilpatrick slightly bettered his primary margin, taking 54 percent of the vote in the final returns.

Kilpatrick said his goal as mayor would be to structure programs for the city around the simple theme of "Kids, Cops, Clean." His hope was that cleaner streets and better public safety would help spur business investment in the city, hurt for years by job losses in the auto industry and more recently by the US recession that began in the mid-to-late 2000s. Although the city is about 80 percent black, Kilpatrick hopes to encourage what had been a slow shift back to diversity as more young whites and Hispanics return to the developing downtown area. The "kids" portion of the theme refers mainly to Kilpatrick's goal of improved after-school programs.

Kilpatrick called for a new, high-tech police headquarters for Detroit, estimating the cost at as much as $75 million. He said it would serve as a symbol of Detroit's commitment to modernize its crime-fighting efforts, following the lead of other major cities such as New York City and Baltimore, Maryland. He also approved the sale of former Detroit House of Correction properties as a quick fix to help alleviate the city's budget shortfall.

Kilpatrick's personal life came under scrutiny in 2003, as allegations surfaced of him throwing parties at the mayor's mansion. Unfortunately for Kilpatrick, these allegations were only a sign of things to come. Rumors of marital infidelity began to hamper his political reputation. In March 2008, he was charged with perjury, in addition to being charged with seven other felony accounts. These included misconduct in office and obstruction of justice. The allegations resulted in state and city wide calls for Kilpatrick's resignation.

In May 2008, the Detroit city council approved a measure requesting that Michigan governor Jennifer Granholm become involved in the legal effort to remove Kilpatrick from the mayor's office. Granholm responded by saying that the matter was better dealt with by city officials. The city council also approved impeachment proceedings aimed at removing Kilpatrick from office.

On September 4, 2008, Kilpatrick pleaded guilty to charges of obstruction of justice and resigned from the office of mayor. Kilpatrick served ninety-nine days in jail and later took a position at a Detroit computer company. He was re-incarcerated in 2010 after violating his probation.

Impact

Kilpatrick, despite departing office in disgrace, did contribute to the revitalization of Detroit following the collapse of the city's auto manufacturing industry. He sold vast swaths of state-owned land to ease budget woes, and brought new retail business to the area's Compuware complex. But his staggering accruement of over $210,000 in debt on a city-issued credit card, and the controversy surrounding his second term, will likely be Kilpatrick's most lasting legacy.

Further Reading

Bunkley, Nick. "Kilpatrick Is Indicted in Criminal Ring." *New York Times* 16 Dec. 2010: 24. Print.

Chappell, Kevin. "Redemption Road." *Ebony* 66.9 (2011): 110–11. Print.

Goldman, Andrew. "The Infamous Kwame Kilpatrick." *New York Times Magazine* (2011): 11. Print.

John Pearson

■ *Kitzmiller v. Dover Area School District*

The Case: US federal district court ruling that requiring the teaching of intelligent design violates the Establishment Clause in the First Amendment to the Constitution

Date: Decided on December 20, 2005

The Dover (PA) Area School District had required science teachers to include a statement that intelligent design (ID) is a viable alternative to evolution. Federal judge John E. Jones III ruled this requirement unconstitutional. He further stated that ID is a form of creationism and therefore represents religious doctrine.

Dover is a small town located just outside of York, Pennsylvania. The school board election of 2001 resulted in the selection of several Christian fundamentalists, most notably William Buckingham and Alan Bonsell. Led by Buckingham and Bonsell, the Dover Area School Board voted in October 2004 to require a statement be added to the biology curriculum that students "be made aware . . . of other theories of evolution including . . . intelligent design." An "anonymous" donor, later revealed to be Buckingham, purchased sixty copies of the creationist science book *Of Pandas and People* (1993) to be made available for students.

In December 2004, the American Civil Liberties Union, representing Tammy Kitzmiller as lead plaintiff and ten other parents, filed suit, alleging an attempt to insert religion into the science curriculum using intelligent design as a "wedge." The school board was represented by the Thomas More Law Center, a Christian law center established by Domino's Pizza magnate Tom Monaghan. The trial was held between September 26 and November 4, 2005, before Judge John E. Jones III in Harrisburg, Pennsylvania.

Witnesses for the plaintiffs included a number of prominent biologists in the field of evolution. The first, and among the most important, witness for the defense was Professor Michael Behe, a biochemist with expertise in the blood-clotting pathway. Behe attempted to argue that intelligent design is legitimate science, though he conceded that no peer-reviewed articles exist to support his claim. Nor could Behe propose how ID could account for biological complexity other than through a "designer."

On December 20, 2005, Jones ruled that ID is not science and that the statement required by the Dover school district represented a religious belief. He further fined the district over $2 million to ensure no such further lawsuits would be necessary.

Impact

The decision and the penalty imposed on the Dover Area School Board effectively ended any further attempts to insert religious doctrine into secondary school curricula. While Jones's ruling did result in some criticism, primarily from members of the Discovery Institute, a fundamentalist Christian organization which works to research alternatives to evolution, most legal scholars have felt his decision to be the final word on the subject.

The eight members of the school board who had voted to institute the statement were defeated in their reelection bids four days after the completion of the trial. The plaintiffs accepted a bid by the new board to pay slightly more than $1 million in fees and damages in settling the lawsuit.

Further Reading

Dembski, William, and Jonathan Witt. *Intelligent Design Uncensored: An Easy-to-Understand Guide to the Controversy.* Downers Grove: InterVarsity, 2010. Print.

Lebo, Lauri. *The Devil in Dover: An Insider's Story of Dogma v. Darwin in Small-Town America.* New York: New, 2008. Print.

Slack, Gordy. *The Battle Over the Meaning of Everything: Evolution, Intelligent Design, and a School Board in Dover, PA.* San Francisco: Jossey, 2007. Print.

Richard Adler, PhD

■ Knowles, Beyoncé

Identification: American singer, actress
Born: September 4, 1981; Houston, Texas

Knowles's success in music and movies during the 2000s made her a superstar. After gaining acclaim as a member of Destiny's Child, she launched a solo career. Beyoncé became an award-winning solo artist with numerous top-selling albums. In addition to her success as a musician, she is also a successful actor.

Singer Beyoncé Knowles—known as Beyoncé—started the millennium as a member of the popular

Beyoncé Knowles. (©iStockphoto.com/Kevin Winter for NAACP)

R&B group Destiny's Child. In 2001, the group won two Grammy Awards for the song "Say My Name" from the album *The Writing's on the Wall.* The group's third album, *Survivor* (2001), earned another Grammy for its title track. In 2001, Beyoncé made her acting debut in MTV movie *Carmen: A Hip Hopera.* Her first major film role came in 2002, when she starred as Foxxy Cleopatra in Mike Meyers's *Austin Powers in Goldmember.* She then pursued a solo singing career, releasing *Dangerously in Love* (2003), which produced the smash single "Crazy in Love." The album went multi-platinum, and won five Grammy Awards. The following year, Beyoncé recorded *Destiny Fulfilled* (2004) with Destiny's Child before the group disbanded.

In 2005, Beyoncé and her mother, stylist Tina Knowles, created a clothing line, House of Deréon, which was named for Beyoncé's grandmother. The following year, Beyoncé released her second album, *B'Day* (2006), which won a Grammy for best contemporary R&B album. She then starred in the film adaptation of the musical *Dreamgirls* (2006) with Jennifer Hudson, Jaime Foxx, and Eddie Murphy. The same year, she teamed with Steve Martin and Kevin Kline in a remake of the 1963 film *The Pink Panther.* In 2007, the *Beyoncé Experience* concert tour appeared at venues throughout the world.

Beyoncé returned to the big screen in 2008 as singer Etta James in a musical biopic, *Cadillac Records*, which profiled Chicago's famed Chess Records, the record label that served as a hotbed of American blues and jazz records from the 1940s to 1960s. Also in 2008, Beyoncé released her third album, *I Am . . . Sasha Fierce*, which produced the singles "Single Ladies (Put a Ring on It)" and "If I Were a Boy." Beyoncé married rapper and record producer Jay-Z in April 2008. In early 2009, she sang Etta James's iconic song "At Last" at President Barack Obama's inaugural ball. She then released her fourth solo album, *I Am . . . Yours.* Beyoncé next appeared in the film *Obsessed* (2009), in which she portrays the wife of a man stalked by another woman.

Impact

Beyoncé is one of the most successful entertainers of her generation. In addition to her work as an entrepreneur, she is also a philanthropist. Over the course of her career, Beyoncé has helped to raise millions of dollars for children's charities and victims of natural disasters. Critics have credited her for helping to evolve the R&B genre, and for imbuing her music with an empowering message.

Further Reading

Allmusic. "Beyoncé Biography." *Allmusic.* Rovi, 2012. Web. 10 Sep. 2012.

Easlea, Daryl. *Crazy in Love: The Beyoncé Knowles Biography.* London: Omnibus, 2011. Print.

Knowles, Beyoncé. "Beyoncé Knowles' NYABJ Award-Winning *Essence* Article: 'Eat, Play, Love.'" *Essence.* Essence Communications, 3 May 2012. Web. 10 Sep. 2012.

Angela Harmon

■ Koons, Jeff

Identification: American artist
Born: 1955; York, Pennsylvania

Koons is an American artist who turns ordinary objects into art. One of his most popular pieces is a stainless steel sculpture of a giant balloon dog with a mirrored finish. He broke *an art market record in 2007, when one of his works sold for $23.6 million, only to surpass that price following year, when another work sold for $25.7 million.*

While critical opinion remains mixed on whether American artist Jeff Koons's pieces are really art or just kitsch, he remains widely popular. Some of his best-known works include mirror-finished balloon animals, large statues of pop-culture icons (such as the Pink Panther and singer Michael Jackson), inflatable bunnies, and provocative images of Koons and his former wife.

At the start of the millennium, Koons designed the sculpture *Split-Rocker*, a sculpture made of ninety thousand living, flowering plants. It was exhibited in the Château de Versailles in France from October 2008 to April 2009. Koons is one of only a few living artists to have their work exhibited at Versailles. Over the course of his career, Koons's work has been exhibited at galleries and exhibitions worldwide, including the Metropolitan Museum of Art in New York, and the Neue Nationalgalerie in Berlin.

In 2007, Koons set a world record when his piece, *Hanging Heart*—an enormous stainless steel heart sculpture—sold at auction for $23.6 million, the most amount of money ever for a piece by a living artist; less than a year later, *Balloon Flower* fetched over $1 million more. During the 2000s, Koons was awarded the Skowhegan Medal for Sculpture (2002), and Officer of the French Legion of Honor (2007). In 2007, the artist founded the Koons Family Institute on International Law and Policy. The decision to create the institute was inspired by a long custody and child support battle Koons endured with his ex-wife, Ilona Staller.

Impact

Although some critics have theorized that Koons's pieces are not really art, this has not affected his success as an artist. He continues to create new work and show his pieces internationally. He has also served as a curator of art exhibitions.

Koons, a father of eight who is married to artist Justine Wheeler, has actively promoted the Family Institute. He has said his balloon sculptures were created to connect with his estranged son, Ludwig, who was raised in Italy by his first wife following their divorce. Koons's work on behalf of children has increased awareness of child custody and abduction issues.

Further Reading

Anthony, Andrew. "The Jeff Koons Show." *Guardian*. Guardian News and Media, 10 Sep. 2011. Web. 11 July 2012.

Schneider, Eckhard, et al. *Jeff Koons*. Taschen, 2009. Print.

Segal, David. "Jeff Koons Makes a Heartfelt Return to the Art World." *San Francisco Chronicle*. Hearst Communications, 16 Nov. 2007. Web. 12 July 2012.

Angela Harmon

■ Krugman, Paul

Identification: American economist
Born: February 28, 1953, Albany, New York

Paul Krugman is an American economist, professor, author and op-ed columnist for the New York Times. *He was the 2008 recipient of the Nobel Prize in Economics for his work in international trade theory and economic geography.*

Since 2000, Paul Robert Krugman has taught economics at Princeton University, having previously taught at Yale University, the Massachusetts Institute of Technology, and Stanford University. Krugman has contributed articles to both *Slate* and *Fortune* magazines, and in 2000, he joined the *New York Times* editorial team and maintains a column twice per

Paul Krugman. (Courtesy The Commonwealth Club/Photograph by Ed Ritger)

week. He has also written for *Harvard Business Review, Foreign Policy, The Economist, Harper's* and *Washington Monthly*.

In addition to his columns, essays and articles, Paul Krugman has authored, coauthored or edited over twenty books, including textbooks on economics and international trade and finance. These include *Peddling Prosperity: Economic Sense and Nonsense in an Age of Diminished Expectations* (1995), *The Accidental Theorist and Other Dispatches from the Dismal Science* (1998), *The Return of Depression Economics* (1999), *Fuzzy Math: The Essential Guide to the Bush Tax Plan* (2001), *The Great Unraveling: Losing Our Way in the New Century* (2003), and *The Conscience of a Liberal* (2007).

In 2000, Krugman won the H.C. Recktenwald Prize in Economics, and in 2004, he was given the Prince of Asturias Award for Social Sciences, which is awarded by the King of Spain. Most notably, in 2008, Paul Krugman was chosen as the winner of the 2008 Nobel Prize for Economics by the Royal Swedish Academy of Sciences.

A self-described liberal, he has frequently used his column to critique the economic dealings of both the Bush and Obama administrations. During the early and mid-2000s, Krugman criticized the Bush administration's tax cuts as well as the lack of regulation in the mortgage and other financial markets. In early 2009, much of Krugman's work focused on criticism of the economic recovery plans designed by the administration of US President Barack Obama, arguing that the stimulus would be insufficient to restart the economy. Krugman was also critical of the policies discussed by the G-20 countries at their 2010 summit in Toronto, Canada. Although G-20 leaders pledged to cut their deficits in half by 2013, Krugman stated that this action would only further exacerbate unemployment numbers worldwide.

Impact

Krugman is one of few thinkers in his field who could be called a "popular economist." His presence in *The New York Times* in addition to his prolific written output has helped established Krugman as one of the most revered economists working today. While Krugman's critics are many, his opinion continues to play a vital role in public discourse on economics.

Further Reading

MacFarquhar, Larissa. "The Deflationist." *New Yorker* 86.2 (2010): 38–49. Print.

Spruiell, Stephen. "Professor Ahab." *National Review* 62.19 (2010): 29–32. Print.

Zandi, Mark. "Paul Krugman." *Time* 173.18 (2009): 135. Print.

Colin Post

■ Kurzweil, Ray

Identification: American computer scientist, inventor, entrepreneur, author, and futurist
Born: February 12, 1948; New York, New York

Ray Kurzweil's theory of singularity represents one of the most provocative predictions for the future of artificial intelligence and humanity, while his practical inventions have improved many lives. Together, his predictions and inventions have inspired additional research and advancements in technology, science, and beyond.

Ray Kurzweil's theory of singularity, the subject of the 2005 bestselling book *The Singularity Is Near: When Humans Transcend Biology* and a later documentary film, is a pioneering, although controversial, concept in contemporary artificial-intelligence research and futurist discussions. Based on the rapid speed at which advancements are being made in artificial intelligence, nanotechnology, and genetics, increasing at an exponential rate of growth, Kurzweil predicts twenty-thousand years of progress will be made during the twenty-first century. According to him, by 2045 artificial intelligence will surpass human intellectual capability and humans and machines will merge into one, a moment that represents the singularity. At that time, humans would become immortal as their hearts, lungs, kidneys, and other organs are replaced with tiny robots.

To prepare for the singularity, Kurzweil has been attempting to extend his life span by taking a multitude of daily supplements and undergoing weekly intravenous injections. Additional health initiatives and advice is outlined in *Fantastic Voyage: Live Long Enough to Live Forever* (2004), a book he cowrote with Terry Grossman, his business partner in Ray and Terry's Longevity Products, manufacturer of related nutritional supplements.

Ray Kurzweil. (Courtesy Tim Wilson)

In 2005, Kurzweil, a recipient of the 1999 National Medal of Technology and Innovation and a 2002 inductee in the National Inventors Hall of Fame, teamed with the National Federation of the Blind (NFB) to introduce the world's first portable electronic reading machine, the K-NFB Reader. As with the award-winning Kurzweil Reading Machine, developed in the 1970s with his improved optical character recognition (OCR) software, the portable reader, a Nokia phone equipped with a camera, translates text into voice, offering unparalleled convenience for the blind, learning disabled, and others with reading impairments.

Impact

As an inventor and an entrepreneur whose patents include flatbed scanners and music synthesizers, Kurzweil has improved the lives of the general public, while his advancement of OCR software that allowed for the development of his reading machines is considered the greatest invention for the blind since Braille. His theory of singularity has wielded major influence in contemporary computer science, inspiring conferences and other scholarly initiatives among scientists in academia, government, and business, while also challenging a generation of scholars to consider the future of artificial intelligence and its effect on humanity.

Further Reading

Kushner, David. "When Man and Machine Merge." *Rolling Stone* 19 Feb. 2009: 56–61. Print.

Shapiro, Kevin. "This is Your Brain on Nanobots." Rev. of *The Singularity Is Near*, by Ray Kurzweil. *Commentary* 120.5 (2005): 64–68. Print.

Wolf, Gary. "Stayin' Alive." *Wired* 16.4 (Apr. 2008): 160–67. Rpt. in *The Best American Science and Nature Writing 2009*. Ed. Elizabeth Kolbert and Tim Folger. Boston: Houghton, 2009: 306–15. Print.

Sally Driscoll

■ Kyoto Protocol

Definition: The first international environmental treaty intended to combat climate change

By the end of the decade, the Kyoto Protocol had united 190 industrialized nations, developing countries, and countries in economic transition, including the Russian Federation and the Baltic States, to pledge support for environmental policies intended to halt climate change.

Formally adopted on December 11, 1997, in Kyoto, Japan, the Kyoto Protocol is an international treaty developed under the United Nations Framework Convention on Climate Change (UNFCCC) to collectively cut emissions of carbon dioxide, methane, nitrous oxide, and other greenhouse gases associated with climate change. The treaty went into effect on February 16, 2005, after ratification by Russia satisfied the mandate that required representation from countries totaling at least 55 percent of the world's greenhouse gas emissions, based on 1990 carbon dioxide levels. The treaty assigned emissions reduction targets to each signatory, averaging about 5.2 percent during the first commitment period (2008–12). Special provisions were granted to India, China, and other developing countries, as their later period of industrialization meant less contribution to global warming during the period covered by the treaty. The treaty also provided for emissions trading to offset reduction targets, and Clean Development Mechanisms (CDM) for additional emissions-reduction projects in developing countries.

By the end of the decade, 190 countries were signatories, including latecomers Australia (2007), Iraq (2009), and Turkey (2009). While the United

Oxfam's Kate Raworth explains the Graph of Climate Injustice on the tenth anniversary of the Kyoto Protocol. (Courtesy NG Swan Ti/Oxfam)

Impact

As the first international environmental treaty, the Kyoto Protocol has raised public awareness about the need for global participation to combat the detrimental effects of climate change. The agreement has also helped to encourage governments to set policies for cap-and-trade systems, invest in green technologies, and work on making the switch from coal to natural gas. Thousands of projects have been initiated by the agreement, such as energy initiatives that use solar panels, and tax credits for energy-efficient vehicles. Many of these projects are occurring in the United States. However, criticism of the United States for refusing to ratify the treaty has been widespread, as the United States is responsible for about one-fourth of the world's greenhouse gas emissions. Additional criticism has come from some environmentalists who believe the treaty represents too little, too late, while cynics believe the treaty is misguided or simply a futile attempt at cooperation.

States was one of the initial signers, President George W. Bush withdrew support in 2001 because the treaty did not require India and China to commit to reductions, and because of its perceived detrimental effect on the U.S. economy, making the United States the only signatory to the treaty not to have ratified it. Since 1997, parties have met periodically to reassess standards and discuss cooperation. Meetings regarding the Kyoto Protocol have taken place in Montreal (2005), Bali (2007), and Copenhagen (2009). The 2009 Copenhagen Accord affirmed the scientific opinion that the global average temperature increase should not exceed 2 degrees Celsius above preindustrial levels.

Further Reading

Allen, Leslie. "Will Tuvalu Disappear Beneath the Sea? Global Warming Threatens to Swamp a Small Island Nation." *Smithsonian.* Smithsonian Institution, August 2004. Web. 11 Sep. 2012.

Kyoto Protocol. United Nations Framework Convention on Climate Change, 2012. Web. 11 Sep. 2012.

"Q&A: The Kyoto Protocol." *BBC News.* BBC, 16 Feb. 2005.

Sally Driscoll

L

■ Lady Gaga

Identification: American singer-songwriter
Born: March 28, 1986; New York, New York

Lady Gaga rapidly rose to fame late in the 2000s following the release of the album The Fame. *The album and its follow-up EP,* The Fame Monster, *produced several hit singles and garnered the singer a large number of loyal fans. Known for her flamboyant style on and off the stage, Lady Gaga also became an influential figure in fashion by the end of the decade.*

Singer-songwriter Lady Gaga, born Stefani Joanne Angelina Germanotta, began her career after dropping out of New York University's Tisch School of the Arts in 2005 to concentrate on music. She performed with the Stefani Germanotta Band for a time before pursuing a career as a solo artist. Def Jam Recordings signed her to a record deal in 2006, but the company ended the contract a few months later.

In 2007, Interscope Records hired Lady Gaga as a songwriter for such well-known artists as the Pussycat Dolls and Britney Spears. After hearing her sing, R & B singer Akon signed her to his Kon Live label. Lady Gaga released her debut album, *The Fame*, in 2008. The singles "Just Dance" and "Poker Face" reached number one on the Billboard Hot 100 charts, while the album's third and fourth singles, "LoveGame" and "Paparazzi," also made their way into the top ten. The album won the Grammy Award for best electronic/dance album and was nominated for album of the year.

Lady Gaga opened for the New Kids on the Block during their 2008 tour and headed the Fame Ball Tour the following year. In late 2009, she released the EP *The Fame Monster*, which produced the singles "Bad Romance," "Telephone," and "Alejandro." The album later won the Grammy Award for best pop vocal album, and "Bad Romance" won the awards for

Lady Gaga. (©FilmMagic)

best female pop performance and best short form music video.

Impact

By the end of the 2000s, Lady Gaga had established a dedicated fan base known as "little monsters." She continued to create popular music, receiving additional critical and commercial recognition following the 2011 release of her second full-length album, *Born This Way*. She has received numerous awards for her music and been recognized by the Gay and Lesbian Alliance Against Defamation for her support of causes related to the LGBT community.

Further Reading

Blasberg, Derek. "Lady Gaga: The Interview." *Harper's Bazaar.* Hearst Communications, 13 Apr. 2011. Web. 11 July 2012.

Hutton, Jen C. "God and the 'Gaze': A Visual Reading of Lady Gaga." *International Contemporary Art* 104 (2009): 5–8. Print.

"Lady Gaga." *Elle.* Hearst Communications, 1 Dec. 2009. Web. 11 July 2012.

Angela Harmon

■ Large-scale forest death

Definition: The death of a large tract of forest due to a variety of reasons

During the 2000s, an alarming number of US forests rapidly died off. Many of these forests were located in the western and southwestern United States, specifically in the Rocky Mountain region. The causes of this mass loss of trees include tree-killing insects, forest fires, drought, diseases, and climate change. By the end of the decade the mortality rate of trees and forests in the United States reached over a million acres.

Frequent fires, insects, and other lethal factors ravaged forests in the western and southwestern United States in the 2000s. Over the course of the decade, over a million acres had been lost. Dendrologists and other scientists believe that the catalyst for many of this large-scale forest death is climate change. Ecologists and entomologists have stated that the increase in temperature caused by climate change is associated with forest fires and the outbreaks of bark beetles. These beetles, also known as mountain pine beetles, burrow into pine trees and lay their eggs. The beetles feed on the tree and their larva kills it. Because of climate change, the life cycle of these beetles has increased from two weeks to several months, leading to a sharp increase in the destruction of pine trees. From 2000 to 2009 the Rocky Mountains in the United States and Canada lost nearly 70,000 square miles of forest.

In 2005 ecologists in Colorado noted that aspen trees were dying off in large numbers. By 2008, about 553,000 acres were dead. They named this phenomenon "sudden aspen decline" (SAD). They believe climate change and drier temperatures caused SAD. Ecologists in Oregon and California also noticed a

Stand of Fraser fir killed by the balsam woolly adelgid. (USDA Forest Service/©Bugwood.org)

similar mass death of oak trees, although they believe a disease brought on by fungus-like organism caused these large-scale deaths.

Record levels of dry weather, extremely windy weather, and drought helped cause a series of devastating wildfires in California in 2007, 2008, and 2009. Dry lightning during the summer of 2008 sparked more than two thousand fires. Some of the largest fires occurred around the Santa Cruz Mountains and the Big Sur region of the Santa Lucia Mountains. In June 2008 fires around Big Sur burned over 160,000 acres before merging with other fires, totaling in over 225,000 acres lost. Smoke from the fires caused a significant amount of air pollution, which led to an increase in the number of people with eye and throat irritation.

Impact

The large-scale forest deaths of the 2000s had harmful effects on ecology, climate, and human health. Forests are home to a diverse community of trees, plants, animals, and microorganisms. The death of forests means the loss of their ecosystems. The decimation of forests in Colorado has led to a decrease in rainfall and an increase in temperature for that region. Wildfires in California during the decade killed several people and countless animals. The various effects caused by the forest deaths of the 2000s will continue to be felt into the next decade.

Further Reading

Bulwa, Demian. "Myriad Wildfires Pollute Air, Pose Health Risks and Keep on Spreading." *San Francisco Chronicle.* Hearst Communications, 27 June 2008. Web. 23 Oct. 2012.

Thomas, Peter A., et al. *Fire in the Forest.* Cambridge: Cambridge UP, 2010. Print.

Patrick G. Cooper

■ Late 2000s recession

Definition: A global recession beginning in 2007 caused largely by a sudden collapse of the "housing bubble"; also known as the Great Recession

During the 2000s, low interest rates for mortgages, coupled with the expansion of credit to first-time homeowners with limited incomes, rising gas prices, and abysmal consumer confidence spurred one of the worst recessions in US history. This recession caused the collapse of several major banking institutions. The recession ended in 2009, but the economic trend continued to cost jobs, to lower incomes, and to slow growth.

The early twenty-first century was marred by a severe recession that began shortly before (and was exacerbated by) the terrorist attacks of September 11, 2001. In an effort to restart the stagnant economy, the US Federal Reserve significantly lowered interest rates, encouraging Americans to use greater access to credit to purchase real estate. This activity helped restart the economy. However, the willingness of financial institutions to expand credit to first-time homeowners (many of whom did not previously have the credit and/or the income to purchase homes) artificially inflated housing prices, creating a "housing bubble." In 2007, this bubble collapsed, triggering a severe global recession.

A recession may be defined as a period during which economic growth declines significantly, as

manifest in a fall of a nation's gross domestic product. The Great Depression of the 1930s was the most severe recession in American history. However, the late 2000s recession was, in the minds of most observers, the worst such trend since the Depression. The late 2000s recession was evident in a wide range of areas. Unemployment rates rose significantly, especially during the 2007–8 period. The construction industry was especially hard-hit, given that new home construction was at a minimum.

The recession occurred primarily because it was not readily understood or anticipated. The signs of a coming recession were indeed manifest—monthly jobs reports were showing consistent losses and the housing market (and relevant construction) was declining rapidly. However, the government's response was simply to lower interest rates, hoping that the reduction would stimulate growth within a few months. The focus was on inspiring consumer confidence before the sluggishness that was affecting the financial sector seeped into the lives of private citizens. However, consumer confidence was already disappearing quickly, and it became clear that the fundamental causes of the recession were more extensive and severe than previously assessed. The downturn was attributed to a number of factors.

Low Interest Rates

In many ways, interest rates are indicators of a pending recession. Some economists argue that recessions are cyclical, and that careful monitoring of interest rates can help signal the next phase of a fiscal cycle. This theory is supported by the fact that low interest rates were in place at the start of the recession. In fact, interest rates were lowered during the previous recession (which began in 2001) as a means of reinvigorating the economy. As the economic environment improved by the middle of the decade, however, the Federal Reserve opted to slowly raise interest rates again, keeping in tune with the recovery.

Policymakers, businesses, and private citizens typically welcome low interest rates. Americans are able to borrow more, allowing them to expand their businesses and purchase more goods and even homes. Then again, low interest rates, when weighed against the rates at which banks buy and sell their reserves (the "federal funds rate"), can create an imbalance. In 2006, this imbalance was evident, particularly as oil prices rose and the housing market began to decline while interest rates continued to rise. The

A closing Circuit City store. (Courtesy Ed Yourdon)

Federal Reserve again lowered interest rates when signs of recession became manifest, but oil prices continued to rise and the real estate market contracted. Because of this imbalance, the Federal Reserve's manipulation of interest rates created turmoil in the markets, hastening the recession's development.

Despite the imbalances it can cause, reducing interest rates can have a positive influence on the economy. Lower interest rates can inspire more investment and purchases, from homes to groceries. They help increase consumer confidence, which fuels commerce and the economy as a whole. The problem, however, was that economists did not yet have a handle on the nature of the housing bubble's collapse, which was at the core of the recession.

Subprime Lending

The subprime mortgage crisis was arguably the factor that worsened the recession. Ironically, this crisis was caused by market demand.

The federal government's stated desire for Americans to purchase their own homes (a decades-long theme) helped foster the development of an industry within the financial sector, one that contributed heavily to the late 2000s recession. Lenders have long offered competitive mortgage rates to credit-worthy consumers. However, by the 2000s, lenders' eyes turned to a sector of the population that previously could not afford to purchase homes. Subprime lenders took advantage of a lack of government oversight and a federal push for homeownership (which helped spur economic recovery after the 2001–4 recession), offering mortgages to people with credit problems and/or low incomes. The risks associated with these loans became liabilities when the real estate market began to collapse. More and more subprime-mortgage customers were unable to keep up with their payments, which meant that banks were losing great sums of money used to fund their reserves. It has been widely accepted that the practice of subprime lending contributed heavily to the financial collapse of several major banking institutions, the global markets, and clients with whom they did business.

The subprime crisis has been viewed by many as a "contagion" that would ultimately impact foreign economies as well. The impacts may be viewed in two general arenas, within the financial sector and outside the banking industry. In the former, economists at first believed many major banks outside of the United States might be able to withstand the subprime crisis. For example, the major international financial institutions of Japan (such as the Bank of Japan) appeared to have deep reserves and strong assets. Additionally, like the financial institutions of India and China, Japan's banks were becoming increasingly decoupled (not dependent on connections with Western economies). However, the subprime crisis was so severe and sudden that it caused a sharp drop in stock markets, meaning even the Japanese banks with investments in those markets were forced to raise new capital to offset that decline. Even India and China were not entirely immune, although their state-supported and heavily insulated institutions fared far better during the recession. These economies suffered moderately because, as foreign investors lost major sums in American and other markets, they sold their holdings in Indian and Chinese companies to offset their losses.

Outside of the financial sector, the subprime crisis had a more indirect—but nonetheless significant—impact. As American consumers struggled to address the debts caused by subprime mortgages, demand for foreign imports dropped markedly. Japan, which long held a trade surplus with the United States (particularly in the automotive and information-technology manufacturing industries), saw business come to a virtual standstill.

The decline in foreign imports was particularly evident in (but by no means localized to) luxury industries. In India, for example, the major corporation Tata had purchased a number of foreign businesses, including Jaguar's luxury sport utility vehicle the Land Rover (which had been in high demand only a few years prior), only to see those businesses underperform as the result of a lack of demand. The trend was global: Consumer demand became stagnant and trade was stifled, causing job losses and economic downturns in nations all over the world.

Credit and Debt

In the years leading up to the start of the Great Recession, available credit expanded in the United States. Mortgages were one such area in which credit was expanded. Consumers took advantage of historically low interest rates not only to purchase homes but also to pay for other products and services. The market accommodated this expansion, as the financial, insurance, and real estate sectors continued to grow to meet an enlarging customer base. Meanwhile, the rising price of homeownership, along with an economy that limited personal income growth (if income was not reduced) and the consistently increasing price of oil, meant that Americans were less able to pay down their credit debts.

There is evidence that suggests that the government's deregulation efforts in the years prior to the mid-2000s made it possible for an expansion in credit availability. Several policy initiatives (including the Gramm-Leach-Bliley Act of 1999) relaxed regulations on the financial sector. These deregulatory acts made it possible for financial institutions to introduce new, innovative tools that could make credit more accessible for consumers. Such an environment enabled more Americans to add what could be viewed as an additional source of income to their households. Within the context of the late 2000s recession, however, this fact shrouded the severity of the situation facing the economy.

In fact, statistics on real income growth during the early to mid-2000s were misleading—most of the data included individual credit along with wages

and assets. Although some citizens (namely those at the higher end of the income scale) saw actual increases in their income during the period leading up to the start of the recession, the vast majority of people experienced reductions in their incomes (a fact clouded by their credit).

Meanwhile, consumers continued to purchase goods and services using their credit. These expenditures helped charge the manufacturing and retail sectors, but only for a time. The increasing number of indebted consumers (whose disposable incomes could not compensate for their purchases) triggered a "negative credit shock" (a sudden decline in available credit). The negative credit shock brought business (which relies on credit to facilitate commerce) to a virtual standstill.

Impact

The recession of the late 2000s had a profound and extensive impact on the global economy. One of the most visible areas in which this impact was evident was in the housing market. Low-income homeowners who obtained subprime loans were increasingly unable to repay their mortgages, causing a sharp increase in foreclosures. Meanwhile, the housing crisis meant that banks lost funds used to invest in markets in the US and abroad. This issue meant that banks could not cover their own debts, causing the collapse of several financial institutions and the near-collapse of several others.

The extreme financial losses reported at some of the world's largest banks caused a ripple effect abroad, as central banks across Europe and Asia were unable to compensate for the loss of their American banking partners. As banks struggled to keep open their doors, they could not invest in or support businesses, causing employers to lay off a high number of staff. Unemployment exacerbated the situation, as more people were unable to pay their mortgages and personal debt. Consumers' financial situations gave way to low consumer confidence, which stymied both American and international commerce and trade.

By the end of the 2000s, several governments launched initiatives to consolidate and protect financial institutions as well as to spur economic growth. However, a number of economists predicted that the recession would last at least a few years into the next decade. While the official end of the recession was 2009, the effects of the recession lingered into the next decade: consumer confidence remained low, unemployment rates did not improve significantly, and housing sales stayed stagnant.

Further Reading

Carr, Fred M., and Jane A. Beese. "The Federal Reserve Rate Manipulations from 2000–2007 and the Housing Mortgage Crisis of 2008." *Journal of Economics and Economic Education Research* 9.2 (2008): 107–15. Print. Describes the effects of the Federal Reserve's interest-rate policies on the American economy, leading up to the 2007 recession.

Dore, Mohammed, and Rajiv Singh. "The Role of Credit in the 2007-2009 Great Recession." *Atlantic Economic Journal* 40.3 (2012): 291–313. Print. Examines the role the expansion of credit played in the recession by increasing apparent rates of personal income and later triggering a negative credit shock that undermined financial institutions and markets.

Duffie, Darrell. *How Big Banks Fail and What to Do about It.* Princeton: Princeton UP, 2010. Print. Describes the significance of large banks with a presence in global markets. These banks, the author argues, played a major role in the global financial crisis of the late 2000s.

Hetzel, Robert L. *The Great Recession: Market Failure or Policy Failure?* New York: Cambridge UP, 2012. Print. Uses a macroeconomic perspective, describing the credit crisis of the latter 2000s as part of an economic cycle that has persisted since the nineteenth century.

Krugman, Paul. *The Return of Depression Economics and the Crisis of 2008.* New York: Norton, 2009. Print. Traces the causes of the recession of the late 2000s to issues with the US banking regulatory system.

Lambert, Thomas E. "Falling Income and Debt: Comparing Views of a Major Cause of the Great Recession." *World Review of Political Economy* 2.2 (2011): 249–61. Print. Discusses how American consumers' efforts to borrow more to pay for the rising cost of living, coupled with the practice of subprime lending and other factors, fueled consumer debt and the Great Recession as a whole.

Mishkin, Frederic S. "Over the Cliff: From Subprime to the Global Financial Crisis." *Journal of Economic Perspectives* 25.1 (2011): 49–70. Print. Describes the impact of subprime lending on American financial institutions, contributing significantly to the recession.

Michael P. Auerbach

■ Ledger, Heath

Identification: Actor
Born: April 4, 1979; Perth, Australia
Died: January 22, 2008; New York, New York

Heath Ledger was an Australian actor best known for his award-winning performances as Ennis Del Mar in Brokeback Mountain *(2005) and the Joker in* The Dark Knight *(2008). Ledger died of a prescription drug overdose at the age of twenty-eight.*

In 1999, Australian actor Heath Ledger landed a role as Patrick Verona in the film, *Ten Things I Hate about You,* in which he starred opposite Julia Stiles. Ledger, reluctant to take a role that would typecast him as a teen film star, took the job because of his limited offers. However, the film was wildly successful, and Ledger was noticed for the first time in the United States.

In 2001, Ledger appeared in *A Knight's Tale,* which became a box-office hit. He subsequently starred in

Heath Ledger. (©iStockphoto.com/Jon Kopaloff)

The Four Feathers (2002), which was panned by critics and was a box-office disaster. Taking more varied and difficult roles, he acted in a succession of films, including *The Lords of Dogtown* (2005), *The Brothers Grimm* (2005), *Brokeback Mountain* (2005), and *Candy* (2006).

Brokeback Mountain not only solidified Ledger's reputation as a serious actor but also earned him an Oscar nomination. In the film, Ledger plays the part of a homosexual cowboy opposite Jake Gyllenhaal. The film caused a cultural stir, as it sensitively handled the relationship between two men who were unable to live their lives openly. Both Ledger and Gyllenhaal were praised for their performances; Ledger won several awards, including the 2005 New York Film Critics Award for best actor and the 2006 International Award for best actor as presented by the Australian Film Institute.

Ledger's performance as Bob Dylan in the 2007 film *I'm Not There* was well received. He costarred in the film with Christian Bale, and the two were slated to perform together again in Christopher Nolan's neo-comic-book action movie *The Dark Knight* (2008).

Ledger's performance as the Joker in *The Dark Knight* was rumored to be legendary, but months before the film was released in July 2008, Ledger was found dead in his Manhattan apartment. He had been filming *The Imaginarium of Doctor Parnassus* (2009) in London, where he had reportedly been having trouble sleeping and had been relying on sleep aids. Ledger had returned to Manhattan in January, and at 3:00 p.m. on January 22, 2008, he was found unresponsive in his bedroom by his housekeeper and was pronounced dead shortly after.

An autopsy following his death cited the prescription drugs oxycodone and hydrocodone in the form of sleeping pills as the cause of death, but results as to whether the death was a suicide or an accidental overdose were inconclusive. A second autopsy, on February 6, ruled out suicide, concluding that the death was the result of an accidental overdose.

Impact

Ledger's early death at age twenty-eight signified a premature end to a well-respected and promising film career. Upon the release of *The Dark Knight*, film critics overwhelmingly praised Ledger's portrayal of the Joker, with many lauding it as one of the greatest on-screen performances of all time. Ledger was posthumously awarded the Academy Award for best supporting actor in 2008.

Further Reading

Norris, Chris. "(Untitled Heath Ledger Project)." *New York* 41.7 (2008): 50–58. Print.

Sperling, Nicole. "Heath Ledger: The Mourning After." *Entertainment Weekly* 977 (2008): 12–13. Print.

Taddeo, Lisa. "The Last Days of Heath Ledger." *Esquire* 149.4 (2008): 126–31. Print.

Anne Whittaker

■ Lindh, John Walker

Identification: American terrorist
Born: February 9, 1981; Washington, DC

John Walker Lindh is a United States citizen who was captured by US forces while fighting for the Taliban in Afghanistan. Known as "The American Taliban," Lindh was charged with aiding a terrorist organization, pleading guilty in July 2002.

John Walker Lindh spent the first ten years of his life in Silver Spring, Maryland, with his father, Frank, an attorney, his mother, Marilyn, and his two sisters. In 1991, when his family moved to San Anselmo, California, where he first studied Islam and Middle Eastern culture at Tamiscal High. In 1998 he graduated early from Tamiscal after Spike Lee's film *Malcolm X* (1992) inspired him to attend the Islamic Center of Mill Valley, convert to Islam at age sixteen, and change his name to Sulayman al-Lindh. In July, he left the United States to study Arabic in Sanaa, Yemen, where he remained until May of 1999. After a brief hiatus in the United States, Lindh returned to school in Yemen in February 2000.

In November 2000, Lindh moved to Bannu, Pakistan, to attend an Islamic school. Less than six months later, he began training at a military camp in northern Pakistan and in three weeks entered Afghanistan to fight for the Taliban army in a civil war against the Soviet-supported Northern Alliance. Lindh received further military training in a government-run camp that was sponsored by known terrorist Osama Bin Laden, whom Lindh met on more than one occasion. In early September, 2001, Lindh was sent to the front lines in Takhar; it is unclear whether he fought or simply served as a guard.

In the wake of the terrorist acts of the previous September, the United States began an aerial bombing campaign designed to destroy Taliban control over Afghanistan. With American assistance, the Northern Alliance forced a Taliban retreat from Takhar to Herat, where Lindh's army was captured by Northern Alliance general Abdul Rashid Dostum. While captive at Mazar-i-Sharif in a makeshift prison, Lindh was questioned by two undercover Central Intelligence Agency (CIA) agents, to whom he said nothing.

Shortly afterward, the captives revolted, and a bloody confrontation forced their retreat to the basement of the compound. Lindh suffered a gunshot wound to the thigh, and one of the CIA agents, Michael Spann, was killed. On December 1, the basement was flooded with freezing water, driving out the soldiers who were still alive, only eighty-six of the original four hundred to five hundred captives. Lindh, who was among the eighty-six, eventually asked for help from Red Cross officials and American reporters and was dubbed the "American Taliban" after being filmed by CNN reporter Richard Pelton.

After Lindh was discovered in Afghanistan, he remained in US military custody for fifty-four days, during which the conditions of his imprisonment remained unclear. The US government and primary interrogator Christopher Reimann insisted that Lindh's Miranda rights had been respected. Others, including Lindh's parents, Jesselyn Radack of the Justice Department, and a Navy medic who treated Lindh in Afghanistan, claimed that Lindh repeatedly asked for and was denied legal counsel.

Lindh's confession to an unnamed defense intelligence officer also remains in question, as the officer admitted to substituting Lindh's testimony that he trained with "al Ansar," a non-Afghani Taliban fighting force, with "al-Qaeda," the terrorist organization. Finally, several declassified accounts report that Lindh suffered mistreatment by military and intelligence personnel, including being duct-taped naked to a stretcher and left in a storage container for days with minimal food and water. Arguing that Lindh was an enemy combatant, American officials claimed that he was outside the jurisdiction of US civil law and the Geneva Conventions and was treated with as much respect as that position allowed.

Lindh was formally indicted on February 5, 2002, with ten counts of criminal charges, most involving aiding a terrorist organization. Lindh pleaded not guilty. After months of trial preparation, however, on July 15, 2002, he accepted a plea agreement from federal prosecutors in which he pleaded guilty to supplying services to the Taliban and to carrying an explosive during the commission of a felony. He was sentenced to twenty years in prison on October 4, 2002. In September, 2004, Lindh's lawyers appealed to President George W. Bush to have Lindh's sentence commuted.

Impact

The capture and prosecution of John Walker Lindh heightened antiterrorist fervor in the United States in the wake of the September 11 attacks. Politicians and news media alike cited Lindh as the terror within US borders in an effort to drum up support for the American War on Terror. In the years following the plea agreement, further evidence and testimony were attained that suggested Lindh never took up arms against American soldiers and never participated in terrorist activity. Furthermore, his treatment at the hands of the Federal Bureau of Investigation (FBI) and the US military, under the direction of Secretary of Defense Donald Rumsfeld, raised questions about the treatment of suspected terrorist detainees at US facilities around the globe.

Further Reading

Dobb, Edwin. "Should John Walker Lindh Go Free? On the Rights of the Detained." *Harper's Magazine* 304. 1824 (2002): 31–42. Print.

Kukis, Mark. *"My Heart Became Attached": The Strange Journey of John Walker Lindh.* Washington, DC: Brassey's, 2003. Print.

Mayer, Jane. "Lost in the Jihad." *New Yorker* 10 Mar. 2003: 50–60. Print.

Lindsay M. Christopher

■ Literature in the United States

Definition: American literature in the 2000s responded to the upheavals of the decade, particularly America's changing role in the world following the terrorist attacks of September 11, 2001, and the economic crisis of 2008

Throughout the first decade of the twenty-first century, many authors in the United States have embraced elements of genre fiction in their written works, borrowing elements from historical fiction, sci-fi, fantasy, and other popular genres. In the decades just prior to the turn of the century, popular and literary fiction in the United States took two primary paths: popular fiction sought to produce compelling storytelling, while literary fiction focused on offering good writing with plausible characters and realistic settings. In embracing elements from science fiction, fantasy, thrillers, mystery, and other genres, American authors in many ways have returned to a style of writing that was highly regarded in the nineteenth and early twentieth centuries, which sought to provide readers with both good writing and compelling storytelling. Also notable in this decade was the desire of nonfiction authors to create lasting accounts of everything from autobiographies to historical events to current issues facing the nation.

In the 2000s, American literature proved to be both resilient and flexible. Though faced with competition from online media—everything from tweets to blogs—American authors, both well established and new and emerging, found a wide and diverse audience of readers. Many critics believe that numerous pieces of fiction and nonfiction written in this decade not only charmed and engaged a generation of readers but also will be read and discussed for generations to come. Much of the literature in this decade absorbed the outward styles of online writing, being, for example, both to the point and laced with irony. Yet it also exhibited the some of the best traits literature has always had to offer: intelligence, earnestness, and engagement with its readers. The decade also saw the rise of numerous "mega-best sellers," everything from up-all-night, page-turning novels to gripping pop-culture analyses of economics.

Best Sellers

While critics do not consider many best-selling books to be fine writing, such works are nevertheless enjoyed by a wide variety of readers and may, in future generations, be considered classics in their own right. Among the best-selling novels of the decade were the four novels that make up Stephenie Meyer's young-adult vampire series: *Twilight* (2005), *New Moon* (2006), *Eclipse* (2007), and *Breaking Dawn* (2008). After the first novel broke sales records upon its release and became popular with both teenagers and adults alike, publishers lined up to sign (or promote)

their own authors who could write vampire novels or another such similar monster-related fiction. Among the authors who benefited from the decade's vampire-mania was Charlaine Harris, whose first novel in her Southern Vampire Mysteries series, *Dead until Dark*, was published in 2001. It has since spawned numerous sequels and inspired the television drama *True Blood*.

A popular young-adult series of the era was the dystopian adventure trilogy written by Suzanne Collins, comprised of *The Hunger Games* (2008), *Catching Fire* (2009) and *Mockingjay* (2010), in which young boys and girls are selected annually from twelve repressed districts and forced to fight to the death on live television. Other highly popular novels of the era include Dan Brown's *The Da Vinci Code* (2003), a thriller that involved a cover-up within the Roman Catholic Church about Jesus's life, and Khaled Hosseini's novel *The Kite Runner* (2003), which tells the coming-of-age story of a boy living through the tumultuous decades in Afghanistan during the second half of the twentieth century.

Perhaps the most popular nonfiction book by American authors in the 2000s was *Freakonomics*, written by Steven D. Levitt and Stephen J. Dubner and first published in 2005. In it, the authors, who are an economist and a journalist, respectively, apply economic theories to everything from drug dealing to parenting to cheating to the impact of legalized abortion on crime.

Celebrated Fiction

Although the above-mentioned novels were enormously popular with readers and may have lasting value, they are not all among the most critically acclaimed works of fiction of the 2000s. Several titles made numerous best-of lists because readers, critics, and award committees had singled them out as being among the finest of the decade's offerings. Ranked very high among them was Michael Chabon's *The Amazing Adventures of Kavalier & Clay*, which won the Pulitzer Prize for fiction in 2001. The novel explores the lives of two young Jewish cousins who create a popular comic book character just prior to World War II and, through their work on this project, vent their frustrations with the world. The novel brought attention to the importance of popular culture (including comic books) and how they help to create the myths of our modern world. Equally lauded was Jonathan Franzen's National Book Award–winning novel, *The Corrections* (2001), which looked with a satirical but humanist eye at modern society through the filter of a Midwestern family named Lambert. Another important novel of the decade was Cormac McCarthy's *The Road* (2006), a slim volume that explored the relationship of a father and his young son trying to survive in a post-apocalyptic world. It won the Pulitzer Prize for fiction in 2007. Another Pulitzer Prize–winner hailed by critics was Junot Diaz's *The Brief Wondrous Life of Oscar Wao* (2007), which, although relatively short at just 350 pages, performs the feat of more epic-length novels by tracing the history of a family (and a nation) over several generations using multiple narrators.

Other works of fiction that made critics' best-of-the-decade lists include: *The Fortress of Solitude* (2003) by Jonathan Lethem, a coming-of-age novel about a young white boy growing up in a predominantly black neighborhood in Brooklyn during the 1970s; *Empire Falls* (2001), Richard Russo's look at small-town, blue-collar life; *John Henry Days* (2001), Colson Whitehead's searing novel about an opportunistic freelance journalist covering a festival held in honor of the noted black folk hero John Henry; and Kelly Link's masterful collection of fantasy and horror short stories, *Magic for Beginners* (2005).

A number of older American masters of fiction also produced acclaimed works in this decade. Thomas Pynchon published *Against the Day* (2006); Tom Wolfe's *I Am Charlotte Simmons* (2004); Don DeLillo's *The Body Artist* (2001), *Cosmopolis* (2003), and *Falling Man* (2007); John Irving's *The Fourth Hand* (2001), *Until I Find You* (2005), and *Last Night in Twisted River* (2009); and Philip Roth's *The Human Stain* (2000), *The Dying Animal* (2001), *The Plot Against America* (2004), and *Exit Ghost* (2007).

Celebrated Nonfiction

American authors of nonfiction also greatly impressed readers and critics during this decade. Perhaps the decade's most acclaimed work of nonfiction was *The Looming Tower: Al-Qaeda and the Road to 9/11* (2006), Lawrence Wright's exhaustive account of the terrorist attacks of September 11, 2001. Wright's work not only chronicled the way in which terrorist networks planned and executed the attacks, which killed nearly three thousand people, but also described the ways in which US intelligence agencies had failed to prevent them. (An equally popular and critically praised nonfiction work about the attack

was *The 9/11 Commission Report*, the official report of the events leading up to the attacks, which was first published in 2004.) Another penetrating work of nonfiction was *Nickel and Dimed: On (Not) Getting By in America* (2001), an undercover investigation of the working poor by Barbara Ehrenreich, who tried to live for two years on income she earned as an unskilled, minimum-wage worker in the United States. In a different vein, Alan Weisman looked at the ways our planet would change if the human race would suddenly disappear in *The World Without Us* (2007).

Well-crafted memoirs also remained popular with critics and readers. One of the first greatly praised memoirs of the decade was Dave Eggers's *A Heartbreaking Work of Staggering Genius* (2000), which explored his life raising his younger brother after the deaths of their parents from cancer. It was celebrated upon its release for its playful and vibrant writing as well as its ironic and self-reflective style. Another important memoir came from the pen of the celebrated American author Joan Didion, who wrote of the year of her life after her husband's death in *The Year of Magical Thinking* (2005), which was considered by critics to be one of the finest depictions of the grieving process written by an American author.

Impact

The first decade of the twenty-first century was marked by real-life events that greatly altered and inspired literature in the United States: the terrorist attacks of September 11, 2001, and the two economic downturns (the first in 2001, the latter beginning in late 2007) that forced many Americans to re-evaluate their expectations of future success and prosperity. These events were not only written about exhaustively in the nonfiction literature of the era but were also touched upon, either directly or indirectly, in much of the period's fiction. In every era, American literature has explored the individual's place in society, how one adapts to or rebels against the prevalent notions of one's time. American literature continued to display this trait in this decade.

In the 2000s, literature in the United States remained just as vibrant as it had been in decades past. American authors, both new and old, demonstrated that they could adapt to the times and yet maintain their individual literary clarity. Moreover, the changing times have given literature a new importance, as it captures the way life was lived and the way people felt at a given moment, even if that literature takes the form of a personal memoir or genre fiction, such as science fiction or fantasy. Although many cultural observers questioned whether long-form works like novels and histories would survive in an era of short-burst writing like blogs and tweets, American readers have shown that they continue to seek out and read such lengthy works even in a hyperpaced era.

Further Reading

Chabon, Michael. *The Amazing Adventures of Kavalier and Clay.* New York: Random, 2000. Print. In Chabon's Pulitzer Prize–winning novel, two Jewish cousins confront their real-world fears through their creation of the Escapist, a mid-century comic book character who embodies all their hopes and dreams.

Eggers, Dave. *A Heartbreaking Work of Staggering Genius.* New York: Simon, 2000. In Eggers' memoir, he describes in ironic detail how he raised his younger brother following the deaths of their parents.

Didion, Joan. *The Year of Magical Thinking.* New York: Knopf, 2005. Print. Didion, a highly regarded author of novels and literary journalism, describes her life in the year following the death of her husband, the noted writer John Gregory Dunne, as she cared for their ailing daughter, Quintana.

Franzen, Jonathan. *The Corrections.* New York: Farrar, 2001. Print. Franzen's sprawling novel about the Lambert family, which won the National Book Award, looks at contemporary American life through a prism that is both satirical and compassionate.

McCarthy, Cormac. *The Road.* New York: Knopf, 2006. Print. McCarthy's post-apocalyptic novel about a father and son's journey through a wasteland earned the Pulitzer Prize in 2007.

Russo, Richard. *Empire Falls.* New York: Knopf, 2001. Print. This Pulitzer Prize–winning novel is a big, old-fashioned page-turner about people living in a blue-collar town that has seen better days.

Wright, Lawrence. *The Looming Tower: Al-Qaeda and the Road to 9/11.* New York: Knopf, 2006. Print. The definitive source of information pertaining to the terrorist attacks carried out by the al-Qaeda terrorist network on the US mainland on September 11, 2001.

Christopher Mari

■ *The Lord of the Rings* trilogy

Definition: Based on the three-volume novel of the same name by author J. R. R. Tolkien, the *Lord of the Rings* film trilogy is one of the most popular movie franchises of all time, and the three installments were some of the most financially successful films of the 2000s.

The Lord of the Rings *film trilogy is a wildly popular series of fantasy films that won several awards in the film industry. The series is based on the* Lord of the Rings *novels written by J. R. R. Tolkien that were published in the 1950s. The films explore the themes of fate and free will, temptation, and power.*

Director Peter Jackson began developing a *Lord of the Rings* adaptation in 1995 with his wife and producer Fran Walsh. After several years of planning and negotiating with Miramax Films producer Harvey Weinstein, the first film, *The Fellowship of the Ring*, went into development. All three films were shot back-to-back in New Zealand. Jackson and his team created Tolkien's fictional world of Middle-earth in real locations throughout New Zealand as well as on soundstages. *The Fellowship of the Ring* was released on December 19, 2001, followed by *The Two Towers* on December 18, 2002, and *The Return of the King* on December 17, 2003. The films would go on to gross $2.91 billion worldwide.

The films tell the story of several characters, both heroes and villains, and how the One Ring brings them together. The ring gives its owner great power but gradually takes control of him, twisting his free will and causing him to do evil. In the story, the ring is given to a hobbit (a fictional species of small humanoids) named Frodo Baggins (Elijah Wood). Frodo is tasked with taking the ring to Mount Doom, which is the volcano where the ring was created and the only place it can be destroyed. He is joined by the wizard Gandalf (Ian McKellen), the warriors Aragorn (Viggo Mortensen) and Boromir (Sean Bean), as well as fellow hobbits Samwise Gamgee (Sean Astin), Pippin Took (Billy Boyd), and Merry Brandybuck (Dominic Monaghan). The fellowship is complete when the dwarf Gimli (John Rhys-Davies) and the elf Legolas (Orlando Bloom) join. Through the three films, the fellowship travels across Middle-earth, battling the evil wizard Saruman

Ian McKellen (left) as Gandalf with Elijah Wood as Frodo in The Lord of the Rings: The Fellowship of the Ring. *(New Line/ WireImage/Getty Images)*

(Christopher Lee) and his army of orcs and goblins. An unlikely aid comes in the form of a deformed hobbit named Gollum (Andy Serkis), a previous owner of the ring.

Impact

The Lord of the Rings became one of the highest-grossing film trilogies of all time. The films garnered a total of seventeen Academy Awards, with *The Return of the King* winning eleven, including the award for best picture. The films brought about a resurgence in the popularity of Tolkien's work, as well as in fantasy films and literature in general. New Zealand's tourist industry also saw a sharp increase following the release of the films.

Further Reading

Fisher, Jason, ed. *Tolkien and the Study of His Sources: Critical Essays.* Jefferson: McFarland, 2011. Print.

Sibley, Brian. The Lord of the Rings: *The Making of the Movie Trilogy.* New York: Harper, 2002. Print.

—. The Lord of the Rings *Official Movie Guide.* New York: Houghton, 2001. Print.

Patrick G. Cooper

■ *Lost*

Identification: Popular television series about the lives of strangers who crash on a strange island and must cope with the hostility of their environment

Executive Producers: Damon Lindelof (b. 1973); Carlton Cuse (b. 1959)

Date: Aired September 22, 2004–May 23, 2010

The cult television series Lost *introduced viewers to a mysterious island, a group of castaways, and the mythology that enveloped their lives over the course of six successful seasons. Despite a drop in viewership from peaking at nearly eighteen million in 2007 to ten million in its final season,* Lost *earned Emmy and Golden Globe Awards, as well as a devoted fan following.*

Assembling a large international cast in Hawaii, *Lost*'s creators were no strangers to ambition. In what would become the most expensive show on television, executive producers and head writers Damon Lindelof and Carlton Cuse told a story that explored human wants and needs, while also examining the external forces that influence individual lives.

The show opens in the aftermath of a plane crash on an uncharted island. Days turn to weeks, and, as hope of rescue fades, the survivors build a patchwork community, following their oft-repeated mantra: "Live together; die alone." Initially thought to be strangers, flashbacks reveal striking overlaps in the characters' lives. These flashbacks also reveal the circumstances that brought many of the survivors to the island. The series premiered with a large cast of fourteen regular characters. Actors joined and left the show as characters were added or written out. The core characters remained consistent, however, and included surgeon Jack Shephard (Matthew Fox), enigmatic box salesman John Locke (Terry O'Quinn), fugitive Kate Austen (Evangeline Lilly), con artist Sawyer (Josh Holloway), millionaire Hugo "Hurley" Reyes (Jorge Garcia), and island native Ben Linus (Michael Emerson). The island itself also proves to be an unpredictable character with many secrets of its own.

As the survivors attempt to rebuild their lives, hostile forces—ranging from polar bears to the "smoke monster," a destructive island being—divide them. Those determined to leave clash with those resigned to stay. The Others, the original inhabitants of the island, continually target the survivors. Their lives are further fractured when six of them are rescued, only to realize that they must return to the island. Dipping into science fiction, the survivors who were left behind begin jumping through time, ultimately finding themselves in the 1970s. Throughout these struggles, questions of science and faith, of free will and destiny, remain major themes.

Impact

Compared to its predecessors and other shows airing at the time, *Lost* set itself apart through fan involvement. Its complicated mythology and intricate plotting led to elaborate fan websites, wild theorizing, and cross-media tie-ins through publications, podcasts, and an alternate reality game: *The Lost Experience*. Though dramatic, its characters tackle philosophical questions about the mysteries of life beyond mere drama. As the characters questioned their lives, so did the audience. *Lost*'s legacy lives in its marketable spirit—and in its many unanswerable questions.

Further Reading

Hale, Mike. "No Longer 'Lost,' but Still Searching." *New York Times* 25 May 2010: C1. Print.

Ryan, Tim. "High Filming Costs Forced ABC Network Executives to Consider Relocating." *Honolulu Star-Bulletin*. Honolulu Star-Bulletin, 26 Jan. 2005. Web. July 2012.

Terry, Paul, and Tara Bennett. *Lost Encyclopedia*. Indianapolis: Penguin, 2010. Print.

Lucia Pizzo

■ Lost in Translation

Identification: Film about a young American woman and an older American actor who meet in a Tokyo hotel and develop a relationship over several days
Director: Sofia Coppola (b. 1971)
Date: Released on October 3, 2003

Written and directed by Sofia Coppola, daughter of acclaimed filmmaker Francis Ford Coppola, Lost in Translation *was one of the film industry's major critical and financial successes of 2003. Set in contemporary Tokyo, the film explores themes of alienation, attraction, and loneliness. The film received four Academy Award nominations, winning for best original screenplay.*

Writer and director Sofia Coppola drew inspiration for *Lost in Translation* from her own experiences in Tokyo. Following her 1999 film, *The Virgin Suicides*, she stated that she wanted to make a film that was fun and romantic. She collaborated with cinematographer Lance Acord to utilize the vibrant lighting of Tokyo. When she began writing the script, she specifically wrote the part of Bob Harris, an actor going through a midlife crisis, with actor Bill Murray in mind. Coppola's goal was to use the film to explore existential questions against the disorienting background of Tokyo.

Harris is in Tokyo to film a whiskey commercial. He is going through a midlife crisis, and his marriage of twenty-five years is falling apart. At a hotel bar, he meets Charlotte (Scarlett Johansson), who is in Tokyo after joining her photographer husband on assignment. Charlotte is also experiencing trouble in her marriage. The two soon form a bond over discussions concerning marriage, children, and the meaning of life itself. Together, they journey around Tokyo, visiting karaoke bars, pachinko parlors, and various parties. The two characters' Americanism contrasts with the culture of Tokyo, and the nature of their relationship remains ambiguous. In the film's iconic final scene, Harris says goodbye to Charlotte before his return to the United States, whispering something into her ear that is inaudible to the audience.

Impact

Lost in Translation received several award nominations. At the 2003 Academy Awards, it was nominated for best picture, best actor, best director, and best original screenplay. It only won the latter, but the director nomination made Coppola the first American woman to be nominated in the category. Murray won a Golden Globe Award and a British Academy of Film and Television (BAFTA) award for his role as Bob Harris. The film, which cost approximately $4 million to make, earned over $119 million at the box office.

Further Reading

King, Geoff. *Lost in Translation.* Edinburgh UP, 2010. Print. American Indies.

Thompson, Anne. "Tokyo Story." *Filmmaker.* Filmmaker Magazine, 2012. Web. 8 Oct. 2012.

Patrick G. Cooper

■ Low-carb diets

Definition: Food restriction plans that greatly minimize or eliminate specific carbohydrates

Together with fats and proteins, carbohydrates are one of the three macronutrients, or energy-containing nutrients, of the human diet. Low-carb diets, which reduce or eliminate certain carbohydrates, can be short-lived, calorie-restrictive fads, or they can be tiered weight-loss programs that replace carbohydrate calories with another macronutrient.

As the numbers of Americans with metabolic disorders like diabetes climb, low-carb diets that aim to reduce weight by lowering sugar intake outpace the heart-healthy, low-fat diets of the 1990s, such as the

American Heart Association diet. Although varied low-carb programs exist, the Atkins diet of 2002 in large part spurred research efforts to determine the true benefits and risks of these programs.

The starches, refined sugars, and fructose prevalent in American diets are all types of carbohydrates that cause more rapid glucose peaks in the body than complex wheat and grains. When a diet with fewer than a hundred grams of daily carbohydrates is implemented, the body burns its own fat sources instead of using daily carbohydrate intake for energy. However, this ketosis, or fat breakdown, can cause kidney damage and malnutrition. Nonselective carbohydrate elimination and increased protein or fat intake also deprive the body of essential nutrients, such as calcium or folate, and potentially increase heart disease risks.

Careful low-carb diets distinguish between nutritive and damaging carbohydrate sources instead of relying on strict calorie-counting techniques alone. For example, the glycemic index (GI) that was developed in 1980 is a calculation that reflects a carbohydrate's effect on blood sugar levels. The South Beach diet, originally designed to minimize fat intake and heart disease, is one such low-carb variant diet. The program incorporates GI measurements into food recommendations on the premise that carbohydrate-rich processed foods adversely affect satiety, or fullness, and weight as much as trans fat. The 2005 Centers for Disease Control Dietary Guidelines for Americans similarly emphasizes fiber-rich carbohydrate choices instead of limiting amounts of carbohydrate foods.

Low-carb diets by definition limit carbohydrate intake instead of emphasizing better carbohydrate choices, and each low-carb diet has its own restrictions about types and amounts of carbohydrates. Many involve preliminary purges, followed by stepwise reintroduction of particular carbohydrate sources and a final maintenance plan. For example, the 2002 Atkins New Diet Revolution institutes a four-phase program that begins with only twenty net grams of carbohydrates each day from a small selection of foods. According to the American Association of Family Physicians, most low-carb diets reduce carbohydrates to fewer than 20 percent of the day's calories. The US Dietary Association, however, recommended in 2009 that 45 to 65 percent of a daily diet consist of healthy carbohydrates including fiber, whole grains, and fruits.

Impact

Although low-carb diets improved significantly in safety and product selection since their initiation in the 1970s, the programs of the 2000s remained inadequate long-term health solutions for many. Professional research into healthful carbohydrate balance has contributed to more appropriate application of these diets without increasing cardiac or metabolic risks.

Further Reading

Atkins, Robert C. *Dr. Atkins' New Diet Revolution.* New York: Harper, 2002. Print.

Freeman, Janine, and Charlotte Hayes. "Low Carbohydrate Food Facts and Fallacies." *Diabetes Spectrum* 17.3 (2004): 137–40. Print.

US Department of Health and Human Services. "Health Facts: Choose Carbohydrates Wisely." Washington, DC: US Dept. of Health and Human Services, n.d. PDF file.

Nicole Van Hoey, PharmD

M

■ *Mad Men*

Identification: Television series about a fictional advertising agency 1960s-era New York City placed against the backdrop of major political, social, and cultural events of the decade.
Executive Producer: Matthew Weiner (b. 1965)
Date: Premiered July 19, 2007

The period drama Mad Men *premiered on the AMC network in the summer of 2007. The series features a complex narrative centered on the domestic, professional, and psychological struggles of advertising executive Don Draper (Jon Hamm) and the employees of the Sterling Cooper (later Sterling Cooper Draper Pryce) advertising agency.*

Much of the series' first three seasons revolved around Don Draper's efforts to hide his past: it is revealed that as a young man in the Korean War he assumed the name and background of Don Draper, a fellow soldier killed in action. Like many of the show's other major characters, Draper combats both his professional and personal anxieties with excessive alcohol consumption, chain-smoking, and array of adulterous relationships.

While fledgling copywriter Peggy Olson (Elisabeth Moss) and voluptuous office manager Joan Harris (Christina Hendricks) illustrate the new professional opportunities open to women of the era, the firm's other male partners Roger Sterling (John Slattery) and Bert Cooper (Robert Morse) personify a reluctant old guard, loyal to the societal conventions that hinder the ascension of women's roles both at home and in the workplace. These characters are often contrasted with rising young executive Pete Campbell (Vincent Kartheiser).

The agency's professional relationships and struggles to create ad campaigns for its ever-demanding clientele are utilized as a device to narrate

The cast and crew of Mad Men *at the Emmy Awards. Front row (left to right): Elisabeth Moss, Jon Hamm, creator and executive producer Matthew Weiner, and Christina Hendricks.* (Alberto E. Rodriguez/Getty Images Entertainment/GettyImages)

the era's rapidly changing notions towards racism, feminism, and homophobia. In these interactions, it is often Draper's task to assure wary clients that the firm's edgy concepts will win over an audience who is blindly in need of direction, as both consumers and individuals.

The series was awarded the Emmy for outstanding drama series in 2008, 2009, 2010, and 2011—winning the award for each of its first four seasons. *Mad Men* frequently uses historical events to depict changing attitudes in the United States. The series has centered episodes on the election and assassination of President Kennedy, the Cuban Missile Crisis, the civil rights movement, and the growing counterculture. These events act as harbingers of the end of the pre-established cultural boundaries and social hierarchies adhered to by each of the series characters, not only in their personal lives but in the work they create to present their clients to the world.

Impact

Mad Men's popularity is rooted in both the authenticity of its production and the intricacies of its characters. The show received numerous accolades for its accurate reproduction of settings, fashions, and music from the 1960s. In an America of the 2000s so dominated by brand allegiance and mass consumerism, the show also acted as both an entertaining and thought-provoking review of the development of modern American society.

Further Reading

Nilsson, Jeff. *"Mad Men—If It's Not Nostalgia, What Is It?" Saturday Evening Post.* Saturday Evening Post Society, 17 July 2007. Web. 2 July 2012.

Vargas-Cooper, Natasha. *Mad Men Unbuttoned: A Romp Through 1960s America.* New York: Harper, 2010. Print.

John Pritchard

■ Maddow, Rachel

Identification: American radio and television personality

Born: April 1, 1973; Castro Valley, California

Rachel Maddow is the host of MSNBC's The Rachel Maddow Show, which surprised media experts with its quick rise to the top of cable television ratings after it launched in the fall of 2008, just prior to the United States presidential elections.

In 1999, while writing her doctoral dissertation in western Massachusetts, Rhodes Scholar Rachel Anne Maddow responded to an open audition at the local radio station, WRNX in Holyoke. She was so successful at the audition that the station manager offered her a job during the commercial break. Maddow went on to cohost the *Dave in the Morning Show* for a year before she returned to Oxford University to finish her degree in political science. Upon completion of her PhD in 2001, Maddow returned to Northampton, Massachusetts, and the *Big Breakfast* show on WRSI.

When liberal radio station Air America began broadcasting in 2004, Maddow was asked to join talk show hosts Chuck D and Lizz Winstead on *Unfiltered.* When that show was cancelled in 2005, Maddow began hosting her own two-hour radio program, *The*

Rachel Maddow hosts former vice president Al Gore on The Rachel Maddow Show. (Courtesy *The Rachel Maddow Show*)

Rachel Maddow Show. (Air America ceased operations in 2010.) In the same year, Maddow was asked to counter more conservative viewpoints and commentary on MSNBC's *Tucker* and CNN's *Paula Zahn Now.* In 2008, MSNBC hired Maddow as a regular contributor, where she first appeared as a panelist for David Gregory's *Race to the White House* and *Countdown with Keith Olbermann.* She eventually stepped in as substitute host for both programs.

In August 2008, Maddow was offered her own show with MSNBC. *The Rachel Maddow Show* premiered on September 8, 2008. Within weeks, she doubled the ratings for the cable network for that hour, beating her 9:00 p.m. rivals at Fox and CNN. While Maddow's ratings have leveled out, she still leads CNN for that time slot. Her reviews have noted her firm grasp of policy and her polite but relentless style in examining those who appear on her show. Characterized as "postpartisan," Maddow was also credited with applying equal pressure to both those who share her political ideals and those who hold different views.

Impact

As an anchor, Maddow has been recognized for her detailed knowledge of public policy and her fearlessness in questioning guests (often politicians) on their past statements and voting history. Maddow is the first openly gay anchor to be hired to host a prime-time news program in the US, and is considered the ideological foil to cable news anchors like Sean Hannity and Bill O'Reilly.

Further Reading

Kurtz, Howard. "You Were Expecting Olbermann?." *Newsweek* 157.10 (2011): 34–37. Print.

Traister, Rebecca. "Mad For Rachel Maddow." *Nation* 287.5 (2008): 22–24. Print.

Wallace-Wells, Ben. "Rachel Maddow's Quiet War. (Cover Story)." *Rolling Stone* 1160/1161 (2012): 62–116. Print.

Ann Cameron

■ March for Women's Lives

The Event: A peaceful rally mainly focused on defending women's abortion rights
Date: April 25, 2004
Place: Washington, DC

The March for Women's Lives was a demonstration organized mainly in support of women's abortion rights. The event was a protest of anti-abortion policies passed by the George W. Bush administration. However, the demonstration also focused on the broader issue of women's rights. It took place at the National Mall in Washington, DC, and was attended by an estimated one million people.

On April 25, 2004, after a year of planning, the March for Women's Lives attracted supporters from across the country. The National Organization for Women (NOW), which had coordinated the 1992 March for Women's Lives, was joined by NARAL Pro-Choice America, the Planned Parenthood Federation of America, and the American Civil Liberties Union (ACLU) in organizing the event. The Black Women's Health Imperative, the Feminist Majority, and the National Latina Institute for Reproductive Health also acted as sponsors of the march. Many other organizations participated as well, including the National Association of Social Workers (NASW) and the National Association for the Advancement of Colored People (NAAACP).

The event officially commenced at ten in the morning. Entertainers and speakers kept the crowd engaged while more spectators joined the rally. Participants moved down Pennsylvania Avenue, passing the White House and the Capitol before finishing at the National Mall. Many pro-life demonstrators stood on the sides of the march, shouting anti-abortion slogans. US Park Police kept order and ensured that each group stayed within its designated space.

The speakers and performers who attended the event included the leaders of the participating organizations, political figures, social activists, actors, and musicians. Whoopi Goldberg and Lisa Gay Hamilton hosted the event. Actresses Susan Sarandon and Julianne Moore took the stage, and many other celebrities joined the rally to show their support. New York senator Hillary Clinton addressed the crowd and asked participants to vote for a pro-choice president in the upcoming election. Ani DiFranco, Moby, the Indigo Girls, and other musical artists entertained the crowd.

Impact

The March for Women's Lives was considered a success due to its attendance numbers, the diversity of participants, and the media coverage it received. The event also served as an example of inter-organizational cooperation for a common cause. However, the rally failed to influence a repeal of George W. Bush's anti-abortion policies. Although all attendees were urged to use their voting rights to fight such legislation, the administration's policies remained in effect.

Further Reading

"Abortion Activists on the March." *BBC News.* British Broadcasting Company, 26 Apr. 2004. Web. 8 Oct. 2012.

Associated Press. "Top Court Upholds Ban on Abortion Procedure." *NBCNews.com.* NBC News Digital, 18 Apr. 2007. Web. 8 Oct. 2012.

Bennett, Lisa. "Over One Million March for Women's Lives." *National NOW Times.* National Organization for Women, Spring 2004. Web. 8 Oct. 2012.

"History & Successes." *Planned Parenthood.* Planned Parenthood Federation of America Inc., 2012. Web. 8 Oct. 2012.

"Personal Stories: Why We March." *National Organization for Women.* National Organization for Women, 2004. Web. 8 Oct. 2012.

Williamson, Elizabeth. "Abortion Rights Advocates Flood D.C." *Washington Post.* Washington Post Company, 25 Apr. 2004. Web. 8 Oct. 2012.

Miroslav Farina

■ Marianas Trench Marine National Monument

Definition: US national monument created to protect submerged lands and waters around the Mariana Islands archipelago in the Pacific Ocean

In 2009, after being urged by marine conservation groups to improve on an otherwise poor record on environmental policy during his White House tenure, President George W. Bush established three marine protected areas in the Pacific Ocean. The largest of these areas, the Marianas Trench Marine National Monument, protected one of the most unique and unexplored ocean environments on Earth.

The Marianas Trench Marine National Monument, established by President George W. Bush in January 2009, is the second-largest marine monument in the United States. It spans more than ninety-six thousand square miles of ocean and protects submerged lands and waters near the Mariana Islands archipelago, which encompasses the fifteen islands of the US Commonwealth of the Northern Mariana Islands and the US territory of Guam. The monument is divided into three units: the Islands Unit, which includes the marine environment around the three northernmost Mariana Islands, Farallon de Pajaros (also known as Uracas), Maug, and Asuncion; the Volcanic Unit, which consists of the submerged lands within one nautical mile of twenty-one volcanic sites that make up the Mariana Arc; and the Trench Unit, which encompasses the submerged lands within the Mariana (or Marianas) Trench, the deepest underwater canyon in the world. The trench stretches for more than fifteen hundred miles and reaches nearly seven miles below the surface at its deepest point, known as the Challenger Deep. These protected areas are among the most biologically diverse in the Western Pacific Ocean, containing undersea mud volcanoes and thermal vents that have produced unusual forms of life unseen anywhere else, as well as a vast frontier of previously unexplored underwater terrain.

President Bush created the Marianas Trench Marine National Monument as one of three national monuments in the Pacific Ocean, the others being the Pacific Remote Islands Marine National Monument and the Rose Atoll Marine National

Large schools of bigeye jack (Caranx sexfasciatus), present at both Farallon de Pajaros and Maug. (NOAA/Photograph by Jake Asher)

Monument. He designated the sites by way of executive order as permitted under the Antiquities Act of 1906, which allows presidents to protect public lands without congressional approval. Bush's establishment of the three sites, which comprise a total of more than 195,000 square miles, followed his designation in 2006 of the Papahānaumokuākea Marine National Monument, which is the largest marine protected area in the world, covering 140,000 square miles around the Northwest Hawaiian Islands.

Impact

The vast majority of the world's oceans remain unexplored. The Marianas Trench Marine National Monument helps prevent desecration of some of the most biologically fascinating and unexplored areas on Earth. Its designation as a national monument preserves the area for future generations by limiting fishing and other commercial activities, thus giving scientists and researchers the opportunity to better understand how endemic marine species can survive in extremely harsh environments and contributing to efforts to fight and understand climate change. It ultimately improved Bush's standing among marine conservationists and his administration's overall record on the environment and helped him earn a legacy of ocean protection, as he was responsible for protecting more of the world's oceans than any other political leader in history.

Further Reading

Broder, John M. "Bush to Protect Vast New Pacific Tracts." *New York Times.* New York Times Co., 5 Jan. 2009. Web. 28 Nov. 2012.

Weiss, Kenneth R. "Bush to Create New Protected Ocean Monuments." *Los Angeles Times.* Los Angeles Times, 6 Jan. 2009. Web. 28 Nov. 2012.

Chris Cullen

■ Mars Exploration Rover mission

Definition: NASA space mission to explore and study the planet Mars and its potential for life

The question of life on Mars has intrigued mankind for generations. With the development of technologies such as satellites and robotic space rovers, examining the potential for life on the planet became increasingly possible. The Mars Exploration Rover mission was launched to help determine if Mars had supported life in the past. Because water is essential to life as humans know it, the mission sought evidence of water on Mars.

In the summer of 2003, the rovers *Spirit* and *Opportunity* were launched into space to intercept and land on Mars. They landed on opposite sides of the planet in January 2004. The rovers' main objective was to determine if the soil and rocks of the planet contained minerals consistent with past water activity. The mission was part of a long-term Mars exploration program headed by the National Aeronautics and Space Administration (NASA). The rovers were sent to areas of the planet deemed likely to have contained bodies of water in the past. *Spirit* was sent to an area known as Gusev Crater, a possible former lake. *Opportunity* landed on a plain called Meridiani Planum, which, according to previously collected mineral samples, is likely to have once been a wet area.

The rovers were equipped with highly advanced cameras, magnets for gathering dust particles, rock-abrasion tools, and various spectrometers capable of examining the rocks and soil more closely. The devices were meant to enable the rovers to carry out remote geological investigations as thoroughly as a human could.

Three years into the mission, a violent dust storm on Mars blocked out the sun, which powered the rovers' mobility systems. The rovers survived the

The Mars Exploration Rover (MER) Opportunity's Hazard Identification Camera. (NASA/JPL-Caltech)

storm, but NASA was faced with another obstacle when *Spirit* became stuck in the sand in May of 2009. Scientists worked for the remainder of the year to free the rover's wheels but were ultimately unsuccessful. In January 2010, NASA decided to repurpose the *Spirit* as a stationary research platform.

While *Spirit* remained incapacitated, *Opportunity* was busy making key discoveries in the Victoria Crater at Meridiani Planum. The rover discovered that water and wind had affected the land around the crater. Earlier study had determined that the same effects were visible in nearby areas *Opportunity* had explored.

Impact

NASA extended the Mars Exploration Rover mission five times, demonstrating its importance in the history of space exploration. The mission's discoveries have encouraged scientists' extraterrestrial theories at unprecedented levels. Evidence of the past presence of water on Mars further supports the idea that there was once life there.

Further Reading

Fountain, Henry. "Crater Was Shaped by Wind and Water, Mars Rover Data Shows." *New York Times.* New York Times Co., 25 May 2009. Web. 21 Nov. 2012.

Mars Exploration Rover Mission. Caltech/JPL, n.d. Web. 21 Nov. 2012.

McKee, Maggie. "Mars Rover May Not Escape Sand Trap for Weeks." *New Scientist.* Reed Business Information, 12 May 2009. Web. 21 Nov. 2012.

"NASA Extends Mars Rovers' Mission." *NBCNews. com.* NBCNews.com, 16 Oct. 2007. Web. 21 Nov. 2012.

Cait Caffrey

Paul Martin. (Courtesy Dave McLean)

■ Martin, Paul

Identification: Canadian politician and former prime minister

Born: August 28, 1938; Windsor, Ontario, Canada

Canadian political figure Paul Martin is known for having reinvigorated the nation's economy as its minister of finance. Later, as prime minister, he advocated for equal opportunities for Canada's Aboriginal peoples and helped to legalize same-sex marriage in Canada.

From 1993 to 2002, Paul Martin served as Canada's minister of finance, during which time he worked to eliminate the nation's deficit, eventually posting five consecutive years of budget surpluses. Martin, a member of the Liberal Party of Canada, used these credentials to his advantage and ran for prime minister in 2003. He soundly defeated Liberal opponent Jean Chrétien, winning 93 percent of the vote at the Liberal leadership convention.

The following year was turbulent for the Liberal Party. During Chrétien's tenure, the party was suspected of misusing money from a public fund to help communication companies generate commissions. Even after the guilty were identified, Martin and other Liberals faced criticism over the scandal. The Liberal Party lost forty-two seats in the House of Commons in the 2004 election, becoming the minority government.

Despite the losses, Martin managed to introduce the largest tax cuts in Canadian history. He advocated for increased government support of education and research. Martin was also instrumental in introducing the Kelowna Accord in 2005. This series of agreements sought to reduce the economic gap between Aboriginal peoples and other Canadians. He also instituted the Civil Marriage Act, which legalized same-sex unions across the nation.

Despite his achievements, Martin was criticized as being indecisive. An article in the *Economist*, a high-profile international magazine, accused him of being sluggish and lacking the confidence to push his government's agenda, citing examples such as a stalled review of foreign policy. The negative press appeared to influence the 2006 election. Martin was defeated by Conservative opponent Stephen Harper, and he stepped down as party leader.

Martin served as a member of Parliament for La-Salle-Émard in Quebec until he retired in 2008. He released a memoir, titled *Hell or High Water: My Life in and out of Politics* (2009). Late in 2008, Martin was appointed to an economic advisory panel of the newly formed Liberal–New Democratic Party coalition government.

Impact

Paul Martin served twenty years as a member of Parliament. His successes earned him the respect of fellow Liberal Party members and his financial expertise kept Canada's economy afloat in troubled times. He accomplished a great deal during his short time as prime minister. His skills continue to be highly regarded and sought after. Martin serves on a number of bodies, among them the International Monetary Fund's Western Hemisphere Regional Advisory Group.

Further Reading

CBC News. "In Depth: Paul Martin." *CBC News.* CBC, 17 Mar. 2006. Web. 13 July 2012.

CBC News. "Federal Sponsorship Scandal." *CBC News.* CBC, 26 Oct. 2006. Web. 13 July 2012.
"Paul Martin Biography." *The Right Honourable Paul Martin.* PaulMartin.ca, n.d. Web. 13 July 2012.

Cait Caffrey

■ Mashup

Definition: Song composed of excerpts from other songs

Mashups grew in popularity throughout the 2000s as digital music files and audio-mixing tools became more widely available. The mixing of excerpts, or samples, from different songs exposed many listeners to new styles of music but also prompted controversies regarding copyright infringement and intellectual property rights.

The music mashup, a single song that mixes two or more source tracks, became more popular in the 2000s thanks to the increased availability of digital audio-mixing tools and use of the Internet as a platform for distribution of music files. While sampling had long been common practice in many musical genres, particularly hip-hop, "mashing up" different songs into one work had not been as widespread. By the 2000s, the increased accessibility of advanced sound-editing programs such as Sound Forge, WaveLab, Pro Tools, and Cool Edit allowed artists to create complex tracks. Crucial features of such programs included beat mapping, which enabled artists to match the beats between source songs accurately.

The Internet was critical in enabling the distribution of mashups on a large scale and cultivating a dynamic culture of mashup sharing. File-sharing programs such as Napster were particularly important early in the decade, as they allowed users to share both source music files and finished tracks. By the latter half of the 2000s, websites devoted to mashups, such as Mashuptown, allowed artists to share their creations and enthusiasts to find new mashups.

Mashup artists who gained mainstream recognition in the 2000s included Brian Burton, known by the stage name Danger Mouse, and Gregg Gillis, who performed and released albums under the name Girl Talk. Danger Mouse's *The Grey Album*, released in 2004, combined music from the self-titled Beatles album known as *The White Album* with vocals from Jay-

Z's *The Black Album*. The album received significant attention because of its recognizable source material and the widely publicized copyright controversy that followed its release. In contrast to Danger Mouse, who became best known for mashing up songs by only two artists, Girl Talk combined samples from hundreds of source tracks by popular and lesser-known artists to produce multilayered mashup albums such as *Night Ripper* (2006) and *Feed the Animals* (2008).

Mashups tended to change their source works sufficiently or use small enough samples to be considered examples of fair use under US copyright law, which allows for the "transformative" uses of parts of copyrighted works. Despite this, a number of mashup artists became involved in copyright disputes throughout the decade, and several mashup websites shut down in response to legal challenges from record companies.

Impact

The popularity of musical mashups helped give rise to the concept of remix culture, which held that increased access to content and technology was creating a culture focused on recombining and reimagining all types of art, including music. This development inspired discussion about modifying copyright law to reflect new creative and technological realities.

Further Reading
Lessig, Lawrence. *Remix: Making Art and Commerce Thrive in the Hybrid Economy.* New York: Penguin, 2008. Print.
Miller, Paul, ed. *Sound Unbound: Sampling Digital Music and Culture.* Cambridge: MITP, 2008. Print.
Sinnreich, Aram. *Mashed Up: Music, Technology, and the Rise of Configurable Culture.* Amherst: U of Massachusetts P, 2010. Print.

Kerry Skemp, MA

■ McCain, John

Identification: American politician and presidential candidate in 2008
Born: August 29, 1936; Panama Canal Zone

John McCain is the senior United States senator from Arizona. A veteran and former POW, McCain made two failed bids for the White House, most notably as the Republican nominee opposing Barack Obama in 2008.

In December 1998, following a successful career in the US Senate and House of Representatives, John Sidney McCain declared his intention to seek the Republican presidential nomination for the 2000 presidential election. He hoped that his military and political experience would give him an edge over his competitors. However, some critics questioned whether the abuse he endured as a prisoner of war in Vietnam had given him a bad temper, an undesirable quality in a potential president.

Among McCain's campaign promises was a pledge to cut taxes and reform campaign finance in order to reduce the influence of special interest groups in government. He supported a plan to invest 62 percent of the budget surplus in the social security program, and also hoped to reform the military by making it more defense-ready. McCain took a stance on gun control by supporting background checks and trigger locks, but at the same time he promised to uphold the right of law-abiding Americans to bear arms.

Despite a strong showing in early primary races, McCain dropped out of the presidential race when fellow Republican George W. Bush won the "Super Tuesday" primary elections on March 9, 2000. He continues to serve in the Senate, and sponsored the controversial McCain-Feingold campaign finance reform bill, which bans unrestricted "soft money" contributions to political candidates. The Senate passed the bill in April 2001. The bill was challenged by numerous groups, but was ultimately upheld by the Supreme Court in 2003. In 2004, Senator John Kerry suggested John McCain as a possible running mate in the presidential election, but McCain maintained that he supported US President George W. Bush. McCain was reelected to the Senate in 2004.

In April of 2007, McCain officially announced his candidacy for the 2008 Republican Party presidential nomination. McCain trailed Republican colleague Fred Thompson by a few hundred votes in the 2008 Republican Party caucus in Iowa. Nonetheless, the two essentially tied for third place in the overall vote—finishing with 13 percent each. McCain won the 2008 New Hampshire Republican primary, earning 37 percent of the vote. McCain finished second in the Michigan Republican party and he finished third in the Nevada caucus. The McCain campaign earned its first victory in the contest for the Republic presidential nomination in South Carolina, earning over 33 percent of the total vote.

John McCain. (U.S. Army/Photograph by Staff Sergeant Jim Greenhill)

The McCain campaign scored a big victory in the Florida primary, held on January 29. McCain earned 36 percent, which awarded him all of the state's 57 convention delegates. Following the win, many political analysts observed that McCain may have the Republican Party nomination wrapped up if he did well on Super Tuesday in February.

In the 2008 Super Tuesday primaries and caucuses held on February 5, twenty-two states voted. McCain won Arizona, Oklahoma, Connecticut, California, New Jersey, New York, Missouri, Illinois, and Delaware. His success on Super Tuesday earned him a significant lead in the overall delegate count. Following the February 5th vote, many analysts stated that McCain had all but wrapped up the 2008 Republican Party nomination for president.

McCain placed second in the Louisiana primary, but earned victories in Washington DC, Maryland and Virginia on February 12. McCain's sweep of the "Potomac Primaries" helped to further solidify his status as front runner in the contest for the GOP nomination.

On March 4, McCain won Republican primaries held in Ohio, Vermont, Texas, and Rhode Island. His victories in these four states confirmed that he had earned the number of delegates to confirm his nomination as the 2008 Republican Party presidential candidate. At his victory speech, McCain vowed to rally Americans around his campaign prior to the general election in November.

On August 29, 2008, McCain announced that he had selected Alaska Governor Sarah Palin as his running mate for vice president. The selection of Palin surprised many analysts and voters. Palin became the first woman in American history to be selected as a presidential running mate by the Republican Party. Palin is a conservative who is known for her pro-life views and her efforts in battling corruption.

Following the longest presidential campaign in US history, the 2008 presidential election was held on November 4, 2008. The Republican Party ticket of McCain and Palin was defeated in the election, earning 174 Electoral College votes and 55,867,094 ballots in the popular vote. The Democratic Party ticket of Barack Obama and Joseph Biden earned 364 Electoral College votes and 63,112,190 ballots in the popular vote. Obama's victory in the 2008 election made him the first African American president in U.S. history. On the evening of November 4, McCain delivered a concession speech at the Biltmore Hotel in Phoenix, Arizona. He congratulated Obama and commented on the historic nature of his election as president. He also thanked his supporters and his running mate Sarah Palin. McCain pledged to continue serving the country as a member of the US Senate.

In August 2010, McCain won Arizona's Republican Party Senate primary. He was reelected to the Senate in November 2010.

Impact

During his years representing Arizona in the United States Senate, Republican John McCain has earned a reputation for speaking his mind. His outspoken nature has often won him the support of independent voters, while placing him at odds with the more conservative factions of his own party. Since his failed bid for the Republican presidential nomination in 2000, McCain has emerged as a prominent voice for campaign finance reform.

Further Reading

Cooper, Marc. "JOHN McCAIN's LAST STAND." *Nation* 291.7/8 (2010): 11–15. Print.

Cullinane, M. Patrick. "Invoking Teddy: The Inspiration Of John McCain's Foreign Policy." *Diplomacy & Statecraft* 19.4 (2008): 767–86. Print.

Kenski, Henry C. "The 2008 Republican Nomination: John McCain As The Comeback Kid." *American Behavioral Scientist* 55.4 (2011): 502–14. Print.

James Ryan

■ McCarthy, Cormac

Identification: American novelist
Born: July 20, 1933; Providence, Rhode Island

Cormac McCarthy is an American novelist whom many critics believe to be among the great writers of his time. His novels Blood Meridian, No Country for Old Men, *and* The Road *are wildly popular bestsellers.*

Cormac McCarthy was born Charles Joseph McCarthy Jr. on July 20, 1933, in Providence, Rhode Island, but he was raised in the Vestal neighborhood of Knoxville, Tennessee. He borrowed the pastoral imagery and setting, as well as several plot elements, for his first novel, *The Orchard Keeper* (1965), from his boyhood haunts. In 1968, McCarthy's second novel, *Outer Dark*, was published. It was praised upon its publication, and McCarthy began to build a reputation as a major new voice in American fiction.

In 1981, McCarthy was awarded a MacArthur Fellowship, which allowed him to continue working on his fifth novel, *Blood Meridian: Or the Evening Redness in the West* (1985), free from financial burden. This and all of his subsequent novels were set in the American Southwest, a region he captured as vividly and richly as he had the Southern region.

Praised by such contemporary writers as David Foster Wallace and the critic Harold Bloom, *Blood Meridian* is considered to be among the best novels of the twentieth century. However, it received little attention at the time of its publication.

All the Pretty Horses (1992), the book that earned McCarthy widespread fame, was the first novel in his Border Trilogy. The second and third novels, *The Crossing* and *Cities of the Plain*, were published in 1994 and 1998, respectively.

In 2004, McCarthy moved to Santa Fe, New Mexico, from El Paso, Texas. He published the novel *No Country for Old Men* in 2005 and the novel *The Road* in 2006. He also published a play in 2006 entitled *The Sunset Limited*, which he adapted for a television film directed by and starring Tommy Lee Jones. A 2007 film adaptation of *No Country for Old Men*, directed by Joel and Ethan Coen, also starred Jones and would go on to win the Academy Award for best picture and best director. A film adaptation of *The Road* was released in 2009.

Impact

The critical clout garnered by his first few novels has established McCarthy as one of his era's literary greats. He is often listed alongside writers such as Thomas Pynchon, Don DeLillo, and Philip Roth. The popular film adaptations of his later novels have reinvigorated an interest in his earlier works. In 2009, it was reported that McCarthy was at work on three new novels.

Further Reading

Collado-Rodríguez, Francisco. "Trauma and Storytelling in Cormac McCarthy's *No Country for Old Men* and *The Road.*" *Papers on Language and Literature* 48 (2012): 45–69.

Nelson, Christopher R. "A Style of Horror: Is Evil Real in Cormac McCarthy's *Outer Dark?*" *Critique* 53.1 (2012): 30–48.

Skrimshire, Stefan. "'There Is No God and We Are His Prophets': Deconstructing Redemption in Cormac McCarthy's *The Road.*" *Journal for Cultural Research* 15.1 (2011): 1–14.

Craig Belanger

■ Medical marijuana

Definition: The parts of the herb cannabis (or specific chemical compounds from the plant) that are recommended by doctors for medicinal and therapeutic purposes

During the 2000s, US states gradually began legalizing marijuana for medical reasons. Though it remained illegal at the federal level, medical marijuana generated millions in state tax dollars, opening the door for the legalization of recreational marijuana at the state level.

In 1996, California became the first state to pass an initiative legalizing the use of medical marijuana. Previously, all state policies regarding marijuana were based on its classification as a Schedule I drug under the federal Controlled Substances Act of 1970, placing it on par with other strictly controlled Schedule I drugs such as heroin, cocaine, and lysergic acid diethylamide (LSD). Following the precedent set by California and other states in the late 1990s like Alaska, Washington, Oregon, and Maine, a growing number of states began passing initiatives in the 2000s to legalize marijuana for medical and therapeutic use.

Through the end of the first decade of the twenty-first century, the official position of the US Food and Drug Administration (FDA) was that marijuana has no medical use. Marijuana has been used for centuries, however, as a treatment for eye pain, insomnia, and gastrointestinal disorders. More recently, marijuana has been used effectively to treat some of the symptoms of cancer, HIV/AIDS, epilepsy, multiple sclerosis (MS), bipolar disorder, depression, anxiety, and chronic pain.

States that have legalized the use of medical marijuana regulate their own dispensaries, cooperatives, and wellness clinics. Patients with a valid medical marijuana identification card or a recommendation from a doctor obtain various forms and limited quantities of the drug to treat their respective medical condition or illness. (Under federal law, doctors are not allowed to "prescribe" marijuana for medical use, but are instead able to recommend the drug.)

Federal guidelines for medical marijuana prosecution were put in place in 2009, under which prosecutors were directed to focus on cases involving individuals claiming compliance with state laws but who were in fact concealing illegal activity. Despite these guidelines, federal drug agencies continued to lead routine crackdowns on state-sanctioned medical marijuana growers and sellers, mostly over purported tax violations, further increasing the chasm between state and federal law on medical marijuana. As of 2012, a total of eighteen states and Washington, DC, had legalized medical marijuana.

Impact

Marijuana legalization, both for medicinal purposes and recreational use, has remained a divisive issue, with some deeming it to be no more harmful than tobacco or alcohol and others continuing to view it as being as serious as other Schedule I drugs. The growing number of states that have decriminalized marijuana for medical purposes, however, has helped usher in an attitude and perception among the public that the drug is comparatively safe and offers important medical and economic benefits. Echoing this sentiment, in November 2012, Washington State and Colorado became the first US states to pass laws legalizing recreational marijuana use.

Further Reading

Earlywine, Mitch. *Understanding Marijuana: A New Look at the Scientific Evidence.* New York: Oxford UP, 2002. Print.

Johnson, Carrie. "U.S. Eases Stance on Medical Marijuana." *Washington Post.* Washington Post, 20 Oct. 2009. Web. 3 Dec. 2012.

Chris Cullen

■ Medical tourism

Definition: The practice of combining vacation and travel abroad with professional therapeutic or medical care

American doctors and medical facilities are among the best in the world. However, as health care and health insurance costs have spiraled upward in the twenty-first century, American patients are seeking alternatives to meet their medical needs. Medical tourism—also called distance medicine—offers a cost-effective, high-quality option, particularly for those seeking elective surgery.

During the twenty-first century, medical tourism has blossomed. In 2007, some 750,000 Americans journeyed overseas to undergo a variety of procedures—cancer treatments, dental work, organ transplants, or reproductive procedures—at foreign hospitals. Twice as many US patients are expected to visit health care facilities abroad in 2012.

While there are many incentives for patients to seek medical care outside the United States, the primary factor is cost. In the recession-wracked economic climate of the early twenty-first century, many Americans simply cannot afford adequate health insurance and must make partial or full out-of-pocket payments for care. As a result, they cancel regular appointments with doctors, use prescription drugs less often, or postpone treatments to alleviate chronic conditions.

Medical tourism offers a viable alternative for patients, employers, and insurance carriers. Depending upon treatment and location, common medical procedures in foreign environments can save 90 percent or more of the cost at a comparable domestic facility. Low-priced, quality care can be found from Bulgaria to Bolivia. A hip replacement, for example, that might cost $40,000 in the United States, can be accomplished for just $3,000 in India. A full facelift, worth $20,000 in the United States, can be undertaken in South Africa for less than $2,000. A dental bridge that costs more than $5,000 in the United States can be had for $1,000 in Hungary.

A number of organizations help patients who wish to take advantage of overseas savings. Medical tourism packagers assist in matching patient conditions with foreign facilities, arranging travel, documentation, and hotel reservations, and even setting up sightseeing excursions for patients in recovery.

Potential medical tourists should be aware there are certain risks involved with undergoing medical procedures overseas. There may be, for example, local diseases for which patients have no established immunity. Follow-up care is not generally as comprehensive as it is in the United States. And if something should go wrong, a foreign malpractice suit might be extremely complicated, or impossible to undertake. Thorough research is vital for patients to make an informed decision about the pros and cons of seeking health care abroad.

Impact

A rapidly growing industry, medical tourism is expected to expand at an annual rate of more than 30 percent as patients, businesses, and insurance companies become aware of its benefits. To help ensure uniform quality of care, the American Medical Association has advocated a set of guidelines. An official foreign accrediting organization, Joint Commission International (JCI), has also been established. By 2008 JCI had approved more than 220 foreign medical sites worldwide.

Further Reading

Hall, C. Michael, ed. *Medical Tourism: The Ethics, Regulation, and Marketing of Health Mobility.* London: Routledge, 2012. Print.

Reisman, David. *Health Tourism: Social Welfare through International Trade.* Northampton: Elgar, 2010. Print.

Woodman, Josef. *Patients beyond Borders: Everybody's Guide to Affordable, World-Class Medical Travel.* Chapel Hill: Healthy Travel, 2008. Print.

Jack Ewing

■ Medicine

Definition: The medical field witnessed significant and rapid advances during the 2000s, particularly as new technologies were implemented that increase speed, precision, and accuracy in health care

Medicine is an integral part of creating and maintaining a healthy and productive society. Throughout the 2000s, several advances were made in the medical field that significantly improve quality of life, prolong survival rates and life expectancies, and extend care to more patients.

Medicine is a broad topic and there are an incredible number of changes and developments that occur every year, let alone over a decade. In the years between 2000 and 2009, there were major developments in several areas of medicine, including surgical procedures, drugs and vaccines, preventative medicine, and research and technology. There were also significant legal and organizational changes in the field of medicine. One of the most fundamental changes of the decade was the integration of information technology in hospitals and doctors office, which has had widespread applications and significant cost savings.

Drugs and Vaccinations

This decade heralded the arrival of new drugs to treat some of the most complex diseases, such as cancer and the human immunodeficiency virus (HIV). One major advancement in cancer treatment was the continued development of targeted drug therapies, which attack the molecules responsible for the growth of cancer cells. Rather than target cell division, which has the potential to also damage healthy cells as chemotherapy does, targeted therapies focus on the molecules and enzymes specific to cancerous cells. A drug called trastuzumab was approved by the US Food and Drug Administration (FDA) in 1998 for use by women with HER2-positive metastatic breast cancer. HER receptors are molecular proteins that affect gene expression; women diagnosed with breast cancer who had high levels of HER2 receptors experienced a particularly aggressive and fatal form of the disease. However, throughout the 2000s, trastuzumab has significantly improved overall survival compared to traditional chemotherapy—in some cases, trastuzumab has been shown to increase survival by several years.

In 2001, another targeted drug therapy, known as imatinib, was approved for use by the FDA to treat chronic myelogenous leukemia. Imatinib targets a certain enzyme related to cancer growth, and the drug has transformed what was once a fatal diagnosis into a manageable, yet chronic condition. As of 2011, the FDA had approved imatinib to treat ten

different forms of cancer. These targeted therapies, such as trastuzumab and imatinib, have significantly extended the life expectancies of cancer patients and represent a significant advancement in oncologists' understanding of cancer development and growth.

Another disease without a definitive cure is HIV, but with the development of highly active antiretroviral therapy (first introduced in the late 1990s), patients with HIV are now living for decades instead of the handful of years that they could expect in the late 1980s or early 1990s. In this decade, results from the early use of highly active antiretroviral therapy have been tested and retested in order to find the best combinations for each individual, allowing patients to live healthier and longer lives. In 2006, the FDA approved Atripla, the first one-a-day pill for the treatment of HIV; Atripla contains three different antiretroviral compounds, thereby greatly simplifying the treatment regime for patients with HIV.

Also introduced in 2006 was Gardasil, the first vaccine to prevent the human papillomavirus (HPV), one of the most common sexually transmitted infections and a significant risk factor for developing cervical and other cancers. By the end of the decade, nearly 50 percent of all adolescent girls in the United States had received the vaccine. Another vaccine first introduced during the decade was the H1N1 influenza vaccine, which was released in 2009 following the swine flu outbreak of that year. Although vaccine supplies were limited in 2009 to those people with the highest risk of developing complications from the H1N1 virus, the vaccine has since been incorporated into the standard annual influenza vaccine.

Surgical Procedures

In the 1990s, a new surgical technique known as minimally invasive surgery was refined; this procedure requires much smaller incisions, often shorter than a half-inch, than traditional open surgery. With the aid of a laparoscopic camera inserted into the incision, the surgeon is able to perform the surgery in the least invasive way possible. This enables the patient to recover much faster with little pain or discomfort. In the 2000s, this procedure became increasingly sophisticated as robotic tools were able to perform surgeries with improved precision. Also in this decade, an even more radical procedure, known as natural orifice surgery came to prominence. In natural orifice surgery, the procedure is performed

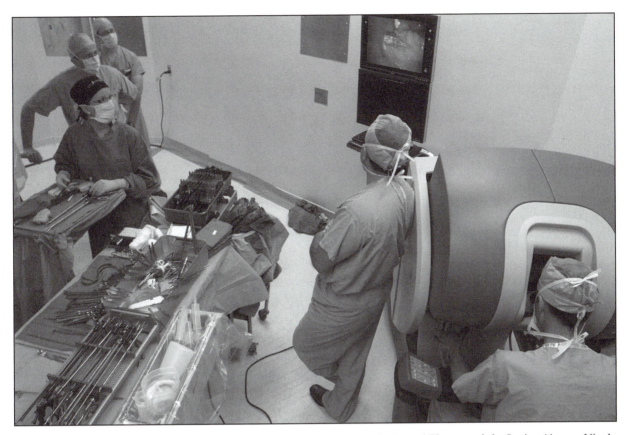

Medical personnel watch a monitor during a laparoscopic prostatectomy. (U.S. Air Force/ Photograph by Senior Airman Nicole Roberts)

through the navel, anus, vagina, or mouth, with no incisions at all.

Another major breakthrough in surgery occurred in 2005, when the first successful face transplant was performed at Amiens University Hospital in France. The patient, a woman named Isabelle Dinoire, had her face viciously mauled by a dog several years prior to the surgery. The transplant grafted a donor's nose, lips, and chin onto Dinoire's face, restoring her ability to smile and use facial expressions. In 2008, surgeons at the Cleveland Clinic in Ohio performed a far more complex face transplant, as they reconstructed part of a patient's bone structure in addition to grafting muscle and tissue.

Research and Technology

Someof the primary reasons such complex surgical procedures were possible in the 2000s were the technological advancements of the past decade, as in robotics-assisted surgery. There were several major breakthroughs in research and technology that are already having widespread applications. It may take several more years before all the possibilities of these new technologies and approaches can be realized.

The most significant of these breakthroughs is perhaps the completion of the mapping of the human genome, a blueprint for what the 23,000 genes that make up a human being actually do. Until 2000, those genes and their specific functions were largely unknown. Through the simultaneous efforts of the Human Genome Project and Celera Genomics, the sequence was completed in 2000. In 2007, Dr. Craig Venter, formerly of Celera, further updated and refined the blueprint. The completed map of the human genome has enabled oncologists to develop the aforementioned targeted therapies for cancer, as scientists can now use tumor genotyping to match patients with the best possible treatments. A number of other applications for this information were in development at the end of the decade.

Another area of research that has advanced significantly is the highly controversial area of stem cell research, both from adults and embryos. While once under a federal ban, research into embryonic stem cells was legalized in the United States in 2009. In 2007 Japanese researchers were able to induce pluripotence in adult stem cells, forcing the cells to express some of the most important properties of embryonic stem cells and thereby greatly increasing the number of stem cells available for research. While few specific advances had been made as of the end of 2009, researchers have stated that their ability to work with and manipulate stem cells has progressed so far that, in the coming decades, human trials and the hoped-for cures and therapies for diseases will come into being.

The creation of functional magnetic resonance imaging, also called fMRI, now allows doctors to more clearly visualize brain activity in order to better understand brain disorders. While the fMRI was originally created in the early 1990s, the information gathered has been put to use in this decade to help understand and treat psychological disorders and brain diseases. While these technologies have specific uses that while likely yield significant advances across the medical field, the overall implementation of informational technology in medicine has improved health care for both patients and doctors, as electronic health records can be easily accessed and shared across different health facilities. The increased reliance on information technology has also had significant cost savings over traditional, paper records. Doctors also have more immediate access to point-of-care information and to information concerning their patients, medications, and medical history. Information technology has even reduced hospital mistakes as bar codes can be used to match each patient to their samples.

Public Health

Public health varies in some instances from the general field of medicine by specifically focusing on services for community health, including sanitation, immunization, and preventative care. One of the largest advances for public health is the nearly 40 percent decrease in deaths due to heart disease. Doctors attribute this to advances in the medical field, such as the introduction of drugs to control high cholesterol and blood-pressure levels, but preventative measures, such as increasing public awareness of the importance of exercise and nutrition in cardiac health, has had an even more significant impact.

Another significant development in public health was the growing number of cities and states that enacted public indoor smoking bans. In 2000, only one major US city—San Jose, California—had enacted a citywide ban on smoking indoors, such as in bars, restaurants, or offices. By the end of the decade, more than half of the fifty largest cities in the United States had enacted a similar ban. Also in 2000, there were no states with a comprehensive statewide ban on smoking indoors. By 2010, twenty-six states had enacted such laws. This will significantly reduce the public's exposure to secondhand smoke, which has been linked to lung cancer, chronic obstructive pulmonary disease, and heart disease.

Health Insurance

Health insurance comes in many forms in the United States, whether privately purchased, through an individual's job, or from a social welfare program. During this decade, the number of people without health insurance grew from previous decades, with an increase of nearly one million additional people without insurance between 2009 and 2010 alone. By the end of the decade, forty-nine million Americans were without health insurance, which was in part due to the rapidly rising costs of health care and the hard economic situation at the end of the decade. Due to the high costs of health care and the growing number of uninsured Americans, the movement for health care reform in the United States gained significant momentum throughout the decade. In 2010, a new health care law, called the Affordable Care Act, was passed into law. Although many of the law's provisions would not go into effect until after 2014, the law would extend health care to the many Americans who could not previously afford private health care on their own and did not qualify for it through their jobs or government programs, or because they suffered from a preexisting condition.

Impact

Advancements in medicine and science made during the 2000s are improving the lives of patients, not only by allowing people to live longer, but by improving their quality of life. With advances in surgery techniques and the overall understanding of the effects of medicine on the body, scientists and doctors and even engineers are continually making discoveries that lead to other breakthroughs. The pace of medical discoveries is accelerating as new technologies enable knowledge to be shared and disseminated among researchers, doctors, and patients.

Further Reading

Cox, Lauren. "The Top 10 Medical Advances of the Decade." *ABC News: Medical Unit.* ABC News Internet Ventures, 17 Dec. 2009. Web. 16 Nov. 2012. This article summarizes ten of the most important medical advances between 2000 and 2010 and their impact on the field.

Fremstad, Shawn. "New Census Numbers Make it Official: 2000–2010 Was a Lost Economic Decade." *Center for Economic and Policy Research.* International Federation of Professional and Technical Engineers, 13 Sept. 2011. Web. 18 Nov. 2012. This article offers an analysis of census data with a section dedicated to health insurance.

Morbidity and Mortality Weekly Report. "Ten Great Public Health Achievements—United States, 2001–2010." *Centers for Disease Control and Prevention.* Centers for Disease Control and Prevention, 20 May 2011. Web. 16 Nov. 2012. A CDC report concerning breakthroughs in public health between 2001 and 2010 and their impact on society and the medical field.

"Secondhand Smoke." *American Cancer Society.* American Cancer Society, 24 Oct. 2012. Web. 18 Nov. 2012. This website explains the dangers of secondhand smoke and provides some information on various smoking bans.

Anna Accettola, MA

■ Microcredit

Definition: The practice of providing small loans to entrepreneurs in deeply impoverished regions as a means of encouraging small business and stimulating economic growth

Since the concept was first introduced in the 1970s, microloans have become a critical element of the fight against global poverty. These small loans, designed to help ease the financial burdens of the poor and stimulate economic growth in impoverished regions, have made it possible for countless people to improve their lives and their communities. However, the commercialization of the microloan business has led to questions about whether lenders benefit more than applicants do.

Microfinancing received a boost in credibility when the Bangladeshi microfinance institution Grameen Bank, considered the first microcredit organization, was awarded the Nobel Peace Prize in 2006. Decades earlier, founder Muhammad Yunus had the idea to offer small loans at low interest rates to impoverished people instead of just giving them money without expecting repayment. Many of these microloans financed small businesses that sustained families and communities.

Recognizing the potential benefits the microfinancing industry offered to the impoverished, many American humanitarian organizations soon joined the cause. Endorsements from celebrities such as Natalie Portman and Robert Duvall helped boost microlending's credibility. Soon, Internet startups were giving Americans the opportunity to help the poor all over the world. Online microlending sites, such as Kiva, MicroPlace, Lend for Peace, and the Microloan Foundation, connected lenders and borrowers on a global level. Established in 2005, Kiva lent over $300 million to over 900,000 borrowers, with a 98.9 percent repayment rate.

Attracted by the possibility of making large profits from small loans and spurred on by the United Nations' International Year of Microcredit in 2005, many banks, financial institutions, and venture capitalists began offering their own microloans. In 2007, over twelve thousand lenders, including Citigroup and eBay, were granting microloans. These institutions became a significant resource for American microloan organizations, some of which were acquired by these banks.

Although the availability of microloans increased, problems related to the industry began to surface. Many institutions significantly raised the microloan interest rates, which incited serious criticism on several levels and caught the attention of Congress. Some international lenders, at least one Kiva partner among them, were charging upward of 70 percent interest, with a few notoriously demanding over 100 percent. The House Financial Services Committee held hearings in January 2010 to determine if some of these institutions were swindling borrowers.

Impact

By the end of 2009, nearly 200 million poor entrepreneurs received microloans, potentially benefitting 641 million of the world's poorest people, according to the 2011 Microcredit Summit Campaign Report. Critics argued that microlending does not serve the most needy; that microlenders' exorbitant interest rates makes them no better than the loan sharks they seek to undercut; and that since most microlenders target female entrepreneurs, who are seen as more reliable borrowers, the practice causes conflicts between the genders. Such criticism has been acknowledged even by proponents, and efforts are underway to reduce interest rates and increase transparency.

Further Reading

CBC News. "Microcredit Lending: Small Loans; Big Payback." *CBC News.* CBC, 10 Nov. 2006. Web. 27 Nov. 2012.

Goldberg, Nathanael. *Measuring the Impact of Microfinance: Taking Stock of What We Know.* Washington: Grameen Foundation USA, Dec. 2005. PDF file.

Islam, Tazul. *Microcredit and Poverty Alleviation.* Hampshire: Ashgate, 2007. Print.

MacFarquhar, Neil. "Banks Making Big Profits from Tiny Loans." *New York Times.* New York Times Co., 3 Apr. 2010. Web. 27 Nov. 2012.

Cait Caffrey

■ Military Commissions Act of 2006

Definition: Federal legislation that allows the US president to identify "enemy combatants" and to detain and try these individuals in military, not civilian, courts

Date: Signed on October 17, 2006

Also known as: MCA

In the war on terrorism, President George W. Bush determined that, in order to effectively combat al-Qaeda, those individuals captured on suspicion of helping that group should be detained and tried as enemy combatants. The Military Commissions Act of 2006 formally allowed the president to carry out this policy.

After the al-Qaeda–backed September 11, 2001, terrorist attacks, President George W. Bush and his administration realized that the nation was facing a new type of enemy. Al-Qaeda did not represent a single nation or government but had members and supporters around the world. With the goal of protecting national security, Bush exercised what he saw as his constitutionally granted executive powers to identify al-Qaeda members as "enemy combatants" and to detain and try them as such in a military commission (court). In 2006, the Supreme Court determined that the Bush administration needed statutory authority to carry out this policy. Congress responded during the same year by passing the Military Commissions Act (MCA).

The MCA generated regulations pertaining to the detention and military trial of such combatants. The charges included material support for terrorism, conspiracy, and participating in war crimes. Unlike in the federal criminal court system, cases did not require a writ of habeas corpus (which permits a judge to review a case on the merits of the evidence against the suspect) before proceeding to the commission.

Most of the individuals detained under the MCA were sent to a special holding facility at Guantánamo Bay, Cuba. Those suspects could be held indefinitely while they awaited trial. The MCA did, however, apply the Fifth Amendment to the detainees, ensuring that they would not be deprived of life, liberty, or property without due process. The MCA also paid deference to the provisions of the Geneva Conventions as well, although neither the United States nor international codes had yet applied its definitions (traditionally referring to military combatants) to terrorists.

Impact

The MCA was a controversial element in the war on terrorism. Civil rights advocates argued that it essentially stripped suspects of their right to a fair trial. They also complained about the length of pretrial detentions at Guantánamo Bay and a perceived lack of humanitarian treatment of detainees there. After his 2009 inauguration, President Barack Obama put a temporary hold on the military commissions in order to review them. In 2009, Congress amended the MCA by passing the Military Commissions Act of 2009, which was signed by President Obama on October 24 of that year. The amendment made a number of key changes to the original act with regard to prisoner rights and the efficiency of the trial process, although the facility in Guantánamo Bay remained operational.

Further Reading

Elsea, Jennifer K. "Comparison of Rights in Military Commission Trials and Trials in Federal Criminal Court". *CRS Report for Congress.* Washington, DC: CRS/Lib. of Cong., 9 May 2012. PDF file.

—. "The Military Commissions Act of 2006: Background and Proposed Amendments." *CRS Report for Congress.* Washington, DC: CRS/Lib. of Cong., 11 Aug. 2009. PDF file.

Richey, Warren. "Obama Endorses Military Commissions for Guantánamo Detainees." *Christian Science Monitor.* Christian Science Monitor, 29 Oct. 2009. Web. 11 Dec. 2012.

Michael P. Auerbach, MA

■ Millennium celebrations

Definition: Celebrations that occurred across the United States that marked the beginning of the third millennium on January 1, 2000

Millennial celebrations in the United States occurred in concert with others around the world on the evening of December 31, 1999, to celebrate the turn of the millennium, which is the span of one thousand years. The evening also ushered in the dawn of the twenty-first century. Celebrations occurred across the United States, with major events held at the Lincoln Memorial, the National Mall, and Times Square.

By the late 1990s, preparations began in the United States to mark the turn of the millennium. President Bill Clinton established the White House Millennial Council in August 1997, with the theme "Honor the Past—Imagine the Future." The council was set up to coordinate millennial activities, under the leadership of then First Lady Hillary Clinton. The council's role was to encourage all Americans to take part in the celebrations, and to this end established the Millennium Communities program. Any community across the United States that planned and held any kind of celebration to mark the millennium was eligible for the honorary designation of Millennium Community. For example, Meridian, Mississippi, renovated a Grand Opera House into an arts education center, while Laredo, Texas, schools created their own time capsules to be opened in 2020.

Fireworks display in San Francisco. (©iStockphoto.com/J. J. Withers)

The Millennial Council also designed and created the National Millennium Time Capsule to commemorate key events and accomplishments of the twentieth century. Winners of various national medals were canvassed for ideas for capsule items, as were students from across the country. Millennium Evenings were also set up by the White House, in order to showcase culture and learning by inviting some of the leading artists and scholars to perform or present, including such distinguished guests as jazz musician Wynton Marsalis, scientist Stephen Hawking, and Nobel Peace Prize–winner Elie Wiesel. Other programs of the council included the Millennium Trails program, designed to recognize and/or create at least two thousand trails across the United States. There was also a desire to preserve the nation's history with the $30 million Save America's Treasures program, designed to preserve historic sites, documents, monuments, and art. Communities and schools were even asked to imagine what human habitation would look like on Mars by the year 2030.

The evening of December 31, 1999, and early morning of January 1, 2000, marked the actual millennial celebrations. The White House hosted a gala at the Lincoln Memorial in Washington, DC, which included notable American artists. It was hosted by Will Smith and produced by Quincy Jones and George Stevens Jr. The Washington Monument was illuminated for the countdown to midnight, and President Clinton addressed the nation by television at about 11:53 p.m. Times Square in New York City was once again teeming with people.

Throughout America, cities and towns held enhanced New Year's Eve celebrations, with the requisite fireworks and countdowns. Although some felt the celebrations were dampened by worries of terrorism and the Y2K computer bug, millennial celebrations in essence turned out to be one big party.

Impact

The impact of millennial celebrations in the United States was relatively short-term. The White House Millennial Council continued its activities until January 1, 2001, in order to avoid the controversy of those who believed that the turn of the millennium actually occurred on the evening of December 31, 2000. There were also numerous community trails, parks, and even some infrastructure built across the country to commemorate the millennium.

Further Reading

Johnson, Dan. "Millennium: The Biggest Party Ever—and You Are Invited!" *Futurist* 32.7 (1998): 41–45. Print.

Robinson, Tracy. "Clinton Transcends the Millennium." *American Spectator* 30.11 (1997): 80–81. Print.

White House Millennium Council 2000. White House, n.d. Web. 10 Dec. 2012.

Lee Tunstall, PhD

■ Miller, Judith

Identification: American journalist
Born: 1948; New York, New York

Judith Miller's work as a journalist became infamous after her reports in the New York Times on the existence of weapons of mass destruction (WMD) in Iraq proved inaccurate. She served time in jail for criminal contempt after refusing to reveal her sources to a Central Intelligence Agency (CIA) leak investigation.

As a journalist at the Washington bureau of the *New York Times,* Judith Miller specialized in issues of national security. She coauthored a book about bioterrorism, *Germs: Biological Weapons and America's Secret War,* which was published shortly after the terrorist attacks of September 11, 2001. Miller and her *New York Times* colleagues were awarded a Pulitzer Prize in 2002 for their coverage of the September 11 attacks and al-Qaeda.

In 2002, Miller also wrote a series of articles for the *New York Times* concerning Iraqi dictator Saddam Hussein's pursuit of a nuclear weapons program. Her primary source was an Iraqi politician, Ahmed Chalabi. Miller later reported that weapons of mass destruction had been found in Iraq but were destroyed. After this story proved untrue, much of Miller's reporting was called into question. The *New York Times* acknowledged that Chalabi's information may have been influenced by his own political agenda. The online magazine *Salon* criticized Miller's reporting on Iraq in 2004. Her reputation was further damaged when members of the Bush administration cited her reports as motivating factors behind their support of the 2003 US-led invasion of Iraq and the war that followed. Miller left the *New York Times* in 2005.

Later in 2005, Miller again found herself at the center of controversy. A judge sentenced her to prison after she refused to divulge the identity of the person who had revealed to her the name a CIA secret agent. Miller served eighty-five days in jail before the source, White House staff member I. Lewis "Scooter" Libby, allowed her to reveal his involvement. She testified to a grand jury in the Libby case shortly after her release. Miller became an adjunct fellow at the Manhattan Institute for Policy Research in 2007 and joined *Fox News* in 2008 as a commentator on national security and terrorism.

Impact

Judith Miller's contributions to American journalism have earned her a Pulitzer Prize and the distinguished DuPont award. She continues to discuss issues of national defense and foreign policy. Miller comments on politics and international events both online and for *Fox News.* Her work during the lead up to the 2003 US-led invasion of Iraq incited an ongoing debate over the media's role and responsibility in society and government.

Further Reading

Foer, Franklin. "The Source of the Trouble." *New York Magazine.* New York Media, 21 May 2005. Web. 8 Oct. 2012.

Joyce, Daniel. "The Judith Miller Case and the Relationship between Reporter and Source: Competing Visions of the Media's Role and Function." *Fordham Intellectual Property, Media and Entertainment Law Journal* 17 (2007): 555–89. PDF file.

Miller, Judith, Stephen Engelberg, and William Broad. *Germs: Biological Weapons and America's Secret War.* New York: Simon, 2001. Print.

Cait Caffrey

■ *A Million Little Pieces*

Identification: Memoir about overcoming substance-abuse addiction that was the subject of a major scandal when parts of it were found to have been fictionalized
Author: James Frey (b. 1969)
Date: Published in 2003

Although there have been other book scandals throughout history, few have reached the magnitude of A Million Little Pieces. *After author Frey was exposed as a fraud, he suffered immense public humiliation and ended up the target of a class-action lawsuit.*

A Million Little Pieces was published in 2003 by Doubleday, a division of Random House, as a memoir that detailed the author James Frey's battle with drug and alcohol addiction. After winding up on a path of self-destruction, he endured various rehabilitation methods until he successfully regained both his health and control of his life. The narrative resonated especially with other addicts who tended to view the book as a self-help manual. Its publication represented a growing interest in the memoir genre and appealed to fans for its captivating narrative, crafty writing, and confessional nature.

In 2005, Oprah Winfrey selected *A Million Little Pieces* for her popular book club, thus ensuring Frey of instant celebrity status and his book a place on the New York Times Best Sellers list. While most readers enjoyed the book at face value, investigators at the *Smoking Gun* website began questioning some of the incidents and dates. Their full investigation, released in early 2006, showed that Frey had misrepresented himself numerous times, including lying about a three-month-long period of incarceration. Frey went on the defensive, refusing to admit he had intentionally deceived his readers and blaming discrepancies on poetic license and faulty memory. Nevertheless, he and his publisher agreed to offer refunds to readers and to include a disclaimer from Frey in future printings. His most public defense took place on the *Larry King Show*,

during which time Winfrey surprised some fans by calling in with her support for Frey.

As the event unfolded, Frey became the target of a seemingly endless barrage of public jokes and vicious hate mail while angry and hurt readers sued for compensation. Frey and Random House eventually settled a class-action lawsuit for $2.35 million. Oprah again invited him to appear on her show, but this time she shamed him mercilessly.

Impact

While Frey eventually recovered and went on to publish additional books, the scandal has become a benchmark in writing and publishing. Publishers are under tighter scrutiny than previously to check facts for accuracy, and writers are more likely to publish a memoir as fiction. The scandal's wider impact also included the instigation of a national dialogue about truth and writers' responsibilities to their readers.

Further Reading

Hamilton, Geoff. "Mixing Memoir and Desire: James Frey, Wound Culture, and the 'Essential American Soul'." *Journal of American Culture* 30.3 (2007): 324–33. Print.

Peretz, Evgenia. "James Frey's Morning After." *Vanity Fair.* 1 June 2008. Web. 31 July 2012.

Wyatt, Edward. "Best-Selling Memoir Draws Scrutiny." *New York Times* 10 Jan. 2006. Web. 31 July 2012.

Sally Driscoll

■ Minimum wage increase

Definition: The lowest rate at which employers must legally pay their workers

The federal minimum wage rate in the United States was stagnant for ten years, from 1997 to 2007, at $5.15 per hour. A series of amendments enacted in 2007 raised the minimum wage rate over the next two years, bringing it to $7.25 per hour.

US president Franklin Delano Roosevelt signed the Fair Labor Standards Act of 1938, which guaranteed a federal minimum wage of twenty-five cents per hour to workers. He enacted this law to reduce the number of Americans living in poverty and to increase spending during the Great Depression. Some states set their own minimum wage rates, which are higher than the federal rate. Others pay workers the federal minimum wage. Regardless, all states must pay their workers the higher of either the state minimum wage or the federal minimum wage. They cannot pay workers less than these rates.

Through the years, amendments have raised federal minimum wage rates. In 1997, the federal minimum wage was set at $5.15 per hour. This rate remained unchanged for the next decade. After a heated debate between the Democratic Congress and President George W. Bush and the Republican Senate, the Fair Minimum Wage Act of 2007 was passed. Under the amendment, the minimum wage rate was increased to $5.85 per hour, effective July 24, 2007. The rate was increased to $6.55 per hour on July 24, 2008, and to $7.25 per hour on July 24, 2009.

The federal minimum wage rate for tipped workers is much lower than it is for nontipped workers. The minimum wage law allows employers to pay tipped workers a reduced minimum wage of $2.13 per hour because these types of workers typically make up the difference in tips. Sometimes, they can make slightly—and, in some cases, drastically—more than the minimum wage once tips are included. Such workers include restaurant servers, bartenders, valets, and hair stylists. Some states, however, require that tipped workers receive higher wages. The states of Alaska, California, Minnesota, Montana, Nevada, Oregon, and Washington require businesses to pay tipped workers the full federal minimum wage in addition to tips. Other states allow employers to pay the reduced minimum, which remained unchanged from the rate of $2.13 set in 1991.

Impact

Raising the minimum wage rate is thought to stimulate the economy because it can increase spending without increasing taxes. It increases the amount of money a person makes, which in turn increases the amount of money a person may be able to spend. The Federal Reserve Bank of Chicago reported in 2007 that a worker would spend about $3,000 for every $1 increase to the minimum wage rate.

Further Reading

"History of Changes to the Minimum Wage Law." *Wage and Hour Division.* United States Department of Labor, n.d. Web. 10 Dec. 2012.

"Minimum Wage Question and Answer." *Raise the Minimum Wage.* National Employment Law Project, n.d. Web. 10 Dec. 2012.

Rampell, Catherine. "Who Is Affected by a Higher Minimum Wage?" *Economix.* New York Times, 24 July 2009. Web. 10 Dec. 2012.

Angela Harmon

■ Minneapolis I-35W bridge collapse

The Event: The collapse of an eight-lane highway bridge that spanned the Mississippi River between Minneapolis and St. Paul

Date: August 1, 2007

Place: Minneapolis and St. Paul, Minnesota

During the evening rush hour on Wednesday, August 1, 2007, a major bridge used by commuters in the Twin Cities suddenly collapsed into the Mississippi River, killing 13 and injuring 145 others. The accident and ensuing investigation shed light on the nation's aging infrastructure and incited a national debate over how to pay for repairs and new construction.

In 2006, the United States Department of Transportation found more than 73,000 bridges to be in need of repair or replacement. The forty-year-old I-35W bridge was undergoing repairs when it collapsed on August 1, 2007. Four of its eight lanes were closed, with concrete work scheduled to begin on the closed portion that evening. The four open lanes of the 1,907-foot-long bridge had bumper-to-bumper traffic when, suddenly, the steel deck truss separated from the southern and northern spans and fell 108 feet into the Mississippi River, plunging 111 vehicles into the water or atop submerged sections of deck. Several spans collapsed onto the land beneath, crushing more cars and a several train cars below. Before emergency workers arrived on the scene, hundreds of people rushed to help, diving into the water to rescue victims, providing first aid, or assisting with evacuations. After a few days of searches, the final death toll totaled 13, with 145 people injured.

At first, many people thought the collapse was caused by an act of terrorism or possibly an earthquake. After a lengthy investigation, aided by video taken by a motion-activated surveillance camera, the National Transportation Safety Board (NTSB)

A Coast Guard vessel patrols a safety zone around the Minnesota bridge collapse site in Minneapolis, August 3, 2007. (U.S. Coast Guard/Photograph by Chief Petty Officer Robert Lanier)

determined that the accident was the result of a design error, blaming the bridge's lack of redundancy and, in particular, the gusset plates for their inability to withstand added weight of the construction loads and heavy traffic on the bridge. In addition, they faulted federal and state transportation agencies for inadequate inspections of the gusset plates and for failing to consider gusset plates in their weight-load statistics, leading to more than one hundred lawsuits. While the incident shocked the nation, the efficiency of the rescue and recovery, as well as individual stories of heroism, lifted spirits. A replacement bridge, St. Anthony Falls Bridge, opened on September 18, 2008, three months ahead of schedule.

Impact

The collapse of the I-35W bridge thrust the nation's aging infrastructure into the limelight. The NTSB made several recommendations to the Federal Highway Administration and the American Associa-

tion of State Highway and Transportation Officials, while the American Society of Civil Engineers (ASCE) prepared the "Report Card for America's Infrastructure," giving most bridges in the United States a grade of "C." While the ASCE also estimated that $9.4 billion a year for twenty years would be needed for their repair, only a small fraction of that estimate was set aside in the years immediately following the incident.

Further Reading

"Interstate 35W Bridge in Minneapolis." *Minnesota Department of Transportation.* Minnesota Department of Transportation, n.d. Web. 3 Aug. 2012.

LePatner, Barry B. "Whitewashing the I-35W Bridge Collapse." *USA Today Magazine* 1 May 2011: 70–71. Print.

National Transportation Safety Board. *Highway Accident Report—Collapse of I-35W Highway Bridge.* Washington, DC: NTSB, 2008. PDF file.

Sally Driscoll

■ Mobile phones

Definition: Any type of handheld telephone that is not directly connected to a land line and uses radio waves for transmission. Also known as a cellular ("cell") phone.

In the years between 2000 and 2009, significant technological advances were made in the development of mobile phones and their programming, features, and capabilities. Consumer use and dependence on cell phones also increased dramatically during the decade. With the increased use of cell phones by more and more people, numerous states throughout the country enacted legislation regulating the use of cell phones while driving.

The first portable telephone was created by Dr. Martin Cooper in 1973 when his company, Motorola, and their competition, Bell Labs, were competing to create and market the new technology. One of original mobile phones available to the public was the Motorola DynaTAC 8000X, released in 1983. It is considered the first generation of modern-day cell phones. The phone weighed almost two pounds, was thirteen inches tall, and was able to make and receive calls but did not have other features that today are considered standard. The phone could store up to thirty phone numbers, and although it held a charge for one hour, it took ten hours to recharge. The retail price in 1983 was $3,500.

The 1990s, which is considered the second generation of cell-phone technology, brought more streamlined and compact mobile phones. In 1996, Motorola released the StarTAC, which could easily fit in a pocket and was the first clamshell, or "flip phone" device. Its design included a hinge that required users to "flip" it open, much like a clam opens its shell, in order to make and receive calls. By 1999, most new cell phones were engineered to fit easily in a user's hand and came with the antenna inside the phone's case. Prior to this, antennas were connected to the outside of the phone. These external antennas were an average of seven inches long and were prone to breaking when extended to their full length.

Technology Innovations

Third generation (3G) cell phones that were produced during the 2000s saw dramatic increases in memory storage capabilities, battery life, available features, and design options; as a result, cell-phone

use by consumers also increased markedly. In 2001, for example, one out of ten people worldwide owned a cell phone; by 2009, six out of ten people owned cell phones.

The first touchscreen phone was unveiled in 2000 by Motorola. The technology was limited at the time, and the display was only available in black-and-white, but it was immensely popular and introduced consumers to the technology that would be commonplace less than a decade later.

In 2001, the Sharp Corporation introduced the first commercially available camera phone. Although it was difficult to buy outside of Japan, the Sanyo 5300 from Sprint, introduced in 2002, was the first camera phone sold in North America. That same year, Sony introduced the Ericsson T68i, which was equipped with limited internet capabilities. Also in 2002, the Danger Hiptop (later purchased by T-Mobile and rebranded as the T-Mobile Sidekick) was released to the public and became an immediate hit mainly for its ability to continuously maintain an Internet connection. It was one of the first phones to offer a full Internet browsing experience with integrated instant messaging, and with its full QWERTY keyboard, the Hiptop/Sidekick was one of the best-selling phones among the hearing impaired.

A drawback to the added technology of the 2000s was that cell phones became increasingly fragile. Complex internal computers were often damaged beyond repair after a phone was dropped or mishandled. Cell phone manufacturers soon tried to introduce phones that were designed with tougher cases to help safeguard the devices. Colorful cases and snap-on protectors were also marketed around this time to provide added protection while also giving consumers a sense that they were customizing or "accessorizing" their cell phones.

Smartphones

A smartphone is any cell phone that includes software functions such as email or Internet browsing. The first smartphone was developed in 1997, but it was not until several years later that the technology was widely available to all consumers. The Kyocera QCP6035, introduced in 2001, was the first mainstream, palm-sized phone and retailed between $400 and $500. In 2002, the Blackberry 5810, which allowed users to receive email and surf the Internet, was launched. The drawback of this phone was that users needed to plug in a headset in order to talk, which kept the 5810 from gaining popularity. The following year, the TREO 600 was released by Palm, and it allowed users to access programs that previously could only be used on a computer. Its increased memory and processing power made it popular for a time, but by 2007, Apple would introduce its breakthrough in mobile phone technology, and the face of the industry was once again changed.

The iPhone
In 2007, Steve Jobs, cofounder and CEO of Apple, Inc., launched a new touchscreen smartphone—the Apple iPhone. Essentially a small, handheld computer that also made phone calls, the iPhone was the second generation of its kind, but this newer model utilized the 3G technology and was the first iPhone to be available outside of the United States. The iPhone 3G included such advanced features as built-in GPS; a multitasking platform that allowed the user to make a call, check e-mail, or get directions at the same time; sync technology for e-mail and calendar; encryption ability to access corporate data; and the Internet browser Safari. Possibly the most industry-altering feature was the introduction of the new App (application) Store, which allowed users to browse and purchase programs to load onto their new iPhones and access with a touch of a finger. To compete with the iPhone, competitors quickly launched the Android, or "droid," platform, available on many types of phones, but programming bugs that were never thoroughly resolved by the end of the decade stalled any major user share that droid phones could have over iPhones. Droid phones did come equipped with an app store, however, which generated a new facet of the mobile phone industry: companies whose sole purpose was to create new applications to sell to consumers. Applications for everything from history databases to the online game sensation Angry Birds could be purchased by consumers for use on their phones.

Manufacturers and Providers
Major advances in mobile phone technology during the 2000s, coupled with the accelerated growth in popularity and use by consumers, forced cell phone manufacturers to constantly offer new and exciting features and designs in order to retain or surpass their market share in the industry. The most common manufacturers during the decade were Nokia, LG, HTC, Samsung, Motorola, and Apple.

Most of these companies did not sell their phones directly to consumers, however, so middlemen, referred to as cell phone providers, marketed and sold products to the public. In order to purchase a phone, a user had to also contract with the provider for a predetermined time period (usually two years) or face a heavy fee-based penalty. As cell phones gained in popularity throughout the decade with the added capabilities and features, price wars were common among providers as they tried to lure consumers to sign their contracts by offering discounts on text messaging, international calling, and bundled packages that offered discounts to families who bought and used several cell phones on the same provider plan.

Legislation
With a growing number of cell phone–related accidents throughout the decade, individual states created and implemented legislation that would impose various penalties for using a cell phone while driving. In 2001, New York was the first state to enact legislation making it illegal for a driver to use a handheld phone. Hands-free phone use, utilizing the speaker or earpiece feature of a phone, while driving was allowed, however, and New York's law became the basis of other laws that were written and enforced across the country. Several states also enacted stricter legislation that banned any use of a mobile phone while driving, including hands-free phones.

In September of 2004, California governor Arnold Schwarzenegger signed the Cell Phone Recycling Act that required all cell-phone providers to accept and then recycle unwanted or unusable cell phones. The law, which was implemented in July of 2006, also stipulated that the recycling of old phone would be at no cost to the consumer.

Impact
Thanks in large part to the technological advancements made in the mobile phone industry during the 2000s, mobile phones have changed the way that people worldwide interact with one another. Individuals are more connected with each other than ever before, which has created debates that are continuing well into the next decade on the benefits and drawbacks of this byproduct of cell phone technology. Cell phones have developed so that their use includes the almost instant ability to access enter-

tainment, emergency personnel, loved ones, bank accounts, online information, navigation tools, current events, and even historical events through mobile applications. Debates also continue regarding the potential health risks from possible radiation that cell phones produce. With the mobile phone industry's ability to continually create smaller and more advanced computer chips and processors, other industries have benefitted. A more innovative society is better able to enhance the quality of life of its residents, but only if individuals remain cognizant of the dangers that can come alongside the benefits of technology.

Further Reading

"Apple Introduces the New iPhone 3G." *Apple.* Apple Inc., 9 June 2008. Web. 11 Nov. 2012. A press release announcing the Apple iPhone, its specifications, and the new Apple Application Store.

Glotz, Peter, Stefan Bertschi, and Chris Locke, eds. *Thumb Culture: The Meaning of Mobile Phones for Society.* Bielefeld: Verlag, 2005. Print. A review of the social and cultural impact of cell phones on society and how they have changed the ways people relate to one another.

Goggin, Gerald. *Cell Phone Culture: Mobil Technology in Everyday Life.* New York: Routledge, 2006. Print. Provides a history of the cultural and technological impact of cell phones throughout the world.

Honan, Mat. "From Brick to Slick: A History of Mobile Phones." *Wired.* Condé Nast, 23 Feb. 2009. Web. 10 Nov. 2012. Presents a photo essay, with accompanying captions that highlight the most significant breakthroughs in mobile phone history.

Klemens, Guy. *The Cellphone: The History and Technology of the Gadget that Changed the World.* Jefferson: McFarland. 2010. Print. Presents a history of cell phone technology from the 1940s through 2010.

Ling, Richard Seyler. *The Mobile Connection: The Cell Phone's Impact on Society.* San Francisco: Kaufmann, 2004. Print. Details the history, growth, and impact of mobile phones on societies across the world.

Sturnquist, Daniel M. *Mobile Phones and Driving.* New York: Nova, 2006. Print. A book on the state-level legislation concerning mobile phones and driving.

Anna Accettola, MA

■ *Modern Family*

Identification: Television mockumentary about the members of an extended family
Executive Producers: Steven Levitan (b. 1962); Christopher Lloyd (b. 1960)
Date: Premiered on September 23, 2009

When Modern Family *premiered in 2009, it became an instant success. The show debuted to high ratings and attracted a growing audience in its first months on the air. Viewers were drawn in by the sitcom's cast of characters and its accurate portrayal of American family life in the twenty-first century.*

Modern Family premiered on the ABC television network on September 23, 2009, to an audience of 12.7 million viewers and widespread acclaim from critics. Created by Steven Levitan and Christopher Lloyd, the family sitcom has featured a diverse cast, including television veteran Ed O'Neill of *Married with Children* fame and Colombian actress Sofía Vergara. The show centers on patriarch Jay Pritchett (O'Neill) and the members of his extended family, who are being filmed as the subjects of a television documentary.

The sitcom's suburban setting is typical of American life in the 2000s; the Pritchett family members' various life circumstances are also familiar. Jay, who is divorced from his first wife, has married a young and beautiful Colombian woman named Gloria (Vergara) and has become stepfather to her twelve-year-old son, Manny. Jay's adult daughter, Claire (Julie Bowen), and her husband, Phil (Ty Burrell), have three children—Haley, Alex, and Luke—and very different attitudes toward parenting. Claire's attempts at being strict are countered by Phil's desire to be easygoing. Jay's adult son, Mitchell (Jesse Tyler Ferguson), who is gay, has adopted a daughter from Vietnam with his partner, Cameron (Eric Stonestreet). Episodes of the show focus on the experiences of the three interconnected families as the adults attempt to raise their children and navigate their relationships with their significant others.

Impact

Since the early years of television broadcasting, the traditional American family has been a popular subject for TV sitcoms. Throughout the twentieth century, divorce, cross-cultural adoption, blended families, and same-sex unions began to redefine the American family. Households that were once considered unconventional became common and accepted. *Modern Family* reflects the changing profile of the American family and updates the family sitcom genre for the twenty-first century.

Further Reading

Bellafante, Ginia. "'I'm the Cool Dad' and Other Debatable Dispatches from the Home Front." *New York Times.* New York Times, 22 Sept. 2009. Web. 4 Sept. 2012.

Bianco, Robert. "Finally, ABC Gives Us a 'Modern Family' We Can Relate To." *USA Today.* Gannett, 23 Sept. 2009. Web. 4 Sept. 2012.

Poniewozik, James. "Yes, We Kin." *Time.* Time Inc., 28 Sept. 2009. Web. 4 Sept. 2012.

Writers of *Modern Family.* Modern Family*: Wit and Wisdom from America's Favorite Family.* New York: Hyperion, 2012. Print.

Kathleen Berlew

■ Mortensen, Viggo

Identification: Danish American actor, poet, and publisher
Born: October 20, 1958; Manhattan, New York

Viggo Mortensen. (©iStockphoto.com/Carlos Alvarez)

Viggo Mortensen gained critical acclaim during the 2000s as one of the stars of The Lord of the Rings film trilogy as well as his collaborations with director David Cronenberg. He also established and ran a publishing company.

Viggo Mortensen, who had roles in several films prior to 2000, gained worldwide recognition as an actor thanks to his role in director Peter Jackson's *The Lord of the Rings* film trilogy, based on the books by author J. R. R. Tolkien. *The Fellowship of the Ring* (2001), the first in *The Lord of the Rings* trilogy, was a success both financially and critically. Mortensen played the character of Aragorn, also known as Strider, a wandering warrior. The next two films in the trilogy, *The Two Towers* (2002) and *The Return of the King* (2003), also did well. Mortensen was nominated for several best actor awards for his role in the films. He was also noted for doing many of his own stunts in the trilogy and for insisting on using a real steel sword rather than a prop one.

Following *The Lord of the Rings* trilogy, Mortensen worked on a number of other film projects during the decade. This included collaboration with Canadian director David Cronenberg on two crime-thrillers: *A History of Violence* (2005) and *Eastern Promises* (2007). In *A History of Violence,* Mortensen played Tom Stall, the owner of a diner in a small town trying to hide from his criminal past. He received several award nominations for this role. In *Eastern Promises,* Mortensen played Nikolai Luzhin, a member of the Russian mafia. For this role, Mortensen received his biggest nomination yet: an Academy Award nomination for best actor.

Mortensen's final major role in the 2000s was as "the Man" in director John Hillcoat's drama *The Road* (2009), based on Cormac McCarthy's Pulitzer Prize–winning novel of the same name. Mortensen received several nominations for this role as well, winning the Utah Film Critics Association award for best actor.

Outside of acting, Mortensen pursued several artistic endeavors in the 2000s. In 2002, he established a publishing company called Perceval Press. Mortensen released several of his own books of poetry and photography through Perceval Press, as well as CDs of his musical collaborations. In the 2000s, he released eight albums and thirteen various publications of his paintings, poetry, and photography.

Mortensen was politically active in the 2000s, helping to promote Democrat Dennis Kucinich in the 2008 US presidential election. He also helped to endorse Barack Obama during his 2008 campaign for the presidency.

Impact

The Lord of the Rings trilogy made Mortensen one of the most recognizable movie actors in the world. In 2006, he was given an honorary doctorate from St. Lawrence University in Canton, New York, where he had graduated from in 1980. His Perceval Press continues to publish works from artists, poets, and musicians, including Mortensen's own artistic work.

Further Reading

Heller, Zoe. "Viggo Talks and Talks." *T: The New York Times Style Magazine.* New York Times Co., 2 Dec. 2011. Web. 15 Aug. 2012.

Lane, Harriet. "'My Mother is Very Happy about It.'" *Guardian* [London]. Guardian News and Media, 21 Feb. 2008. Web. 15 Aug. 2012.

Siegal, Nina. "Viggo Mortensen Interview." *Progressive.* Progressive Magazine, Nov. 2005. Web. 15 Aug. 2012.

Patrick G. Cooper

■ Murdoch, Rupert

Identification: Australian-American media entrepreneur

Born: March 11, 1931; Melbourne, Victoria, Australia

Rupert Murdoch built a global media empire and transformed both the content and the distribution of news and entertainment around the world. The far-reaching influence of his company, News Corporation, on popular culture, media, and business has garnered both fierce condemnation as well as accolades.

Rupert Murdoch. (Copyright by World Economic Forum swiss-image.ch/Photo by Monika Flueckiger)

In 1973, after two decades of starting and acquiring newspapers in Australia and England, Australian-born Rupert Murdoch moved into the American newspaper market with the acquisition of the *San Antonio Express.* In 1977, he bought several New York publications, including the *New York Post* (sold in 1988, repurchased in 1993) and the *Village Voice* (sold in 1985). He later acquired the *Times of London* and *Sunday Times* (1981), the *Boston Herald* (1982), the *Chicago Sun-Times* (bought in 1983, sold in 1986), and many others.

In 1980, Murdoch formed News Corporation (better known as News Corp.) and began to expand his empire into electronic media. By 1987, News Corp was the world's largest newspaper publisher, and it continued to absorb or control hundreds of mostly media-related corporations.

In 1986 he launched Fox Broadcasting , which became the first TV network to successfully challenge the long-time dominance of networks NBC,

CBS, and ABC. The Fox network changed television standards in both entertainment and journalism, and not without controversy. Its entertainment is often considered vulgar, and its news is criticized as lacking journalistic integrity because of conflicts of interest with Murdoch's business and political commitments.

In 2005, he surprised many by purchasing MySpace, a popular social networking site on the Internet. With control of MySpace, the company assured a strong foothold in the vastly expanding realm of cyberspace, where, according to one critic, it can "host the cultural conversation." In 2007, Murdoch purchased Dow Jones & Company, giving him control of the venerable *Wall Street Journal* and sparking further debate over the morality and ethics of Murdoch's kind of cultural "hospitality."

Murdoch's domination of world media was perhaps inevitable. Journalism-school dean Ben Bagdikian began keeping tally of media ownership in 1984, a year that saw about fifty large corporations controlling more than half of the American media. In successive editions of his book *The Media Monopoly* (1984), that number has fallen dramatically. By 2003, the world's media were dominated by five giant corporations, one of which was Murdoch's News Corp.

Even Murdoch's critics, however, concede that he has made some valuable contributions, such as modernizing the newspaper industry in England and eliminating its union rules, but also, they blame his predilection for sensational infotainment for increasing vulgarity in entertainment and dishonesty in news. One critic argued that "Murdoch uses his diverse holdings . . . to promote his own financial interests at the expense of real newsgathering, legal and regulatory rules, and journalistic ethics." The writer goes on to say that, "If ever someone demonstrated the dangers of mass power being concentrated in few hands, it would be Murdoch."

Murdoch and News Corp. have been embroiled in the News International phone hacking scandal in 2011. As a result of the scandal, , Murdoch stepped down as a director of News International, a subsidiary of News Corp. in July 2012.

Impact

Murdoch's half-century construction of a worldwide media empire has produced a large personal fortune. His estimated net worth of nearly $9.4 billion has come with a price: far-reaching social and cultural effects. The editorial control exercised by Murdoch over his various holdings means that he has been at least tangentially responsible for shaping years' worth of popular culture and mass information to his liking. Murdoch's defenders argue in turn that he is, "in some sense, the best democrat of all." He gives people what *they* want. Media critics counter that Murdoch has defined what the public wants simply by producing one type of content over another. To his supporters, though, Murdoch has put a human (if sometimes ruthless) face on the otherwise impersonal, perhaps inexorable, processes of media change and consolidation in an era of globalization.

Further Reading

Auletta, Ken. "Promises, Promises." *New Yorker* 2 July 2007: 43–51. Print.

Kimmel, Daniel M. *The Fourth Network: How Fox Broke the Rules and Reinvented Television.* Chicago: Ivan R. Dee, 2004. Print.

Wolff, Michael. *The Man Who Owns the News: Inside the Secret World of Rupert Murdoch.* New York: Random, 2010. Print.

___ et al. *Rupert Murdoch, The Master Mogul of Fleet Street: 24 Tales from the Pages of* Vanity Fair. New York: Vanity Fair, 2012. E-book.

Edward Johnson

■ Music industry in the United States

Definition: The combined ranks of artists, promoters, record labels, producers, and distributors that comprise the music business in the United States

Rapid advances in technology changed the way Americans produced, consumed, and shared music in the 2000s. The MP3 format and file-sharing services changed the face of the music industry at a detriment to traditional business models.

The 2000s were a time of great upheaval for the music industry in the United States. The advent of digital music saw the MP3 file format overtake compact discs as the primary mode of music consumption. The entire sales model of the industry was turned on its head in the first decade of the 2000s. File-sharing programs made the Internet an anarchic haven for music sharing, which proved problematic for the industry, but beneficial for independent artists who could now distribute their music, free of industry constraints. With millions of songs being downloaded completely free of cost, the Recording Industry Associations of America began fighting a losing battle against digital music.

Declining Sales

Between 1999 and 2009, total revenue for music sales and licensing in the United States fell from $14.6 billion to $6.3 billion. During the 1990s, the music industry experienced a boom in sales as consumers phased out the cassette format, buying all new music and replacing old catalogs with compact discs. As the Internet became more widely used by the general public, peer-to-peer file sharing systems that allowed users to share media files like music and movies began to gain popularity. Following the shut-down of file-sharing pioneer Napster in 2001, a variety of other peer-to-peer sharing services allowed consumers to access and download unlimited amounts of music entirely for free. The MP3 file format became the standard for compression, transfer, and playback of digital audio and revolutionized the way music was consumed in the United States and the world over.

Portable Media Players & iTunes

In November 2001, Apple Inc. released the first version of its now ubiquitous iPod portable media player. The iPod and similar products—colloquially referred to as MP3 players—allowed music consumers to easily and compactly store thousands of songs for playback. In January 2001, Apple released iTunes—a user-friendly media player that allowed users to build extensive, easily organized digital music libraries. About nine months later, iTunes version 2.0 was released. It included support for the iPod, giving users convenient means to store, transfer, and listen to their music collections. In April 2003, iTunes 4.0 was released, and with it came the groundbreaking iTunes store. Prior to the introduction of the iTunes store, there was no model for monetizing digital music. File-sharing sites facilitated cost-free digital music sharing, but the selection from which to choose was dependent upon users' personal libraries. iTunes—at a charge of ninety-nine cents

per-song—provided new releases and an extensive selection that minimized costs for users, and provided a platform for record labels to profit off digital music. By 2011, digital music downloads via iTunes and similar services accounted for 50.3 percent of music sales in the United States, overtaking physical music sales for the first time in history.

Decline of the Album

From the early days of vinyl up through the demise of the compact disc, consumers primarily bought albums, not singles—with the possible exception of 45s in the 1950s and 60s. But in the 2000s, the MP3 file gave consumers the option of selectively building their music library from individual tracks. File-sharing services and digital music download stores inherently favored a singles-friendly consumption pattern. The album as a packaging unit for music began to decrease in popularity, ushering in a new age of digital one-hit-wonders. Digital album sales began to rise in the late 2000s, but single tracks still accounted for the vast majority of digital music sales.

Impact

The music technology, software, and consumption trends that defined the 2000s changed the music industry forever. Cost-free file-sharing conditioned consumers to expect their music for free. iTunes and similar digital music stores presented a viable digital sales model, at least partially making up for losses from illegal downloads. But by 2010, illegal downloads still accounted for 95 percent of music downloads worldwide. The compact disc market was virtually eliminated by iPods, iPhones, and other portable media players/smartphones. Underwhelming digital profits and anemic physical sales forced record labels and artists to refocus efforts on more profitable aspects of the industry. Live performance, licensing, and merchandise became more important than music sales.

In 2007, British alt-rockers Radiohead released their seventh studio album, *In Rainbows*, as a pay-what-you-want digital download. Many independent artists and select mainstream acts subsequently adopted the pay-what-you-want model. Independent artists in particular benefitted from shifting consumption trends in the 2000s. File-sharing services and music hosting websites like Bandcamp and SoundCloud allowed independent musicians to cheaply distribute their music to literally millions of people.

Further Reading

Elberse, Anita. "Bye-Bye Bundles: The Unbundling of Music in Digital Channels." *Journal of Marketing.* 74.3 (2010): 107–23. *Business Source Premier.* Web. 13 Dec. 2012. Analyzes the effect of unbundling on digital music sales.

Goldman, David. "Music's lost decade: Sales cut in half." *CNNMoney.* Cable News Network, 3 Feb. 2010. Web. 11 Dec. 2012. Examines music sales figures and consumption patterns in the first decade of the 2000s.

Guberman, Daniel. "Post-Fidelity: A New Age of Music Consumption and Technological Innovation." *Journal of Popular Music Studies* 23.4 (2011): 431–54. Print. A study on the role of technological innovation in music consumption patterns.

McCourt, Tom. "Collecting Music in the Digital Realm." *Popular Music & Society.* 28.2 (2005): 249–52. *Academic Search Premier.* Web. 13 Dec. 2012. Explores the collecting of digital music and the history of musical recordings.

O'Donnell, Patrick and Steve McClung. "MP3 Music Blogs: Their Efficacy in Selling Music and Marketing Bands." *Atlantic Journal of Communication* 16.2 (2008): 71–87. Print. Examines the execution and efficacy of MP3 music blogs as a means of marketing and distribution.

Steve Miller

■ MySpace

Definition: The premier online social-networking site for most of the decade, known especially for music

MySpace was one of the most innovative and lucrative websites of the decade and the first social-networking site to gain widespread popularity. By the end of the decade, however, its reputation was in decline, its popularity had been surpassed by Facebook, and it became known mostly as a music and entertainment site.

MySpace was launched by American Internet entrepreneurs Chris DeWolfe and Tom Anderson in August 2003 to compete with Friendster and other social-networking sites. It offered profile pages that could be individually customized, the ability to upload photos and videos, and, most important, an opportunity for members to socialize with friends and other like-minded people, all paid for with advertising revenues. What set it apart from the other social networks was its openness. Members could "friend" any other member, and, if desired, could even fake their own identification. By June 2004, MySpace was claiming one million unique visitors each month, and by July 2005, the site had more than twenty-two million members. That same month, media conglomerate News Corporation bought out MySpace's parent company, Intermix Media (formerly eUniverse Inc.), for $580 million.

Much of the site's success came from a business decision to turn MySpace into a music site where established musicians could promote their recordings and fans could "friend" the musicians. At the time, MySpace had become known as the world's largest online hangout for teenagers, where they could share music, meet potential dates, and chat. It also became known as a hangout for sexual predators. (In 2009, MySpace admitted they had blocked ninety thousand sex offenders during 2007 and 2008.) Lawsuits brought by the families of victimized minors, as well as a 2006 lawsuit brought by Universal Music Group over copyright infringement, and various other lawsuits began to taint the site's reputation.

While MySpace fought back, a formidable competitor, Facebook, was beginning to edge ahead. (Facebook surpassed MySpace in number of users in June 2008.) In 2009, DeWolfe stepped down as the website's CEO and MySpace went on to lay off the majority of its employees by 2011. As the decade came to a close, the future of MySpace was uncertain, but appeared to be focused on music and entertainment. In 2011, News Corporation sold MySpace at a significant loss; the advertising firm Specific Media bought out the social-networking site for $35 million.

Impact

As the first social-networking site to host millions of people with billions of hits worldwide each day, MySpace set the bar for future business collaborations and innovation. It built an unprecedented community of established and amateur musicians, many of whom were given a boost through MySpace Records or special concerts. After several high-profile incidents involving sexual predators, MySpace supported the passage of the Keeping the Internet Devoid of Sexual Predators Act of

2007, which requires sex offenders to register their email addresses and instant-messaging aliases with the National Sex Offender Public Registry.

Further Reading

Angwin, Julia. *Stealing MySpace: The Battle to Control the Most Popular Website in America.* New York: Random, 2009. Print.

Matt, Krantz. "The Guys behind MySpace.com." *USA Today.* Gannet Co. Inc., 13 Feb. 2006. Web. 9 Aug. 2012.

Sally Driscoll

N

■ Natalee Holloway disappearance

Definition: Natalee Holloway was an eighteen-year-old high school student from Mountain Brook, Alabama, who disappeared while on a trip to the Caribbean country of Aruba in 2005.

The disappearance of Natalee Holloway became an international news story. The search for Holloway involved the FBI, Dutch soldiers, hundreds of volunteers, and the Aruban police. The case sparked a media sensation in the US, and was covered extensively on every major news channel. Although several people were arrested during the investigation, they were all released, and no one was formally charged.

Natalee Ann Holloway (born October 21, 1986) travelled to Aruba for a five-day trip with 124 fellow graduates of Mountain Brook High School on May 26, 2005. She was last seen leaving a nightclub in Oranjestaf the morning of Monday, May 30. Witnesses say she left with Joran van der Sloot, a Dutch student studying in Aruba, and brothers Satish and Deepak Kalpoe. Later that day, Holloway never showed up at the airport for her flight home and was reported missing.

Van der Sloot and the Kalpoe brothers were picked up for questioning. In their statements they said that they dropped Holloway off at the hotel she was staying at around 2:00 am. The men were released, but because of eyewitness testimonies and varying statements, they would be questioned many more times throughout the investigation. A massive investigation was launched with thousands of Aruban civil servants and volunteers joining the Aruban police in the search for Holloway. Dutch marines and US law enforcement agents also joined the search.

Law enforcement officials continued surveillance on Joran van der Sloot and the Kalpoe brothers. Several other individuals were arrested and questioned, but all were released. After his initial release, Van der Sloot gave interviews with the media and changed his story several times. At one point he told authorities he sold Holloway into sexual slavery, but he later recanted this testimony.

The tremendous amount of media coverage of the case in the United States led to some controversy. Critics stated that the continuous coverage of the investigation was proof of the "missing white woman" theory. This idea claims that media coverage of missing white women is excessive, compared to when a man or a non-Caucasian goes missing. In April 2009 the Lifetime Movie Network aired a television movie called *Natalee Holloway*. The film saw the highest ratings ever for that network at the time.

Holloway was declared dead on January 12, 2012. That same month, Van der Sloot pled guilty to the 2010 murder of a woman in Peru and was sentenced to life in prison.

Impact

The disappearance of Holloway caused a media sensation as law enforcement officials from different countries searched for her. The investigation received widespread criticism, as did the US media's coverage of the case. The Holloway disappearance was one of the most followed and publicized news stories of the 2000s.

Further Reading

Garrison, Larry and Dave Holloway. *Aruba: The Tragic Untold Story of Natalee Holloway and Corruption in Paradise.* Nashville: Nelson, 2006. Print.

Holloway, Beth. *Loving Natalee: A Mother's Testament of Hope and Faith.* New York: HarperOne, 2007. Print.

Patrick Cooper

■ National debt

Definition: Total amount a national government owes

The national debt grew dramatically during the 2000s as two fiscal recessions and relatively slow economic growth fostered larger deficits. The United States' entry into military conflicts in Afghanistan and Iraq further increased the nation's debt. Congress took a number of steps throughout the decade to cut spending, raise revenues, and avoid reaching the debt ceiling.

Since the establishment of the United States, the federal government has been able to operate with budget deficits by borrowing money to finance them. However, the national debt—the total amount the government owes—cannot be allowed to reach the same level as the gross domestic product (GDP), or else it could surpass the country's level of economic growth. To prevent this, the government has in place a statutory "debt ceiling," which limits the size of the debt and prevents this issue from becoming reality. The placement of this ceiling can be adjusted in response to increased budgetary needs.

During the 2000s, the possibility of reaching this ceiling became a significant concern because tax revenues, the government's primary source of income, dwindled while budgetary needs increased. The US economy experienced a recession early in the decade, and following the terrorist attacks of September 11, 2001, military and homeland security spending increased dramatically. The United States began an extremely expensive military campaign in Afghanistan, and in 2003, American troops were deployed to Iraq as well, putting further strains on the military budget. High unemployment and low production in the United States resulted in the collection of fewer tax revenues to pay for those conflicts, particularly as a second recession began in 2007. As a result of these factors, the national debt increased by more than 6 trillion dollars over the course of the decade.

In response to the country's increasing budgetary needs, Congress voted to raise the debt ceiling eight times between 2000 and 2009, ending the decade with a debt limit of more than 12 trillion dollars. Decreasing spending was also a major goal, and Congress launched a series of budget reforms that reduced targeted spending and modified the budget items that were typically guaranteed, such as those going to certain defense endeavors.

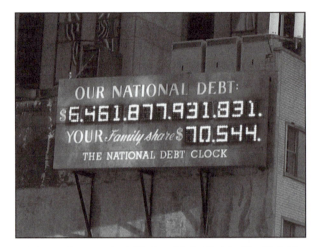

The Durst Organization's National Debt Clock in New York City. (Courtesy Wally Gobetz)

Impact

Despite efforts to reduce the national debt, the United States owed a total of 11.9 trillion dollars by the end of the decade. An issue of significant concern among those in government as well as the public, the national debt would become a key talking point during both the 2010 midterm elections and the 2012 presidential election.

Further Reading

Christensen, Jane R. *The National Debt: A Primer.* Hauppauge: Nova, 2004. Print.

Labonte, Marc. *The Magnitude of Changes That Would Be Required to Balance the FY2006 Budget.* Washington: Congressional Information Service, 2005. Print.

Michael P. Auerbach

■ National Do Not Call Registry

The Law: Database formed upon passage of the Do-Not-Call Implementation Act
Date: Signed March 11, 2003

Established following the passage of the Do-Not-Call Implementation Act of 2003, the National Do Not Call Registry collected the phone numbers of individuals who did not wish to receive unsolicited sales calls. Telemarketers were prohibited from calling numbers listed within the registry except under specific circumstances, and violation of these regulations resulted in heavy penalties.

Although the US government implemented the Telephone Consumer Protection Act (TCPA) in 1991, requiring telemarketers to set up their own do-not-call lists and limit calls to between the hours of 8:00 a.m. and 9:00 p.m., unsolicited calls remained a concern and annoyance for many Americans in the early 2000s. Despite legislation and the establishment of state do-not-call registries, the number of telemarketing calls increased from an estimated 18 million calls per day in 1991 to 104 million calls in 2002.

Lawmakers had long discussed developing a national do-not-call registry, but the cost was viewed as prohibitive, and existing computer software did not meet the needs of such a registry. However, advancements in technology soon made the development of a registry possible, and on March 11, 2003, President George W. Bush signed the Do-Not-Call Implementation Act. This act authorized the Federal Trade Commission (FTC) to create the National Do Not Call Registry and charge telemarketing companies a fee to access the database. Regulated jointly by the Federal Communications Commission (FCC) and the FTC, the registry went into effect after the US Court of Appeals ruled that its provisions were constitutional.

To add their residential or mobile phone numbers to the registry, consumers could either call a designated toll-free number or fill out an online form. Listings remained active for five years, during which time many telemarketers were prohibited from calling. The law did not apply to calls from political campaigns, nonprofit organizations, organizations conducting surveys, or companies with whom an individual had already established a business relationship. In 2007, the Do-Not-Call Improvement Act made listings permanent, while the Do-Not-Call Fee Extension Act extended the FTC's authorization to collect fees from telemarketers.

Impact

In the National Do Not Call Registry's first year of operation, more than 62 million phone numbers were registered. By the end of the decade, that number had grown to roughly 190 million. The FCC fined dozens of companies for violations over the course of the decade, notably levying a $5.3 million penalty against the satellite service provider DirecTV. While the regulation of telemarketing benefited consumers, it also resulted in the loss of jobs in the telemarketing industry and led some companies to consider new tactics such as spam e-mail marketing, which remained a significant concern into the next decade.

Further Reading

Bacon, Perry, Jr., and Eric Roston. "Stop Calling Us." *Time* 28 Apr. 2003: 56. Print.

Clark, Kim, et al. "Give It Up!" *US News and World Report* Dec. 2005: 96. Print.

Horvath, August, et al. "Telemarketing Practices." *Consumer Protection Law Developments.* Chicago: ABA, 2009. Print.

Sally Driscoll

■ National Endowment for the Arts

Definition: Federal government agency responsible for supporting visual and performing arts, literature, and arts education

During much of the 2000s, the National Endowment for the Arts operated under a severely limited budget and restrictions imposed by the US Congress. Despite these difficulties, the agency worked to raise the literacy rate and bring cultural programs to underserved populations through a variety of projects.

The National Endowment for the Arts (NEA) began the 2000s with a budget of $97.6 million, down from a peak of nearly $176 million in 1992. Drastic cuts took place during the late 1990s as part of a congressional initiative to decrease government spending. In addition to decreasing the agency's budget, Congress prohibited the NEA from funding individual visual artists, a decision based on the controversial nature of certain previous NEA-funded visual art projects, and stipulated that more federal funds be given to state art agencies and used for arts education.

In 2001, NEA chair Bill Ivey transferred leadership to Michael Hammond, who died unexpectedly only a week after taking the position. Dana Gioia succeeded him as chair and worked within these limitations to implement new programs that carried out the mission of the NEA without being divisive. One of the first initiatives introduced during Gioia's

National Endowment for the Arts Funding

Funding and Grants	2001	2002	2003	2004	2005	2006	2007	2008	2009
Funds available (in millions)	94.0	98.6	101.0	105.5	108.8	112.8	111.7	129.3	186.8
Grants awarded (number)	2,093	2,138	1,925	2,150	2,161	2,293	2,158	2,219	3,075

Source: U.S. National Endowment for the Arts, Annual Report, and U.S. National Endowment for the Humanities, Annual Report.

tenure was Shakespeare in American Communities, a program of professionally produced plays that brought classic theater to underserved communities, including Native American reservations. Another program, Operation Homecoming: Writing the Wartime Experience, a partnership between the NEA and the Department of Defense, sponsored creative writing workshops and literary projects for returning veterans. American Masterpieces: Three Centuries of Artistic Genius featured music, dance, and theatrical performances; visual art exhibits; and educational programs that emphasized the contributions of minorities. Poetry Out Loud, a collaboration with the Poetry Foundation, encouraged an appreciation for poetry among high school students, while The Big Read brought communities together to enjoy quality books and worked to combat the falling literacy rate.

By 2008, the NEA's budget had increased to $144 million, but the economic recession of the period affected funding and limited new initiatives by Gioia's successor, Rocco Landesman. However, the American Recovery and Reinvestment Act of 2009 included a $50 million appropriation to save jobs in the arts, bringing the NEA's projected budget for 2010 to $167.5 million.

Impact

The programs funded by the NEA during the 2000s tended to feature noncontroversial subjects and themes and shifted from serving mostly city-based organizations to benefiting a broader cross-section of the population. A number of these initiatives remained active into the next decade, continuing to promote the arts and arts education throughout the United States.

Further Reading

Binkiewicz, Donna. *Federalizing the Muse.* Chapel Hill: U of North Carolina P, 2004. Print.

McCarter, Jeremy. "Will Act for Food." *Newsweek* 19 Jan. 2009: 48. Print.

Sally Driscoll

■ Native Americans

Definition: Throughout the 2000s, the Native American population in the United States continued to struggle with economic and health-related problems on reservations, while also gaining new ground in strengthening tribal governments and communities

Despite continuing to face hardships such as poverty and health issues, the Native American population in the United States showed substantial growth in the strength of their tribal governments, in the gaming industry, and in the preservation of their cultures. Through the 2002 Executive Order on Tribal Colleges and Universities, continuing education on reservations was greatly improved.

According to the US census, 5.2 million people reported that they were Native American or Alaska Native in 2010. This equals 1.7 percent of the US population. More than 2.3 million of the 5.2 million stated that they were of mixed race, while the remainder stated that they were Native American or Alaska Native only. Of these 5.2 million people, approximately 1 million lived on reservation lands.

In the 2000s, the US government federally recognized 565 tribal governments, with many more undergoing the process of filing for federal recognition. These tribes have the right to form their own governments and to enforce laws within their reservations. The largest tribes in the United States—those with more than 100,000 respondents in the 2010 census—are the Navajo, Cherokee, Sioux, Choctaw, Chippewa, Mexican American Indian, Blackfeet, and Apache. Complications with recognizing tribal governments have arisen because many individual states recognize tribes that the federal government does not.

In 2007 a book was published by the Harvard Project on American Indian Economic Development called *The State of the Native Nations: Conditions under US Policies of Self-Determination*. The book identified several factors contributing to the low quality of life on reservations. These factors include the lack of access to capital and the lack of education and opportunities to gain business experience.

Alongside the poverty issue are the nutrition and health problems plaguing Native American reservations. There are higher-than-average rates of diabetes, tuberculosis, and suicide among Native Americans, particularly those who live on reservations. Outside of their reservations, many Native Americans state that they still face prejudice. A 2007 focus group study conducted by the nonpartisan Public Agenda organization found that most non-Native Americans are unaware of the contemporary issues facing Native Americans.

Government Relations

On November 6, 2000, President George W. Bush signed Executive Order 13175, which mandated that all government agencies engage in "regular and meaningful consultation and collaboration with tribal officials in the development of federal policies that have tribal implications." The purpose of the order was to strengthen the relation between the federal and tribal governments and it has greatly improved the decision-making process regarding tribal and federal policies.

To help promote Native American education, the US government also passed the Executive Order on Tribal Colleges and Universities. This order, signed by President Bush on July 3, 2002, acknowledged that tribal colleges and universities need to be supported by all "federal government departments and agencies." The order established the President's Board of Advisors on Tribal Colleges and Universi-

ties, which is responsible for overseeing long-term development efforts and endowment building for tribal colleges and universities. There are thirty-three fully accredited tribal colleges and universities in the United States, completely operated by Native American tribes. By 2003, enrollment in these institutions had increased to 30,000 students, compared to 2,100 in 1982.

Senator Sam Brownback of Kansas introduced a historic joint resolution in 2004. The purpose of this resolution (Senate Joint Resolution 37) was to issue an apology to all Native peoples for "official depredations and ill-conceived policies" by the US government in their dealings with Native American tribes. President Barack Obama signed this resolution into law in 2009.

A major class-action case concerning Native Americans was settled in December 2009. The class-action lawsuit *Cobell v. Salazar* was filed against the US Department of the Interior, specifically the Bureau of Indian Affairs (BIA). The BIA is responsible for the handling of Native American trust accounts and the lawsuit claimed these accounts had been mismanaged. The suit created a settlement fund of $1.4 billion that was to be distributed to class members. In addition, the suit established a $2 billion fund that allowed federally recognized tribes to purchase and consolidate land interests.

The Gaming Industry

The Native American gaming industry saw substantial growth in the 2000s. The BIA was pressured in the 2000s to further regulate the Native American gaming industry on reservations. The Indian Gaming Regulatory Act was introduced in 1998 and many felt that these laws needed to be updated. Many Native American tribes believed these government regulations violated their tribal sovereignty.

In 2003 the Federal Bureau of Investigation (FBI), the National Indian Gaming Commission (NIGC), and several other government offices formed the Indian Gaming Working Group (IGWG) to help address criminal activity in the Native American gaming industry. The following year, the Native American gaming industry generated over $22 billion. Over 600,000 jobs have been created due to the Native American gaming industry and much of the income generated goes to creating more jobs. For example, in 2005 Cherokee Nation Enterprises gave 75 percent of their profits to the Jobs Growth

Fund, which helps expand businesses within the Cherokee Nation.

Impact

The Native American population in the United States achieved significant progress in the 2000s. The improved cooperation and collaboration between the federal government and tribal communities have helped to improve educational, economic, and health outcomes for Native Americans. Through the Executive Order on Tribal Colleges and Universities, the landmark apology signed by President Barack Obama, and other initiatives, the US government has signaled its willingness to rectify past injustices and strengthen its relationship with tribal governments and communities.

Further Reading

Fixico, Donald L. *Bureau of Indian Affairs (Landmarks of the American Mosaic)*. Westport: Greenwood, 2012. Print. Written by a professor of Native American studies at Arizona State University, this work looks at the history of the Bureau of Indian Affairs and examines the relationship between Native Americans and the US government.

Light, Steven Andrew, and Kathryn R. L. Rand. *Indian Gaming and Tribal Sovereignty: The Casino Compromise*. Lawrence: UP of Kansas, 2007. Print. This book accounts the laws and politics of the Native American gaming industry. It examines the political interests and legal rights behind the regulations as well as the importance of tribal sovereignty.

Owings, Alison. *Indian Voices: Listening to Native Americans*. New Brunswick: Rutgers UP, 2011. Print. This book presents an oral history of what it is like to be a Native American in the twenty-first century.

Treuer, David. *Rez Life: An Indian's Journey Through Reservation Life*. New York: Atlantic Monthly, 2012. Print. This book examines contemporary life on reservations and looks at the relationship between Native Americans and the US government.

Patrick G. Cooper

■ Netflix

Definition: American company that delivered DVD rentals through the mail and streamed video over the Internet for a set monthly fee

Netflix challenged traditional models of DVD rental throughout the 2000s, allowing subscribers to receive rented DVDs by mail and return them at any time without paying additional fees. The company also introduced online streaming of content during the decade, enabling subscribers to watch films and television programs instantly.

Launched in the late 1990s by entrepreneurs Reed Hastings and Marc Randolph, Netflix was one of the first companies to rent DVDs to customers online. The process was simple: Netflix users paid a monthly subscription fee to gain access to thousands of films and television shows on DVD. To order a DVD, they made a selection online, and the DVD was delivered to them in the mail. They could keep a DVD as long as they wished without incurring late fees. However, they could not order another DVD until they returned the previous one in the mail in a prepaid envelope. As the service became popular, Netflix introduced a number of subscription plans that allowed customers to rent multiple DVDs at a time for a higher monthly fee.

In 2007, Netflix began to offer streaming content as part of its subscription plans. Customers could initially stream only a limited number of hours of video. However, Netflix introduced unlimited streaming for most subscribers early the following year. Subscribers were also soon able to stream content to a wide variety of devices other than computers, including the Xbox 360, Blu-ray Disc players, the PlayStation 3, and certain television sets.

Netflix experienced dramatic increases in subscribership and revenue throughout the 2000s. At the end of 2002, 857,000 subscribers were using its service. By 2006, that number rose to 6.3 million. At the end of the fourth quarter of 2009, Netflix had a record 12.3 million subscribers. The company reported total revenues of $444.5 million, up from $45.2 million in the fourth quarter of 2002. Although Netflix faced competition from Walmart and Blockbuster, both of which introduced online DVD rental services, it continued to dominate the market throughout the decade. As the 2000s came to a close, Netflix's greatest competition appeared to be the growing number of online streaming video providers, including Hulu, and the DVD rental company Redbox, which distributed its DVDs via vending machines.

Impact

The success of Netflix demonstrated that renting DVDs to customers online and streaming videos to customers' computers and other devices was profitable, paving the way for other video rental companies to offer online rental and streaming services. The increasing popularity of Netflix's services, particularly its streaming service, fell within a growing overall trend toward quick, on-demand delivery of content. By the end of the decade, films and television shows, as well as video games, books, and other media, were available nearly instantly via the Internet, emphasizing the period's changing attitudes toward content delivery and consumption.

Further Reading

Knee, Jonathan A. "Why Content Isn't King: How Netflix Became America's Biggest Video Service—Much to the Astonishment of Media Executives and Investors." *Atlantic Monthly* July–Aug. 2011: 34–38. Print.

Srikanth, Deepti. "Netflix' Competitive Strategy: The Business Lessons." *IBSCDC Case Studies* 8 Feb. 2009: 1–18. Print.

Jamie Aronson Tyus

■ Newmark, Craig

Identification: American entrepreneur
Born: December 6, 1952; Morristown, New Jersey

Craig Newmark founded the innovative free online classified site Craigslist, which by the 2000s allowed users throughout the United States and a number of other countries to find housing, browse job openings, sell household items, and make connections in their communities. He was an active advocate for many causes throughout the decade, including open source software, fact-checking and investigative journalism, and government transparency.

Craig Newmark is an entrepreneur best known for founding Craigslist, an online community that features events, forums, and classified postings. After moving to San Francisco, California, Newmark created an e-mail list to share news about local events in San Francisco with friends. As the number of recipients increased and many list members began to request information beyond event listings, such as

Craig Newmark. (Courtesy J. D. Lasica)

job openings, Newmark expanded the list and transitioned it into a website, which he named Craigslist. The site gained a strong user base by the end of 1997. Its popularity was due in part to Newmark's stance on advertising and pricing; he chose not to allow banners advertisements or pop-up ads on the site, and he did not charge users to post most types of listings. In 1999, Newmark left his job in information technology and began working on the site full time.

Although his net worth was estimated in the hundreds of millions, Newmark preferred to characterize Craigslist as a "community service" rather than a business and credited chief executive officer Jim Buckmaster with much of the site's success. Newmark continued to work on Craigslist occasionally throughout the 2000s, though his involvement declined as Buckmaster took over. By the end of the decade, he worked primarily in customer service rather than in an executive capacity.

Newmark also became known for his philanthropic endeavors during the decade. As Craigslist grew, he devoted more time and money to various causes, most prominently citizen journalism, free speech, net neutrality, and open-source software. Some of the many organizations that Newmark supported throughout the 2000s include DonorsChoose, FactCheckED, and the Wikimedia Foundation.

Impact

Newmark's development of Craigslist changed the way people found local events, items, and housing in the 2000s, and the site remained one of the most popular websites in the United States into the following decade. As a philanthropist, Newmark played a significant role in supporting a number of organizations, largely through outreach initiatives.

Further Reading

Masum, Hassan, and Mark Tovey. *The Reputation Society: How Online Opinions Are Reshaping the Offline World.* Cambridge: MITP, 2012. Print.

Vinjamuri, David. *Accidental Branding: How Ordinary People Build Extraordinary Brands.* Hoboken: Wiley, 2008. Print.

Weiss, Philip. "A Guy Named Craig." *New York* 16 Jan. 2006: 8. Print.

Kerry Skemp

■ Newspaper industry

Definition: Large media conglomerates and smaller publishers that publish print or electronic newspapers

The newspaper industry experienced declines in readership and revenue during the 2000s, in part because of the increasing popularity of online news sources and advertising venues. As the decade progressed, newspaper companies used cost-cutting tactics and experimented with electronic publishing in the hope of remaining competitive in a changing industry.

Few areas of the communications industry experienced changes in the 2000s as significant as those in newspaper publishing. The continued proliferation of the twenty-four-hour cycle, spurred by the growth of numerous cable television news networks and thousands of news-oriented websites in combination with the burgeoning culture of real-time amateur reporting via online social networks such as Twitter, began to pose a significant challenge to the continued economic feasibility and cultural relevance of print news publications. Throughout the decade, the newspaper industry struggled to retain readers, cut costs, and remain a relevant part of American media.

Declines in Traditional Newspaper Revenues

A 2006 report by the Pew Research Center outlined a steady increase in the revenue of newspapers in the United States from 1950 to 1999, with revenue increasing an average of 7 percent per year during that span. But by 2006, the annual growth of newspaper revenue slowed to just half of a percent per year. The resulting financial crisis was the worst faced by the newspaper industry since the Great Depression. The downturn in sales led to a historic restructuring of the newspaper industry's corporate establishment and a cultural reconsideration of the role of news in everyday life.

Newspaper revenue suffered primarily because of the decade's stagnant economy and an exodus of readers to free, Internet-based news platforms that were accessible across a variety of devices, from personal computers to mobile phones. But declining readership and sales were not the industry's only problems. Another major cause of the industry's plummeting revenue throughout the early 2000s was the proliferation of websites hosting classified advertisements for employment opportunities, goods, and services, which had long been one of the major profit generators for newspapers. Similar declines in traditional advertising revenue were seen across the media spectrum throughout the decade.

Consumers began to use more localized online job marketplaces as well as free online community platforms such as Craigslist as an alternative to newspapers for civic engagement. Major international auction and employment sites such as eBay and Monster also aided in the deflation of newspaper classified advertising profits. By the mid-2000s, newspapers could no longer remain competitive with online alternatives that allowed both commercial customers and individual consumers to connect with vastly larger audiences around the clock at dramatically lower rates. In response to this, some newspaper publishing companies joined forces to gain market share in the new online marketplace. Media companies such as the Tribune Company, Gannett Company, and Washington Post Company joined forces to form Classified Ventures, which founded the online automotive marketplace Cars.com, among other initiatives. The financial struggles of the newspaper industry resulted in the closure of several prominent daily newspapers that could no longer remain solvent. These included the *Rocky Mountain News* and the *Tucson Citizen*. Other national daily print newspaper titles, notably the *Christian Science Monitor*, ceased daily print operations to become online-only entities.

A newsroom on World Photo Day 2005: work on the electronic edition continues past the print deadline. (Courtesy Atle Brunvoll)

Changing Culture of Print News

The proliferation of online news publications, photo-sharing applications, and individual blogs throughout the decade began to change the very notion of news as well as how the public consumed and interacted with it. The concept of printed news became perceived by some as antiquated as more readers opted for the portability, ease of access, and breadth of knowledge provided by digital news sources that were available from all over the world. A particular concern on the part of many readers was the fact that print newspapers could not be updated quickly as events occurred and were thus rendered dated as soon as they were printed, while online news sources could report on events seconds after they occurred.

Daily missives from print reporters with expertise in particular locales began to lag significantly in the face of niche online communities that boasted an array of insights from both professional and amateur writers. Blogs and niche websites allowed writers of varying professional backgrounds and abilities to disseminate news across a breadth of subject matter, from politics to pop culture, music, and sports, at a grassroots level. The decade also witnessed a major fluctuation in the previously established roles of print reporters. Many well-known print journalists across politics, sports, and general news became frequent commentators on television programs and guest bloggers on various news websites. The new, multifaceted role of print journalists represented a significant departure from the tradition of reporters dedicating large portions of their careers working for specific print titles.

Cost-Cutting Measures and Industry Restructuring

Newspaper companies and the major media conglomerates that controlled numerous daily newspapers used various corporate restructuring strategies throughout the decade in an attempt to adapt to the changing news marketplace. Major media conglomerates such as the Gannett Company began to reorganize the corporate structure of their newspapers by 2006. Such efforts included melding editorial duties across titles and departments as well as consolidating newspaper graphics, photo editing, and layout responsibilities into singular positions. Other newspapers, such as the *Boston Globe*, the *Cleveland Plain Dealer*, and the *New York Times*, took steps such as freezing pensions; eliminating print production employees, newsroom employees, and journalists; and downsizing domestic corporate headquarters and closing foreign bureaus.

Many newspaper companies began to explore the feasibility of outsourcing foreign news operations through the use of syndicated reporting from part-time foreign correspondents. Firms such as Global-Post began to offer major daily newspapers access to reportage submitted to their online database by their network of freelance journalists in stations across the world. Cuts to domestic staff also took place at newspapers across the United States. In 2008, newspapers eliminated six thousand full-time newsroom workers, 11 percent of the industry's entire newsroom workforce. According to the United States Congressional Research Service, the layoffs represented the largest single-year decline in US newspaper employees since 1978. The physical size of newspapers also began to shrink throughout the decade, a reflection of both cost-cutting measures and the reduced amount of advertising and classified space in daily print editions. This move allowed newspapers to shift from outdated printing technology to more cost-effective and heavily automated printing processes.

New Revenue Streams

By the mid-2000s, all surviving major North American newspapers had established some kind of online presence. But replacing losses in traditional advertising revenue with new digital revenue streams presented a tremendous challenge, one that would not be fully met by the decade's end. The establishment of "pay walls," barriers that blocked readers from accessing exclusive online content without a paid subscription, helped many newspaper companies recoup a small fraction of the revenue lost from the decline in readership, sales, and advertising.

Other new avenues for profit began to redefine the very definition of newspapers in the digital landscape. Newspaper websites began to focus on interactivity during the decade, particularly by creating a variety of online community forums for readers. These efforts transformed newspaper websites from simple news portals into community hubs complete with detailed event calendars, live chats with staff writers and local community figures, and contests and giveaways. Many major publications, such as the *Boston Globe*, partnered with national retail firms to establish online retail outlets selling souvenir merchandise from their regions in addition to memorabilia from regional sports teams.

The end of the decade saw many prominent newspapers embrace a move to "e-editions," or electronic replica publications. Publishing in electronic format gave the newspaper industry a presence in the emerging market of books and periodicals to be read on electronic reading devices such as the iPad, Kindle, and Nook. Unlike basic websites, electronic editions preserved the traditional format of newspapers, retaining distinctive fonts and layouts, and allowed readers to peruse electronic newspapers just as they would print editions, yet without the physical constraints of paper.

Impact

By the end of the 2000s, the newspaper industry was left with more questions than answers regarding the future of print news. Seeking to develop a feasible business model that would allow newspapers to co-exist with the world of digital news dissemination, several major newspaper firms established protocol to share market research data in order to develop an industry-wide solution. By early in the next decade, six major media companies representing more than one hundred newspapers agreed to share detailed sales and marketing information with think tanks such as the Pew Research Center's Project for Excellence in Journalism. The goal of such research was to establish new industry protocols and strategies pertaining to digital advertising, hybrid subscription models spanning print and digital platforms, and efforts to promote the continued legitimacy and necessity of daily newspapers in the eyes of consumers.

Further Reading

Farrell, Mike, and Mary Carmen Cupito. *Newspapers: A Complete Guide to the Industry*. New York: Lang, 2010. Print. Gives an overview of the newspaper industry, providing historical context for the events of the 2000s and discussing their effects on the field.

Fitzgerald , Mark, and Jennifer Saba. "Turn and Face the Change—With Newspaper Industry in Crisis." *Editor and Publisher* (2008). *Center for Communications and Community*. University of California, Los Angeles, 22 Aug. 2008. Web. 19 Nov. 2012. Discusses some of the ways in which the newspaper industry needed to change in the 2000s in order to survive.

Kirchhoff, Suzanne. *The US Newspaper Industry in Transition*. Washington: Congressional Research Service, 2001. Print. Summarizes the effects of the economic downturn, online news and advertising, and other factors on newspaper publishing and discusses the US government's response.

McChesney, Robert, and John Nichols. *The Death and Life of American Journalism: The Media Revolution That Will Begin the World Again*. New York: Nation, 2012. Print. Argues that the decline of print media during the 2000s was due not to the Internet or the decade's economic troubles but to the public's dissatisfaction with commercial news.

Meyer, Philip. *The Vanishing Newspaper*. Columbia: U of Missouri P, 2009. Print. Suggests strategies newspaper publishers could use to preserve their particular form of journalism.

John Pritchard

■ No Child Left Behind Act of 2001

The Law: Standards-based education-reform law to improve the public school system

Date: Enacted January 8, 2002

The reauthorization of the Elementary and Secondary Education Act, known as "No Child Left Behind," sets perfor-

mance standards and goals for public schools in states. The law targets underperforming schools to ensure quality public education for all students. The economy and the difficult standards involved, however, left states with the decision to pursue exemptions and significant reforms.

The 2000s was a significant decade with regard to public policy and education in the United States. When President George W. Bush assumed office in 2001, one of the centerpieces of his administration was education reform. Throughout his campaign, Bush called for more standards and loftier goals for the nation's public schools, suggesting repeatedly that there were inequities in the system. His goal was that there would be "no child left behind."

Issues and Standards

The central issue at hand when Bush campaigned was that a significant percentage of US school districts were underperforming—dropout rates were high, fewer children were attending college, and the overall quality of education children were receiving was noticeably lower than that found in districts with relatively more wealth. The issue was particularly visible in the nation's urban and rural districts: Buildings were old, classrooms were overfilled, teachers were undertrained, and resources were limited in areas serving predominantly minority and/or poor residents.

Taking these facts into consideration, many reformers advocated for parental choice: If the school in which their children was inadequate, parents should have the right and ability to send their children to a higher performing school within the district (such as charter schools—public schools that follow parameters set by school boards and parents, as opposed to those set by the government) or private schools. Other reformers called for the government to intervene and impose higher standards on the underperforming schools, incentivizing them to improve with the promise of more federal funds. These standards included testing for students and greater systems of teacher accountability.

These reforms were met with considerable skepticism by some groups. Teacher unions, for example, took exception to the idea that they might be held accountable for their respective school's underperformance. Other parties expressed concern that charter schools and "vouchers" (financial assistance programs) for private schools would

siphon money and students away from public schools and make it difficult to improve those districts.

When Bush won the presidency, he and his administration pushed ahead with the "no child left behind" approach. They targeted the Elementary and Secondary Education Act, introduced by President Lyndon B. Johnson in 1965, as the vehicle for these sweeping reforms. The Bush administration would reauthorize (provide new funding and direction for) the act, including provisions that intensified demands on states to impose improved school standards, which would be tracked through testing at the third and eighth grade levels as well as in high school, and increased accountability for teachers. Congress made some modifications to the Bush initiative, but what would become known as the No Child Left Behind (NCLB) Act was passed in 2002 with bipartisan support.

The Debate over NCLB

The centerpiece of the NCLB was the requirement that states develop strong standards in reading and math, set goals for student proficiency, and test students to ensure that they are meeting those standards. The federal government would not set these standards, nor would they administer any testing. These tasks would be managed by the states, although they would be funded by the federal government. If the federal government's assistance was insufficient for states to develop these tests, the states could seek an exemption from NCLB. Furthermore, the federal government would be expected to compile data on how the states' standards are being met.

There have been two sets of objections to NCLB. The first is over whether testing improves schools. In this regard, opponents complain that testing does not increase graduation rates or educational quality; rather, they argue, NCLB only creates an environment that stresses preparation for tests of basic skills. Teachers and students, according to these parties, are too focused on passing basic competency tests and not focused on comprehensive, top-quality education. The second argument against NCLB was one based on the economic realities of the 2000s. In 2001, a severe recession hit the US economy, and only a few years after that recession ended, the worst recession since the Great Depression took hold in 2008. In these situations, the states have suffered greatly, enduring budget deficits and major revenue losses. To spend more state resources on school testing, opponents of NCLB say, would take money away from other budget priorities.

This latter argument became one of the most echoed statements against NCLB during the 2004 election. Democrats called for significant changes to the law, with some even calling for its outright repeal. However, rivals for the Democratic presidential nomination had a great deal of difficulty challenging a law for which they had voted in 2002. Opponents to the law could only argue that changes needed to be made to the law, but few could offer specifics on those modifications.

By the end of the Bush administration's second term, NCLB remained controversial, given the states' economic plights. The recession continued to tear into state revenues, and although Bush had increased federal spending on education, many states used those funds for other priorities. When President Barack Obama took office in 2009, he spoke of the need for equal educational opportunity and accountability (themes that echoed Bush's NCLB ideals earlier in the decade). His only modification to NCLB was granting waivers to states who were financially unable to comply with the law.

Impact

The development of the NCLB stemmed from many years of perceived underperformance in US public schools (particularly those serving the nation's poor and minority populations). The act (and indeed the forces behind it) called for increased testing on schools to identify and monitor student development. The act was a major shift in policy, significantly increasing federal funding to the states so that this testing could proceed. It also called for greater accountability from teachers and administrators, a component that was not well-received by teachers unions. Despite the controversy such provisions created, the bill was passed in bipartisan fashion. In fact, even though doubts lingered about the program's effectiveness and cost to states two years after its passage, there were no calls for its repeal.

One of the most impactful education public policies introduced in the 2000s, the No Child Left Behind Act was significant because it increased the federal role in public school reform. Although it maintained the states' rights to create and enforce standards, the NCLB demonstrated a desire by Washington to take a more active role in improving public schools. The motivations were clear: to level the field between poor and wealthy school districts and ensure that all young people have access to the best quality of education. The debate over NCLB's costs and effectiveness continued throughout the 2000s, but the act itself was neither repealed nor dramatically changed.

Further Reading

Chapman, Laura H. "An Update on No Child Left Behind and National Trends in Education." *Arts Education Policy Review* 109.1 (2007): 25–36. Print. Provides an overview of the key provisions of the NCLB and the effectiveness of the act as of 2007.

Cross, Christopher T. *Political Education: National Policy Comes of Age.* New York: Teachers Coll. P, 2010. Print. Updated version. Provides an overview of what advocates viewed as the justification for the increased federal role in public education as found in NCLB.

McGuinn, Patrick J. *No Child Left Behind and the Transformation of Federal Education, 1965–2005.* Lawrence: UP of Kansas, 2006. Print. Describes how NCLB came into being, giving an overview of the figures, issues, and political environment involved with the development and the passage of the law.

Ravitch, Dianne. *The Death and Life of the Great American School System: How Testing and Choice Are Undermining Education.* New York: Basic, 2011. Print. Offers a critique of the proficiency standards required in the NCLB.

Rjobelen, Erik W., and Michelle R. Davis. "Bush's Agenda Will Get a Second Term." *Education Week* 24.11 (2004): 1–27. Print. Describes how the NCLB was expected to continue (despite some political opposition) during President Bush's second term.

Therrien, William J., and Leah Washburn-Moses. "Impact of No Child Left Behind's Highly Qualified Requirements on Both Rural and Non-Rural Schools in Ohio." *Rural Special Education Quarterly* 28.1 (2009): 11–19. Print. Provides an update on the effects of a special-education requirement of NCLB on districts in Ohio.

Michael P. Auerbach

■ Nobel Prizes

Definition: Prizes for contributions in any of six categories awarded annually by the Nobel Foundation

The Nobel Prize was established in the will of Alfred Nobel to be awarded annually to persons making the most important contributions in the fields of chemistry, literature, peace, physics and physiology or medicine. The first prizes were awarded in 1901. A prize in economic sciences was established in 1969.

The Nobel Prize is arguably the most prestigious of international awards. While the original intent was to award individuals in five categories for achievements that year, the award has evolved into also awarding organizations and groups of individuals, reflecting developmental changes in each category. In 1968 the Swedish central bank Sveriges Riksbank established a prize for work in economic sciences. The first award was in 1969.

In the 2000s sixty-eight North Americans were awarded individual or joint Nobel Prizes. A Nobel Prize in Economics went to an American every year during the 2000s. An American received the Nobel Prize in Chemistry every year but 2007. In physics an American won a prize nearly every year as well. In the category of physiology and medicine, the United States was represented in eight of the ten years. The Nobel Peace Prize went to three Americans: former President Jimmy Carter, former Vice President Al Gore (with the United Nations Intergovernmental Panel on Climate Change), and President Barack Obama. No American has won a Nobel Prize in Literature since 1993.

Chemistry

During this decade an American received the Nobel Prize in Chemistry every year but one. The 2000 award in chemistry was presented jointly to Alan J. Heeger and New Zealand-born American Alan G. MacDiarmid, along with Japan's Hideki Shirakawa "for the discovery and development of conductive polymers." In 2001 half the award was presented to William S. Knowles and Ryoji Noyori, of Japan, for their study of "chirally catalyzed hydrogenation reactions," and half to K. Barry Sharpless for his work on "chirally catalyzed oxidation reactions." The 2002 award was jointly awarded to John Fenn and Japan's Koichi Tanaka, who received half based on their

President Barack Obama receives the Nobel Peace Prize. (MFA Norway/ Photograph by Per Thrana)

"development of soft desorption ionization methods for mass spectrometric analyses of biological macromolecules"; the other half went to Switzerland's Kurt Wüthrich. The 2003 Prize in Chemistry was jointly awarded to Peter Agre for his work in deciphering the channels in cell membranes and to Roderick MacKinnon for his studies of the structures of ion channels in membranes. The 2004 Prize was awarded jointly to Irwin Rose with Aaron Ciechanover and Avram Hershko (both of Israel) for their study "ubiquitin-mediated protein degradation" in cells. The 2005 award was jointly awarded to Robert Grubbs and Richard Schrock—along with Yves Chauvin, of France—for "development of the metathesis method in organic synthesis." The 2006 award went to Roger Kornberg for his research into eukaryotic cell transcription. Kornberg's father, Arthur Kornberg, had been the recipient of the 1959 Prize in Physiology or Medicine. The 2008 award was jointly awarded to Martin Chalfie and Roger Tsien, with Japan's Osamu Shimomura, for their discovery of the cellular "green fluorescent protein." The 2009 Prize was awarded jointly to Thomas Steitz, Indian-born American

North American Nobel Prize Winners, 2000-2009

Year	Chemistry	Economic Sciences	Literature	Peace	Physics	Physiology or Medicine
2000	Alan J. Heeger*	James J. Heckman Daniel L. McFadden			Jack S. Kilby*	Paul Greengard*
2001	William S. Knowles K. Barry Sherpless*	George A. Akerlof A. Michael Spence Joseph E. Stiglitz		The United Nations*	Eric A. Cornell Carl E. Wieman*	Leland H. Hartwell*
2002	John B. Fenn*	Vernon L. Smith*		Jimmy Carter	Raymond David Jr.	H. Robert Horvitz*
2003	Peter Agre Roderick MacKinnon	Robert F. Engle III*				Paul C. Lauterbur*
2004	Irwin Rose*	Edward C. Prescott*			David J. Gross H. David Politzer Frank Wilczek	Richard Axel Linda B. Buck
2005	Robert H. Grubbs Richard R. Schrock*	Thomas C. Schelling*			Roy J. Glauber John L. Hall*	
2006	Roger D. Kornberg	Edmund S. Phelps			John C. Mather George F. Smoot	Andrew Z. Fire Craig C. Mello
2007		Eric S. Maskin Roger B. Myerson		Intergovernmental Panel on Climate Change Albert Arnold Gore Jr.		
2008	Martin Chalfie Roger Y. Tsien*	Paul Krugman				
2009	Thomas A. Steitz*	Elinor Ostrom Oliver E. Williamson		Barack H. Obama	George E. Smith*	Carol W. Greider*

*Prize shared with non-North American

Venkatraman Ramakrishnan, and Israeli Ada Yonath for their studies of cell ribosomes.

Economic Sciences

The 2000 Prize in Economic Sciences was awarded to James Heckman "for his development of theory and methods for analyzing selective samples" and Daniel McFadden "for his development of theory and methods for analyzing discrete choice." The 2001 award went jointly to George Akerlof, Michael Spence, and Joseph Stiglitz for "analyses of markets with asymmetric information." The 2002 award was divided between Daniel Kahneman for applying psychological research to economics and Vernon Smith for applying laboratory research in economic science. The divided 2003 awardees included Robert Engle III for "methods of analyzing economic time series." The 2004 award went jointly to Edward Prescott and Norway's Finn Kydland for "contributions to dynamic macroeconomics." The 2005 award was jointly to Robert Aumann and Thomas Schelling for "enhancing our understanding of conflict and cooperation through game-theory analysis." The 2006 award went to Edmund Phelps for "analysis of intertemporal tradeoffs in macroeconomic policy." The 2007 Prize was awarded jointly to Eric Maskin, Roger Myerson, and Russian-born American Leonid Hurwicz for work in design theory. The 2008 award went to Paul Krugman for his "analysis of trade patterns." The 2009 Prize was divided between Elinor Ostrom for "analysis of economic governance, commons" and Oliver Williamson for "analysis of economic governance, boundaries of the firm."

Peace

The Nobel Peace Prize went to an American in 2002, 2007, and 2009. The 2002 award went to President Jimmy Carter for his long efforts towards finding peaceful solutions to conflicts and his advocacy for the advancement of human rights. Carter is the first former president to win the prize for work undertaken after leaving office. The 2007 award went jointly to former Vice President Al Gore and the United Nations Intergovernmental Panel on Climate Change for efforts to educate about climate change. Gore was recognized for raising awareness about the human role in climate change and the measures that can be undertaken to counteract this change. The 2009 Prize went to President Barack Obama for his efforts in international diplomacy. This prize was

controversial, as Obama had not yet served a full year in office when the prize was announced and had only been in the office for two weeks when he was nominated. The Nobel Committee defended their choice, citing Obama's commitment to nuclear nonproliferation and multilateral view on international relations, also citing his willingness to cooperate and engage in mediation. Some critics called the award premature, while others saw it as a condemnation of his predecessor's (President George W. Bush) administration.

Physics

In 2000 the award was divided and Jack S. Kilby won the Nobel Prize in Physics for his work in development of the integrated circuit. The 2001 Prize was awarded jointly to Eric Cornell and Carl Wieman, along with Germany's Wolfgang Ketterle, for "Bose-Einstein condensation in dilute gases of alkali atoms," and studies of the properties. The 2002 award was also divided, with half going to Raymond Davis Jr. and Japan's Masatochi Koshiba for detecting cosmic neutrinos. The 2003 award went jointly to Anthony Leggett, a dual citizen in the United States and United Kingdom, and Russia's Alexei Abrikosov and Vitaly Ginsburg for their work on superconductors. The 2004 award was jointly given to David Gross, H. David Politzer, and Frank Wilczek for discoveries in strong interactions. The 2005 award was divided, half to Roy Glauber for "contributions to quantum theory of optical coherence," and half to John Hall and Germany's Theodor Hansch for "contributions to laser-based precision spectroscopy." The 2006 award jointly awarded John Mather and George Smoot for discoveries in "cosmic microwave background radiation." The 2008 Prize was divided and half went to Yoichiro Nambu, a Japanese-born American, for discovering the "mechanism of spontaneous broken symmetry." The 2009 Prize was divided, half to Chinese-born American Charles Kuen Kao for "achievements concerning the transmission of light in optical fibers," and half to Willard Boyle and George Smith—from Canada and the United States, respectively—for inventing the Charge-Coupled Device (CCD) sensor.

Physiology or Medicine

In the 2000s Americans won a Nobel Prize in Physiology or Medicine every year but 2005 and 2008. The 2000 award was presently jointly to Paul

Greengard, Eric R. Kandel, and Sweden's Arvid Carlsson, "for their discoveries concerning signal transduction in the nervous system." The award in 2001 went jointly to Leland Hartwell and Great Britain's Tim Hunt and Sir Paul Nurse for their work in understanding the cell cycle. The 2002 Prize was awarded jointly to H. Robert Horvitz with South Africa's Sydney Brenner and Britain's John Sulston for their studies of apoptosis (programmed cell death) and regulation of organ development. The 2003 Prize was awarded to Paul Lauterbur and Great Britain's Sir Peter Mansfield for "discoveries in magnetic resonance imaging." The 2004 Prize was awarded to Richard Axel and Linda Buck for their work in deciphering the olfactory system. The 2006 Prize was awarded to Andrew Fire and Craig Mello for discovering interference RNA and its role in gene regulation. Italian-born American Mario Capecchi, British-born American Oliver Smithies, England's Martin Evans shared the 2007 Prize for application of embryonic stem cells in modification of genes. In 2009 the Prize was awarded to Carol Greider, Australian-born American Elizabeth Blackburn, and Canadian American Jack Szostak for discovery of chromosomal telomeres and the enzyme telomerase.

Impact

Despite the occasional insertion of politics into the decisions, the Nobel Prize represents one of the few awards in which the prestige and honor are universally recognized. More recent awards have addressed issues such as climate change and human rights as well as fundamental research in the sciences.

Further Reading

Feldman, Burton. *The Nobel Prize: A History of Genius, Controversy and Prestige*. New York: Arcade, 2001. Print. A history of the prize, including its origins. The author provides insights into controversies as well.

Meyers, Morton. *Prize Fight: The Race and the Rivalry to be the First in Science*. New York: Palgrave Macmillan, 2012. Print. A study of the controversies between scientists, particularly the historical attempts to receive credit (and notoriety) for their work.

Pratt, David. *The Impossible Takes Longer: The 1000 Wisest Things Ever Said by Nobel Prize Laureates*. New York: Walker, 2007. Print. The author has compiled numerous insightful quotes, including some which are humorous.

Scientific American Presents: Nobel Prize Winners on Medicine. New York: Kaplan, 2009. Print. A collection of articles from the magazine. The articles are primarily historic but do provide description of the winners' research.

Worek, Michael. *Nobel: A Century of Prize Winners*. Richmond Hill: Firefly, 2010. Print. Highlighted are some two hundred winners, describing not only their work, but also trivia about the awardees. Addressed primarily to younger readers.

Richard Adler

■ Northeastern blackout of 2003

The Event: A massive power outage that affected the northeastern United States and parts of Canada
Date: August 14–17, 2003
Place: northeastern United States and Canada

On August 14, 2003, much of the northeastern United States and parts of Canada were plunged into darkness after a massive cascade electrical failure. The power outage affected both major cities and small towns, leaving millions of customers without electricity for up to four days.

The blackout originated in northern Ohio, where a simple fault resulted in a widespread cascade failure that affected a large portion of the power grid across the Northeast. The initial fault, which occurred around 2:00 p.m., was the result of a high-voltage power line coming into contact with some overgrown trees. The line had softened and sagged from the intense heat caused by the electricity flowing through it. The contact with trees resulted in the power line being automatically shut down, as per normal safety protocols. At this point, the fault should have triggered an alarm at FirstEnergy Corporation's control room, but the alarm system failed, and technicians at the utility company remained unaware of the situation.

In order to compensate for the now-inoperative power line, other high-voltage power lines began to take on increased power loads. Three of these lines also began to sag and brushed into trees, leading to more faults. As the remaining operating lines attempted to shoulder the extra burden, the system quickly became overtaxed. At 4:05 p.m., the rest of the FirstEnergy system shut down, triggering a cascade failure that caused widespread power outages in parts of New York, New Jersey, New England, and Canada.

Without electric-powered public transportation, New Yorkers take to the city's streets and bridges, including the Brooklyn Bridge. (Courtesy Chris Kreussling)

Impact

The blackout left approximately fifty million people without power. While most customers had their power restored within two days, some were left in the dark for up to four days. The incident also resulted in close to $6 billion worth of damage and led to eleven deaths.

After a task force found that the blackout was caused by a combination of human error and equipment failures, Congress adopted the Energy Policy Act of 2005, which granted the Federal Energy Regulatory Commission (FERC) the authority to approve and enforce reliability standards. As of 2008, FERC had approved ninety-six such standards, some of which directly address the factors that led to the 2003 blackout, such as overgrown trees, inadequate training, and power grid fault survivability.

Further Reading

Blackout August 14, 2003, Final Report. New York Independent System Operator (ISO), Feb. 2005. Web. 11 Sept. 2012.

"The Economic Impacts of the August 2003 Blackout." *ELCON.* Electricity Consumers Resource Council, 9 Feb. 2004. Web. 11 Sept. 2012.

Final Report on the August 14, 2003, Blackout in the United States and Canada. US-Canada Power System Outage Task Force. US Department of Energy, Apr. 2004. Web. 11 Sept. 2012.

Minkel, J. R. "The 2003 Northeast Blackout—Five Years Later." *Scientific American.* Scientific American, 13 Aug. 2008. Web. 11 Sept. 2012.

Jack Lasky

■ Nuclear proliferation

Definition: The spread of nuclear weapons and weapon-making material, whether through the development of new weapons-manufacturing programs or the sale of existing weapons or material capable of being used to make weapons

Nuclear proliferation often refers to the development or acquisition of nuclear weapons by countries that are not nuclear weapons states, as defined by the Nuclear Nonproliferation Treaty of 1968. This has been one of the most significant issues of the twentieth and twenty-first centuries, due to its potential to cause global devastation. By the twenty-first century, the threat of global nuclear war had largely subsided, but it was replaced by fear of nuclear terrorism and the use of nuclear weapons technology by unstable political regimes.

The Nuclear Nonproliferation Treaty (NPT) of 1968 is an agreement between 189 member nations to cooperate in preventing the spread of nuclear weapons, promoting nuclear disarmament among nations that have nuclear weapons, and promoting beneficial and nonmilitary use of nuclear technology. The NPT has been signed by more nations than any defense or military treaty in global history. Under the NPT, the United States, Russia, France, Great Britain, and China are designated as nuclear weapons states and are the only regions permitted to develop nuclear weapons technology.

Another major landmark in nuclear nonproliferation was the 1972 Anti-Ballistic Missile Treaty (ABM) limiting the use of antiballistic missiles. Under the terms of the treaty, the United States and Russia agreed to limit their antiballistic missile systems to two sites each.

American and Russian Nuclear Disarmament

Following World War II, the United States and Russia (then the Soviet Union) competed in the development of nuclear weapons, leading to a nuclear arms race that continued into the early 1990s, when political developments in Russia led to a renewed interest in disarmament. At this point, leaders in the United States and Russia began negotiating a nuclear weapons reduction program known as the Strategic Arms Reduction Treaty (START I). START I was initially proposed under US president Ronald Reagan in 1982, officially signed in 1991, and became effective as of 1994.

In January 1993, US president George H. W. Bush signed a new disarmament agreement with Russian president Boris Yeltsin, known as the START II agreement, which called for the banning of multiple independently targetable reentry vehicles (MIRVs), a type of nuclear weapon containing several missiles.

Efforts toward nuclear disarmament were complicated by the United States' efforts to create a national missile defense (NMD) system, consisting of interrelated measures designed to counter nuclear attacks. This effort began under the Reagan administration, but in 1999, the United Nations passed a resolution calling for the United States to abandon the program.

The 2000s saw both major accomplishments and setbacks in the efforts to achieve reduction in nuclear weapons within the United States, China, and Russia. In March 2000, Russia and the Netherlands agreed to dismantle old nuclear warheads and to dispose of nuclear weapons material. Also that year, the Russian Federation voted to ratify the START II initiative.

Following the 2000 US presidential election, President George W. Bush announced that the United States would continue its efforts to develop an NMD system, despite objections from China and Russia. After the September 11, 2001, terrorist attacks against the United States, the nation adopted additional measures to research antimissile technology. In December 2001, Bush withdrew the United States from the 1972 ABM treaty. In response, Russia announced in 2002 that it would withdraw from the START II program.

By 2002, both Russia and the United States had completed reduction of their respective nuclear arsenals to the levels called for in the START I agreement, with each country eliminating more than 70 percent of its nuclear weapons. In May of that year, the United States and Russia negotiated the Strategic Offensive Reductions Treaty (SORT), which limited the strategic arsenals of both countries but not to the levels originally called for in the START II agreement or the initial ABM treaty.

Throughout the remainder of the decade, the United States and Russia cooperated in several nuclear initiatives, including an agreement to share information and technology related to preventing nuclear terrorism. Talks between the two nations continued regarding the future of nuclear proliferation, and Russia continued to object to the United States' NMD program. Difficulties in negotiations led to a failure to reach a new agreement to replace the START I program, which was set to expire in December 2009.

Russian president Dmitri Medvedev and US president Barack Obama agreed to continue heeding the protocols of the START I agreement until a new agreement could be reached. The New START treaty was signed in April 2010 as a replacement of SORT and a continuation of START I. New START calls for further reductions in the overall nuclear arsenal of both countries within seven years—down to between one thousand and fifteen hundred missiles each from the two thousand or more missiles allowed under the SORT agreement.

North Korean Nuclear Program

In 1994, the United States and North Korea signed the Agreed Framework, which limited nuclear weapons within North Korea in return for US financial aid and help in transitioning North Korea's nuclear energy technology to "light water reactors." The agreement was set for an intended completion date of 2003, but in October 2002, North Korea announced that it had begun a nuclear weapons development program. In December, the International Atomic Energy Agency (IAEA), a UN agency that promotes nonmilitary nuclear technology and nuclear disarmament, announced that several detectors installed in the Yongbyon research reactor in North Korea had been disabled.

In 2003, North Korean leader Kim Jong-Il announced that North Korea was withdrawing from the NPT agreement and reactivating its nuclear research facilities. North Korea also officially withdrew from its 1992 pact with South Korea to prevent a stockpile of nuclear weapons on the Korean peninsula. The United States and other nations threatened economic and political sanctions against North Korea if the country did not abandon its nuclear program; however, the United States' invasion of Iraq and criticism of Kim Jong-Il's leadership complicated efforts to reach an agreement.

North Korea eventually entered the Six-Party Talks, along with representatives of the United States,

South Korea, China, Russia, and Japan, in 2003, but negotiators failed to reach an agreement. A second set of negotiations took place in February 2004 in China but again failed to result in an agreement. While North Korea proposed a nonaggression agreement with the United States, US representatives wanted North Korea to comply with the agreements in the Six-Party group.

In 2005, North Korea announced that it had produced weapons-grade plutonium from its Yongbyon nuclear reactor, making North Korea a nuclear weapons state under the IAEA definition. Further information revealed that North Korea had obtained nuclear weapons plans and technology from Pakistan, due to corruption in Pakistan's military and political structure. North Korea then announced in September 2005 that it would abandon its nuclear program and return to the NPT. However, talks with the United States broke down, and in 2006, North Korea announced that it would not return to negotiations unless the United States agreed to lift trade restrictions against North Korean companies.

North Korea conducted a test of a nuclear device in October 2006, prompting a strong international reaction and efforts to begin a new set of talks. Six-Party negotiations at the end of the year failed to progress. In January 2007, the United States and North Korea reached an agreement through which North Korea would cease its nuclear program and disarm in return for energy aid from the United States and allies. In return, North Korea agreed to shut down the Yongbyon nuclear facility and to allow UN inspections. The United States further agreed to unfreeze more than $20 million in aid to North Korea. IAEA inspectors verified that the Yongbyon nuclear plant had been shut down in July 2007.

In April 2009, North Korea attempted to launch a satellite into orbit, claiming that the launch was part of efforts to contribute to space exploration. However, opponents in the United States and several European nations believed that North Korea was testing technology that might later be used to launch intercontinental ballistic missiles. The United States accused North Korea of violating UN agreements, and North Korea withdrew from further negotiations with the United States, stating the intention to reinitiate its nuclear weapons program.

North Korea reactivated its nuclear facilities in 2009 and expelled UN inspectors. In May of that year, the country announced its second nuclear weapons test.

Iranian Nuclear Program

In the wake of the 2001 terrorist attacks against the United States, the global international community became more concerned about nuclear terrorism, the potential for a radical group to obtain a nuclear weapon for use in terrorist attacks against another nation. This brought increased scrutiny on nations suspected of developing or attempting to trade in nuclear material and technology. In 2003, the IAEA reported that Iran had undisclosed nuclear technology and had failed to report some nuclear development initiatives. In late summer 2003, IAEA inspectors found traces of weapons-grade uranium at an Iranian weapons facility. Iran issued a public statement claiming that its nuclear program was intended to produce energy for civilian use and not for the development of weapons technology.

In early 2004, Iran agreed to suspend any nuclear weapons development activities, but in 2005, it announced that it would continue its uranium enrichment program. In 2009, Iran announced that it had finished construction of a second uranium enrichment facility near the city of Qom.

In 2010, news surfaced about a malicious computer worm called Stuxnet. It was eventually revealed that the virus had infected thousands of computer systems in Iran and had, in fact, interfered with the operation of centrifuge systems essential to the country's uranium enrichment process. According to some sources, Stuxnet was part of a joint US-Israeli cyberweapons program called Operation Olympic Games, designed to carry out cyberwarfare operations against international enemies. The US government denied any involvement.

Impact

The continuation of the nuclear disarmament process initiated in the 1970s continued in the 2000s, though the United States' concern over the potential for nuclear terrorism led to setbacks in the schedule for disarmament and significant disagreements between the United States and allies, including Russia and China. Despite these setbacks, global nuclear armament was reduced by more than

30 percent during the decade, and many stronger nuclear nonproliferation agreements were reached. The 2010 New START program is considered a significant step in overall arms reduction in comparison to the START 1 agreement.

Concern over nuclear weapons peaked in the 2000s with the threat of nuclear weapon use by terrorist groups. The United States and allied nations believed that North Korea could eventually represent a legitimate threat with the potential for nuclear war, while nuclear programs in Iran, Pakistan, Syria, and North Korea raised concerns about the potential for nuclear weapons or technology to be sold to terrorist groups. Though negotiations and economic sanctions failed to stop North Korea or Iran from developing weapons technology, negotiations did continue into the following decade, with some gains made through agreements to trade energy and other aid in exchange for the reduction of nuclear programs.

Further Reading

Blix, Hans. *Why Nuclear Disarmament Matters.* Cambridge: MIT P, 2008. Print. General introduction to historical and modern issues surrounding nuclear disarmament in the United States and globally. Contains a section discussing the future of disarmament measures.

Huntley, Wade L., Kazumi Mizumoto, and Mitsuru Kurosawa, eds., *Nuclear Disarmament in the Twenty-First Century.* Hiroshima: Hiroshima Peace Inst., 2004. Print. Summarizes and explains the START I and START II programs and other developments in nuclear disarmament up to 2004.

Lodgaard, Sverre, ed. *Nuclear Disarmament and Non-Proliferation: Towards A Nuclear-Weapon-Free World?* New York: Routledge, 2010. Print. Provides a detailed introduction to issues surrounding nuclear disarmament and nonproliferation efforts. Discusses the development of nuclear weapons in North Korea and Iran and the threat of nuclear terrorism.

"Nuclear Non-Proliferation: Chronology of Events." *IAEA.org.* International Atomic Energy Agency, 2009. Web. 16 Aug. 2012. A chronology of major events in nuclear nonproliferation from 1945 to 2009, including developments in Iranian and North Korean weapons technology.

Ogilvie-White, Tanya, and David Santoro. *Slaying the Nuclear Dragon: Disarmament Dynamics in the Twenty-first Century.* Athens: U of Georgia P, 2012. Print. Thorough overview of nuclear disarmament and nonproliferation progress and issues covering both the George W. Bush and Obama administrations up to 2011.

Paul, Thazka Varkey. *The Tradition of Non-Use of Nuclear Weapons.* Stanford: Stanford UP, 2009. Print. Discusses nuclear development policies in the United States, Russia, China, and India. Also discusses the traditions and philosophies that have prevented the use of nuclear weapons.

Pollack, Jonathan D. *No Exit: North Korea, Nuclear Weapons, and International Security.* London: International Inst. for Strategic Studies, 2011. Print. Provides a historical review of North Korea's military development and nuclear energy programs from the end of the Korean War to 2009.

Micah Issitt

O

◼ Obama, Barack

Identification: US president, 2009–
Born: August 4, 1961; Honolulu, Hawaii

Democrat Barack Obama was elected as the forty-fourth president of the United States in November 2008. He became the first African American in US history to be elected to the office of president. Obama's election was the culmination of a career in law and public service, and his rise to prominence in American politics was a particularly unique story, one that has become known worldwide for its cultural significance.

Barack Hussein Obama was born in Hawaii in 1961 to Ann Dunham, an eighteen-year-old Caucasian student from Kansas, and Barack Obama Sr., a University of Hawaii student from Kenya. After graduating from Columbia University in New York, Obama came to Chicago to work at the grassroots level. He first worked with a church-based job-training program in Chicago's poor South Side. He also worked in school reform and city services reform programs in the same area.

After three years of community work in Chicago, Obama returned to the East Coast where he attended law school at Harvard University. There, he was the first African American editor of the prestigious *Harvard Law Review* and graduated magna cum laude.

After an unsuccessful try for a House of Representatives seat in 2000, Obama announced in 2004 that he would run for the US Senate. Obama had served as an Illinois state senator for six years before deciding to run for the Senate. He won the 2004 election by nearly 70 percent and became only the third African American to hold a US Senate seat since Reconstruction in the 1860s. His unique background appealed not only to liberal white and African American voters within Chicago but also to rural white voters in southern and central Illinois.

Obama stated two goals as the main focus of his Senate career. The first included making sure that children receive basic services such as healthcare,

Barack Obama. (Official White House Photo/Photograph by Pete Souza)

early childhood education, decent housing, and good teachers. The other was to demonstrate the value of diversity in the world.

Following his keynote address at the Democratic National Convention in August 2004 and first-time election to the Senate in November 2004, Obama was singled out as a major political leader. Early supporters of Obama suggested that his growing popularity had as much to do with his humility, compassion, and integrity as it did with his political agenda.

Excerpt from Barack Obama's Inaugural Address, delivered on January 20, 2009

"My fellow citizens, I stand here today humbled by the task before us, grateful for the trust you have bestowed, mindful of the sacrifices borne by our ancestors. I thank President Bush for his service to our Nation, as well as the generosity and cooperation he has shown throughout this transition.

Forty-four Americans have now taken the Presidential oath. The words have been spoken during rising tides of prosperity and the still waters of peace. Yet every so often, the oath is taken amidst gathering clouds and raging storms. At these moments, America has carried on not simply because of the skill or vision of those in high office, but because we the people have remained faithful to the ideals of our forebears and true to our founding documents.

So it has been; so it must be with this generation of Americans.

That we are in the midst of crisis is now well understood. Our Nation is at war against a far-reaching network of violence and hatred. Our economy is badly weakened, a consequence of greed and irresponsibility on the part of some, but also our collective failure to make hard choices and prepare the Nation for a new age. Homes have been lost, jobs shed, businesses shuttered. Our health care is too costly. Our schools fail too many. And each day brings further evidence that the ways we use energy strengthen our adversaries and threaten our planet.

These are the indicators of crisis, subject to data and statistics. Less measurable but no less profound is a sapping of confidence across our land, a nagging fear that America's decline is inevitable, that the next generation must lower its sights. Today I say to you that the challenges we face are real. They are serious, and they are many. They will not be met easily or in a short span of time. But know this, America: They will be met.

On this day, we gather because we have chosen hope over fear, unity of purpose over conflict and discord. On this day, we come to proclaim an end to the petty grievances and false promises, the recriminations and worn-out dogmas that for far too long have strangled our politics."

Obama announced his candidacy for the presidency on February 10, 2007. Obama's rising star captivated both the general public and political analysts, although some questioned whether or not he would be able to turn that support into a strong and viable candidacy.

Obama publicly announced that he had secured the Democratic Party nomination for president on June 3, 2008. Headlines worldwide proclaimed his victory as historic; he became the first African American to earn the nomination of a major political party in the United States.

On August 23, Obama announced that he had selected Delaware senator Joe Biden as his running mate on the 2008 Democratic Party ticket. The Obama campaign stressed Biden's experience in foreign policy in supporting his preparedness to be vice president.

Obama was elected US president on November 4, 2008. He earned 365 Electoral College votes—far surpassing the 270 needed to claim victory. In the popular vote, Obama and Biden received 69,456,897 votes. Republican Party candidates Senator John McCain of Arizona and Governor Sarah Palin of Alaska earned 173 Electoral College votes and 59,934,814 overall. Obama's victory in the 2008 election made him the first African American president in US history. On the evening of November 4, Obama delivered a victory speech at Grant Park in Chicago, Illinois, to an audience of hundreds of thousands of his supporters. Obama congratulated his opponent McCain and commented on the historic nature of his election to the office of president. He also spoke of the need for national unity in the years ahead.

Obama took office as the forty-fourth US president on January 20, 2009. His first months as president were marked by efforts to resuscitate the US economy following the 2007–8 global financial crisis. Obama signed the American Recovery and Reinvestment Act on February 17, 2009, which initiated a nearly $800 billion economic stimulus package.

Although critics of the plan stated that the spending program was too far-reaching and costly, some economic improvements were reported in the months following its passage into law.

In addition, President Obama committed more US troops to the war in Afghanistan, stating that deteriorating conditions on the ground in the region made increased US military involvement a necessity. In October 2009, President Obama was awarded the Nobel Peace Prize. In its announcement of the award, the Norwegian Nobel Committee recognized Obama's efforts toward nuclear nonproliferation and diplomatic cooperation.

In November 2009, President Obama made his first visit as commander in chief to Asia, which included stops in China and South Korea. In China, Obama discussed continuing friendly economic relations with China while stressing the importance of human rights for people worldwide.

Obama's second major initiative as president was the reform of the US health care system. In campaigning for reform, he voiced his support for the establishment of a universal health care system that would provide health coverage for all Americans. Although the legislative and political debate surrounding health care reform was one of the most contentious and partisan in modern American history, Obama signed the Patient Protection and Affordable Care Act into law in March 2010. While the president's supporters lauded the passage of the bill, critics claimed the legislation represented the establishment of a health care system that would be co-opted by the federal government.

In September 2010, President Obama announced the end of US combat operations in Iraq. The last American combat brigade left Iraq in August 2010 after seven years of war.

Impact

In addition to being the first African American president in history, Obama has been celebrated for many achievements, including health care reform, helping to end the wars in Iraq and Afghanistan, and the historic assassination of Bin Laden—the mastermind behind the September 11, 2001, terrorist attacks. He is the recipient of the Nobel Peace Prize for his work in international diplomacy, becoming only the third US president to receive this award. Obama's presidency is also significant for the African American community, as he was able to overcome significant and deep-rooted racial boundaries to hold the highest ranking position in the US government. Obama was reelected to the presidency on November 6, 2012.

Further Reading

Bair, Barbara. *How Race Survived U.S. History: From Settlement and Slavery to the Obama Phenomenon.* New York: Verso, 2008. Print.

Hendricks, John Allen, and Robert E. Denton Jr., eds. *Communicator-in-Chief: How Barack Obama Used New Media Technology to Win the White House.* New York: Lexington, 2012. Print.

Maraniss, David. *Barack Obama: The Story.* New York: Schuster, 2012. Print.

Obama, Barack. *The Audacity of Hope: Thoughts on Reclaiming the American Dream.* New York: Random, 2006. Print.

Karen Hunter

■ Obama, Michelle

Identification: First Lady of the United States, 2009–
Born: January 17, 1964; Chicago, Illinois

Michelle Obama is the wife of Barack Obama, the forty-fourth president of the United States. With her husband's election in 2008, she became the first African American First Lady. She holds a law degree from Harvard Law School and a master's degree from Princeton. An accomplished attorney who moved from the private sector to public service in the areas of urban planning and development, youth advocacy, and community affairs, Obama showed herself to be an able and confident campaigner during her husband's quest for the presidency and subsequent bid for reelection.

Michelle Obama was born Michelle LaVaughn Robinson on January 17, 1964, in Chicago, Illinois. She grew up on Chicago's South Side. Later, as one of the few black students at Princeton, she felt acutely aware of a racial divide on campus. She studied sociology and African American studies, spending her free time running a community literacy program for children. After Princeton, she applied and was accepted to Harvard Law School in 1985. She felt the same racial divide there, and she spent her free time recruiting black undergraduates to Harvard from other schools.

Michelle Obama. (Library of Congress, LC-DIG-ppbd-00357/Photograph by Joyce N. Boghosian)

In 1996, Michelle began her career with the University of Chicago. She was named associate dean of student services and helped the university develop its first community-service program. She was then offered the position of vice president of community and external affairs for the University of Chicago's medical center. This promotion raised some eyebrows, as she was appointed to the high-paying post just two months after her husband was elected to the US Senate in 2004; the university was accused of trying to ingratiate itself with the new senator. Regardless, in this position, she was able to increase volunteering tremendously. Hospital employees increasingly volunteered in the community and community members increasingly volunteered at the hospital. In the fall of 2007, she took a leave of absence from this position to campaign with her husband.

The Obama family decided to stay in Chicago when Barack was elected to the Senate. Obama wanted her daughters to have stability, and Chicago was their home and where her mother lived. Not until 2005, after the publication of her husband's book *The Audacity of Hope* did the family's financial situation improve. In that year, the couple earned some $1.67 million, which was more than their past seven years' income combined. They paid off their student loans and purchased a home for $1.65 million during this time. There was some controversy with this purchase, as the Obamas bought adjacent land, to enlarge their yard, from Rita Rezko, the wife of Tony Rezko, a Chicago real estate developer, restaurateur, and fund-raiser who was convicted of fraud and bribery in 2008.

As her husband's presidential campaign progressed, Obama took on a central role, giving speeches and attending events. She has been compared to both Cherie Blair, the wife of former British prime minister Tony Blair, and Jackie Kennedy, the First Lady from 1961 to 1963. She tried to spend only one night away from home when she campaigned, and her mother watched the children while she traveled. She claimed not have political aspirations, denying she would run for her husband's former Senate seat.

After Barack Obama's inauguration as president of the United States in January 2009, Michelle Obama had a central role in his administration as First Lady. She has championed the organic-food movement, organizing the creation of an organic garden at the White House. Obama has also worked to increase awareness of childhood obesity in the United States, urging parents and children alike to make more informed decisions about what they eat and to remember to exercise regularly.

Impact

Obama was the first African American First Lady of the United States. She played a central role in her husband's campaign for presidency, giving a number of keynote speeches. During her time as First Lady, she launched the Lets Move! campaign that is aimed at promoting children's health with a healthy diet and physical activity. She is also an important advocate for poverty awareness. Obama has become a popular culture icon and has been a positive role model for African American women.

Further Reading

Obama, Michelle, and Lisa Rogak. *Michelle Obama in Her Own Words: The Views and Values of America's First Lady.* New York: Perseus, 2009. Print.

Swarns, Rachel L. *American Tapestry: The Story of the Black, White, and Multicultural Ancestors of Michelle Obama.* New York: Harper, 2012. Print.

Lee Tunstall

■ Obesity

Definition: The condition of having excess body weight from fat, not from muscle or bone

Obesity is best characterized by body mass index (BMI), a secondary measurement that accounts for both height and weight to determine an individual's adipose tissue, or fat stores. An adult BMI of 30 or greater reflects obesity, whereas BMI of 25 to 29 indicates pre-obese extra weight.

Obesity has long been acknowledged as a negative contributor to quality of life and especially to cardiac and metabolic health, and continued professional effort goes into understanding the causes of and solutions for increased weight. Three factors, alone or in tandem, are accepted causes of obesity: genetic predisposition, low physical activity levels, and poor diet. Although genes can set the stage for obesity in some families, the imbalance of calories eaten and calories expended through exercise is the actual culprit in most cases.

Epidemic Levels of US Obesity

Worldwide obesity rates climbed ever higher, to epidemic levels by 1998. Rates in the United States led the epidemic, with the greatest obesity rate of any nation. American obesity is particularly associated with affluent modern living, in which food is abundant and people are more sedentary. However, obesity is just as problematic in low-income populations, in part as a result of poor quality food choices. In 2008, barriers to appropriate nutrition in lower-income populations were more clearly defined to include fewer healthy food markets within an urban neighborhood and lower rates of daily physical exercise.

By 2005, 24 percent of the adult population in the United States was obese by BMI according to the Centers for Disease Control and Prevention (CDC). This prevalence contrasts greatly with the 7 percent obesity of 1980, and it signifies a reversal of the increased life expectancy observed during the 1990s in the United States. Moderate obesity remained more common than extreme obesity diagnoses dictated by BMIs reaching and exceeding 40. However, by 2009, any obese diagnosis was cause for lowered life expectancy in adults. Research supported overall reduction of life expectancy by at least three years with moderate obesity; mortality could come ten to fifteen years sooner for people with extreme obesity.

Morbidity and Mortality

Rates of obesity-related cardiovascular disease and diabetes have doubled in the United States since 1980. The trend of increased weight and poor insulin control by the body has combined to form a metabolic syndrome, in which excess fat tissue around the waist is an acknowledged contributor to long-term cardiac morbidities such as stroke, hypertension, and atherosclerosis. In addition to the diseases traditionally associated with obesity, multiple organ systems in the body experience negative effects of excess body weight. For example, extra pressure surrounding joints can worsen osteoarthritis, and middle-body fat continues to worsen pulmonary function; obesity has also been linked to greater rates of all-cause mortality, an indicator of overall damage. Though causes remain unclear, obesity also appears relevant to the formation of endometrial, breast, and colon cancers, to liver disease, and to polycystic ovarian syndrome.

Treatment Options

As a result of the growing number of disease risks associated with obesity, diet and surgical treatment methods exploded. In 2002, the new Atkins Nutritional Approach diet encouraged a nutrition program that severely restricted carbohydrate intake in

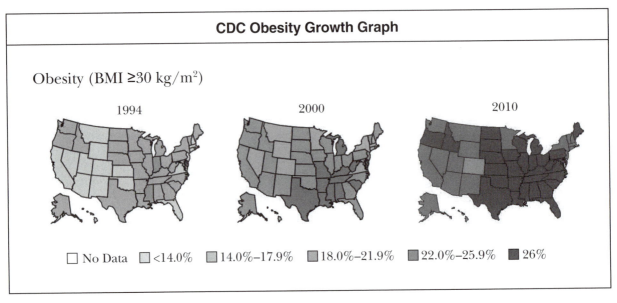

CDC Obesity Growth Graph

Obesity (BMI ≥30 kg/m²)

1994   2000   2010

☐ No Data   ☐ <14.0%   ☐ 14.0%–17.9%   ☐ 18.0%–21.9%   ☐ 22.0%–25.9%   ■ 26%

Source: CDC's Division of Diabetes Translation.

an effort to prevent metabolic consequences of obesity. Instead of the 45 to 65 percent carbohydrate intake outlined for daily nutrition by the US Department of Agriculture (USDA), low-carb programs minimized carbohydrate sources to as low as 20 percent of daily food intake. By 2010, Americans received 35 percent of their daily calories from solid fats and sugars, two of the least healthy food categories, and the concept of carbohydrate avoidance became favored over the low-fat diet recommended by the American Heart Association in the 1990s.

As diseases related to sugar intake outpaced concerns about cardiac risks from fat, the marketed dietary options for removing carbohydrates from daily intake grew. By 2005, American adults spent nearly forty million dollars annually on short-term diet programs—such as the South Beach Diet, the Zone program, and evolving versions of the Atkins regimen—that tout prepackaged supplements, pills, or prepared meals along with self-help instructional books.

For long-term control of severe obesity, Americans additionally turned to gastric-bypass and lap-band surgical procedures. These surgeries aim to constrict daily calorie intake by limiting the stomach's physical capacity to hold food or by adjusting the route of food through the intestinal tract to minimize its processing and absorption. Although gastric bypass surgeries can reduce weight by more

than 50 percent, the procedures require careful food intake afterward to maintain nutrition, and their long-term safety and effectiveness outlook remains conflicted. Prevention of obesity through diet and exercise remain the standard of care for people with high BMIs.

Childhood Obesity

For the first time since obesity rates have been tracked in the United States, excess weight and its health complications have extended into childhood. Although obesity in children was rare in the 1980s, it is now considered the most common nutritional disease in twenty-first-century children. Obesity rates have tripled in children from 1980 to 2008, and the exponential increases seen in the United States have not been matched by those in other developed countries, such as England, Scotland, or Spain. Type 2 diabetes, a disease once associated with adults, and cardiovascular diseases such as high blood pressure or cholesterol are being identified and treated in children as well. The result of the climbing weight and morbidities is a new generation of adults who are already battling extra fat and poor health, leading to a greater risk of early mortality.

To counter this trend, preventive nutritional and physical activity efforts have been a focus of the twenty-first century. Movements to reduce sugar in schools and to improve cafeteria lunch offerings were among the first efforts at instilling healthy habits and choices. In 2007, fruit and vegetable intake in teenagers was well below the five servings per day suggested by the USDA; school-centered behavior change and education is seen as the most cost-effective preventive measure with long-term efficacy. To reduce the cost and quality of life impacts of obesity in the younger generation, emphasis on physical activity and healthy foods, rather than mandated meals or repeating dietary restrictions, has become the focus. The 2008 Let's Move campaign, developed by First Lady Michelle Obama, instituted a well-rounded approach to the obesity trend in youth. To complement the physical activity experiences touted by Let's Move, the program provides brochures, educational programs, and adult guidance toward nutritional efforts to prevent obesity from developing at all. The program encourages common sense, plain-language initiatives to help children develop healthy relationships with food and to make strong nutritional choices. Sample meal and budget shopping plans, as well as examples of balanced plates that observe USDA daily serving suggestions, have been made available online for parents, schools, and other caregivers.

Impact

The poor activity and dietary habits led to obesity in nearly one quarter of American adults in 2005 and to more than one third of adults by 2008, according to the CDC. If Americans continue the trend, half of the population will be obese by 2030, and life expectancy will continue to drop. However, this future can be countered with aggressive efforts that encourage physical activity and improved nutrition. Prevention is recognized as the most important way to reduce youth and adult obesity and mortality. Public health efforts toward this goal might include future initiatives for wellness care insurance coverage and expanded employer programming.

Further Reading

Berg, Frances M. *Underage and Overweight: America's Childhood Obesity Epidemic—What Every Parent Needs to Know.* Long Island City: Hatherleigh, 2003. Print. A nutritionist's introduction about childhood obesity and recommendations to caregivers for raising a generation of youth who make appropriate food choices for better health.

Brownell, Kelly, and Katherine Battle Horge. *Food Fight: The Inside Story of The Food Industry, America's Obesity Crisis, and What We Can Do About It.* New York: McGraw, 2004. Print. A consumer-oriented discussion about how American food choices contribute to the country's disproportional obesity rates, guided by two nutrition experts.

"Dietary Guidelines for Americans." *Department of Health and Human Services Center for Nutrition Policy and Promotion.* USA.gov, 16 Nov. 2012. Web. 12 Dec. 2012. A definitive update to nutrition recommendations that began in 1980, that incorporates goals and standards identified during the start of the twenty-first century to counter the obesity epidemic.

Koplan, Jeffrey P., Catharyn T. Liverman, and Vivica I. Kraak, eds. *Preventing Childhood Obesity: Health in the Balance.* Washington: National Academies, 2005. Print. Evaluates and reports on obesity as a rising childhood epidemic followed by identified causes and approaches to counter the trend.

Lyznicki, James M., Donald C. Young, Joseph A. Riggs, and Ronald M. Davis. "Obesity: Assessment and Management in Primary Care." *American Family Physician* 63.11 (2001): 2185–97. Print. Review of a twenty-first-century approach to medical counseling and correction of obesity, with an emphasis on addressing body mass and diet choices directly with patients.

Nicole Van Hoey, PharmD

■ *The Office*

Identification: Television comedy about the employees of Dunder Mifflin, a paper company
Executive Producer: Greg Daniels (b. 1963)
Date: Premiered on March 24, 2005

The Office premiered on the television network NBC in 2005. After a slow start, the show soon found an audience and became one of the most popular comedies of the decade. The show won a number of awards during the 2000s, including several Emmy Awards.

The Office is based on the British television series of the same name, created by Ricky Gervais and Stephen Merchant. Executive producer Greg Daniels reimagined the show for American audiences in 2005. The mockumentary-style comedy focuses on the employees of the Scranton, Pennsylvania, office of paper company Dunder Mifflin, which is led by inept regional manager Michael Scott (played by Steve Carell). The cast includes a wide variety of characters, such as sales representative Jim Halpert (John Krasinski), office receptionist Pam Beesly (Jenna Fischer), and assistant to the regional manager Dwight Schrute (Rainn Wilson). As the series progresses, the characters develop new relationships with their coworkers that help contribute to the show's awkward humor. By the end of 2009, the show had completed its fifth season.

Although *The Office* averaged only about 5.4 million viewers in its first season, the show soon began to attract the attention of viewers and critics. By the end of the decade, the series averaged about 8.2 million viewers. In 2006, the series won the Emmy Award for outstanding comedy series, and Carell received the Golden Globe for best actor in a comedy series. *The Office* won many other awards throughout the decade, including the Screen Actors Guild Award for outstanding performance by an ensemble in a comedy series in 2007 and 2008 and the Television Critics Association Award for outstanding achievement in comedy in 2006 and 2007.

Impact

The Office helped launch the careers of several actors, including Carell, Krasinski, and Wilson, who found work in numerous feature films in the wake of the show's success. In addition, the show's mockumentary format was soon adopted by other comedies, including NBC's *Parks and Recreation*, cocreated by Daniels, and ABC's *Modern Family*. *The Office* also affected the real city of Scranton, Pennsylvania; although the show was shot in California, Scranton enjoyed increased attention and tourism thanks to fans eager to visit some of the places mentioned by characters on the show.

Further Reading

Clarke, Jayne. "Scranton Welcomes Fans of *The Office*." *USA Today*. Gannett, 29 July 2009. Web. 3 Aug. 2012.

Pastorek, Whitney. "*The Office*: Working Overtime." *Entertainment Weekly*. Entertainment Weekly, 30 Sept. 2007. Web. 3 Aug. 2012.

Wisnewski, J. Jeremy. The Office *and Philosophy: Scenes from the Unexamined Life*. Malden: Blackwell, 2008. Print.

Rebecca Sparling

■ Oil crisis

Definition: An increase in the price of oil from $20 per barrel in the early part of the 2000s to an all-time high of $145 per barrel in 2008; the price then decreased sharply during the recession that began in 2008.

When the price of oil skyrocketed to $145 per barrel, it caused an economic shock and fear that a peak in oil production had been achieved. This led the United States to reevaluate its energy policies in terms of energy independence and security and to develop unconventional methods of oil production, along with investigating alternative resources and renewable energy production.

The 2000s, a decade of bubbles and busts, also saw tremendous volatility in oil prices. The oil crisis of the 2000s began in 2003 with the gradual increase of oil prices. This was due to many international issues that were going on, including the US war against Iraq, which caused many in the United States to worry about an oil supply disruption. The US dependence on foreign oil peaked in 2005 and then decreased gradually throughout the decade. When oil skyrocketed in price in 2008, the price of gasoline rose to over $4 per gallon, which caused many Americans to rethink their driving and other energy use habits. There were also allegations of financial speculation driving up the price of oil. As the 2008 recession took hold, the price of oil fell drastically to $40 per barrel by December of that year and then increased gradually, but it did not return to peak 2008 levels. Demand for oil in the United States was substantially reduced during the recession as the economy slowed down and energy needs were reduced.

The Run-Up of Oil Prices

There would have been no oil crisis in the United States during the 2000s without the price increases that occurred. At the turn of the twenty-first century, oil prices seemed to be holding steady at between $25 and $30 per barrel. After the terrorist attacks of September 11, 2001, there were fears that oil prices would increase, but they remained fairly steady. What did begin to drive oil prices up was the US invasion of Iraq in 2003. Oil production in the Middle Eastern country was disrupted; it went from six million barrels per day in 2002 to one million barrels per day in

2004 to 2005. Although oil prices declined slightly during this time, by 2005 prices were back at record highs of about $66 per barrel. America's oil imports also peaked in 2005. This coincided with a booming economy in the United States, so the effects were not as noticeable as they would have been in a depressed economy.

In August 2005, Hurricanes Katrina and Rita hit the US Gulf Coast and disrupted oil production in the Gulf of Mexico. Nine oil refineries were closed down, and thirty offshore oil platforms were either destroyed or damaged. In 2006, new tensions in the Middle East between Lebanon and Israel, as well as missile tests in North Korea, drove up the price of oil to $78 per barrel, once again resulting from fears of disruption to oil imports to the United States.

In 2008, the price of oil increased steeply, peaking at $145 per barrel. Financial speculation was suspected; the theory was that traders simply drove up a speculative price bubble that eventually popped. There was evidence both for and against this theory, without a definitive conclusion as to whether speculators had an impact on oil price volatility.

A Supply-Demand Problem

Apart from oil disruptions and financial speculation, many also believed that oil production had peaked around the world and that with demand increasing, the diminishing supply would cause an economic crisis. Production in the United States had peaked around 1970 and had been declining ever since. Many other oil fields around the world had been in production for some time and were in production decline. At the same time, demand was rapidly increasing around the world for oil, as the emerging economies of India and China in particular were in need of much more oil to fuel their factories and vehicles. This shrinking supply and increasing demand set the stage for the price shock of 2007 to 2008.

The theory that world oil production has peaked and that a gradual decline in supply is inevitable is known as "peak oil." This peak oil theory is controversial and states that oil and gas reserves are finite—in other words, they cannot be replaced once they are extracted—and that there is a point at which oil extraction will meet the peak production totals and decline thereafter. When the oil price spike of 2007

to 2008 occurred, many saw this as a sign that peak oil production had been achieved. In 2005, a Peak Oil Caucus was formed in the US Congress, made up of both Democrats and Republicans. After 2005, concerns about peak oil subsided as oil production flattened. Offshore oil drilling policy was also relaxed in 2008, and calls for drilling in the Alaskan Arctic National Wildlife Refuge were renewed as a means to move toward energy independence and therefore security.

Impact

The oil crisis jolted many Americans into awareness of the importance of reducing energy consumption. Higher gasoline prices led Americans to purchase smaller, more fuel-efficient cars, and to drive less, at least in the short term. This led to an economic crisis with US automobile manufacturers, which in turn led to a government bailout of two of the Big Three companies. Smaller hybrid and electric cars began to be developed and marketed by major automobile manufacturers. The United States also moved toward researching and supporting more ways to reduce energy consumption and to develop alternative and renewable energy sources.

A longer-term impact of the oil price shock was that the United States began seriously considering how to achieve energy independence as a means for national energy security. Interest in domestic and offshore oil production was renewed. Improved and cheaper hydraulic fracturing (fracking) processes to unlock shale oil found across the United States launched a new domestic oil boom that continued into the 2010s. By the end of 2009, with oil hovering around $80 per barrel, the United States was in a new and sustained high-price oil environment and needed to find new policies to reduce dependence on more costly foreign oil.

Further Reading

Behr, Timo. "The 2008 Oil Price Shock: Competing Explanations and Policy Implications." *GPPi Global Energy Governance Project* 1 (2009): 1–30. PDF file. Explains how global oil markets reached new highs in 2008 and what effects this could have on world economies.

Fattouh, Bassam. "Price Formation in Oil Markets: Some Lessons from 2009." *Arab Energy Club.* Arab Energy Club, 8 Mar. 2010. Web. 14 Dec. 2012.

Discusses oil price fluctuations in 2009: steep increases in the first half of the year and stabilized prices in the second half.

Hamilton, James D. "Causes and Consequences of the Oil Shock of 2007–08." *Brookings Papers on Economic Activity* (2009): 215–83. PDF file. A highly academic paper on the causes and consequences of the oil crisis, using advanced economic theories and models.

"Peak Oil Primer." *Energy Bulletin*. Post Carbon Institute, 20 Oct. 2011. Web. 14 Dec. 2012. Provides basic information on the peak oil theory.

Sachs, Jeffrey D. "Why the Oil Crisis will Persist [Extended Version]." *Scientific American*. Nature America, 22 Sept. 2008. Web. 14 Dec. 2012. An article by the director of the Earth Institute at Columbia University that details the oil price crisis and calls for better car and city design.

Lee Tunstall, PhD

■ Olympic Games

Definition: Notable performances and events surrounding prominent North American athletes and sports teams in the five biannual international Olympic sports competitions held in locations throughout the world in the 2000s

The Olympic Games entered the 2000s riding a surge of popularity thanks to improving digital technologies in both computing and broadcasting that allowed spectators to follow the games closer than ever before. Record television audiences and rampant interest in the biannual events would place the games as a key event symbolizing a newly emerging global culture.

Sydney 2000

The Olympic Games of the 2000s would begin with the 2000 summer games hosted by Sydney, Australia. The event played host to over 10,600 athletes who competed in three hundred events, making the Sydney games the largest in Olympic history at the time.

The United States led all nations with a total of ninety-three medals at the 2000 Summer Olympics, while Canadian athletes earned fourteen medals and Mexican Olympians earned six medals. Mexico's lone gold medalist at the games was weightlifter Soraya Jiménez, who placed first in the women's lightweight competition. The Canadian men's doubles tennis team, comprised of Sébastian Lareau and Daniel Nestor, would defy expectations when they defeated Australia to earn the gold medal.

The 2000 Summer Olympics would mark another memorable entry onto the world stage for the US men's basketball team. Led by National Basketball Association (NBA) stars such as Vince Carter, Kevin Garnett, and Jason Kidd, the team would lead the Americans to a 5–0 record at the games.

The United States would in fact lose several of its medals from the Sydney Olympic Games seven years after the conclusion of the event. US women's track star Marion Jones would ultimately confess to taking performance enhancing drugs during the competition, which would result in her and her US track teammates being stripped of their medals.

Salt Lake City 2002

The 2002 Olympic Games were held in Salt Lake City, Utah. The planning and anticipation of the games was significantly marred by the discovery of a widespread bribery scandal in 1999. Numerous investigations by both the International Olympic Committee (IOC) and US Federal officials revealed extensive evidence proving that several IOC members willingly accepted bribes in the form of cash, gifts, and other financial investments in exchange for awarding the games to Salt Lake.

The Salt Lake games were further hampered by a financial crisis that threatened the event. Over a billion dollars in federal funds from the United States government were ultimately allocated for the games. A majority of the infrastructure of the Salt Lake Olympics concentrated on widespread security apparatus, as the games were the first to take place in the wake of the September 11, 2001, terrorist attacks.

Canada would dominate both the men's and women's ice hockey tournaments at the 2002 Winter Olympics, winning gold medals in each tournament. The Canadian men's team was propelled by National Hockey League (NHL) stars Mario Lemieux, Steve Yzerman, and Jarome Iginla.

The record ten gold medals won by American athletes at the 2002 Olympics, the most of any host

Leading Medal Winners of the Olympics for the Decade

Country	Gold	Silver	Bronze	Medals Won
United States	128	123	113	364
Russia	95	86	106	287
China	115	60	66	241
Germany	65	71	75	211

nation at the time, were highlighted by victories by women's figure skater Sarah Hughes, women's snowboarder Kelly Clark, and men's short track speed skater Apollo Anton Ohno.

Athens 2004

The 2004 Summer Olympics marked the return to the event's birthplace in Athens, Greece. With 201 nations competing, the Athens games eclipsed the previous record for the largest Olympic Games set in Sydney in the year 2000. Nearly four billion spectators watched the 2004 games on television, the largest global television audience for any Olympic Games.

The Mexican Olympic delegation was highlighted by women's cyclist Belem Guerrero, who earned a silver medal in the women's points race event. Canada's Kyle Shewfelt would win gold in the men's gymnastics floor exercises, becoming the first Canadian to win a gold medal in the event.

While the US men's basketball team would finish a disappointing third place, American swimmer Michael Phelps had one of the most successful Olympic Games of any athlete ever. Phelps won a total of eight medals, including six gold medals.

The US women's softball team took home gold by defeating their competition by an aggregate score of 51–1. The 2004 games would mark the next-to-last Olympic appearance of the decade for both softball and baseball, which would be eliminated from the competition by the International Olympic Committee in 2005, making their final appearance in the 2008 games.

Turin 2006

The 2006 Winter Olympic Games in Turin, Italy, were the first to allow spectators in North America and worldwide to connect to live video coverage on their mobile phones. Although no athletes from Mexico qualified to participate in the 2006 winter games, the delegations from Canada and the United States each put in distinctly memorable performances.

Canadian skeleton rider Duff Gibson of Canada became the oldest Olympian ever to earn a gold medal at the winter games when he took gold in the men's skeleton racing competition. The US delegation in Turin was headlined by gold medal performances from both the men's and women's snowboarding teams. American Shaun White won gold in the men's half-pipe competition, while Hannah Teter placed first in the women's competition. The success of the men's and women's snowboarding teams paralleled a renaissance in the sport of snowboarding in the United States throughout the decade.

Shani Davis of Chicago, Illinois, became the first person of African American descent to win a gold medal at the Winter Olympic Games when he won the men's 1000-meter speed skating competition.

Beijing 2008

The city of Beijing was awarded the 2008 games over four other candidate cites, among them Toronto, Canada. Athletes from the host nation China topped all other participating nations with fifty-one gold medals, despite numerous memorable performances from athletes from the United States, Mexico, and Canada. Mexican tae kwon do participants Guillermo Pérez Sandoval and Maria del Rosario Espinoza won gold medals in their respective events, the first tandem of Mexican athletes to ever win gold in the Olympic tae kwon do competition.

Much as he had been four years previously in Athens, the American swimmer Michael Phelps was the star of the Beijing Olympic Games, earning eight gold medals in numerous men's swimming competitions. The Canadian men's crew team followed up their World Championship with a gold medal at the Beijing games, the first world champion crew team to follow one honor with the other in thirty-five years.

Future of the Olympic Games in North America

Quebec City, Canada, and San Juan, Puerto Rico, each submitted formal applications for the 2002 Winter Olympics and 2004 Summer Olympics respectively, although neither bid advanced in the nomination process. Toronto, Canada, and Havana, Cuba, each submitted bid applications for the 2008 Summer Olympic Games, which were ultimately awarded to China. While Havana did not receive serious consideration, Toronto was a finalist and finished second behind chosen host city Beijing, with twenty-two second-round nominations.

Numerous North American cities were among the applicants to host the Olympic Games of the 2000s, and several were in competition to play host to the games scheduled to take place in the next decade. Chicago, Los Angeles, and San Francisco were all early candidates bidding for the 2016 Summer Olympic Games. While Los Angeles and San Francisco would eventually retract their bids, Chicago's case for the games became one of the most publicized events in the sports business industry during the 2000s.

Bolstered by support from President Barack Obama, prominent American athletes such as Michael Jordan and Michael Phelps, as well as media icons like Oprah Winfrey, Chicago was widely considered a favorite for the nomination. Despite four years of work and an investment of nearly $50 million dollars to land the 2016 Olympic Games, the International Olympic Committee chose Rio de Janeiro, Brazil. Even though Chicago's defeat was a shock for Americans, sports business insiders expected that prominent cities from both Canada and the United States would continue to place bids for future games in decades to come.

Impact

The Olympic Games of the 2000s were a reminder not only of the tremendous technical gains made throughout the world in broadcasting and information technology, but also of the tremendous amount of modern infrastructure that hosting an Olympic Games can bring to cities throughout the world.

As such, many sports business analysts throughout the 2000s contended that the IOC will continue to use the Olympic Games as a potential development tool in their attempt to unite citizens in every corner of the world into the Olympic movement. However,

New York and Chicago's failed bids to host the Olympic Games, as well as the United States' failed bid for the 2022 World Cup, led to some skepticism as to how prominently major North American cities would fare in future Olympic hosting competitions.

As trends in architecture and civil engineering shifted to a more environmentally conscious focus by the mid-2000s, the Olympic Games took on a new role as a potential with which to introduce renewable energies and green technologies to host cities on a massive scale.

The dominance of North American athletes in the Olympic Games of the 2000s further strengthened the role of Olympic athletes as no simply sporting greats, but as key societal role models and cultural icons.

Further Reading

"Factsheet: The Games of the Olympiad." *Olympic.org.* International Olympic Committee, 30 May 2012. Web. 26 Nov. 2012. A brief overview of the Summer Olympics hosted from 1896 up to the present.

"Factsheet: The Olympic Winter Games." *Olympic.org.* International Olympic Committee, 3 July 2012. Web. 26 Nov. 2012. A brief overview of the Winter Olympics hosted from 1924 up to the present.

Horne, John, and Gary Whannel. *Understanding the Olympics.* New York: Routledge, 2012. Print. A discussion of the Olympic Games movement in the past and present, as well as speculations about the future of the games. Covers the social, cultural, historical, political, and economic aspects of the Olympic Games.

"Olympic Games." *Olympic.org.* International Olympic Committee, n.d. Web. 26 Nov. 2012. The official website for the Olympic Games. Includes information and recaps on past games as well as news about future games. Information is categorized by sport, athlete, country, and general information about the games and the IOC.

"Olympic History Interactive Timeline." *CBS News.* CBS Interactive, n.d. Web. 26 Nov. 2012. A historical timeline of the Olympic Games, from its origin in ancient Greece up to the Summer Olympics of 2008.

"Past Olympic Host City Election Results." *GamesBids. com.* Games Bids Inc., n.d. Web. 26 Nov. 2012. A list of election results for Olympic Games host cities from 1928 onward.

Schauss, Gerald P., Stephen R. Wenn, eds. *Onward to the Olympics: Historical Perspectives on the Olympic*

Games. Waterloo: Wilfrid Laurier UP, 2007. Print. A history of the Olympic Games. Compares the ancient games to the modern movement, discusses the economic and organizational aspects of the games, and focuses on the types of athletes who participate.

John Pritchard

■ The Omnivore's Dilemma

Identification: A nonfiction book that studies the evolution of the modern omnivore
Author: Michael Pollan (b. 1955)
Date: Published in 2006

In The Omnivore's Dilemma: A Natural History of Four Meals, *Michael Pollan focuses on the diets of omnivores and the evolution of the modern American meal. In order to help readers understand where the different components of their meals come from, Pollan investigated contemporary diets, including those that consist of industrial foods, organic foods, and foods people forage for themselves. Through these efforts, Pollan hoped to answer one question: What should Americans eat for dinner?*

Author Michael Pollan set out to discover the source of modern American cuisine for his book *The Omnivore's Dilemma.* Pollan traveled around the United States to explore the nation's dining habits. He wanted to understand how Americans decide what they should or should not eat. His book compares the various types of food available,

Author Michael Pollan (second from right) with the Underground Food Collective. (Courtesy Lee Davenport)

Michael Pollan

Author Michael Pollan was born in 1955 and grew up in Long Island, New York. He attended Bennington College, Oxford University, and Columbia University, where he earned a master's degree in English. For several years, Pollan was the executive editor of *Harper's Magazine* and was a contributing editor and columnist for *House & Garden* magazine. He began contributing articles to *The New York Times Magazine* in 1987.

Pollan often writes about the strained relationship between people and nature, and he has published several books about gardening, home buying, and amateur construction. *Second Nature: A Gardener's Education (1991),* was the recipient of the QPB New Vision Award and was included on the American Horticultural Society's list of the Best Gardening Books of the Twentieth Century. In 1997, he published *A Place of My Own: The Education of an Amateur Builder,* which described his diligent effort to construct a small building with his own hands. *The Botany of Desire: A Plant's-Eye View of the World,* published in 2001, was on The New York Times Best Seller list and the recipient of the Borders Original Voices Award for the Best Nonfiction Work of 2001. It deals with the concept of coevolution, specifically people's relationships with certain plants.

Pollan also wrote many acclaimed essays and articles. He received the John Burroughs Prize in 1997 for the Best Natural History Essay and the 2000 Reuters-IUCN Global Award for Environmental Journalism for his writing on genetically modified crops. His reporting on animal agriculture earned him the 2003 Genesis Award from the Humane Society of the United States. His essays have been included in anthologies such as *Best American Essays, Best American Science Writing,* and the *Norton Book of Nature Writing.* His articles have also appeared in numerous journals, including *Gourmet* and *Vogue.*

examines the origin of an array of feasts, and acknowledges the dilemma consumers face when confronted with so many conflicting dietary opinions.

To better understand what goes into Americans' meals, Pollan sampled a series of dishes and then located the original source of each ingredient that made up these meals. He visited food-science laboratories, organic farms, fast-food chains, and Iowa's cornfields in search of answers. Pollan's objective was to help his readers truly understand just what they were eating and how it arrived at their dinner tables. He also explains the link between personal food preferences and hereditary evolution. Another point that Pollan particularly emphasizes is how people's diets affect not only their health but also the health of the planet.

Impact

The Omnivore's Dilemma was a finalist for the National Book Critics Circle Award and won the James Beard Award for best food writing. The book was also chosen as one of the ten best books of 2006 by the *New York Times* and the *Washington Post*. Despite these achievements, many critics questioned Pollan's spin on America's food-production process. His criticisms of industrial farming, in particular, garnered some backlash from those in the business. These reactions did not hinder the book's success, however; it was even included in Washington State University's freshman reading program in 2009. That same year, Pollan published an adaptation of the book for young readers.

Further Reading

"About Michael Pollan." *Michael Pollan*. Michael Pollan, 2010. Web. 4 Sept. 2012.
"Author Michael Pollan: 'The Omnivore's Dilemma.'" *NPR*. National Public Radio, 14 Apr. 2006. Web. 4 Sept. 2012.
Hurst, Blake. "The Omnivore's Delusion: Against the Agri-intellectuals." *The American*. American Enterprise Institute, 30 July 2009. Web. 4 Sept. 2012.
"The Ten Best Books of 2006." *New York Times*. New York Times, 2007. Web. 4 Sept. 2012.

Cait Caffrey

■ Online gambling

Definition: Betting money on games of chance using the Internet

The progress of technology during the 2000s allowed for a more interactive experience and safer online transactions, which attracted players to Internet gambling websites. Legislative bodies and financial institutions resisted the expansion of online gambling, however, and many restrictions were enacted to limit these activities.

In 2000, US Internet gambling revenue reached $2.2 billion. By the end of the decade, that number had risen to $6.3 billion. Furthermore, revenue projections—should favorable legislation be enacted—rose as high as $14 billion.

The major impediment to the growth of online gambling in the United States was its vague legal status. Initially, the 1961 Wire Act was used to hinder such activities. The act banned the use of telecommunication wires to transmit wagers but did not explicitly prohibit betting via the Internet, which had yet to be created. The US Department of Justice mainly prosecuted online sports betting, since the Wire Act clearly made it illegal to wager remotely on sports events. In October 2006, the Unlawful Internet Gambling Enforcement Act (UIGEA) was passed. The act banned financial transactions related to illegal online gambling, without clearly defining online gambling. The legal situation was further complicated by often conflicting legislation at the state level. UIGEA permitted online gambling within state boundaries and tribal grounds, leaving legislation in the hands of local authorities.

The Department of Justice used both the Wire Act and UIGEA to prosecute and seize assets from offshore online gambling. These actions resulted in the withdrawal of some of the larger, more reputable operators from the US market. Following the adoption of UIGEA, online gambling revenue dropped significantly. The market recovered, and smaller, less-respectable operators filled the gap.

Online gambling in the United States also faced the hostile credit and banking industry. Major credit card companies and issuing banks blocked transactions related to online gambling and refused to license gambling websites. The vague legal status of online gambling, as well as the high credit risk of such transactions, forced financial institutions to implement advanced security measures, such as transaction coding systems, to avoid authorizing such dealings.

Impact

In spite of restrictive legislation, legal actions, and hostile financial institutions, online gambling in the United States persisted and increased its participant base and revenue. Some of the reasons for its rise could be found in the inability of the legislative system to clearly define the legal status of online gambling. Such impediments to the industry in the United States shifted the global center of online gambling to Europe.

Further Reading

"Internet Gambling: An Overview of the Issues." *GAO*. US Government Accountability Office, 2 Dec. 2002. Web. 14 Dec. 2012.

Stewart, David O. "Online Gambling Five Years after UIGEA." *American Gaming Association*. American Gaming Assn., 18 May 2011. Web. 14 Dec. 2012.

"United States Gambling Data." *Antigua-US WTO Dispute over Internet Gambling*. Antigua Online Gaming Assn., n.d. Web. 14 Dec. 2012.

Miroslav Farina

■ Online music services

Definition: A type of website or computer software that offers downloadable and/or streaming music in exchange for a fee. Some services are subscription based, while others charge per-track access. Although some online music services use pirated music content in violation of copyright and trade laws, most of the best-known online music services operate in accordance with established regulations.

Online music services reinvented the ways in which the people access music. Music fans worldwide have embraced them for their ease of use, wide selection, and convenience. In the first part of the decade, when online music services were in their early stages of development, the music business was slow to adapt to them, fearing a loss of control over music content and its traditional sales model. By the end of the decade, however, sales figures and popular culture proved that digital music would become the central industry sales model and the major revenue source for music business entities.

In the late 1990s, the consumer market began to demonstrate an interest in digital music files. Napster, an illegal file-sharing program, was the primary means of acquisition. Besides ripping tracks from CDs that they owned, consumers had few legal means to obtain files for use on early digital media players.

Faced with decreasing sales, record labels were forced to adapt to a business model that centered on an entirely new method of music consumption.

Early Years

One of the earliest online music services was eMusic, which offered legal music downloads from artists not under contract with major music labels. For a monthly fee, users could download thirty songs from the site's catalog. Following the shutdown of Napster in June 2001, other Internet services began to appear. In December 2001, listen.com launched the music streaming service Rhapsody. For a monthly fee of $5.95, Rhapsody users gained unlimited access to the company's catalog of independent artists and recording labels.

In 2002, Universal Music Group and Sony Music Entertainment unveiled Pressplay, which offered its users access to a library composed of artists from the companies' respective record labels, as well as songs from British-based EMI's catalog. Like eMusic, the service offered the ability to cache (store) up to thirty songs per month and to burn them onto CDs. The songs could not be transferred to digital media players, however, and when users cancelled their subscriptions, they lost the ability to listen to their cached songs. The service was discontinued after being acquired by the software company Roxio in 2003.

The Internet media company RealNetworks released RealOne Music (also known as MusicNet) in January 2002. RealOne Music featured songs and albums from BMG, Warner Music Group, and EMI. Subscribers were granted access to one hundred streams per month as well as the ability to have one hundred songs cached onto their computers at any given time, but transfer to digital players was restricted.

In 2002, Rhapsody began expanding its collection to include tracks from major record companies. By the end of June, the service featured music from all five major labels. Although major labels had already been making sections of their catalogs available to online music services, very few popular bands and performers were involved in the music-streaming venue.

In August of 2002, Pressplay retooled its subscription plans and introduced a tier that allowed users to download ten tracks per month. Unlike the cached tracks available from other services, these song files were purchased by the consumer and available to them even after a subscription cancellation. Songs downloaded from Pressplay could also be transferred to digital music players.

In April 2003, Apple launched the iTunes Music Store. Unlike other services, iTunes was not subscription based; instead, Apple sold individual downloads of songs and albums to users, who could then transfer their purchases to their iPods, Apple's line of digital music players. Notably, songs purchased from the service were incompatible with other companies' digital media players. Response to the store was overwhelming, and Apple sold over 250,000 songs during iTunes' first full day of operation.

RealNetworks purchased Rhapsody in August 2003, discontinuing RealOne Audio; later that year, Roxio—the company responsible for the software behind Pressplay—purchased Universal and Sony's stakes in the company and relaunched it under the Napster brand, which they had also acquired. Both services allowed users to purchase permanent downloads of single songs.

While most services charged for subscriptions or individual downloads, some companies attempted to direct attention from piracy with free, ad-supplemented music services. Perhaps the best-known example of free streaming online music is Pandora Radio, which was launched in 2000. Pandora users input an artist or genre they wanted to hear, and the application plays songs it determines are similar to the selection. The free version of Pandora Radio features advertisements and imposes limits on how many times a user can skip a song. These limitations are lifted for users who pay for a Pandora subscription.

Slacker Radio, introduced in 2007, took a similar approach. Like Pandora Radio, Slacker Radio allows nonpaying users to create stations based around artists or songs. However, Slacker Radio also features a number of curated stations; instead of playing songs based on the genre or artist of a "seed" song, stations feature songs chosen by DJs or people in the music industry. Like Pandora, Slacker Radio also uses track selection limitations and advertisements on its free service.

Several online music services developed during the 2000s have since folded. These include Ruckus Network, GarageBand.com, BitPass, Sony Connect, and Yahoo! Music Unlimited.

Criticism

Many music consumers reacted apprehensively to legal online music services, as the restrictions placed on them seemed too strict, especially when compared to the unlimited free music offered by pirate music websites and services. At the same time, music business companies scrambled to make sure their intellectual property rights and revenue stream were protected. In 2004, Microsoft introduced PlaysForSure, a digital rights management (DRM) implementation that allowed users to freely cache and transfer music to certified devices. PlaysForSure prevented users from keeping the music after their subscriptions expired, transferring music to unauthorized devices or users, and burning songs to CDs. Services such as Rhapsody and the revamped Napster abandoned their first-party DRM solutions in favor of the more accessible PlaysForSure. In response, hackers released software that removed the DRM from cached files, allowing them to be shared and played without restrictions.

Apple's own DRM system, FairPlay, incorporated similar user restrictions, though it was aimed more specifically at preventing piracy than limiting what a user could do with downloaded files. Users were allowed to burn any track they purchased to a CD as many times as they wanted, songs could be transferred to as many iPods as had been authorized by the user, and up to five computers could be authorized to play purchased songs. Despite the more user-friendly implementation, FairPlay still drew criticism. In response, Apple removed the DRM from EMI's songs in 2007 and from all music files sold in the store in 2009. From that point on, any song purchased from iTunes could be played on any compatible digital music device.

Meanwhile, artist availability remained a routine complaint on the part of music consumers throughout the 2000s. High-profiles artists such as AC/DC, Led Zeppelin, Pink Floyd, and The Beatles were not available on early legal online music services, usually due to licensing and royalty disputes. This changed when purchase-driven services such as the iTunes Music Store debuted, though many major artists were frequently absent from subsequent subscription-based services. In November 2010, Apple and EMI announced that The Beatles catalog would become available on iTunes.

Impact

Online music services have supplanted the traditional music consumption model that involved consumers purchasing physical copies of artist's work at physical stores. Perhaps in response to the uncertain and often chaotic early days of digital music, sales of vinyl records increased in the late 2000s. Although large recording labels continued to make compact discs available, digital music has become the industry's core media, led by Apple's iTunes Store. Spotify, a music streaming service based in Sweden, launched in the United States in 2011. Unlike other ad-based services, it allows users to select specific songs or albums on demand. Other new services, such as Rdio and MOG, offer similar features. In 2011, Apple, Google, and Amazon all introduced services that allow users to upload their music—regardless of where or how it was obtained—to a central server (referred to as "the cloud") and stream or download music to other devices. Amazon's and Apple's offerings charge a fee, while Google's is as a free service with a 20,000-song limit. As the world of online music services continues to evolve, the fiscal side of the music business faces challenges as illegal pirate Internet networks and file sharing software continue to provide unlimited, free music.

Further Reading

Bargfrede, Allen, Cecily Mak, and Jonathan Feist. *Music Law in the Digital Age.* Boston: Berklee, 2009. Print. Explores the application of copyright law to digital music.

Breeding, Andy. *The Music Internet Untangled: Using Online Services to Expand Your Musical Horizons.* Watertown, MA: Giant Path. 2004. Print. Summarizes and recommends various online music services.

Burkart, Patrick, and Tom McCourt. *Digital Music Wars: Ownership and Control of the Celestial Jukebox.* Lanham, MD: Rowman, 2006. Print. Describes the effect on the recording industry of consumers acquisition of digital music.

Kwong, Sze Wan, and Jungkun Park. "Digital Music Services: Consumer Intention and Adoption." *Service Industries Journal* 28.10 (2008): 1463–81. Print. Analyzes consumer use of digital music services.

Van Tassel, Joan M. *Digital Rights Management: Protecting and Monetizing Content.* Amsterdam: Focal, 2006. Print. Demonstrates and discusses DRM strategies and implementation.

Leland Spencer

■ Open source code

Definition: Open source code is a set of computer program codes written by programmers who freely distribute them so others can modify and expand on them.

The open source approach to computer software allows for free access and distribution of software's source code, which allow for copying, modification, and further distribution. The idea behind an open source code is that by allowing others to modify a source code without having to go through licensing restrictions, computer programs can evolve more quickly. Participants in this open source culture believe in cooperating with other programmers to further computer technology rather than focus on solely making a profit from it.

Source codes are made up of the lines of codified instructions that programmers write for computers to interpret. The idea of sharing source codes came about when the Internet was relatively new. In 1998, the computer services company Netscape Communications Corporation published the source code to their popular web browser Navigator. That same year, the Open Source Initiative (OSI) was formed. This group of computer programmers, founded by Bruce Perens and Eric S. Raymond, dedicates itself to the promotion of open source software. Open source software includes the source code and commonly comes with an open source license, which is a copyright license that makes the source code available to users and allows them to modify, customize, and redistribute the software. Through an open source license, users do not have to pay the software's original author.

OSI has put forth a definition of open source that includes free distribution, open source codes, integrity of the author's source code, and no discrimination against fields of endeavor. Under this open source definition, copyright restrictions are either nonexistent or more lenient. Shortly after founding the OSI, the group separated itself from the "free software movement," stating that their goals, such as the promotion of open source software within large software businesses, were more pragmatic than the idealistic members of the free software movement.

Some popular examples of open source software include the web browser Mozilla Firefox, the Apache HTTP Server, and GNU/Linux operating system. In the late 2000s, the popular computer software company Google started its own open source project that allows users to view Google-created source codes. The project also supports educational programs for students working toward programming degrees. By the end of the decade there were several websites dedicated to publishing and promoting open source code.

Impact

The use of open source code within software has led to many advantages in computer programming. Open source code allows for people other than the original programmers to test the software and to spot bugs in it that need to be fixed. Open source code also allows users to customize the level of security the software provides them. The customization of open source code has allowed businesses and schools to make their software more efficient. It has also helped build and strengthen the community of programmers and users who are interested in improving computer software.

Further Reading

Moody, Glyn. *Rebel Code: Linux and the Open Source Revolution.* New York: Basic, 2002. Print.

St. Laurent, Andrew M. *Understanding Open Source and Free Software Licensing.* Sebastopol: O'Reilly, 2004. Print.

Patrick G. Cooper

■ O'Reilly, Bill

Identification: American television host; author
Born: September 10, 1949; New York City, New York

Bill O'Reilly is credited with popularizing the opinion-driven newscast genre with his program The O'Reilly Factor. *The show, on which the host frequently discusses a variety of controversial issues, averages millions of viewers, making O'Reilly one of the most popular talk-show hosts on cable television.*

Bill O'Reilly (Courtesy World Affairs Council of Philadelphia)

Bill O'Reilly joined Fox News as host of *The O'Reilly Report* in 1996. The program's ratings were initially below average, but they quickly rose during the 2000 presidential election. O'Reilly's brusque style of interviewing proved popular with audiences. He was soon the top-rated cable news host, earning higher ratings than CNN's *Larry King Live.* In 1998, the name of O'Reilly's show was changed to *The O'Reilly Factor* and viewership continued to grow.

In light of his television success, O'Reilly launched *The Radio Factor* in early 2002, which had a discourse similar to his television program. The project never fared as well as *The O'Reilly Factor*, however. Nonetheless, O'Reilly has been able to translate his television notoriety into publishing. He released eight nonfiction books during the 2000s, each dealing with his opinions on American politics, family, and culture. He released a children's book, *The O'Reilly Factor for Kids*, in 2004. Several of O'Reilly's books, including *The No Spin Zone* (2001), and *Who's Looking Out for You?* (2003), have reached the top spot on the New York Times Best Sellers list.

O'Reilly has become well-known for his public disputes with various celebrities, among them actor George Clooney and politician and former comedian Al Franken. Some media analysts have criticized O'Reilly's bombastic style and have accused him of narrow-mindedness and intolerance. Comedian Stephen Colbert's *The Colbert Report*, which first aired in 2005, is a direct parody of O'Reilly's program. *The Daily Show*, hosted by comedian Jon Stewart, has regularly used O'Reilly's show (and interviews with O'Reilly himself) as fodder. Despite the criticism, *The O'Reilly Factor* continued to receive top ratings throughout the 2000s. By the end of the decade, more than three million viewers were watching his newscast every night.

Impact

O'Reilly's political commentary is considered a major weight in the world of broadcast news. He is widely considered an influential figure in conservative politics in America. In 2012, he published the book *Killing Kennedy: The End of Camelot*.

Further Reading

Boedeker, Hal. "Fox News Dominates July Ratings; Bill O'Reilly Again Tops—and Nancy Grace Makes Impressive Gains." *Orlando Sentinel*. Orlando Sentinel, 28 July 2009. Web. 12 July 2012.

Cowles. Gregory. "Inside the List." *New York Times*. The New York Times Company, 24 Sept. 2010. Web. 12 July 2012.

Johnson, Peter. "Cable Rantings Boost Ratings." *USA Today*. USA Today, 3 Oct. 2006. Web. 12 July 2012.

Cait Caffrey

■ Organic food industry

Definition: The industry that produces food grown and processed without pesticides, food additives, and genetically modified organisms

The organic food movement began in response to the twentieth-century introduction of chemicals and pesticides to the food industry to increase yield. The organic food industry grew steadily in the United States after the passage of the Organic Foods Production Act of 1990, which helped set strict standards for organic food production. In the 2000s, many Americans, inspired by new books and films on food production and consumption, began seeking alternatives to the conventional food supply chain, including organic foods.

The Organic Foods Production Act of 1990 implemented national organic standards and established the National Organic Standards Board. The board makes recommendations to the National Organic Program (NOP) of the United States Department of Agriculture (USDA) to help regulate the organic food industry. The NOP, established in 2000, is in charge of developing and regulating organic food standards, which ensure that companies use the correct practices when growing and producing organic products. The NOP verifies that the players within the organic food industry—including farmers, ranchers, distributors, and processors—comply with these standards and become certified by accredited agents.

The organic food industry is heavily regulated by the USDA, which frequently inspects and audits organic companies to ensure that regulations are followed and organic products are labeled correctly. All organic products must carry the USDA organic seal, which verifies that the product is at least 95 percent organic or has been made with certified organic ingredients. The seal means the crops have been harvested without exposure to radiation, sewage sludge, synthetic fertilizers, pesticides, or genetically modified organisms. The seal also ensures that animals are raised according to standards that protect their health and well-being. Farmers raising livestock cannot use antibiotics or growth hormones and must feed the animals a 100 percent organic diet. The animals must also be provided with an outdoor pasture. Animals that have been cloned do not qualify as organic products.

Labeling

As awareness of food production methods grew in the 2000s, food labeling became an important issue. Consumers often had difficulty understanding the differences between the profusion of labels and health claims, especially those denoting organic and nonorganic food products. In addition to carrying the USDA organic seal, products from livestock—including meat, eggs, and milk—may also have other labels regulated by the USDA. Products that contain any of these various labels may or may

Farmers' market in Jackson, Mississippi. (Courtesy Natalie Maynor)

not be organic. If a product is labeled "natural," for example, but does not contain a USDA organic seal, it is not an organic product. Products that are 70 percent organic can carry the label "made with organic ingredients" but cannot bear the USDA organic seal.

Animal products could bear a number of different labels in addition to or instead of organic. A product labeled "free range" means that the livestock was permitted unlimited access to indoor/outdoor areas and fresh food and water. "Cage-free" means the livestock was not kept in caged areas, but was permitted unlimited access to indoor areas. Products labeled "natural" do not contain any artificial ingredients and are minimally processed. This labeling applies to meat and egg products only. "Grass-fed" livestock are fed primarily grass. Unlike organic grass-fed livestock, these animals may be fed grass that has been treated with pesticides and may be given antibiotics and/or hormones. A "no-added hormones" label means that the livestock has been raised without the use of hormones or steroids. Other labels, such as "pasture-raised" and "humane," may or may not be regulated by non-USDA independent certifying organizations.

Industry Growth

The organic food industry grew steadily through the 2000s in the United States to become one of the fastest-growing segments in the food market. According to the Organic Trade Association, organic foods accounted for almost $14 billion in sales in 2005. By the following year, this number had risen to $17.7 billion. Sales continued to increase, even when the US economy entered a recession during the late 2000s. In 2009, organic foods accounted for $26.6 billion in US sales and $54.9 billion in global sales. The United States led the global market in organic food sales, with Germany and France not far behind.

The wider availability of organic foods at large grocery chains was cited as one of the main reasons for the continued increase. At first, organic foods could be found only at small specialty grocery stores and farmers markets. People also began choosing more organic products because of an increased awareness of health issues, the environmental impact of food manufacturing, and food and animal safety concerns.

Impact

During the 2000s, people increasingly chose organic products because they believed these products were better for both their health and the environment. Organic foods do not contain potentially toxic chemicals such as pesticides, which can leave a residue on produce and affect its taste and appearance. Organic foods also do not contain food additives, such as artificial sweeteners, colorings, flavorings, and preservatives. Organic farmers are prohibited from using chemical pesticides, which can wash from farmlands into waterways where they may contaminate the water supply and soil, kill wildlife, and destroy vegetation. Instead, organic farms use such practices as hand weeding and crop rotation, which are designed to benefit the environment and reduce pollution.

Further Reading

Dunn-Georgiou, Elisha. *Everything You Need to Know about Organic Foods.* New York: Rosen, 2002. Print. Traces the development of the organic food movement in the United States and outlines the parameters set for food to be considered organic by the USDA.

Fromartz, Samuel. *Organic, Inc.: Natural Foods and How They Grew.* Orlando: Harcourt, 2006. Print. Tracks the changes in Americans' awareness of the food they consume and looks at the sources of organic food.

Langley, Andrew. *Is Organic Food Better?* Chicago: Heinemann, 2009. Print. Looks at the range of opinion on and facts about organic foods. Good starting place for discussing the topic of organic foods.

"Organic Foods: Are They Safer? More Nutritious?" *Mayo Clinic.* Mayo Foundation for Medical Education and Research, 7 Sept. 2012. Web. 26 Nov. 2012. Provides medical research on organic foods, including information on nutrition and health.

Organic Trade Association. "Quick Overview: Organic Agriculture and Production." *Organic Trade*

Association. Organic Trade Assn., 16 Feb. 2011. Web. 21 Nov. 2012. Provides information about the organic trade industry and how organic food is produced.

Angela Harmon

■ Organized crime

Definition: Criminal activities conducted by organized groups to operate illegal businesses, corrupt the political or law enforcement process, or materially affect legitimate business through extortion or other criminal tactics

Although activities of traditional organized crime groups in North America were curtailed by the end of the twentieth century, new organizations arose to take their place in running sophisticated criminal networks that challenged law enforcement agencies and affected economic prosperity both the United States and Canada.

During the 2000s, the face of organized crime changed but the central problem persisted in both the United States and Canada. As a result of a 1970 statute, the Racketeer Influenced and Corrupt Organization (RICO) Act, which allowed the United States government to prosecute individuals suspected of engaging in organized crime activities, by 2000 the influence of traditional organized crime groups like the Italian American Mafia in areas such as gambling, prostitution, racketeering, drug trafficking, and other corrupt practices was substantially circumscribed. Nevertheless, the threat from organized crime to law-abiding citizens' safety and security and to the economic health of the United States and Canada continued, as other criminal groups arose or were strengthened.

The Changing Face of Organized Crime

The criminal organizations that posed the most serious threats in North America during the period from 2000 to 2009 were ones based in South Asia, Russia, Latin America, and Africa. These groups differed from the Mafia in three important ways. First, they were transnational. Aided by improved communications, especially the Internet, these groups often operated in two or more countries, sometimes on two or more continents. Second, the command-and-control structure of new groups was notably different from the hierarchical organization of traditional groups like the Mafia. While a formal organization may have made it easier for leaders in the Mafia to control operations, the existence of that structure also allowed law enforcement officials to identify group members and negate activities once leaders were apprehended. By contrast, new criminal groups tended to have a less formal structure and be more willing to outsource activities to other groups. It was not uncommon for law enforcement officials to discover that local street gangs in the United States were being employed by Mexican or Colombian drug lords who managed a sophisticated and often decentralized supply network that involved several different groups in South, Central, and North America. Even traditional organizations like the Mafia began contracting with violent gangs like the Hells Angels to carry out violent activities such as contract murder. A third important change was the growth of government sponsorship of organized crime. In a number of countries, especially Third World countries, government leaders gave protection to criminal networks in exchange for a share of profits. A handful of officials also made enormous personal profits from illegal sales organized by criminal networks.

Criminal Activities and Practices

As they had done for decades, between 2000 and 2009 organized criminal groups continued to engage in what may be termed traditional activities: loan sharking, union infiltration to skim profits, gambling, drug trafficking, prostitution, and extortion of legitimate businesses. Theft for resale continued to provide a lucrative source of illegitimate profits, from mundane items such as cigarettes to sophisticated computer hardware and software. Organized crime also became heavily involved in the sale of stolen prescription drugs and fraudulent medicines. At the same time, activities that had been practiced on a modest scale in the past were stepped up, particularly human trafficking. The desire for foreign nationals to enter the United States or Canada presented a lucrative opportunity for criminal organizations to develop sophisticated networks to smuggle in immigrants, often collecting exorbitant fees for their services. Additionally, sophisticated networks were created to bring in young women for the sex trade; these women frequently were abused and even enslaved by those who arranged their entry into the country. Another form

of trafficking also became popular: the illegal sale of natural resources. Criminal groups stole exotic wildlife, precious metals and gems, and particularly energy resources such as oil and natural gas for resale to customers willing to overlook the source of these commodities.

The growing pervasiveness of the Internet allowed criminal groups to capitalize on sophisticated scams to prey on unsuspecting victims who believed they were engaging in legitimate electronic business transactions. Criminal groups also created systems for engaging in identity theft, allowing them to steal from individuals' financial accounts without having to engage in any direct contact with victims. The same electronic systems that have permitted the transfer of funds internationally between banks in different countries have also been used by organized crime for money laundering. In 2009, more than eleven million people in the United States were victimized, at a cost of $54 billion.

Perhaps the most disturbing trend is the growing link between organized crime groups and revolutionary or terrorist organizations. Frequently these arrangements involve transfer of weapons, often from the United States. For example, in 2008 an international arms dealer was arrested and charged with supplying arms to the Revolutionary Armed Forces in Colombia (FARC). Two years earlier, United States customs agents uncovered a smuggling ring that was obtaining weapons and military equipment in the United States for shipment to the Tamil Tigers in Sri Lanka.

Law Enforcement Efforts

The growth of translational organized crime posed significant challenges for law enforcement agencies in North America. To be effective in eliminating these groups or at least minimizing their effectiveness, cooperation among agencies of different nations became mandatory. While such cooperation existed between the United States, Canada, and their traditional political allies, it was not always forthcoming from states that have not had close relationships with, or were openly hostile toward, Western governments. Some of these nations refused assistance or openly abetted criminal groups whose victims were predominantly in First World countries.

A related problem posed by the growth of international criminal syndicates was the requirement for the United States and Canada to shift resources away from fighting traditional forms of organized crime to deal with newer, more complex forms of illegal activity. As a consequence, during the 2000s older groups such as the Mafia were able to begin rebuilding organizations decimated by federal efforts during the last three decades of the twentieth century. The success of these rebuilding efforts was highlighted in 2011 when the Federal Bureau of Investigation launched a coordinated effort against the Mafia that resulted in more than 120 arrests.

Impact

The economic impact of organized crime during the 2000s was staggering. The United Nations Office on Drugs and Crime estimated that in 2009 transnational organized crime generated $870 billion in income. As the largest economy in the world, the United States suffered the greatest loss, though the nature of international activity makes it difficult to quantify that loss precisely. Not always noted, however, is the human impact of organized crime: the victims often suffered irreparable physical or emotional harm, particularly those swept up in sex trafficking or caught in immigration schemes that went awry. The need to focus law enforcement resources on organized crime placed great strain on national security, particularly in the United States, which is a particular target of terrorist groups.

Further Reading

Albanese, Jay S. *Transnational Crime and the 21st Century: Criminal Enterprise, Corruption, and Opportunity.* New York: Oxford UP, 2011. Print. Provides an overview of organized criminal activity in the first decade of the twenty-first century, explaining the relationship between criminals and government officials and exploring the many illegal activities in which organized groups participate.

Camilleri, Jason D. *Organized Crime: Challenges, Trends, and Reduction Strategies.* Hauppage: Nova Science, 2011. Print. Describes trends in organized criminal activity and its impact on the economic and security of the United States; suggests government actions required to counter threats.

Finckenauer, James, and Ko-lin Chin. "Asian Transnational Organized Crime and Its Impact on the United States: Developing a Transnational Crime Research Agenda." *Trends in Organized Crime* 10.2 (2006): 18–107. Print. Discusses an in-depth study on organized crime in Asia and its effect on the United States in terms of issues like human trafficking and the drug trade.

Larkin, Erik. "Organized Crime Moves into Data Theft." *PC World* 27.7 (2009): 33–34. Print. Examines the increasing incidence of data theft and cybercrime as related to criminal organizations.

Liddick, Donald R., Jr. *The Global Underworld: Transnational Crime and the United States.* Westport: Praeger, 2004. Print. Describes the many international organized crime groups and the wide variety of criminal operations that have a significant impact in the United States and Canada.

Nicaso, Antonio, and Lee Lamothe. *Angels, Mobsters, and Narco-Terrorists: The Rising Menace of Global Criminal Empires.* Mississauga: Wiley, 2005. Print. Systematic examination of the various criminal cartels operating throughout the world, focusing on organization and preferred forms of criminal activities.

Laurence W. Mazzeno

■ *The Osbournes*

Identification: Reality television show about the personal life of heavy metal icon Ozzy Osbourne and his family

Executive Producers: Jonathan Taylor; Jeff Stilson (b. 1959)

Date: March 5, 2002–March 21, 2005

The Osbournes *gave viewers a look into the personal lives of former Black Sabbath lead singer Ozzy Osbourne and his family. The show quickly became MTV's most popular and highest-rated program. It was also nominated for several awards and won an Emmy for outstanding nonfiction show in 2002.*

American producer and director Jonathan Taylor created the reality television series *The Osbournes*, which aired for four seasons on MTV from 2002 to 2005. Taylor served as coexecutive producer and executive producer for the entire series. Jeff Stilson served as executive producer until 2004. In 2005 Lois Curren, Greg Johnston, and one of the show's stars, Sharon Osbourne, shared the role of executive director for several episodes.

The Osbournes featured the family of Ozzy Osbourne, former lead singer and songwriter of the heavy metal band Black Sabbath and creator of the musical festival Ozzfest. On stage, Ozzy—also known as the Prince of Darkness—is known for his dark persona. On *The Osbournes*, viewers see Ozzy as a gentle man and loving husband and father. The show also featured Ozzy's wife and former band manager, Sharon, a television personality; their son Jack, an actor and documentary film maker; and their daughter Kelly, a singer and television personality. Oldest daughter Aimee declined to participate in the show.

The first episode introduced the Osbournes as they moved into their new Beverly Hills estate. Subsequent episodes focused on the family's relationships, struggles, careers, and daily activities. Viewers quickly learned about the family's numerous pets and the love-hate relationship between siblings Jack and Kelly.

Prior to filming the second season, Sharon was diagnosed with colon cancer, and she decided to continue filming in order to document her battle and treatments. During filming of the third season, Ozzy was seriously injured in an all-terrain vehicle accident, which became the major storyline for the season. The fourth and final season featured more of the family's difficulties, including Kelly's and Jack's battles with drugs and alcohol.

Impact
The Osbournes was one of the first reality television shows of the new millennium to focus solely on the daily life of a celebrity family. Such programs allowed viewers into the personal, day-to-day lives of celebrities, which many believe is their appeal. Rather than showcasing themselves as a perfect family, the Osbournes allowed the world to witness their various struggles, which most viewers could relate to and empathize with. Critics believe that *The Osbournes* paved the way for the success of other celebrity-family reality shows, such as *Gene Simmons Family Jewels* (which first aired in 2006) and *Keeping Up with the Kardashians* (which first aired in 2007).

Further Reading
Osbourne, Ozzy. *I Am Ozzy*. New York: Grand Central, 2011. Print.

Osbourne, Sharon. *Sharon Osbourne Extreme: My Autobiography*. London: Time Warner, 2005. Print.

Angela Harmon

■ Osteen, Joel

Identification: American televangelist, Christian author, and pastor of one of the largest churches in the United States
Born: March 5, 1963; Houston, Texas

Beginning in 1999, Joel Osteen turned Lakewood Church, located in Houston, Texas, into one of the largest, fastest-growing Christian congregations in the United States. His televised ministry is seen by seven million of people weekly in the United States and is broadcast in more than one hundred countries worldwide.

In 1959, Joel Osteen's father, John, founded Lakewood Church as a nondenominational charismatic church in Houston, Texas. Joel Osteen attended Oral Roberts University in Tulsa, Oklahoma, but left without a degree in 1982 when he returned to Houston to found a television ministry for his father's church. For seventeen years, he produced the television programming for Lakewood Church, broadcasting his father's sermons weekly. When John Osteen suffered a heart attack in January 1999, Joel preached his first sermon, filling in for his father. When his father died a short time later,

Joel Osteen. (Courtesy cliff1066)

Joel became the senior pastor for the Lakewood Church.

Since 1999, Lakewood Church has become one of the largest congregations in America. In 2001, the church began proceedings to obtain a long-term lease on the former Compaq Center, which had been the home of the Houston Rockets professional basketball team. After spending more than $90 million in renovations, the church began using this sixteen-thousand-seat facility in 2005, the largest regularly used church building in the United States. Each weekend, as many as forty thousand people attend the multiple worship services there. Osteen's weekly television broadcasts are seen by millions in the United States and worldwide.

Osteen has also written several best-selling books, beginning with *Your Best Life Now: 7 Steps to Living at Your Full Potential*, which was released in 2004. Osteen's preaching and writing emphasizes a positive, upbeat message about the goodness of God and the unlimited potential of believers who put their trust in him. While Osteen's message and methods resonate with many believers, evangelical Christian critics have suggested that he preaches a form of the "prosperity gospel" that promises success and wealth to believers, but deemphasizes personal responsibility, sacrifice, and Christian service.

Impact

Osteen is widely recognized as a leading example of a modern religious entrepreneur. His congregation has become one of the largest in the United States, his television ministry ranks among the largest in terms of viewership, and several of his books have become national best sellers. Despite criticisms that his ministry is overly focused on materialism and personal gain, Osteen's broadcasted services represent the most-watched religious program in the United States.

Further Reading

Lee, Shayne, and Phillip Luke Sinitiere. *Holy Mavericks: Evangelical Innovators and the Spiritual Marketplace.* New York: New York UP, 2009. Print.

Van Biema, David, and Jeff Chu. "Does God Want You to be Rich?"" *Time* 18 Sept. 2006: 48–56. Print.

Young, Richard. *The Rise of Lakewood Church and Joel Osteen.* New Kensington: Whitaker, 2007. Print.

Mark S. Joy

■ Oz, Mehmet

Identification: Turkish American surgeon, television personality, and author
Born: June 11, 1960; Cleveland, Ohio

Oz spent many years as a cardiovascular surgeon and has used his medical expertise to educate the general public about important health issues. He became a celebrity health expert after appearing on several television and radio shows to offer medical information and advice. Oz's self-help book became a best-seller and he has since launched a series of other books on personal health.

Cardiothoracic surgeon Mehmet Oz has performed countless heart and lung operations and currently serves as director of the Cardiovascular Institute and Complementary Medicine Program at New York Presbyterian Hospital. In 2001 he became professor of surgery at Columbia University, and in 2003 he and his wife, Lisa, developed the show *Second Opinion with Dr. Oz*, which aired on the Discovery Health Channel.

In 2004 Oz began appearing as a medical expert on *The Oprah Winfrey Show*. His regular appearances generated immediate popularity for the surgeon and the talk show, and Oz appeared in more than fifty-five shows over five seasons. In 2003 he founded the nonprofit organization HealthCorps, a health

Mehmet Oz. (Courtesy Be the Change Inc./Jim Gillooly/PEI)

mentor program for high school students. He appeared on other television programs, including *Good Morning America*, *Today*, and *The View*, to discuss preventative and complementary health topics. He has written hundreds of columns and articles for various publications, among them *Esquire*, *O, The Oprah Magazine*, and *Time*. In 2005, he became the host of a radio program on Sirius XM satellite radio's Oprah Radio channel. Also that year, he published *YOU: The Owner's Manual: An Insider's Guide to the Body That Will Make You Healthier and Younger*, with Michael F. Roizen. The book made the New York Times Best Sellers list and led to a series of YOU books by the authors. *Time* magazine named Oz to its "100 Most Influential People" list in 2008, and he was included on *Esquire*'s "Seventy-Five Most Influential People of the Twenty-First Century" list. In 2009 Oz launched his own medical television show, *The Dr. Oz Show*, and has since won two Daytime Emmy Awards for outstanding informative talk show host.

Impact

Mehmet Oz has endeavored to educate as many people as possible about preventative medicine and public health issues throughout the 2000s. He used his celebrity status and media appearances to further his message and was an integral part of Oprah Winfrey's mission to educate and improve lives.

Further Reading

Bruni, Frank. "Dr. Does-It-All." *New York Times Magazine*. New York Times Co., 16 Apr. 2010. Web. 10 July 2012.

Dr. Oz Show Official Website. "Mehmet Oz, MD." *The Dr. Oz Show*. ZoCo1 LLC, n.d. Web. 10 July 2012.

PBS. "Faces of America with Henry Louis Gates, Jr.: Dr. Mehmet Oz." *PBS*. WNET.org Properties, n.d. Web. 10 July 2012.

Angela Harmon

P

■ Palin, Sarah

Identification: American politician and governor of Alaska

Born: February 11, 1964; Sandpoint, Idaho

Republican Sarah Palin was the youngest person and the first woman to serve as governor of Alaska. After taking office in 2006, she was both praised for her personality and politics and criticized for her relative inexperience.

The daughter of two school teachers, Sarah Heath Palin was born in 1964 in Sandpoint, Idaho. She attended the University of Idaho, where she earned a degree in journalism. She worked in the media before pursuing a career in politics.

Palin was criticized by both Democrats and Republicans for her lack of political experience. However, she described herself as being a "hard-core conservative." She opposes gay marriage and abortion and praised the concept of teaching the theory of creationism in public schools. Throughout her career, Palin made a point of differentiating her conservative ideals from what she saw as corrupt elements within her own party.

In 2002, Palin ran unsuccessfully for the office of lieutenant governor of Alaska. She was defeated by fellow Republican Loren Leman, but she finished as the runner-up in overall voting.

Former governor Frank Murkowski appointed Palin to the role of commissioner on Alaska's Oil and Gas Conservation Commission. Palin gained prominence in this position by playing the role of whistleblower, calling attention to the ethics violations of her Republican colleagues. Her actions resulted in the resignation of Randy Ruedrich, chairman of the state's Republican Party. Palin resigned from her position in protest of what she considered a lack of ethics among the members of the commission.

Palin went on to defeat Murkowski in Alaska's Republican gubernatorial primary in 2006. She de-

feated Democratic challenger and former governor Tony Knowles in the general election. Palin was forty-two years old when elected and, thus, became the youngest governor in the history of the state. She is also the first woman to hold the office of governor in Alaska.

In July 2007, *The Weekly Standard* named Palin "the most popular governor" in the United States and the "GOP's newest star." The article praised Palin's integrity and her often-contentious relationship with the rest of the Republican Party.

Governor Palin sought to rein in what she viewed as the excesses of the Murkowski administration. She grounded a private jet once used by Murkowski and announced the plane was for sale. Palin also overturned Murkowski's last-minute appointment of Jim Clark to the board of directors of the Alaska Natural Gas Development Authority. She stated that Clark, Murkowski's former chief of staff, did not share her views on the state's pipeline development projects.

After taking office, Palin moved quickly to make her vision of Alaska a reality. She unveiled a plan to create a "subcabinet" of advisors that would focus on climate change and greenhouse gas emissions in the state. Palin also signed into law her own legislation, known as the Alaska Gasline Inducement Act (2007), which outlined a plan to build a natural-gas pipeline in the state's northern region. In June 2007, Governor Palin signed the largest budget in Alaska's history. The $6.6 billion budget also included the second-largest cuts in the state's construction projects since Alaska became a state.

On August 29, 2008, US senator and presidential candidate John McCain announced that he had selected Palin as his running mate for vice president. The selection of Palin surprised many analysts and voters. Palin became the first woman in American history to be selected as a presidential running mate by the Republican Party. Palin was selected by the McCain campaign for being a

John McCain with running mate Sarah Palin at the Republican National Convention. (©iStockphoto.com/Ethan Miller)

staunch conservative, known for her pro-life views and her efforts in battling corruption. Shortly after Palin's selection as the 2008 Republican Party vice presidential candidate, it was announced that Palin's seventeen-year-old daughter Bristol was pregnant. In an official statement, Palin said that she and her husband were proud of their daughter. Although an engagement between Bristol Palin and her boyfriend, Levi Johnston, was announced, it was subsequently canceled.

The election to decide who would become the forty-fourth president of the United States was held on November 4, 2008. Senator McCain and Governor Palin were defeated by Democratic Party challengers Senator Barack Obama and Senator Joe Biden.

On July 3, 2009, Palin announced that she was resigning from the office of governor on July 29. The news came as a shock to Palin's colleagues in the Republican Party because she was scheduled to remain in office through 2010. Reaction to the announcement was mixed. It was unclear at the time of the announcement whether Palin intended to leave politics for good or whether she was making early moves to run for the presidency in 2012.

Impact

In November 2009, Palin published a book entitled *Going Rogue*, which details her experience as a candidate in the 2008 election. She continued to make regular appearances at events held by the conservative Tea Party movement. Throughout 2011, Palin undertook a nationwide bus tour with her family, visiting various locations of political and historical interest. During the tour, she conducted fund-raising through her political action committee SarahPAC. Although it had been previously speculated that Palin would announce a presidential campaign for the 2012 election, she announced in October 2011 that she would not be running.

Further Reading

Heath, Chuck Sr., and Chuck Heath Jr. *Our Sarah: Made in Alaska.* New York: Hatchette, 2012. Print.

Palin, Sarah. *Going Rogue: An American Life.* New York: Harper, 2009. Print.

McGinniss, Joe. *The Rogue: Searching for the Real Sarah Palin.* New York: Crown, 2011. Print.

Joshua Pritchard

■ Partial-Birth Abortion Ban Act

The Law: Federal legislation that banned abortions in which the fetus is partially delivered prior to the termination of the pregnancy

Date: Enacted on November 5, 2003

The Partial-Birth Abortion Ban Act sought to restrict a controversial abortion procedure known as dilation and extraction. In 1995, the National Right to Life Committee coined the term "partial-birth abortion" to describe the procedure and began a campaign to ban it. Their efforts culminated in the adoption of this legislation in 2003, the first federal law to criminally outlaw a method of abortion since the US Supreme Court legalized abortions in 1973.

Initially introduced in 1995 by US Representative Charles Canady, the Partial-Birth Abortion Ban Act was vetoed twice by President Bill Clinton in 1996 and 1997. Reintroduced by Senator Rick Santorum in 2003, Congress passed the act with bipartisan support, and President George W. Bush signed it into law. In addition to detailing the partial-birth abortion procedure, in which a fetus is partially delivered before a doctor punctures its skull to terminate the pregnancy, the act emphasized the physician's intent. Doctors found guilty of *intentionally* carrying out a partial-birth abortion could be fined or jailed.

Like many aspects of the abortion debate, terminology holds political weight. Terms often used to describe this abortion procedure include *partial-birth abortion, dilation and extraction,* and *intact dilation and evacuation.* Pro-life and pro-choice proponents claim the medical and political superiority of their preferred terms, but the procedure largely remains the same. Regardless of terminology, this abortion method is most often performed during the second trimester and, according to the reproductive health nonprofit Alan Guttmacher Institute, accounted for 0.2 percent of all abortions performed in the United States.

Citing vague terminology and insufficient protection for women in cases where the mother's health is in danger, opponents brought the law before the Supreme Court in *Gonzales v. Carhart* (2007). The court issued a close ruling in favor of the law, upholding its constitutionality and affirming that it provides adequate protection for women whose lives were at risk. Dissenters, including Justice Ruth Bader Ginsburg, voiced their opposition to the ruling, viewing the act as a threat to women's health.

Impact

The importance of the Partial-Birth Abortion Ban Act has been interpreted variously. Some view the act as a step toward overturning *Roe v. Wade,* fearing the eventual outright illegalization of all abortion procedures. Others question the wisdom of allowing the government to interfere in the doctor-patient relationship. Still others view the act's health exception for women as too lenient, since it includes mental as well as physical health concerns. They fear that these exceptions will create a loophole through which to obtain partial-birth abortions.

Most tangibly, the Partial-Birth Abortion Ban Act has altered the way doctors perform abortions after the first trimester of pregnancy. In order to protect themselves from liability, doctors have increased the use of an abortion method in which they first fatally inject the fetus with drugs prior to its extraction.

Further Reading

Feldt, Gloria. *The War on Choice.* New York: Bantam Dell, 2004. Print.

Johnson, Douglas. "The Partial-Birth Abortion Ban Act—Misconceptions and Realities." *National Right to Life Committee,* 5 Nov. 2003. Web. 19 July 2012.

Rovner, Julie. "'Partial-Birth Abortion:' Separating Fact from Spin." *NPR.* NPR, 21 Feb. 2006. Web. 19 July 2012.

Lucia Pizzo

■ *The Passion of the Christ*

Identification: A controversial film depicting the final hours in the life of Jesus Christ, including his torture, crucifixion, and resurrection
Director: Mel Gibson (b. 1956)
Date: Released on February 25, 2004

One of the most controversial and financially successful films of the 2000s, Mel Gibson's The Passion of the Christ *aimed to accurately depict the final twelve hours in the life of Jesus Christ. Gibson cited the Gospels of Matthew, Mark, Luke, and John from the Bible's New Testament as his main source material for the film. The film drew great controversy for its graphic violence and alleged negative depiction of Jewish people.*

The third film directed by Mel Gibson, *The Passion of the Christ,* was the fifth-highest grossing film of 2004 and easily the most controversial. Gibson, a traditionalist Catholic, decided that the Biblical languages of Aramaic, Latin, and Hebrew would be the only spoken languages in his film to maintain historical accuracy and enhance the experience for audiences. Gibson consulted several theological advisors during filming to ensure accuracy. Gibson and his production company, Icon Productions, completely covered the cost to produce and market the film—approximately $45 million. The film was released on February 25, 2004, on Ash Wednesday, which, for Catholics and other Christians, marks the beginning of Lent.

Actor Jim Caviezel played Jesus Christ and Romanian actress Maia Morgenstern played Mary, the mother of Jesus. The film depicts several events described in the Gospels of the New Testament, including Judas's betrayal of Jesus to the temple guards, Jesus carrying the cross, and Jesus's resurrection. Gibson intentionally made the scenes depicting Jesus's torture exceptionally graphic so that the audience would see how much Jesus suffered and realize the enormity of his sacrifice to mankind. The graphic violence was the reason the film received an R rating. An edited version of film, called *The Passion Recut*, removed some of the most graphic scenes and was released in 2005 so that younger audiences could see it in theaters.

A great amount of controversy surrounded the film. Many people believed that the film was anti-Semitic. People argued that Gibson ignored decades of contemporary religious scholarship and held onto the belief that Jews pursued Jesus and blackmailed the Romans into killing him. Some scholars believed that despite his intention to be historically accurate, Gibson took great artistic interpretation with his film.

Impact

The Passion of the Christ went on to become the highest grossing R-rated film of all time, earning more than $600 million worldwide. The film was nominated for and won several awards, including the People's Choice Award for favorite movie drama. Several members of the cast and crew converted to Catholicism after the film completed shooting, citing their experiences on set as the reason. The film brought traditional Catholicism into the public dialogue for a great amount of time leading up to and following its release.

Further Reading

Bartunek, John, and Mel Gibson. *Inside the Passion: An Insider's Look at* The Passion of the Christ. Ascension, 2005. Print.

Duncan, Ken, and Mel Gibson. *Photography from the Movie* The Passion of the Christ. Tyndale House, 2004. Print

Patrick G. Cooper

■ Paul, Ron

Identification: American politician and presidential candidate in 2008
Born: August 20, 1935; Pittsburgh, Pennsylvania

Republican Ron Paul has represented Texas in the US House of Representatives since 1997. A former member of the Libertarian Party, he is also a military veteran and a physician. He is a strict constitutionalist who believes in small government, and he has proposed that individual income tax and the Internal Revenue Service be abolished.

Ron Paul. (Courtesy Gage Skidmore)

Paul earned his medical degree in 1961 and completed his residency at Henry Ford Hospital and the University of Pittsburgh. Paul successfully campaigned for the Libertarian Party nomination for president in 1988, bringing the Libertarian message of civil liberties and small government to a wider national audience. The notoriety that Paul gained during his presidential candidacy helped him to establish the Foundation for Rational Economics and Education (FREE), a think tank devoted to promoting the Libertarian concepts of personal economic freedom, free trade, and isolationist foreign policy.

Paul returned to Congress as a representative for Texas in 1996 after winning an unexpected election victory against Republican Greg Laughlin. Throughout his career, Paul has also authored numerous books, including *A Foreign Policy of Freedom* (2007). Paul and his wife Carol have five children and live in Lake Jackson, Texas.

In February 2007, Paul announced that he would seek the Republican Party nomination in the 2008 US presidential election. After his announcement, Paul gained a dedicated and motivated group of supporters through the Internet. Political analysts said that Paul's campaign developed an effective web-based marketing and fundraising system.

Although Paul campaigned for the Republican Party nomination, his political philosophy remained vested in libertarian ideals. He strongly opposed increased taxes and increased government spending. He also opposed the proposition of a national identification card system and the widely debated Patriot Act, which allows for government surveillance of people suspected of involvement in alleged terrorist activities. Paul believed that legislation related to abortion in the United States should be handled by state governments.

As the 2008 Iowa caucus approached, it became clear that Paul was the candidate who had found a way to make the most of web-based fundraising, raising $20 million in the last quarter of 2007. Paul placed fourth in the 2008 Republican caucus in Iowa, earning 10 percent of the overall vote. In the 2008 New Hampshire Republican primary, Paul finished fifth overall, earning 8 percent of the vote. He finished fourth in the Michigan Republican primary with just over 6 percent of the vote. Paul finished second behind Mitt Romney in the Nevada caucus, earning nearly 14 percent of the total voting. He placed fifth in the South Carolina primary, earning approximately 4 percent of the vote. Paul also earned 4 percent of the vote in the Florida primary.

In the 2008 "Super Tuesday" primaries and caucuses held on February 5, twenty-two states voted. Paul did not win the vote in any state. Paul finished fourth or fifth in the majority of states, behind Romney, Mike Huckabee, and John McCain. Paul did finish third in Utah.

Paul finished behind Huckabee and McCain in primaries held in Louisiana; Washington, DC; Maryland; and Virginia. On March 4, McCain won the Republican primaries held in Vermont, Texas, Rhode Island, and Vermont. These victories confirmed McCain's nomination as the 2008 Republican presidential candidate. Paul did not officially suspend his 2008 presidential campaign until June 13, 2008.

Paul published the book *End the Fed* in 2009. In July 2011, he announced that he would not seek reelection to Congress so that he could focus all his energy on another bid for the Republican Party presidential nomination. He finished third in the 2012 Iowa Republican caucus and second in the 2012 New Hampshire Republican primary, earning 22.9 percent of the vote. He finished in fourth place behind his GOP colleagues Newt Gingrich, Romney, and Rick Santorum in the 2012 South Carolina Republican primary. On Super Tuesday, March 6, 2012, Paul did not finish first in any of the ten states that held GOP primary elections.

Impact

Ron Paul is a three-time candidate for the president of the United States, running under both the Libertarian and Republican parties. He also served as a medical officer in the US Air Force. Paul is the author of many books, including *Liberty Defined* (2011), *End the Fed* (2009), and *Pillars of Prosperity* (2008). During his tenure in Congress, Paul served on the House Banking Committee and established FREE.

Further Reading

Doherty, Brian. *Ron Paul's Revolution: The Man and the Movement He Inspired.* New York: Harper, 2012. Print.

Paul, Ron. *Liberty Defined.* New York: Hachette, 2011. Print.

___. *The Revolution: A Manifesto.* New York: Hachette, 2008. Print.

Joshua Pritchard

■ Paulson, Henry

Identification: American banker and US secretary of the treasury, 2006–9

Born: March 28, 1946; Palm Beach, Florida

Hank Paulson, Jr. was named the United States treasury secretary in June 2006. Paulson worked at the White House in the 1970s, under President Richard Nixon, then left to work at the investment bank Goldman Sachs. He rose to the top of the bank and presided over its transition from a private to a public bank. He left the bank in June 2006 to become treasury secretary. Secretary Paulson saw a severe decline of the US and world economy, which many claimed was the worst since economic crisis since the Great Depression of the 1930s.

In 1998, Goldman Sachs chairman Henry (Hank) Merritt Paulson forced out his cochairman, Jon Corzine, and became the investment bank's chief executive officer (CEO). He then guided the bank through its transition from a private to a public entity by issuing an initial public offering (IPO), whereby the bank offered its shares for sale to the public for the first time. He was also one of the proponents of taking more risk at investment banks and he was well compensated for his efforts. Paulson earned $30 million in 2004 and $37 million in 2005; his personal fortune is estimated to be $700 million. With this wealth, he has supported numerous Republican political candidates, donating over $336,000 to the party between 1998 and 2006.

Henry Paulson (left) and Ben Bernanke. (©iStockphoto.com/Alex Wong)

Paulson has also donated $100 million of his money to a family foundation which supports conservation and environmental education. This interest in conservation also led him to follow his wife onto the board of directors of Nature Conservancy, where he spent two years as chair. There, he leveraged his connections in China as cochair of the organization's Asia-Pacific Council. He worked with the People's Republic of China president (1993–2003) Jiang Zemin to preserve the Tiger Leaping Gorge in Yunnan province. His other volunteer work included his role as founding chairman of the advisory board of the School of Economics and Management of Tsinghua University in Beijing, and membership on the boards of the Peregrine Fund, Catalyst, and J. L. Kellogg Graduate School of Management at Northwestern University. Paulson also served on the board of the dean's advisors of the Harvard Business School.

On June 28, 2006, President George W. Bush named Henry Paulson at the seventy-fourth secretary of the Treasury. He was unanimously confirmed by Congress on July 10, 2006. He played a prominent role in the global financial crisis that began in 2006, but boiled over in 2008. With the burst of the housing bubble in 2006, mortgage holders began defaulting on their loans, lenders failed, and mortgage-backed security values began to fall. The repercussions were seen in Wall Street firms and at Freddie Mac and Fannie Mae, government sponsored companies that hold almost half of US home mortgages.

In the spring of 2008, Paulson developed plans to stabilize and work out deals to shore up the financial markets. He oversaw the demise of three of Goldman Sachs's main rivals, namely Lehman Bros,

Merrill Lynch and Bear Stearns, and has also engineered government bailouts for other failing entities. In September, Freddie Mac and Fannie Mae were purchased by the federal government for $200 billion. This was followed by an $85 billion bailout of the insurer American International Group (AIG), for which the American taxpayer received an 80 percent stake in the company.

Later that month, Paulson requested $700 billion from Congress for the Troubled Asset Relief Program (TARP). This program was initially designed to buy troubled assets ("toxic loans") from banks, and Paulson warned it was necessary to ensure that banks would continue to loan money to one another. The House of Representatives initially rejected his plan, finding that the proposal gave too much authority to the secretary, with not enough accountability. After a tense week of negotiations, the three-page proposal became a 400-page bill that was passed first by the Senate and then by the House. In November 2008, Paulson announced that he had changed course and decided to invest directly in banks to encourage lending.

Throughout this process, Paulson has been accused of trying to protect wealthy shareholders, like himself, who many feel are responsible for the economic collapse. He has been accused of socializing debt and privatizing profits. Questions regarding the allocation of the initial half of the TARP program have also arisen, with taxpayers and legislators wanting specific information as to how the money is being spent. Paulson has been reluctant to disclose the names of banks and the amounts that they have received because this information may cause the public to lose faith in a given institution's solvency. Paulson has emphasized that the primary goal of government action in the bailout has been to create stability and public confidence in the markets.

In November 2008, Paulson told reporters that he would not be spending the remaining $410 billion of the TARP funds, hoping to hold the funds for emergency use.

Impact

Paulson served as US treasury secretary until January 2009. During his tenure, he created a number of programs, including the Hope Now Alliance that helped homeowners after the mortgage crisis. He was succeeded by Timothy Geithner. After leaving government, he took a position at the Paul H. Nitze School of Advanced International Studies at Johns Hopkins University in Baltimore, Maryland. In February 2010, Paulson published a memoir entitled *On the Brink: Inside the Race to Stop the Collapse of the Global Financial System.*

Further Reading

Paulson, Henry M. *On the Brink: Inside the Race to Stop the Collapse of the Global Financial Crisis.* New York: Hachette, 2010. Print.

Sorkin, Andrew Ross. *Too Big to Fail: The Inside Story of How Wall Street and Washington Fought to Save the Financial System—and Themselves.* New York: Penguin, 2009. Print.

Zuckerman, Gregory. *The Greatest Trade Ever: The Behind-the-Scenes Story of How John Paulson Defied Wall Street and Made Financial History.* New York: Crown, 2009. Print.

Lee Tunstall

Randy Pausch's "Last Lecture" at Carnegie-Mellon University. (Courtesy Wil Paredes)

■ Pausch, Randy

Identification: American professor
Born: October 23, 1960; Baltimore, Maryland
Died: July 25, 2008; Chesapeake, Virginia

Randy Pausch was a professor of computer science, human-computer interaction and design at Carnegie Mellon University (CMU). He was also an expert on virtual reality, the cocreator of a graduate program in computer-mediated digital technologies, and the director of the research group that developed the Alice software project. In 2007, Pausch became an Internet and media sensation when a speech he delivered at CMU, titled "Last Lecture," became an uncommonly popular video after it was posted on YouTube. Pausch gave the speech after having been diagnosed with pancreatic cancer and being told he had just months to live. In the speech, Pausch encouraged listeners to pursue their childhood dreams and delivered an inspiring message of hope, humor and determination.

In 1997, Randolf Frederick Pausch left the University of Virginia to accept a position as associate professor of computer science, human-computer interaction and design at Carnegie Mellon University

(CMU). He was promoted to full professor in 2000. At CMU, Pausch started an innovative new course in virtual reality programming that brought together undergraduates in diverse fields, including art, drama, design, and computer science. The course, called "Building Virtual Worlds," was an immediate and dramatic success. It proved so popular, in fact, that Pausch and his colleague Don Marinelli, a professor of drama at CMU's School of Fine Arts, decided to work together to build an interdisciplinary masters program around it. The result was the Entertainment Technology Center (ETC). The center quickly gained a reputation for turning out graduates—skilled artists and computer scientists—who were prepared for jobs in the fields of video game, entertainment and virtual reality technology.

Pausch considered the software program known as Alice to be his most important professional legacy. Alice uses a three-dimensional interactive interface to teach high school and college students basic computer programming skills as they develop animated movies and video games. Pausch began working on developing Alice while he was at CMU. Caitlin Kelleher, a graduate student Pausch mentored, has since developed a version of Alice designed specifically to reach middle-school aged girls.

It is a fairly common practice on university campuses for professors to be invited to deliver a "last lecture" to faculty and students—a talk that encapsulates the most important lessons from their careers. Faculty members are typically asked to speak as if this were to be the last lecture they will ever give. Just a few weeks before Pausch was scheduled to deliver his own last lecture, he received the news that he had incurable pancreatic cancer and had a mere three to six months to live. On September 18, 2007, he went ahead with his talk—rather than being a sober speech, it was an exuberant celebration of life. Pausch spoke of his delight in his successes, the debts he owed others, and the importance of following one's dreams. His lecture was delivered to an audience of only a few hundred in an auditorium in CMU, but after a journalist and CMU alumnus wrote a column about the speech and provided a link to an online video of it, Pausch became an instant celebrity.

Not long after he spoke at CMU, Pausch stopped teaching and retired to his home in Virginia. He spent the last several months of his life co-writing a book based on his talk, entitled *The Last Lecture*, and spending time with his family. Pausch died on July 25, 2008, at the age of forty-seven. He was survived by his wife, Jai, his sons Dylan and Logan, and his daughter Chloe.

Impact

In addition to being a notable professor, Pausch also worked for Walt Disney Engineering, Electronic Arts (EA), Google, and Media Matrix. He led the development of Alice, computer software that is used to create three-dimensional computer animation, and he is the author of five books and more than seventy articles. In 2007, he was inducted as a Fellow into the ACM and received the ACM Special Interest Group on Computer Science Education Award.

Further Reading

Marinelli, Donald. *The Comet & the Tornado: Reflections on the Legacy of Randy Pausch.* New York: Sterling, 2010. Print.
Pausch, Randy. *Dream New Dreams: Reimaging My Life After Loss.* New York: Crown, 2012. Print.
___. *The Last Lecture.* New York: Hyperion, 2008. Print.

M. Lee

■ Pelosi, Nancy

Identification: Speaker of the United States House of Representatives, 2007 to 2011
Born: March 26, 1940; Baltimore, Maryland

US congresswoman Nancy Pelosi grew up in a political family, Both her father and brother served as mayor of Baltimore, and her father also served in the US House of Representatives. Rather than following immediately in their footsteps, Pelosi first took time to raise a family and relocate to California, where she began working for a local Democratic committee before becoming a member in the US House of Representatives.

Nancy Pelosi was born Nancy D'Alesandro in March 1940, the daughter of prominent congressman Thomas D'Alesandro and his wife Annunciata. Nancy attended Catholic high school in Baltimore, and graduated from the Institute of Notre Dame in 1958. She earned her bachelor of arts degree in political science from Trinity College in Washington, DC, in 1962.

Pelosi's politics had always been in line with her constituents in the San Francisco area. Firmly entrenched in the left of the political spectrum, she campaigned for gay rights, abortion access, health care for the poor, and human rights around the world. Taking a seat in a congress composed of more moderate Democrats from other less liberal parts of the country was a balancing act for Pelosi. While she easily won re-election term after term, making sure she was not shunned within the party for some of her more controversial causes took considerably more work.

Pelosi had a seat on the House Appropriations Committee, but her big political break came in October 2001, when she was elected the Democratic Party whip. With this position, she became the party's second in command and was distinguished as the highest-ranking woman in Congress. The whip is responsible for strategizing with party members to get legislation passed that furthers the party goals. One of the first tests of her ability in this role was the campaign finance reform bill that Congress passed in 2001. Pelosi worked with members of the House and the Senate through every new amendment and voting shift to keep the bill from being stopped by Republicans.

In the November 2002 congressional elections, Democrats lost control of the House of Representatives, giving the Republicans a twenty-four-seat

Nancy Pelosi. (Courtesy Talk Radio News Service)

majority. Former Democratic majority leader Dick Gephardt left his post to concentrate on his 2004 presidential bid, and Pelosi worked hard to gain support from her fellow Democrats for the job. Despite opposition from Congressman Martin Frost from Tennessee, Pelosi was elected House Minority Leader on November 14, 2002. She was the first woman both to hold such a rank in Congress and to be elected to the top post in a major political party.

In November of 2006, Pelosi was chosen as the first female Speaker of the House after the Democratic Party regained majority of control in Congress. Pelosi was an ardent and vocal supporter of the health care reform initiative of 2009. Following the passage of the Patient Protection and Affordable Care Act (PPACA) in March 2010, Pelosi's work was praised by US president Barack Obama, who called her one of the best Speakers in the history of the US Congress. Following the November 2010 midterm elections, the Republican Party regained control of Congress, forcing Pelosi to step down as Speaker of the House.

Impact

Pelosi was the first woman to serve as the Speaker of the House—making her the highest-ranking female

politician in American history. She is known for her advocacy for women's rights, gay rights, and human rights. Pelosi was an important supporter of health care and played a role in passing Obama's Patient Protection and Affordable Care Act.

Further Reading

Peters, Ronald M., Jr., and Cindy Simon Rosenthal. *Speaker Nancy Pelosi and the New American Politics.* New York: Oxford UP, 2010. Print.

Povich, Elaine S. *Nancy Pelosi: A Biography.* Westport: Greenwood, 2008. Print.

Sandalow, Marc. *Madam Speaker: Nancy Pelosi's Life, Times, and Rise to Power.* New York: Rodale, 2008. Print.

Brenda Kim

■ Pharmaceutical industry

Definition: The industry that researches, develops, manufactures, and markets prescription and over-the-counter drugs earned enormous profits and drew criticism throughout the 2000s

The United States has the largest pharmaceutical industry in the world. Fueled by the aging population, technological advances, and global competition, the industry expanded tremendously in the 2000s. Research and development continued to grow during the decade. The pharmaceutical industry was affected during the 2000s, however, by numerous lawsuits regarding the safety of medications.

The pharmaceutical industry has created an abundance of different drugs to treat an array of ailments. Because of this, many health-care providers began to rely less on invasive surgeries and other procedures and more on treating ailments with prescription medications. The pharmaceutical industry came into the forefront during the 1980s and 1990s as it focused on developing more drugs, including those to treat cancer, heart disease, and AIDS. During the next two decades, pharmaceutical companies relied heavily on research and development of new drugs and various ways to market and distribute them.

Billions of dollars go into the research and development of new drugs each year. The high cost is due to the high risk involved and the many steps pharmaceutical companies must take to develop and test new drugs. Creating and developing a new drug cost more than $1.3 billion in 2005, according to the US pharmaceutical industry's advocacy group Pharmaceutical Research and Manufacturers of America. In addition to the high cost, time is a factor when developing drugs. It takes an average of twelve years to develop a new drug, and while patents exist for medications, they typically only last twenty years. Other drug companies can release generic versions of name-brand drugs once a patent expires. Also, research is expensive because only a tiny percentage of newly developed drugs make it to clinical trials, and even fewer reach the human testing phase. Only about 10 percent of all new drugs make it to human testing, and only 2 percent will be approved for use. Many scientists—including biochemists, chemists, molecular biologists, pharmacologists, physiologists, statisticians, and toxicologists—are involved in the research of new drugs. They are needed to study every aspect of a drug from its makeup to how it works.

New Drug Development

Drug companies must go through several stages to develop a drug. During preclinical research, scientists research diseases and ailments and develop experimental drugs to combat these diseases and ailments. These experimental drugs are then tested in laboratories and animal studies. After this step is complete, the drug company must file an investigational new drug application (IND) with the US Food and Drug Administration (FDA), which monitors and regulates the pharmaceutical industry. If the IND is approved, the drug company can move to clinical trials.

During phase I of the clinical trials, drugs are administered to a small number of patients, and the safety and tolerability of the drugs is studied. If successful, the drug moves to phase II, which tests the effectiveness of a drug. During this phase, researchers determine many factors about the medication, including its safety and risks as well as its dosage. If the drug is deemed effective and safe, it will move to phase III. During this phase, the drug is administered to a larger number of people to confirm its safety and effectiveness. After these steps are complete, the pharmaceutical company must file a new drug application (NDA), which contains all of the information regarding the new drug. If the FDA approves the drug, it can be made and distributed. It must also undergo phase IV of the process, in which drug

companies continue studying a drug to determine if any long-term side effects exist.

Drug Safety and Lawsuits

Throughout the 2000s, many lawsuits were filed against pharmaceutical companies regarding the safety of certain drugs. Sometimes through continued research, drug companies find that their drugs have harmful side effects that were not apparent during the initial testing. This was the case with pharmaceutical giant Merck and its painkiller Vioxx. The company found that those taking Vioxx showed an increased risk of heart attack and stroke, so it pulled the drug off the market in 2004. In 2007 the company settled thousands of lawsuits concerning Vioxx. The following year, Johnson & Johnson settled hundreds of lawsuits filed by patients using the Ortho Evra birth-control patch. The lawsuits claimed that the patch caused blood clots, heart attacks, strokes, and death in some cases. Other lawsuits during this time questioned the safety of drugs such as Wyeth's Prempro and Premarin hormone-replacement drugs, AstraZeneca's antipsychotic drug Seroquel, and Pfizer's antiseizure medication Neurontin.

Impact

The pharmaceutical industry has had many positive as well as negative impacts on American consumers and physicians. It has developed many drugs that have greatly improved the quality of life for those suffering from diseases and ailments. It continues to research and develop drugs that in the future could impact those suffering from incurable diseases, such as AIDS. The industry has been blamed, however, for not fully testing drugs that have been found to have harmful side effects, including death. It also is often criticized for pushing unneeded drugs on Americans through aggressive marketing and advertising campaigns.

Further Reading

California Biomedical Research Association. "Fact Sheet: New Drug Development Process." *California Biomedical Research Association.* California Biomedical Research Association. Web. 30 Nov. 2012. PDF file. A fact sheet explaining the new drug development phases.

Gavura, Scott. "What Does a New Drug Cost?" *Science-Based Medicine.* Science-Based Medicine, 14 Apr.

2011. Web. 30 Nov. 2012. An article exploring the costs of developing new drugs.

Helfer, Adam. "Drugging America: The Drug Industry Exposed." *Washington Times.* Washington Times LLC, 27 Mar. 2011. Web. 3 Dec. 2012. An interview with a former pharmaceutical representative who speaks critically of the industry's aggressive marketing tactics.

Schmit, Julie. "More Drugs Get Slapped with Lawsuits." *USA Today.* USA Today, 23 Aug. 2006. Web. 1 Dec. 2012. Describes recent legal challenges to a number of pharmaceutical companies.

Wadman, Meredith. "Merck Settles Vioxx Lawsuits for $4.85 Billion." *Nature.* Nature Publishing Group, 13 Nov. 2007. Web. 30 Nov. 2012. This article describes the legal challenges to Merck regarding the side effects linked to Vioxx.

Angela Harmon

■ Phelps, Michael

Identification: Olympic swimmer
Born: June 30, 1985; Towson, Maryland

At the age of fifteen, Michael Phelps became the youngest swimmer since 1932 to compete for the United States in the Olympic Games. Afterward, he went on to compete in three Olympics, winning a total of eighteen gold medals, the most by any Olympian in the modern era.

Michael Fred Phelps was born on June 30, 1985, in Baltimore, Maryland, to Fred and Debbie Phelps. In 1999, at the age of fifteen, Phelps earned a spot on the US Olympic team for the 2000 Summer Olympic Games in Sydney, Australia. In securing his position, he made history as the youngest swimmer on the Olympic team since thirteen-year-old Ralph Flanagan competed in the 1932 Los Angeles Olympic Games. Phelps's performance in Sydney was not quite as impressive as his Olympic trials, however; he placed fifth in the 200-meter butterfly.

At the Phillips 66 National Championships in August 2001, Phelps set a new world record in the 200-meter butterfly. He then took first place in the 100-meter butterfly. Later that same year, he won the 200-meter butterfly in the Pan Pacific Swimming Championships in Fukuoka, Japan.

At the 2002 US National Championships, Phelps came in first in four events: the 100-meter and

Michael Phelps. (Courtesy J. D. Lasica)

200-meter butterflies and the 200-meter and 400-meter medleys. He established a new world record in the 400-meter medley with a time of 4:11:09. By the end of 2002, Phelps was the world's best swimmer in three events. He had won gold medals in the 200-meter and 400-meter individual medleys and a silver medal in the 200-meter butterfly in the 2002 Pan Pacific games. He also helped the US four-man team win the 400-meter medley with a world-record time of 3:33:48. His leg of the race was the fastest ever in the history of the event.

At the Spring Nationals, Phelps became the first individual to win in three different swimming categories at one national event. In Barcelona, he medaled six times and set five new world records, and at the Summer Nationals, he became the first man to claim five national titles in a single swim meet. By the end of the year, Phelps's success had won him a $9-million-endorsement contract with Speedo and worldwide attention.

The following summer, Phelps qualified for six individual and two relay-team events for the 2004 Olympics in Athens, Greece. The publicity around his Olympic qualification focused on the possibility of Phelps matching or beating Mark Spitz's 1972 record of seven gold medals during a single Olympics. At the age of nineteen, Phelps set two Olympic records and won six gold and two bronze medals at the Athens Olympics, but he did not break Spitz's record.

In 2005, Phelps enrolled at the University of Michigan and began working toward a degree in sports marketing and management. His coach took a varsity coaching job at the school, and Phelps began working as his assistant while continuing to train. However, Phelps was not permitted to participate in collegiate swimming because of his endorsement deals.

Phelps qualified for eight events for the 2008 Olympic Games in Beijing, China, positioning him once again to strive for Spitz's 1972 record. By the end of the Olympics, Phelps had set seven world records and one Olympic record and had accomplished his goal as an Olympian. He had broken Spitz's thirty-six-year-old record by winning a total of eight gold medals in a single Olympics. He not only surpassed Spitz's total medals but also competed in a wider variety of events. While Spitz had only competed in freestyle and butterfly events, Phelps competed in all four swimming strokes—the freestyle, butterfly, breaststroke, and backstroke.

At the 2012 Olympic Games in London, England, Phelps won four gold and two silver medals. He retired from competitive swimming soon after the games.

Impact

Phelps is the most decorate Olympian of all time, with twenty-two medals, eighteen of which are gold. In the 2008 Olympic Games in Beijing, Phelps won eight gold medals—setting the record for most in a single Olympics. Phelps also set thirty-nine world records and is the most successful Olympic swimmer in history. In addition to his athletic success, Phelps founded the Michael Phelps Foundation, an organization devoted to swimming and promoting a healthy lifestyle.

Further Reading

Phelps, Michael. *Beneath the Surface: My Story.* New York: Sports, 2004. Print.

—. *No Limits: The Will to Succeed.* New York: Simon, 2008. Print.

Zuehlke, Jeffrey. *Michael Phelps (Amazing Athletes).* Minneapolis: Lerner, 2005. Print.

Lynn-nore Chittom

■ Phishing

Definition: The act of using various communication devices such as e-mail and telephones in an attempt to trick individuals into either revealing their personal information, including passwords and social security numbers, or installing malicious software (malware)

Phishing is used by identity thieves to acquire the confidential personal and financial information of victims. The term is a variation of "fishing" and refers to identity thieves fishing for victims. Identity thieves, also referred to as "phishers," pose as representatives from banks, credit card companies, or other financial institutions and e-mail or call victims requesting their personal information. Phishers offer several fraudulent reasons for why the victim must enter their personal information. Phishing raised many concerns over online security in the 2000s.

Phishing first became popular during the early days of America Online (AOL), one of the first prevalent Internet providers. Phishers would pretend to be AOL employees and send users instant messages requesting their passwords for confirmation purposes. Once they procured users' passwords, phishers could use them to access their accounts for spamming or other nefarious purposes. AOL eventually put policies into place to delete the accounts of anyone involved with phishing and to quickly detect any instant messages that contained phishing-related words.

After AOL's security increased, phishers started to pretend to be financial institutions such as banks and credit card companies. The first known phishing attempt in which the perpetrator pretended to be a financial institution was in June 2001. A phisher posed as e-gold, a website that allowed users to instantly transfer gold currency. Although this attempt was unsuccessful, it was used by phishers as a test to develop more successful methods.

Following the terrorist attacks on September 11, 2001, phishers began sending out fraudulent identification check e-mails. Recipients were asked to enter their personal information to confirm their identities for reasons of national security. These attempts were also seen as failures but were used to test new methods of phishing.

Online Phishing

After the unsuccessful phishing attempts in the early part of the 2000s, phishers started implementing more sophisticated methods to acquire victims' personal information. By 2004, phishing was seen as a serious and lucrative criminal activity. It led to heightened online security, increased awareness, and several lawsuits and government actions.

Many phishers pose as social media websites such as Facebook. They send users e-mails claiming that they noticed a security issue on the account and that, as a result, users must fill out legal forms, such as terms of use or copyrights law forms. These phishers typically state that if users do not comply and fill out the form, their account will be terminated. A link is usually included in the e-mail that is disguised with a legitimate address, such as Facebook's web address; in reality, the link will download an executable file if clicked. This kind of trickery is how phishers get victims to download malicious software that exposes personal information and passwords.

Oftentimes phishers include company logos in their e-mails to make them look legitimate. There are several ways to tell whether an e-mail is a phishing scam or not. Many times words are misspelled or threats of account deletion are made.

In 2006, phishers began using e-mails to pose as the US Internal Revenue Service (IRS). In response, the IRS issued several consumer warnings about the use of the IRS logo for phishing and identity-theft purposes. Several of these IRS-related e-mail phishing scams claimed that the individual was owed a tax refund. The individual was then asked to enter personal information in order to receive the money owed them. The IRS established several ways for consumers to report suspicious e-mails that might be phishing scams.

Some phishers set up fraudulent or replica websites to pose as financial institutions. Once one of these fake websites was visited, users could unknowingly receive malicious software. Even on legitimate websites, phishers could alter the sites' scripts and security aspects to fool users. This was a particularly successful phishing method because the fraudulent websites were nearly undetectable to average online users.

In 2006, this type of phishing was done on the website PayPal, which allows users to easily transfer money to other bank accounts. Phishers used the PayPal website to trick users into going to a uniform resource locator (URL) hosted on the legitimate PayPal website. Phishers created a warning message that appeared when users visited the website that said the user's account was disabled because it may have been accessed unlawfully by a third party. Users were then redirected to a fraudulent PayPal login page that looked extremely similar to the actual login page.

This technique was also frequently used on the websites of banks. When users visited the sites, a pop-up window would appear that requested their personal login information for security purposes. Financial institutions responded by increasing online security measures through the use of security questions and images. For example, in 2008, Bank of America implemented a SiteKey system on its website in which users choose an image that appears every time they login. If the image does not appear during the login process, the user has been led to a fraudulent site. Other companies hit with phishing attacks during the 2000s included Best Buy, the United Parcel Service (UPS), and First Union Bank.

File-sharing websites and services such as RapidShare were also used by phishers to harvest information or leave computers vulnerable for later attack. Phishers would use fake websites or alter legitimate ones to sell users RapidShare upgrades that did not exist. Sometimes phishers would send out e-mail newsletters posing as file-sharing websites or would post in forums, encouraging users to pay for fake upgrades. Both of these phishing methods were used to steal victims' credit card information.

A majority of online phishing in the 2000s was traced to the Russian Business Network (RBN). RBN is a cybercrime organization based in Russia that performs identity theft on a large scale. It undertook some of the largest and most successful phishing scams of the decade, oftentimes selling personal information to criminals for use in identity theft. RBN developed malicious software such as the MPack, which is a kit that was sold to hackers to infect hundreds of thousands of personal computers.

Phone Phishing

Phishers also used phones to acquire personal financial information. This method became known as "vishing." Sometimes they would e-mail messages posing as financial institutions or Internet providers. At other times, phishers would steal a list of phone numbers from financial institutions and call the victims themselves. Once victims were on the phone, they would be asked to enter their debit card pin number, Social Security number, or other personal information. The phone numbers victims called would be owned by the phishers, who typically used a voice-over Internet protocol (VoIP) to disguise the location of their numbers, making phishers difficult to locate. A VoIP allows phishers to make and receive phone calls using their computer and Internet connection.

Phishers could even use VoIPs to disguise the caller identification on the victims' end. They could call a victim and have the caller identification information correspond to that of a trusted bank or other entity. This made vishing hard to monitor.

Other phishers used phones to pose as technical support departments from Internet providers or software companies such as Microsoft. Phishers used this method to install malicious software (commonly known as "malware") to gain access to sensitive information. Frequently, once the malicious software had been installed, phishers would charge victims to remove it from their computer. Phishers also used this method to adjust settings on victims' computers to leave them vulnerable to further unlawful access.

In response, financial institutions, Internet providers, and software companies released several warnings stating that they would never call and request information or make charges via the phone. They stated that if anyone calls claiming to be from their institution, that individuals should hang up and report the number.

Combating Phishing

The sharp rise in phishing during the 2000s and the massive financial losses it caused led to several antiphishing responses on public and federal levels. The most basic method of combating phishing was to educate the public on how to recognize these scams. The IRS released several consumer warnings throughout the decade, and software companies, including Microsoft, published materials online to inform the public about phishing. Along with online consumer warnings, the IRS released informational videos and podcasts and provided consumers with e-mails and telephone numbers they could contact if they suspected they were the target of phishing attempts.

Because of phishing, several websites, financial institutions, and other entities changed the way they handled e-mails and information online. For example, PayPal began to include users' login names in e-mails to let them know they were not being phished. Typically, phishing e-mails would address users with generic greetings, such as "Dear PayPal user." In a similar fashion, banks started to include partial account numbers in e-mails. However, studies conducted in 2006 found that including personal information in an e-mail did not prevent phishing, since phishers typically used the same tactics to bait victims.

Many popular Internet browsers implemented measures for what became known as "secure browsing." Several Internet browsers began to include antiphishing technology as part of their browsers and services. If a user attempts to visit a website that is not recognized as secure by Firefox, for example, a warning box will appear or Firefox will simply block the website.

E-mail servers such as Gmail increased their e-mail spam filters to help combat phishing. Many of these filters utilize language processing to recognize and block e-mails that include common phishing words and sentences.

The US Federal Trade Commission (FTC) set up services to help reduce telephone phishing scams. Their services encouraged users to report suspicious phone calls and phone numbers. The FTC then passed on this information to appropriate law-enforcement officials. Individuals could also register their phone number on the National Do Not Call Registry, which limits the number of telemarketers and potential phishers that can call the number.

Federal responses

In 2004, the FTC filed a lawsuit against a seventeen-year-old in California who was suspected of perpetrating phishing scams to acquire credit card information. This was the first law-enforcement action brought against a phisher. In 2006, the Federal Bureau of Investigation enacted an operation code-named Cardkeeper that led to the arrest of seventeen people involved with international phishing scams in the United States, Poland, and Romania. This group allegedly stole identities, credit card information, and bank information. Four suspects from the group were arrested in the United States and were in possession of machines used to encode cards with victims' bank information.

On December 16, 2003, US president George W. Bush signed the Controlling the Assault of Non-Solicited Pornography and Marketing Act (CAN-SPAM Act). This act established national standards for the distribution of commercial e-mail. The FTC was given authority to enforce the provisions put forth by the act. It was created to reduce the amount of unwarranted and unwanted e-mails, including phishing-related messages. Although many critics saw it as a failure, the first individual convicted under its provisions was sentenced in 2007. This individual, Jeffrey Brett Goodin, sent thousands of e-mails posing as the

AOL billing department and requesting users' personal information. He was sentenced to serve seventy months in prison.

Impact

Phishing raised several concerns about the security of valuable personal information that is frequently used online by banks and other entities. During the 2000s, various phishing methods managed to successfully rob victims of billions of dollars. Businesses affected by phishing also lost billions of dollars. Phishing was the most successful cybercrime method of the decade and changed the way information is distributed online. Its rise also led to an increase in awareness and heightened security on several fronts.

Further Reading

Jakobsson, Markus, and Steven Myers, eds. *Phishing and Countermeasures: Understanding the Increasing Problem of Electronic Identity Theft.* Hoboken: Wiley, 2006. Print. Presents information from several authorities on phishing from a variety of perspectives.

James, Lance. *Phishing Exposed.* Rockland: Syngress, 2006. Print. Discusses the various techniques used by phishers.

Krebs, Brian. "Shadowy Russian Firm Seen as Conduit for Cybercrime." *Washington Post.* Washington Post, 13 Oct. 2007. Web. 14 Dec. 2012. Examines RBN and its involvement with various cybercrimes, including phishing. Offers an international perspective.

Lininger, Rachael, and Russell Dean Vines. *Phishing: Cutting the Identity Theft Line.* Hoboken: Wiley, 2005. Print. Presents information on phishing prevention for average Internet users and helps readers to identify phishing attempts.

"Phishing." *OnGuardOnline.gov.* Federal Trade Commission, n.d. Web. 14 Dec. 2012. Provides an overview of phishing, examples of fraudulent e-mails, and methods of addressing phishing scams and reporting them.

Patrick G. Cooper

■ Photography

Definition: The 2000s saw the introduction of camera phones and the increasing sophistication and affordability of digital cameras

The 2000s decade represented one of the most transformative periods in the 170-year history of photography. Known as the "digital revolution," by the end of the decade almost all photographers had switched from film cameras to digital equipment, making film processing and the darkroom virtually obsolete as new uses for photography and new perspectives on the art emerged in society.

The 2000s decade represented the digital revolution, an era of vast technological advancements in photographic equipment, resulting in an exciting time for photography enthusiasts. The first widely affordable digital single-lens reflex (DSLR) cameras appeared on the consumer market, with the popular Nikon D1 in 1999 and Canon's Digital Rebel in 2000, steering a new generation of amateur photographers toward digital photography. By 2004, US sales of digital cameras had surpassed the sales of film cameras, prompting Polaroid to discontinue production of its popular instant film in 2008—to the outrage of many photography enthusiasts. By the end of the decade, the average camera's resolution had significantly improved, and digital cameras were offering high-definition video, wi-fi capability, and many other improved functions. Point-and-shoot cameras shrunk in size and their features became increasingly sophisticated, guaranteeing effortless and near-perfect exposures. The first cell phones equipped with cameras appeared on the US market in 2002, and by the end of the decade had made the sharing of instant snapshots a ubiquitous activity. During the 2005 London bombings, nearly all news footage of the event was captured by amateur photographers using cell-phone cameras.

New ways of storing and presenting photo collections were made possible by the introduction of Flickr in 2004 and other Internet sites, digital frames, and digital photo albums. The art of digital photography was at first considered a separate entity from traditional photography, until digital cameras became the standard tool. Some of the most memorable photographs from the decade include the documentary shots of the terrorist attacks on the World Trade Center and images taken by embedded photographers during the Iraq War.

Impact

By the end of the decade, almost all photographers—professional and amateur—had switched to digital equipment and techniques, resulting in the closing of thousands of photo-processing centers. In 2009,

Kodak announced it would no longer make Kodachrome, previously one of the most successful brands of color film, officially signifying the end of an era. The digital revolution ushered in new applications for photography in medicine, science, and other disciplines, while in the arts it meant a shift in aesthetic values, largely related to the ability to manipulate photo files in Adobe Photoshop and other software. The ease of sharing photos via e-mail, social-networking sites, and online albums united individuals, but also had some unwelcome results, including lawsuits over copyright infringement and privacy issues.

Further Reading

Dijck, van José. "Digital Photography: Communication, Identity, Memory." *Visual Communication* 7.1 (2008): 57–76. Print.

Ritchin, Fred. *After Photography.* New York: Norton, 2008. Print.

Sally Driscoll

■ Photovoltaics

Definition: The conversion of solar radiation into electricity for use in powering a variety of devices

Solar power research expanded greatly in the 2000s, leading to the development of photovoltaic (PV) panels that were increasingly cost competitive with traditional power sources. Leading up to the decade, PV power had limited applications due to its high cost per watt, and PV technology was often used to power simple devices, such as calculators and watches, or highly specialized and expensive systems such as telecommunications satellites. Through the 2000s, PV technology was increasingly used to power residential homes, communications centers, and other complex systems.

"Photovoltaics," or "PV," is another term for solar cells that can convert sunlight directly into electricity. The conversion is known as the PV effect. As manufacturing and installation costs dropped throughout the 2000s, solar panels increasingly came to be used in residential and commercial buildings. Homes that utilize PV power commonly have about ten to twenty solar panels positioned in the direct path of the sun. Commercial buildings and business that utilize PV power sometimes use hundreds of solar panels in a large interconnected PV system known as a "solar array."

Solar panels in Lovell, NV. (Courtesy Scott)

While most PV panels are installed directly onto the buildings they power, several solar power plants have been constructed in the United States. The Martin Next Generation Solar Energy Center in Martin County, Florida, was constructed in 2008 for the Florida Power and Light Company (FPL). The FPL expects the plant to drastically reduce carbon emissions and gas consumption from their nearby electrical power plant.

During the decade, the US government created incentives for individuals and businesses to install solar panels. The Energy Policy Act of 2005 established a 30 percent investment tax credit for businesses and individuals who installed solar energy systems in 2006 and 2007. In 2008, the tax credit was extended for one additional year. Also in 2008, the US Department of Energy's Solar America Initiative announced they would invest $17.6 million in six early-stage PV power projects collectively known as the PV Incubator. The goal of the PV Incubator was to fund prototype PV technology for commercial use. Despite these investments and incentives, the United States steadily lost its share of the PV market through the 2000s. In 2010, the United States accounted for only 8 percent of total PV production worldwide, compared to 44 percent in 1996.

Environmental issues such as global warming and carbon emissions became key political topics during the 2000s. Some advantages of PV power are that it does not produce carbon emissions, reduces air pollution, and is an unlimited resource. The high cost of the technology is the biggest disadvantage, as is the large amount of space the technology needs in order to be efficient. Despite these disadvantages, the use of PV power continued to increase throughout the decade.

Impact

Improved PV technology quickly changed the energy industry in the United States. A 2008 report from the Solar Energy Industries Association stated that solar energy capacity in the United States had increased by 17 percent in 2007. By the end of the decade, approximately 2,528 megawatts of PV power had been installed across the country. A report produced by Clean Edge, an energy-consulting firm, projects that 10 percent of US electricity needs could be met by solar power by 2025.

Further Reading

Harris, Arno. "A Silver Lining in Declining Solar Prices." *Renewable Energy News*. RenewableEnergy-World.com, 31 Aug. 2011. Web. 14 Dec. 2012.

Nelson, Jenny. *The Physics of Solar Cells (Properties of Semiconductor Materials)*. Imperial College P, 2003. Print.

"U.S. Solar Industry Year in Review 2008." *SEIA*. Solar Energy Industries Association, 2008. Web. 14 Dec. 2012.

Patrick G. Cooper

■ Pickens, T. Boone

Identification: American entrepreneur and activist
Born: May 22, 1928; Holdenville, Oklahoma

Throughout his career as a businessman, T. Boone Pickens has been an oil man, corporate raider, activist shareholder, hedge fund manager, political activist, and a reluctant environmentalist. In 2008, Pickens launched his own campaign for the Pickens Plan, which calls for massive wind farms to be built on the Great Plains to generate electricity. Pickens argues that this would reduce America's dependence on foreign oil and leave the country more financially and physically secure. However, the difficulties that would have to be overcome for the Pickens Plan to work are considered immense.

Thomas Boone Pickens Jr. founded Mesa Petroleum in 1964 and helped it become one of the largest independent oil corporations in the world. In 1997, Pickens started BP Energy Fund (now known as BP

T. Boone Pickens (right) with Harry Reid. (UNLV Photo/Geri Kodey)

Capital Management), a hedge fund firm that looked after two energy funds: Capital Commodity and Capital Equity. As a successful hedge fund manager, Pickens used some of his money for philanthropic, or charitable, efforts, the largest of which was his $165 million gift to his alma mater, Oklahoma State University, in 2006. Despite his good intentions, his gift was criticized, largely because, as a condition of the gift, Pickens had authority over where the gift was invested. Almost as soon as the gift was given to the university, it was reinvested in BP Capital. Adding to the mix, Pickens used his gift as a tax write-off. Directing the money into his own investment group assured him of indirect financial gain from a tax-exempt gift. While some saw this as an ethical conflict of interest, the gift and its investment were not illegal under US federal law.

The 2004 US presidential campaign between Texas governor George W. Bush and Senator John Kerry (D-MA) saw active involvement from Pickens, a lifelong conservative. As with many others during that election, Pickens was caught up in the antagonism that pitted the Republicans against the Democrats in a particularly divisive election. One of the most controversial elements surrounding the election were the 527 groups, named for the part of the US tax code that gives them tax-exempt status. A 527 group is allowed to raise funds and work to elect a candidate they favor as long as their efforts are independent and are not coordinated with the party or candidate they favor.

Pickens funded approximately $3 million worth of television ads for the Swift Boat Veterans, adding heated rhetoric to the political debate. He was so confident of his position that he dared the public to prove that the Swift Boat Veterans accusations were wrong and promised anyone who could do so $1 million. When a group of veterans presented Pickens with ten inaccurate charges against Senator Kerry, Pickens reneged on his $1 million prize offer.

Pickens is unapologetic about his position during the 2004 election, but by 2008 his political motivations had moved him closer to the Democrats than would have been conceivable four years earlier. During 2008, as the Iraq War dragged on, emerging economies increased their demand for oil and multinational oil companies cut back on oil exploration projects. As a result, global oil supplies dwindled, sending the price of oil higher and higher. This sparked a heated debate about the oil industry and the issues upon which oil has a direct impact, such as environmentalism, national security, foreign policy and the economy. Pickens believed that the government was on the wrong track concerning energy sustainability, and as a result, he introduced his own strategy called the Pickens Plan.

The Pickens Plan argues that the United States needs to reduce its dependency on foreign oil, which would in turn reduce the need for military action in the Middle East. Pickens argues that reducing foreign oil imports will create jobs in the United States and help stimulate the economy, which was sent reeling after several financial crises. Pickens calls for large tracts of land from Texas to the Canadian border to be converted into wind farms, which would convert wind energy into electricity to power the major urban centers in the country. According to the plan, this would in turn free up the natural gas that is currently being used in homes to power automobiles and trucks. Pickens believes that this plan would reduce American dependence on foreign oil by up to 40 percent, and save approximately $300 billion a year. As of 2008, the United States held 3 percent of global oil reserves, consumed 20 percent of the world's annual oil production, and spent $700 billion per year importing foreign oil.

However, the Pickens Plan would require a significant restructuring of North American power grids, and would require American car manufacturers to increase their production of natural gas-powered cars. The plan also means that service stations would have to invest heavily in natural gas pumping stations. To offset these concerns, Pickens plans to invest $10 billion to build a wind energy farm in Texas, and has invested $58 million in a print and media advertising campaign to deliver his message. Pickens believes that the energy crisis cannot be solved through further drilling for oil. He believes that the root problems of the country's energy supplies must be addressed and an alternative energy industry must be developed.

His advocacy for wind energy, cleaner burning gas and the reduction of crude oil has brought him approval from leading Democrats such as Senator Harry Reid (D-NV) and former Vice President Al Gore, as well as the environmental group Sierra Club. Despite these unusual allies, Pickens does not consider himself an environmentalist and favors an integrated solution with increased nuclear power plants and offshore oil drilling as a short-term remedy. Pickens does believe that climate change is a real threat, but his concerns are focused mainly on the American economy and security, with environmentalism as a side effect of his goals. As the largest private owner of natural-gas fuelling stations, Pickens is poised to reap huge financial benefits from natural gas fueling stations and wind farms.

As of 2009, Pickens continues to make appearances throughout the world in support of alternative energy projects.

Impact

In addition to his success in business, Pickens has played a significant role in politics—donating over $5 million to President Bush and other Republican candidates and groups. Pickens was involved in promoting and spreading the awareness of alternative energy. He established the Pickens Plan, legislation that called for an increase in domestic energy sources and a decrease in the dependence on foreign oil and natural gas. He is also a philanthropist who has donated over $700 million to charities, including Oklahoma State University.

Further Reading

Breslau, Karen. "The Pickens Profile You Haven't Read." *Newsweek.* Newsweek/Daily Beast Co. LLC, 9 Aug. 2008. Web. 15 Nov. 2012.

Egan, Timothy. "The Oil Man Cometh." *New York Times.* New York Times Co., 24 July 2008. Web. 15 Nov. 2012.

Strom, Stephanie. "Billionaire Gives a Big Gift but Still Gets to Invest It." *New York Times.* New York Times Co., 24 Feb. 2006. Web. 15 Nov. 2012.

                                                                Ian Paul

■ Piracy

Definition: An act of theft committed at sea that usually involves violent struggle

Twenty-first century pirates wield heavy artillery and are much more dangerous than their more colorful and storied predecessors. Modern pirates have been known to hijack ships and to take hostages. During the late 2000s, a surge of highly violent piracy threats prompted the United States to take action.

During the 2000s, acts of piracy were most often committed against transport vessels that held valuable cargo. In some instances, pirates hijacked commercial cruise ships and other liners, robbing passengers and crews of their belongings. Pirates were also known to take crew members and even passengers hostage, demanding hefty ransoms. Global piracy was rampant at the beginning of the twenty-first century. By 2005, however, the number of pirate hijackings around the world had decreased by nearly half.

Though pirate attacks were decreasing on a global scale, the reverse was true in certain regions. The number of pirate attacks off the coast of Somalia quadrupled between 2007 and 2009. Somali pirates generally held ships hostage for ransom. Somalia is along the coast of the Gulf of Aden, which acts as a passageway for more than thirty-three thousand commercial ships annually; 279 pirate attacks occurred within the Gulf of Aden between 2007 and 2009, and 87 were successful. The attacks threatened international maritime trade and cost nations millions of dollars in ransom payments. The Somali threat became so severe that the United States—concerned about its maritime industry—decided to take action against these outlaws.

Somali Threat

The United States was directly affected by the Somali threat in November of 2005 when a boat full of Somali pirates opened fire on the American-owned cruise liner the *Seabourn Spirit.* The ship managed to change direction and escape, but the attack drew attention to the dangers of piracy.

Negotiations between the pirates and authorities proved mostly ineffective. In April 2009, Somali pirates stormed the decks of the US-flagged container ship MV *Maersk Alabama*, which was carrying food supplies to eastern Somalia. The pirates took the ship's captain hostage, holding him in a lifeboat for four days before American snipers fatally shot the kidnappers. The MV *Liberty Sun*—another American cargo ship carrying aid supplies—was attacked just a few days later, though the effort was unsuccessful. *Maersk Alabama* was attacked by Somali pirates for a second time in November of 2009, but the crew thwarted the assault. The attacks warranted a more concentrated effort at fending off pirates in the Gulf of Aden.

US Response

Beginning in 2005, the United States developed the National Strategy for Maritime Security, partnering with other affected nations to aid in the safety of the world's oceans. In its efforts to keep Somali pirate attacks at bay, the United States engaged in a number of confrontations throughout the late 2000s. In March 2006, a Somali pirate died in an exchange of fire with two US Navy warships, part of a force tasked with securing the region against piracy. Another US Navy ship attempted to engage Somali pirates in international waters after the pirates hijacked a Danish vessel in June 2007. The military ship was forced to abandon its pursuit when the hijackers took the boat into Somali waters, however.

In December 2008, the US National Security Council issued the Countering Piracy off the Horn of Africa: Partnership and Action Plan. After the pirate attacks in 2009 against the *Maersk Alabama* and *Liberty Sun*, American officials called for more peacekeeping efforts between the United States and Somalia as well as an expansion of forces dedicated to patrolling the oceans against piracy. The government also asked the shipping industry to reassess its self-defense strategies to better safeguard ships.

Impact

Despite global prevention efforts, pirate attacks plagued many areas, especially those sandwiched between the Red Sea and the Indian Ocean. The increase in pirate attacks along the Somali coast brought together many nations in an attempt to protect maritime commerce. Many more countries continued to join in the US fight against piracy as they recognized the necessity of defending the world's oceans.

Further Reading

UN Office on Drugs and Crime. "Maritime Piracy." *United Nations Office on Drugs and Crime.* UNODC, 2009. PDF File. Global analysis of the incidence of maritime piracy in 2009.

US Bureau of Political Military Affairs. "United States Actions to Counter Piracy off the Horn of Africa." *US Department of State.* US Dept. of State, 1 Sept. 2009. Web. 4 Dec. 2012. Overview of the US response to piracy.

US Bureau of Public Affairs, Office of the Spokesman. "Taking Diplomatic Action against Piracy." *US Department of State.* US Dept. of State, 13 May 2009. Web. 4 Dec. 2012. Diplomatic action taken by the Contact Group on Piracy off the Coast of Somalia.

US Department of Transportation Maritime Administration. "Countering Piracy off the Horn of Africa: Partnership and Action Plan." *National Security Council.* National Security Council, 2008. PDF File. Plan of action set in motion by the United States and partnering nations to address the surge in marine piracy.

White House. "The National Strategy for Maritime Security." *White House.* White House, 20 Sept. 2005. Web. 4 Dec. 2012. Strategy developed during the administration of US President George W. Bush in response to various maritime threats.

Cait Caffrey

■ *Pirates of the Caribbean* series

Identification: A series of fantasy adventure films based on the classic Walt Disney theme-park attraction of the same name

Director: Gore Verbinski (b. 1964)

Date: Released on July 9, 2003; July 7, 2006; May 25, 2007

The Pirates of the Caribbean *film series of the 2000s capitalized on the rising use of modern technology in Hollywood productions to help revive interest in the long-dormant pirate genre. It became not only a monstrous critical and commercial success but also a cultural phenomenon.*

The *Pirates of the Caribbean* film franchise helped reinvent and breathe new life into a long-forgotten pirate genre that had once flourished during the golden age of Hollywood in the 1930s and 1940s. Based on the eponymous log flume–style boat attraction at several Walt Disney theme parks, the film series flaunted state-of-the-art digital effects like computer-generated imagery (CGI) and three-dimensional (3D) animation, as well as a large number of big-name stars, creating mass appeal for audiences young and old.

The first installment of the series, *Pirates of the Caribbean: The Curse of the Black Pearl*, was released in 2003. Directed by Gore Verbinski, produced by Jerry Bruckheimer, and written by Ted Elliott and Terry Rossio, the film follows an entertainingly eccentric and wily rum-swilling pirate, Captain Jack Sparrow (Johnny Depp), as he embarks on a quest with a blacksmith, Will Turner (Orlando Bloom), to rescue Turner's love interest, Elizabeth Swann (Keira Knightley), the strong-willed and beautiful daughter of Governor Weatherby Swann (Jonathan Pryce) of Port Royal, Jamaica, who has been kidnapped by Sparrow's nemesis, the nefarious pirate Captain Hector Barbossa (Geoffrey Rush). The film unexpectedly became a major commercial hit, grossing over $650 million worldwide. It also gained much critical success, earning five Academy Award nominations, including one for best actor for Depp, whose memorably iconic portrayal helped catapult him from a highly respected but largely unbankable idiosyncratic actor to one of Hollywood's biggest and highest-paid stars.

The unexpected success of *The Curse of the Black Pearl* and the growing 2000s trend of Hollywood film franchises and reboots inevitably led to back-to-back sequels, *Dead Man's Chest* (2006) and *At World's End* (2007), both of which were again directed by Verbinski, produced by Bruckheimer, and written by Elliott and Rossio. The films continue the adventures of Sparrow, Turner, and Swann as they encounter a wide range of colorful and villainous characters on the high seas, including Davy Jones (Bill Nighy), an undead pirate captain; Tia Dalma (Naomie Harris), a beautiful and exotic voodoo priestess; and Sao Feng (Chow Yun-fat), the pirate lord of the South China Sea. Though not as critically well-received as their predecessor, *Dead Man's Chest* and *At World's End* grossed a combined $2 billion in worldwide box-office receipts, instantly making *Pirates* one of the most financially successful film franchises in history. Further installments in the franchise included *On Stranger Tides* (2011), a standalone sequel directed by Rob Marshall and based on a 1987 historical novel of the same name.

Impact

Pirates were largely a forgotten subject in Hollywood before *Pirates of the Caribbean* brought them back to the cultural forefront, aided by innovative story-telling, top-notch acting, and modern advances in film technology. The unlikely global hit has become a multibillion-dollar brand consisting not only of films and theme-park rides but also books, video games, toys, clothes, and a plethora of other branded merchandise. The film series has become one of the most lucrative in the history of film, and Johnny Depp's Jack Sparrow character has become a pop-culture icon on par with Robin Hood.

Further Reading

Corliss, Richard, and Rebecca Winters Keegan. "The Year of the 3Quel." *Time* 15 Jan. 2007: 44–46. Print.

Rottenberg, Josh. "Days of Plunder." *Entertainment Weekly* 18 May 2007: 28–34. Print.

Chris Cullen

■ Pixar Animation Studios

Definition: A film production studio that created the most critically acclaimed and financially successful computer-animated films of the decade

Through breakthrough technology and powerful story-telling, Pixar Animation Studios revolutionized computer-animated films in the 2000s. The studio's films have made billions of dollars worldwide, garnered several film industry awards, and created cultural icons of their characters. Despite being acquired by Walt Disney Pictures in 2006, Pixar was able to remain an independent entity.

Founded in 1979 as part of the Computer Division of the Lucasfilm production company, Pixar has since grown into one of the most successful studios in the history of cinema. After years of producing commercials and short films, Pixar released its first feature film, *Toy Story*, in 1995, which was also the

Pixar Animation Studio. (Courtesy Mike Turner)

first feature-length computer-animated film. A distribution deal with Walt Disney Productions (also known as Walt Disney Pictures) allowed Pixar to continue producing films and shorts, including *Toy Story 2*, which broke box-office opening weekend records in the United States.

Pixar's first film of the 2000s was *Monsters Inc.*, a film about monsters who harvest the screams of children as their energy source. The commercial and critical success of this film helped Pixar expand to over six hundred employees. It also won Pixar an Academy Award of Merit for significant advances in the field of motion picture rendering. This was followed in 2003 with *Finding Nemo*, about a tropical fish and his son, which broke box-office opening weekend records and won an Academy Award for best animated feature. Pixar broke its previous box-office records in 2004 with *The Incredibles*, about a family of superheroes. This also won the Academy Award for best animated feature. In 2006, Pixar released *Cars*, in which all of the characters were vehicles. This same year Walt Disney Productions purchased Pixar, and part of the agreement was that Pixar would be allowed a measure of independence in their film output and in their employee regulations. In 2007, the studio released *Ratatouille*, which revolved around a rat who dreamed of being a chef, and was followed by *WALL•E* in 2008 and *Up* in 2009, all three of which also won Academy Awards for best animated feature. *Up* was also the second animated film in history to be nominated for best picture and was the best reviewed film of 2009.

Alongside their breakthrough visual effects and animation, Pixar's films are critically acclaimed for their mature handling of serious themes such as friendship, responsibility, and commitment. In particular, *Up*, which centers on an elderly widower learning to enjoy life again, was applauded for the ways in which it addressed death.

Impact

Pixar set new standards for computer-animated films throughout the 2000s. The studio advanced animation technology and also proved computer animation was a respected medium that could be utilized to tell a sophisticated story capable of engaging both children and adults. Its RenderMan computer software has become a film industry standard for computer-animated visual effects. Following Pixar's success, several film studios started their own computer animation branches.

Further Reading

Paik, Karen. *To Infinity and Beyond!: The Story of Pixar Animation Studios*. San Francisco: Chronicle, 2007. Print.

Price, David A. *The Pixar Touch: The Making of a Company*. New York: Vintage, 2009. Print.

Patrick G. Cooper

Valerie Plame Wilson. (Courtesy truthout.org/Photograph by Troy Page)

■ Plame scandal

Definition: The public disclosure of Valerie Plame Wilson as a spy for the US Central Intelligence Agency (CIA) and the subsequent grand-jury investigation into who leaked this information

Valerie Plame Wilson was a spy for the CIA for nearly two decades when her cover was blown in a 2003 issue of the Washington Post. *This revelation led to a four-year special investigation headed by the US Department of Justice Office of Special Counsel to identify the source that leaked the information about Plame's classified identity. The scandal raised many questions about the 2003 invasion of Iraq.*

The CIA recruited Valerie Plame Wilson, best known as Valerie Plame, in 1985. In 1998, she married diplomat Joseph C. Wilson IV. In February 2002, Wilson was sent to Niger to investigate possible sales of uranium to Iraq for use in weapons. The CIA sent Wilson after Plame recommended him, stating that her husband was on good terms with former Niger prime minister Ibrahim Assane Mayaki. After meeting with Mayaki, Wilson told the CIA that Niger never sold uranium to Iraq but that it was approached about doing business with the country. Despite Wilson's claims, US president George W. Bush began giving speeches in October 2002 stating that Iraq had been caught attempting to purchase hundreds of tons of uranium.

On July 6, 2003, Wilson published an article in the *New York Times* titled "What I Didn't Find in Africa." In the article, Wilson states that the federal government exaggerated the threat posed by Iraq and that intelligence reports about the country's nuclear weapons program were false. On July 14, 2003, an article by journalist Robert D. Novak was published in the *Washington Post* titled "Mission to Niger." In the article, Novak revealed that Plame was a covert CIA agent.

The disclosure of Plame's identity set off an investigation by CIA director George Tenet, the Federal Bureau of Investigation, and the US Department of Justice into who leaked the information concerning Plame's identity to Novak. Experts believed that the disclosure of Plame's identity compromised every network and relationship she had created over her career. Lead suspects in the investigation were Karl Rove, the White House deputy chief of staff, and

Lewis "Scooter" Libby, chief of staff for Vice President Dick Cheney.

Libby was charged with two counts of perjury and making false statements and one count of obstruction of justice. In March 2007, he was found guilty on all counts except one count of making a false statement. President Bush commuted Libby's sentence.

Impact

Following the disclosure of Plame's identity, several debates ensued over the extent of the damage it would cause in the foreign intelligence community. The Bush administration was heavily criticized for what many saw as its protection of people such as Libby and Rove. Several members of Congress called for Rove to disclose his role in the affair. The Plame scandal demonstrated the sensitive nature of the intelligence community and raised questions about the 2003 invasion of Iraq.

Further Reading

Novak, Robert D. "Mission to Niger." *Washington Post.* Washington Post, 14 July 2003. Web. 2 Nov. 2012.

Wilson, Joseph C., IV. "What I Didn't Find in Africa." *New York Times.* New York Times, 6 July 2003. Web. 2 Nov. 2012.

Wilson, Valerie Plame. *Fair Game: My Life As a Spy, My Betrayal by the White House.* New York: Simon, 2007. Print.

Patrick G. Cooper

David Plouffe. (Official White House Photo/Photograph by Pete Souza)

■ Plouffe, David

Identification: American political strategist
Born: 1967; Wilmington, Delaware

A renowned political strategist, David Plouffe is regarded as the architect behind President Barack Obama's successful 2008 election campaign. With a forward-thinking approach to politics, his strategies throughout more than two decades in politics are known for taking into consideration the bigger picture and goals well beyond the next obstacle.

In 2000, David Plouffe was named executive director of the Democratic Congressional Campaign Committee. That same year, he joined colleague David Axelrod's political consulting firm AKPD Media in Chicago. Plouffe became a partner there, helping manage Democrat Barack Obama's Senate campaign in 2004. Plouffe's partnership with Axelrod and Obama would come to define his career as a political strategist.

In 2008, Senator Obama named Plouffe as campaign manager of his 2008 presidential bid. Political analysts now consider the campaign to be one of the most remarkable in American political history. Many considered Obama to be a long shot in the presidential race, given that he had served only one term as a US senator and attained the majority of his political experience as an Illinois state legislator. In addition, one of Obama's Democratic Party rivals in the race was Senator Hillary Clinton of New York, a former First Lady and a politician with a formidable network of fundraisers and allies.

Plouffe began the campaign with an aggressive effort focusing on the Iowa caucuses, the first voting event in the presidential nominations. He had previously worked for a senator in Iowa and was familiar with the intricacies of caucus procedure. Beginning in early 2007, Plouffe focused the campaign's message of hope and change on Iowa, and Obama won the caucus.

As the primary season unfolded, Plouffe enacted a strategy that focused not only on Super Tuesday, the day in which a large number of states conduct primary elections, but smaller states with fewer delegates at play. Obama's strong showing on Super Tuesday and success in smaller states allowed him to acquire enough delegates to win the primaries.

During the general election campaign against Republican Arizona senator John McCain and Alaska governor Sarah Palin, the Obama team made use of technology and the Internet as a way to spread its message and raise funds in a way never before seen in presidential politics. The Obama campaign's website allowed supporters to donate any amount of money they could afford, and the strategy proved incredibly lucrative. Analysts also praised the campaign for its discipline and avoidance of any major political missteps. With a wealth of staff members and with funds donated through the web, Plouffe helped lead Obama to victory in November 2008 presidential election. Obama thanked Plouffe in his acceptance speech on election night. In 2009, Plouffe published a book about his experience in the campaign entitled *The Audacity to Win*, which became a *New York Times* best seller.

Impact

Despite his shyness and distaste for the spotlight, David Plouffe is regarded as one of the most brilliant political minds of his generation. In 2009, he served as an outside advisor to the Obama administration.

Plouffe's use of technology, in particular the fundraising aspect of the Obama campaign website, greatly influenced the political campaigns of American politicians vying for seats in every level of government. His deft use of social media websites, such as Facebook and Twitter, during Obama's 2008 presidential campaign has inspired politicians from all parties nationwide.

Further Reading

Barnes, James A. "Obama's Inner Circle." *National Journal.* National Journal Group Inc., 31 Mar. 2008. Web. 8 Oct. 2012.

"David Plouffe: White House Senior Adviser (Since January 2011)." *Washington Post.* Washington Post, n.d. Web. 8 Oct. 2012.

Goldman, Julianna. "Obama's Aide Plouffe Plots Victory from Background." *Bloomberg.com.* Bloomberg, 16 June 2008. Web. 8 Oct. 2012.

Cait Caffrey

■ Police brutality

Definition: The use by police officers, security personnel, or correctional facility personnel of excessive force without just cause, which violates the civil rights of suspects

Cases of police brutality in the United States increased in the years following the September 11, 2001, terrorist attacks. Law enforcement agencies were given increased powers to wage the War on Terror, resulting in excessive force and racial profiling of people of color and foreign ethnicities. Another spike in abuse of police authority occurred in New Orleans, Louisiana, in the aftermath of Hurricane Katrina. Though experts generally acknowledged an increase in police brutality, accused officers were infrequently charged and rarely found guilty.

In a 2007 report, the Civil Rights Clinic at the DePaul University College of Law found that police abuse and brutality in the United States had worsened since the beginning of the decade. Police departments across the United States had become more militarized after September 2001. Military-grade equipment and weaponry—including heavy machine guns, bazookas, and attack helicopters—were adopted by many divisions. Many law-enforcement officers also received robust military and tactical training by special-forces operatives. The factor that contributed most to the increase in police brutality, however, was a slow change in officers' self-perception—the traditional image of a public servant and a peacekeeper was being replaced by that of a soldier. In contrast to traditional police officers, soldiers react more aggressively to even subtle threats and do not concern themselves with due process and the civil rights of suspects.

An imposing group of police officers stand over a man. (Courtesy Caren Litherland)

Use of Excessive Force

By the 2000s, the use of Tasers had spread through police departments as an alternative to deadly force. Tasers, electroshock weapons meant to subdue suspects, were more likely to be used without just cause because they were viewed as nonlethal. From 2001 to 2007, however, more than 150 suspects died after being stunned with the device. Tasers were used by officers against the elderly, pregnant women, and even children. Reports indicated the weapons were used with greater frequency on people of color.

Suspects of color were significantly more likely than Caucasians to become victims of police abuse. In many cases, the suspects were unarmed and were cooperating with the authorities when they were either shot and killed or severely beaten. Police officers often falsified reports and planted evidence, such as weapons or drugs, to justify their misconduct.

Other minority groups that suffered frequently from police brutality were individuals with disabilities, juveniles, and members of the lesbian, gay, bisexual, and transgender community. Those with disabilities were often unable to comprehend and fully comply with police orders, and such encounters often resulted in fatalities. Cases in which the suspect belonged to more than one frequently targeted group usually resulted in the individual's wrongful death. In one such instance in 2002, a Dominican man with epilepsy had a seizure in front of police officers. Instead of providing assistance, they pinned him to the ground, suffocating him to death. He was a person of color, with dreadlocks, and the officers assumed the man was a drug addict acting violently. In the same year, a mentally disabled gay African American man was dancing in the street with a pair of knives when he was killed by police.

Prosecution

In the first ten months of 2007, 66 percent more law-enforcement prosecutions took place than in

This new world of law enforcement had a greater need for police officers. The overall security of the United States demanded a well-staffed police force, but recruits were not readily available. Many of the young men and women suitable for police service had instead joined the military. This shortage forced many departments to relax some standards and promote less-experienced officers to higher-ranking positions, leading to greater likelihood of lapses in supervision.

all of 2002. Furthermore, this constituted an increase of 61 percent over the numbers ten years earlier. The most alarming statistic, according to experts, was the number of cases denied prosecution—98 percent in 2005.

The process of filing a complaint about police brutality was difficult at many police precincts. Those in law enforcement existed in a culture of cooperation and cover-up. A certain "them-against-us" mentality often led police officers to falsify reports and to overlook the misconduct of their colleagues. A report focusing on the Chicago police department, for example, found that, in 2004, only 0.48 percent of all excessive-force complaints were deemed valid.

Juries and courts were more likely to dismiss police wrongdoing as justifiable because of the nature of the victims, who were often either engaged in some criminal activity or fit the profile of such criminals. In many cases, the offending police officers were cleared of all charges in spite of existing evidence against them and often returned to active duty. Some of those officers later committed additional acts of police brutality.

Impact

The low prosecution rate and even lower disciplinary action rate of police brutality cases led to increased activism among citizens. Many human-rights advocates organized into watch groups and started programs of citizen countersurveillance of the police. They would record on video instances of excessive force by law-enforcement officials. Some of those activists suffered retaliatory actions by police officers.

Further Reading

Gallagher, Ryan. "Study: Police Abuse Goes Unpunished." *Medill Reports.* Medill School Northwestern U, 4 Apr. 2007. Web. 29 Nov. 2012. Study about the prosecution of police abuse in Chicago.

Johnson, Kevin. "Police Brutality Cases on Rise since 9/11." *USA Today.* USA Today, 17 Dec. 2007. Web. 29 Nov. 2012. Includes statistics about police brutality cases from 2001 to 2007.

Lendman, Stephen. "Police Brutality in America." *Baltimore Chronicle.* Baltimore News Network, 13 July 2010. Web. 29 Nov. 2012. Reviews reports of police brutality in the United States.

Ritchie, Andrea J., and Joey L. Mogul. "In the Shadows of the War on Terror: Persistent Police Brutality and Abuse of People of Color in the United States." *DePaul College of Law Civil Rights Clinic.* DePaul College of Law Civil Rights Clinic, Dec. 2007. Web. 29 Nov. 2012. Report prepared for the UN Committee on the Elimination of Racial Discrimination.

Rizer, Arthur, and Joseph Hartman. "How the War on Terror Has Militarized the Police." *The Atlantic.* Atlantic Monthly Group, 7 Nov. 2011. Web. 29 Nov. 2012. Discusses how militarizing law enforcement changes the mind-set of police officers.

Miroslav Farina

■ Political talk radio

Definition: A radio talk show format that is political in nature

The rise of political talk radio in the 2000s was attributed to two major events: the abolishment of the Fairness Doctrine in 1987 and the adoption of deregulation guidelines from the Telecommunications Act of 1996. The format also received a boost in the mid-2000s with the introduction of podcasts and satellite radio.

In addition to entertaining its listening audience, a primary goal of political talk radio during the 2000s was to sway public opinion. All political talk radio shows followed the same format. A host talked about current political events and voiced his or her opinions, usually sparking criticism or approval from listeners who would then call to the program and speak to the host to voice their reactions and opinions on the subject.

Political talk radio's popularity surged in the 1980s and the 1990s largely due to the repeal of the Fairness Doctrine, which stated that all sides of an issue or debate must be represented. Under the Fairness Doctrine, many radio stations stayed away from airing political talk radio shows, which typically were conservative. In 1987 the doctrine was abolished, paving the way for radio broadcasters to air potentially one-sided and/or politically themed shows.

In the late 1990s, political talk radio benefited from the passage of the Telecommunications Act of 1996, which changed the rules on owning various media outlets. Because of this, many political radio programs became nationally syndicated, or aired throughout various national outlets, further popularizing the genre.

Polarizing Talk

The number of stations across the United States that carried talk radio surged from 400 in 1990 to more than 1,400 in 2006, according to *Inside Radio*. By 2009 this number swelled to more than 3,500 stations, according to the Pew Research Center for the People and the Press. Most of these stations carried political shows, which remained the most popular genre of talk radio through the end of the 2000s. The number of listeners of political talk radio kept growing as well. The Pew Project for Excellence in Journalism estimated that more than forty million people listened to political talk radio by the end of 2009.

Rush Limbaugh quickly became one of the most listened to political commentators following the legislative changes. By 2006 he was broadcast on hundreds of stations and had 13.5 million listeners, according to *Talkers Magazine*. While the majority of political commenters and political talk radio shows were conservative throughout the 2000s, liberal (also referred to as "progressive") talk radio did exist. Founded in 2003, Democracy Radio was founded in 2003 and helped launch the career of liberal commentator Ed Schultz. Other popular liberal hosts during the 2000s were Stephanie Miller and Randi Rhodes.

In 2004 the station Air America Radio debuted to compete with conservative programming. The station featured liberal commentators such as comedians Al Franken and Janeane Garofalo and author Rachel Maddow. Although it had many well-known commentators, it never captured a significant audience, and with mounting debts and a financial scandal in 2005, the station filed for bankruptcy in October of 2006. Democracy Radio later became a part of Air America. Air America's last full year of operation was in 2009. A few of Democracy Radio's shows still ran in syndication on other stations as of 2009.

Podcasts and Satellite Radio

Around 2004, podcasting, a new type of medium for distributing audio content, became widely used to listen to audio files. Listeners typically used computers or portable media devices, such as MP3 players or iPods, to listen to podcasts. This new type of medium changed the way people listened to political talk radio. Instead of missing programs aired at inconvenient times, audiences were able to download their favorite podcasts and listen to them at their convenience.

The introduction of satellite radio in 2001 also encouraged the growth of talk radio. These types of radio signals allowed stations to reach a larger geographical area than local radio stations could. The two major satellite radio companies were Sirius and XM Radio, which as of 2006 had almost fourteen million subscribers. The shows of many political commentators, such as Glenn Beck, Laura Ingraham, Stephanie Miller, and Ed Schultz, were aired through syndication on satellite radio during the 2000s.

Impact

The impact of political talk radio was to sway public opinion. Throughout the 2000s, political talk radio influenced politics, and some of the most influential political commentators included Rush Limbaugh, Sean Hannity, Michael Savage, and Glenn Beck. Newt Gingrich's former press secretary, Tony Blankley, argued that Limbaugh had clout when it came to the 2000 election of President George W. Bush. In the *Huffington Post*, President Bill Clinton cited talk radio as one of the key influences in the GOP's 2002 congressional wins. During the 2008 election cycle, Limbaugh launched what he called Operation Chaos, his plan to defeat Democratic frontrunner Barack Obama in the primary elections, by urging Republicans to vote for Senator Hillary Rodham Clinton to keep her in the race, believing that any votes for Clinton would take votes away from Obama. While crossover voting existed in the primary, it could not be proven that it was due to Operation Chaos.

Further Reading

Alterman, Eric, and Danny Goldberg. "Think Again: Listen Up, Progressives: Talk Radio Matters." *Center for American Progress*. Center for American Progress, 11 Mar. 2010. Web. 4 Dec. 2012. A look at the popularity of conservative talk radio.

Berry, Jeffrey M., and Sarah Sobieraj. "Understanding the Rise of Talk Radio." *Cambridge Journals Online*. Cambridge UP, Oct. 2011. Web. 4 Dec. 2012. An article about the popularity of talk radio through the years.

Goodman, Sandy. "Limbaugh Flap Is Latest Proof of Talk Radio's Political Influence." *Huffington Post*. TheHuffingtonPost.com, Inc., 20 Mar. 2012. Web. 5 Dec. 2012. A report about talk radio.

Mills, Ken. "Talk Radio History." *KMA Talk Radio Initiative.* Ken Mills, 2004. Web. 5 Dec. 2012. An overview of the early days of talk radio.

Parker, Jennifer. "Is Limbaugh's Operation Chaos Working?" *Political Punch.* ABC News Network, 6 May 2008. Web. 5 Dec. 2012.

Voices.com. "History of Podcasting." *Voices.com.* Interactive Voices Inc., 2003–2012. Web. 5 Dec. 2012. Provides the history and benefits of podcasting and well as the impact podcasting has on consumers and various media.

Angela Harmon

■ Popular music

Definition: Any musical genre that enjoys widespread success with the general population

Rock, classical, and mashup music have been profiled elsewhere in this volume. This article describes trends in the genres of electronic dance music, hip-hop, and Christian rock—all of which underwent significant changes in style and prevalence during the 2000s.

The 1990s were the age of alt-rock. Labeled as an "alternative" to popular Top 40 music, alt-rock bands like Nirvana, Pearl Jam, Nine Inch Nails, Smashing Pumpkins, and R.E.M. became radio staples, redefining the popular music landscape. The trend of diversification in popular music continued into the 2000s. Thanks to the Internet, independent artists were able to reach a wider audience and a seemingly endless variety of genres and subgenres began to emerge. Three genres in particular—electronic dance music, Christian rock, and hip-hop—experienced fundamental shifts in style and popularity during the 2000s.

Electronic Dance Music

Long considered a European phenomenon, electronic dance music, or EDM, began a rapid ascent to popularity in the United States during the 2000s. The EDM label comprises a vast number of subgenres and styles that typify the electronic music scene. British big beat acts—named for their massive techno instrumentation and four-on-the-floor rhythms—like Fatboy Slim, The Prodigy, and The Chemical Brothers saw brief success in the United States during the 90s, but EDM failed to catch on in the mainstream.

Consequently, America's electronic music scene remained largely underground until the early 2000s, when the concept of the superstar DJ became widely accepted. Because the majority of EDM production is done on computers, live EDM performances typically consist of a lone DJ spinning prerecorded tracks. Thanks to new American outdoor music festivals like Bonnaroo, in Tennessee, and Coachella, in California, EDM DJ/producers like Diplo, Daft Punk, and Deadmau5 became popular festival acts, widening their fan bases in the process. EDM-specific festivals like the Electric Daisy Carnival, and the Electric Zoo Festival also experienced success in the 2000s.

During the first decade of the twenty-first century, Europe-born dance trends like dubstep and trance saw widespread mainstream success in the United States. Dubstep DJ Skrillex, real name Sonny Moore—a former member of the post-hardcore band From First to Last—became a countrywide sensation during the 2000s, eventually earning five Grammy nominations at the Fifty-Fourth Grammy Awards in 2012. EDM eventually began to seep into Top 40 pop music, with artists like Rihanna, The Black Eyed Peas, and Kanye West utilizing EDM elements in their songs.

Christian Rock

The Christian rock genre—characterized by religious lyrical and thematic content—saw a surge of popularity in the 1990s, with crossover acts like Jars of Clay and Audio Adrenaline experiencing mainstream success. Christian rock of the 90s was generally of the Top 40 alt-rock breed, but by the early 2000s Christian rock as a genre began to broaden its horizons. Metalcore band Underoath, for example, took the Christian rock ethos and adapted it to a hardcore metal sensibility. A far cry from the radio-ready Christian rock of the 90s, Underoath and similar Christian bands screamed lyrics over heavy, dissonant guitar riffs and brutally relentless, but precise drum beats. As some bands took Christian rock in a heavier direction, others rode the pop-punk wave to mainstream success. Canton, Ohio's Relient K infused Christian imagery with poppy hooks and distorted guitars, garnering a Grammy nomination for best rock gospel album," and scoring a charting mainstream hit with "Be My Escape," off their 2004 album *Mmhmm.* Christian music festivals, which rose to prominence through the 80s and 90s, saw continued success in the first decade of the 2000s. In 2008, the Creation Festival—an annual, massively successful Christian rock festival founded in 1979—staged a country-wide tour, playing more than thirty cities in the Northeast, South, and Midwest to celebrate the festival's thirtieth anniversary.

Hip-Hop and Rap

Hip-hop and rap underwent a drastic transformation during the 2000s. The ease with which personal computers allowed inexperienced users to produce tracks and record vocals led to an explosion of underground, independent rap music. The relatively localized and formulaic style of the 80s and early 90s gave way to a hip-hop landscape of unprecedented variety and complexity. Radio rappers like Eminem and 50 Cent continued to have mainstream success, and regional styles like Southern crunk and Central American reggaeton received considerable airplay.

The real story of 2000s hip-hop comes from the underground. Alternative hip-hop acts like OutKast, Gnarls Barkley, and Kanye West opened a path to the mainstream for even more underground acts to crossover. MCs like Kid Cudi, Lupe Fiasco, and Lil B were able to parlay independent Internet success into mainstream acclaim. The late 2000s saw an explosion in independent hip-hop artists. Frat-rap upstarts like Asher Roth and Mac Miller released party-ready jams to an audience of new, young hip-hop fans, while provocateurs like Odd Future Wolf Gang Kill Them All (OFWGKTA) continued to push the boundaries of the genre, adopting lo-fi production methods and rapping about increasingly dark subject matter.

The Internet can be credited with delivering independent and underground hip-hop to the masses. Thanks to music hosting sites like Bandcamp and SoundCloud, hip-hop artists were able to release free mixtapes with astounding frequency, turning the traditional distribution model on its head. Previously limited by financial and logistic constraints, established underground rappers like El-P and Aesop Rock began to reach a wider audience via Internet exposure.

Further Reading

Farrugia, Rebekah and Thom Swiss. "Producing Producers: Women and Electronic/Dance Music." *Current Musicology* 86 (2008): 79–99. *Academic Search Premier*. Web 13 Dec. 2012. Focuses on challenges that women DJs and producers face in the industry and argues that more women EDM producers are needed in the industry.

O'Malley, Zack. "DJs Are the New Rock Stars." *Forbes* 20 Aug. 2012. *Business Source Premier*. Web. 13 Dec. 2012. Traces the rise of electronic dance music DJs during the late 2000s.

Reeves, Mosi. "Underground Hip-Hop Acts Surface at a Club Near You." *Billboard* 117.45 (2005): 26. Print. Focuses on the emergence of underground hip-hop acts at mainstream venues.

Sandler, Lauren. "Holy Rock 'N' Rollers." *Nation* 276.2 (2003): 23–25. Print. Discusses how Christian rock bands incorporate the message of Jesus Christ into their music.

Thompson, Paul "An Empirical Study into the Learning Practices and Enculturation of DJs, Turntablists, Hip Hop and Dance Music Producers." *Journal of Music, Technology & Education* 5.1 (2012): 43–58. Print. Examines the technique and process of producing electronic dance music, with a focus on DJs and turntablism.

Steve Miller

■ Powell, Colin

Identification: US secretary of state, 2001–2005
Born: April 5, 1937; New York, New York

A decorated US military officer and the first African American to serve as secretary of state, Colin Powell was at the forefront of US politics for decades. His long career of military and political service under four presidents made him uniquely suited to confront foreign policy issues facing the United States in the aftermath of the September 11, 2001, terrorist attacks.

Colin Luther Powell was born on April 5, 1937, in Harlem in New York City. He was raised in the South Bronx and was educated in the New York public school system. He graduated from Morris High School in 1954 and went on to receive a bachelor of science degree in geology from City College of New York.

During college, Powell was active in the US Army's Reserve Officer Training Corps (ROTC). The ROTC allowed him to exploit his intellect and leadership abilities, and he graduated in 1958 as a cadet colonel, the corps' highest-possible rank. Powell's

Colin Powell. (Courtesy Talk Radio News Service)

performance in the ROTC earned him a commission as a second lieutenant in the Army.

For his service in Vietnam, Powell was decorated with a Bronze Star, a Soldier's Medal, two Purple Hearts, and the Legion of Merit. However, he has been criticized for his role in the events surrounding the infamous 1968 My Lai Massacre, in which American soldiers murdered approximately five hundred unarmed South Vietnamese civilians.

Powell first gained the approval of the American public during the December 1989 invasion of Panama. His demeanor in numerous interviews and television appearances played an important part in convincing the nation that the military action, which was in violation of international law, was justified.

The public became even more aware of Powell in 1990, when the Persian Gulf War captured the world's attention. In response to Iraq's occupation of the small neighboring country of Kuwait, the United States and its allies launched Operation Desert Shield, a rapid deployment of US troops in Saudi Arabia designed to force Iraqi leader Saddam Hussein to withdraw his forces, in August 1990. Powell was the chairman of the Joint Chiefs of Staff during the Persian Gulf War.

On January 20, 2001, Powell became the sixty-fifth US secretary of state. As a member of the conservative administration of President George W. Bush, Powell was often criticized for his moderate views on social issues. Unlike many Republicans, he supported abortion rights and affirmative action, but he also opposed any effort to lift the ban on homosexuals in the military.

As secretary of state, Powell faced his greatest challenge in the wake of the September 11, 2001, terrorist attack on the United States of securing the support of Arab nations for the US-led War on Terror. It was Powell's role to gather multinational support for an invasion of Iraq. In February of 2003, Powell met with the United Nations and announced that the United States had intelligence that Iraq was developing weapons of mass destruction. The announcement was met with both skepticism and support for the US intentions. In March 2003, the Iraqi government was overthrown by US and British troops.

On September 13, 2004, Powell testified before the Senate Homeland Security and Governmental Affairs Committee that the United States had faulty intelligence regarding the weapons of mass destruction possessed by Iraq. The existence of such weapons could not be confirmed, a discovery that plagued the Bush administration. Powell recommended that a position for a national intelligence director be created, in order to avoid this type of conflict again in the future.

After Bush's election for a second presidential term, Powell submitted his resignation. He was replaced by former National Security Advisor Condoleezza Rice. Powell retired to private life but was still influential in government politics, most notably crossing party lines to endorse Barack Obama for president in 2008, and again in 2012.

Impact

Powell is known as the first African American secretary of state and for his role as four-star general in the Army, his success in Operation Desert Storm, and his work after the Cold War. During the George W. Bush administration, he played a central role in diplomacy, and, despite his efforts to avoid physical conflict in the Middle East, he helped orchestrate the Iraq War. Powell has been the recipient of many awards, including two Presidential Medals of Freedom, the Congressional Gold Medal, and the President's Citizens Medal.

Further Reading

Edmonds, A. O. *Colin Powell: American Power and Intervention from Vietnam to Iraq.* Lanham: Rowman, 2009. Print.

Jeffries, Judson. *Soldier: The Life of Colin Powell.* New York: Knopf, 2007. Print.

Powell, Colin, and Joseph E. Persico. *My American Journey.* New York: Random, 1996. Print.

Keira Stevenson

■ Private military companies

Definition: Corporations , often staffed by former military personnel, that provide military and security services, either to private clients or as supplemental forces hired by military organizations; also known as private military contractors or PMCs

The legal and economic status of PMCs was an area of intense debate throughout the 2000s, as thousands of private security personnel were hired by the Department of Defense to supply supplementary security and assistance in Iraq and other conflicts around the world. Because of detailed media coverage of the conflict in Iraq, a number of prominent researchers studied the relationship between military resources and the use of PMC forces to supplement military operations.

Growth of PMCs

The US-led occupation of Iraq began in March 2003. In the aftermath of the occupation, the US State Department began hiring private military contractors to provide additional security and supplementary services. The Iraqi conflict led to the largest proliferation of PMCs in history, and by mid-decade, the number of private military contractors active in Iraq rivaled the number of soldiers and military personnel in the region.

Among the most prominent PMCs operating in Iraq were:

- Kellogg, Brown, and Root (KBR Inc)
- Blackwater USA (Academi)
- DynCorp International
- AQMI Strategy Corp
- CACI International
- Military Professional Resources Inc. (MPRI)

PMCs in Iraq were tasked with providing private security for nonmilitary officials, nonmilitary installations, and nonmilitary convoys, as well as aiding in the training of civilian militia. In addition, PMC companies provided linguistic aides and translators and supplemented construction personnel for military and nonmilitary construction projects. According to official military policy, PMC employees were allowed to respond to attacks with proportionate force, but were prohibited from offensive action by United Nations restrictions.

During the Gulf War conflict of the 1990s, estimates released by the US State Department indicated that there was one PMC employee for every fifty employees of the US Armed forces. In 2003, the number of PMCs increased rapidly and, by 2004, there was one PMC for every ten soldiers active in Iraq.

In 2006, census figures of military and security personnel in Iraq indicated that there were more than 100,000 PMC employees operating in Iraq, including Iraqis, Americans, and other nationals. An article published by the *New York Times* in August 2008 indicated that there were an estimated 180,000 PMC employees active in Iraq. This estimate caused controversy in the media, as estimates released by the Pentagon indicated that there were no more than 25,000 PMC employees active. A report from the Congressional Budget Office in 2008 stated that the US State Department spent more than $100,000 billion in fees to private contractors between 2003 and 2009, representing more than 20 percent of the cost of the Iraqi conflict. Some experts contended that the Congressional Budget Office estimate may be far less than the actual cost of PMC operations in Iraq and elsewhere during the period.

Many of the most prominent PMCs were involved in significant controversies during the Iraq and Afghanistan conflicts. For instance, representatives of CACI International were accused of taking part in the torture of Iraqi prisoners at Abu Ghraib prison. While a number of US Army servicemen were prosecuted for their role in the torture of Iraqi prisoners, Army service investigations found that private security employees were involved in as many as half of the proven cases of abuse and torture, and many were not prosecuted for their role in perpetrating these crimes.

According to the United Nations Mercenary Convention, which went into effect in 2001, member nations are prohibited from recruiting, training, or

A Blackwater Security Company MD-530F helicopter aids in securing the site of a car bomb explosion in Baghdad, Iraq. (U.S. Air Force/ Photograph by Master Sergeant Michael E. Best)

financing "mercenaries" for use in military operations. The use of PMC employees is controversial because some opponents argue that PMCs are synonymous with mercenary organizations. Supporters of PMC activities argue that mercenaries are recruited "to fight" in armed conflicts, while PMC employees are prohibited from engaging in conflict directly, unless attacked, and are specifically employed to serve as security and assistants to military forces.

In addition to controversies surrounding the conduct of PMC employees, some opponents have argued that the expansion of PMC forces has been economically damaging to the Department of Defense. Employees of private military companies are paid substantially higher rates for their services than active military personnel. For instance, Scott Helvenston, one of four Blackwater employees who were killed in an attack in 2004 by dissidents in Fallujah, Iraq, was earning approximately $600 per day, which is significantly higher than the pay offered to low-level soldiers fighting in the conflict.

Another controversial issues surrounding PMCs in the 2000s was the potential for PMC contractors to exert political influence. For instance, in 2001, the top ten PMCs spent more than $32 million in lobbying and spent more than $12 million in donations to political organizations. Throughout the decade, political analysts and media organization expressed concern that PMC political donations might lead to political corruption.

Halliburton and KBR Controversies

Kellogg, Brown, and Root (KBR), which was owned by Halliburton until April 2007, was one of the most controversial PMCs throughout the 2000s because of the extensive links between the company and the George W. Bush administration. Former Vice President Dick Cheney was the CEO of Halliburton prior to becoming vice president. Halliburton was awarded several lucrative no-bid contracts for providing security services in Iraq; some accused the Bush administration of favoring KBR because of the company's connections with Cheney. Halliburton donated more than $700,000 to the Republican Party between 1999 and 2002.

Another KBR controversy occurred in 2008 when former Defense Department civilian official Charles M. Smith told the media that he had been ousted from his position in 2004 when he refused to pay $1 billion in questionable expenses to KBR contractors. Smith's decision to refuse payment came after Army auditors had determined that KBR had failed to properly account for the compensation they were seeking. Following Smith's dismissal, Halliburton received payment from the Defense Department after hiring an independent auditor to review the charges. In 2010, it was announced that the Justice Department was filing suit against KBR for improper costs associated with the company's activities in Iraq.

Also in 2008, it was revealed that KBR had avoided paying hundreds of millions in Medicare and Social Security taxes by hiring employees through shell corporations in the Cayman Islands. According to a March 2008 article published in the *Boston Globe*, more than 21,000 KBR employees were listed as employees of two subordinate corporations located outside of the US tax jurisdiction. The Defense Department was aware of Halliburton's tax loophole since 2004, but claimed that this tax maneuver allowed KBR to charge less for services and thereby resulted in Defense Department savings. Media and political advocates criticized KBR and the Defense Department for favoring Defense Department budget concerns while costing millions to the United States in potential tax revenues.

In 2009, KBR pled guilty to violating the Foreign Corrupt Practices Act (FCPA, 1977) and paid $402 million in fines for using independent agents to distribute $180 million in bribes to Nigerian officials while trying to win lucrative construction contracts. KBR argued that being forced to comply with US laws placed the company at a competitive disadvantage and could prevent the company from winning contracts against non–US-based PMC competitors.

Blackwater Controversies

North Carolina–based Blackwater USA was founded by former naval officer Erik Prince in the 1990s and became one of the world's most prominent PMCs after the company won substantial Defense Department contracts to provide personal security in Iraq from 2003 to 2011. Blackwater's first contract, awarded in 2003, was for providing protection for Ambassador L. Paul Bremer at a cost of $21 million for an eleven-month period. From 2004 to 2008, Blackwater earned $320 million in Defense Department contracts for services in Iraq.

The military conflicts won by Blackwater attracted media scrutiny because of the close ties between Blackwater employees and representatives of the Bush administration. Prince was a White House intern under the first Bush administration, and Prince's family were long-time and substantial contributors to the Republican Party. In addition, Prince's sister was a former chair of the Republican Party, and members of the Blackwater staff served in high-ranking government positions. For instance, Cofer Black, one of Blackwater's chief officers, was a former CIA head of counterterrorism operations.

Between 2004 and 2010, representatives of Blackwater were involved in a number of high-profile controversies, primarily regarding the behavior of Blackwater employees. There were numerous instances throughout the decade of Blackwater employees being accused of assaulting or mistreating civilians and of taking an aggressive or active role in minor conflicts. The 2004 death of four Blackwater employees operating as guards for a supply convoy in Fallujah was also controversial; some in the media speculated that the incident was indicative of the inherent problems with allowing civilian security to operate in unstable areas.

In September 2007, four guards employed by Blackwater Worldwide were involved in a shooting incident in a Baghdad public square that resulted in the death of seventeen Iraqi civilians and more than twenty others wounded. The incident was one of the most controversial events of the Iraqi conflict, outside of the Abu Ghraib prison incident. The four guards involved in the incident were accused of manslaughter, but the case was dismissed in 2009 when a federal judge claimed that the Department of Defense had utilized tainted evidence in their case. In April 2011, an appeals panel found that there was insufficient reason for dismissal of the case and ordered the case to be reopened.

As Blackwater became the subject of increased scrutiny from the media and from political analysts, Prince split the company into at least thirty shell corporations in an effort to continue bidding for contracts while reducing the company's public scrutiny. According to an article published in the *New York Times* in April 2011, since 2001, corporations owned

wholly, or in part, by Prince have won more than
$600 million in classified contracts from either the
Department of Defense or the Central Intelligence
Agency (CIA). Though Blackwater received significant support from the Bush administration, companies owned by Prince continued to enjoy significant
support under the Obama administration, in part
because the Obama administration attempted to
avoid the cost of hiring new companies to take over
operations handled by existing companies in Iraq.

Impact
The proliferation of private military companies
during the Iraq War and in subsequent military conflicts represented, to some analysts, a fundamental
alteration of warfare strategy. While the period from
2001 to 2011 resulted in record military spending
in the United States, a significant portion of this
spending represented the growing reliance on nonmilitary contractors for security, transport, and technical aid. The Defense Department defended the
use of PMCs for a variety of reasons, including insufficient manpower and the need for supplementary
personnel who are able to respond under attack.
However, some analysts questioned the financial
justification of PMC operations, claiming that the
Department of Defense was wasting significant resources that could have been better distributed
among servicemen and women. In addition, contracts won by companies like Blackwater and KBR
raised accusations of government corruption extending to the executive branch.

Some analysts speculated that the use of PMCs
would remain an important part of future military
operations, because PMC employees represented a
necessary supplement to existing military manpower.
However, some raised concerns that the proliferation
of PMCs could threaten the integrity of the US military, as many former special forces operatives chose
to leave the military during the decade in favor of
PMC employment, where they were often able to
earn higher salaries for their services. Given the
higher profits offered by the private sector, some analysts speculated that the armed forces would experience additional difficulty maintaining necessary
manpower for armed service operations.

Further Reading
Bennett, Brian. "Victims of an Outsourced War."
Time. Time Inc., 15 Mar. 2007. Web. 6 Dec. 2012.

Discusses Blackwater history and operations in
Iraq, especially in regard to the death of four
Blackwater employees in Fallujah.

"Blackwater Worldwide." *New York Times.* New York
Times Co., 25 Apr. 2011. Web. 6 Dec. 2012. Overview of Blackwater history and activities during
the 2000s.

Dunigan, Molly. *Victory for Hire: Private Military Companies' Impact on Military Effectiveness.* Stanford:
Stanford UP, 2011. Print. Examines the effect of
PMC involvement on various types of warfare and
military scenarios.

Kinsey, Christopher. *Corporate Security and International
Security: The Rise of Private Military Companies.* New
York: Routledge, 2006. Print. Discusses a variety
of issues surrounding the rise in proliferation of
PMC contractors in military operations. Provides
history of PMCs and mercenary organizations.

Risen, James. "Use of Iraq Contractors Costs Billions,
Report Says." *New York Times.* New York Times Co.,
11 Aug. 2008. Web. 6 Dec. 2012. Discusses the
2008 Congressional Budget Office report about
the numbers of PMC contractors in Iraq and their
expenses.

Singer, Peter Warren. *Corporate Warriors: The Rise of
the Privatized Military Industry.* Ithaca: Cornell UP,
2008. Print. Discusses the history of mercenary
and PMC use in warfare and examines the role of
PMCs in current and future military operations.

Stockman, Farah. "Top Iraq Contractor Skirts US
Taxes Offshore." *Boston Globe.* New York Times Co.,
6 Mar. 2008. Web. 6 Dec. 2012. Discusses KBR and
Halliburton's use of tax shelters to avoid paying
Medicare and Social Security taxes.

Micah Issitt

■ Private militias

Definition: Radical, often illegal paramilitary organizations of like-minded citizens united in common
causes.

*The modern militia movement—extreme, often well-armed,
generally far-right antigovernment groups—sprang up in
the United States in the early 1990s. The movement, linked
to domestic terrorism and other crimes, has since ebbed and
flowed. The first decade of the twenty-first century saw a resurgence of private militias that represented a potential
threat to American welfare.*

Militias have been part of American history since European immigrants first arrived in North America. Colonial governments required troops of able-bodied men to maintain order and repel attacks from American Indians or foreign invaders. After the American Revolution, volunteer militias served as peacekeeping forces until the establishment of a professional standing military in the early nineteenth century. The National Guard, legislated in 1903, obviated the need for state militias. Most states subsequently passed laws prohibiting or regulating paramilitary groups.

Birth of the Militia Movement

The modern militia movement in the United States came to the attention of the mainstream media during the last decade of the twentieth century, following a series of volatile, highly publicized confrontations and legislation enacted to decrease violence. Standoffs over illegal weapons erupted into armed conflict between federal agencies and extremists in Ruby Ridge, Idaho, in 1992, and in Waco, Texas, in 1993, resulting in multiple deaths on both sides. Extreme right-wing groups were outraged, calling such incidents blatant demonstrations of government tyranny.

Private militias, emulating the militancy of 1960s groups such as the Minutemen, Black Panthers, and the Weather Underground, formed to protect themselves against an imagined diabolical plot: a global United Nations takeover and the establishment of a dictatorial New World Order. Militias—many espousing exclusionary doctrines of white supremacy or fundamentalist Christian identity—collected weapons, stockpiled foodstuffs, and engaged in combat training in preparation for the coming apocalyptic conflict. Watchdog groups, especially the Southern Poverty Law Center and the Anti-Defamation League, regularly monitored the activities of hate groups and militias to alert appropriate authorities to their dangers.

An event that galvanized militias occurred in Oklahoma City, Oklahoma, in 1995. Timothy McVeigh and his accomplice Terry Nichols—both associated with paramilitary groups—blew up a federal building, killing more than 160 people in an act of domestic terrorism. This mass murder demonstrated what a single determined individual could do to cause chaos, and boosted the numbers of militias. At the height of the early movement in 1996, there were some 850 paramilitary groups. Every state had at least one.

Militias in the Twenty-First Century

At the beginning of the twenty-first century, the militia movement stalled. One reason was that the "Y2K" computer failure predicted to disrupt American society and begin Armageddon never materialized. Another major factor in the loss of momentum was the election of a staunchly conservative US president, George W. Bush. During the early months of his administration, the Bush team allayed some far-right concerns, and dozens of private militias disbanded.

The trend began reversing in the wake of the terrorist attacks of September 11, 2001. The passage of the Patriot Act in early 2002 gave law-enforcement agencies broader powers, redefined domestic terrorism, and increased scrutiny of paramilitary groups. The act antagonized people on the far left and far right alike, and it made militias more cautious. Many radical organizations splintered into less detectable cells, and grew to rely upon the Internet rather than in-person meetings to communicate or disseminate propaganda.

An economic downturn and widespread unemployment, combined with the 2008 election of the first African American president, caused an upsurge in hate groups and associated militias. The right-wing fringe perceived President Barack Obama as foreign-born, a Muslim, and a socialist. These notions gained validity through the pronouncements of various conservative elected officials, celebrities, and pundits, including Michele Bachmann, Rush Limbaugh, Glenn Beck, Ron Paul, and Sarah Palin, and a new wave of militias began cropping up.

By the end of the first decade of the twenty-first century, the number of private armies in the United States had surpassed one thousand. These groups of armed, self-styled patriots ranged across a broad spectrum. Some were relatively benign activists who worked within the law to uphold constitutional rights and freedoms. Many were bigots oriented toward preserving racial purity. Some were religious zealots. Quite a few believed an apocalypse was coming, and a handful were dangerously radical, feeling no act of violence was too extreme.

Impact

The modern militia movement has flourished by taking advantage of the First Amendment (freedom of speech and assembly) and Second Amendment (right to bear arms), with which courts are reluctant to tamper. Most states have statutes regulating the formation and training of paramilitary groups, the rigorous enforcement of which seems the best method of checking militia activity and maintaining domestic law and order.

Further Reading

Barkun, Michael. *A Culture of Conspiracy: Apocalyptic Visions in Contemporary America.* Berkeley: U of California P, 2006. Examines the American obsession with conspiracies to explain incomprehensible phenomena.

—. *Religion and the Racist Right: The Origins of the Christian Identity Movement.* Chapel Hill: U of North Carolina P, 1996. Explores the history and ideology of belief systems at the core of many militias.

Hamilton, Neil A. *Militias in America: A Reference Handbook.* Santa Barbara, CA: ABC-CLIO, 1996. Historical overview of the rise of militias, complete with time lines and biographies of militia leaders.

Hummel, Jeffrey Rogers. "The American Militia and the Origin of Conscription: A Reassessment." *Journal of Libertarian Studies* 15.4 (Fall 2001): 29–77. Detailed history of American public and private militias from colonial times.

Levitas, Daniel. *The Terrorist Next Door: The Militia Movement and the Radical Right.* New York: St. Martin's, 2004. Discusses the undercurrents of racism and antigovernment thought present throughout American history.

Jack Ewing